The Linux® Kernel Primer

Prentice Hall
Open Source Software Development Series

Arnold Robbins, Series Editor

"Real world code from real world applications"

Open Source technology has revolutionized the computing world. Many large-scale projects are in production use worldwide, such as Apache, MySQL, and Postgres, with programmers writing applications in a variety of languages including Perl, Python, and PHP. These technologies are in use on many different systems, ranging from proprietary systems, to Linux systems, to traditional UNIX systems, to mainframes.

The **Prentice Hall Open Source Software Development Series** is designed to bring you the best of these Open Source technologies. Not only will you learn how to use them for your projects, but you will learn *from* them. By seeing real code from real applications, you will learn the best practices of Open Source developers the world over.

Titles currently in the series include:

Linux® Debugging and Performance Tuning: Tips and Techniques
Steve Best
0131492470, Paper, 10/14/2005
The book is not only a high-level strategy guide but also a book that combines strategy with hands-on debugging sessions and performance tuning tools and techniques.

Linux Programming by Example: The Fundamentals
Arnold Robbins
0131429647, Paper, 4/12/2004
Gradually, one step at a time, Robbins teaches both high level principles and "under the hood" techniques. This book will help the reader master the fundamentals needed to build serious Linux software.

The Linux® Kernel Primer: A Top-Down Approach for x86 and PowerPC Architectures
Claudia Salzberg, Gordon Fischer, Steven Smolski
0131181637, Paper, 9/21/2005
A comprehensive view of the Linux Kernel is presented in a top down approach—the big picture first with a clear view of all components, how they interrelate, and where the hardware/software separation exists. The coverage of both the x86 and the PowerPC is unique to this book.

The Linux® Kernel Primer

A Top-Down Approach for x86 and PowerPC Architectures

Claudia Salzberg Rodriguez

Gordon Fischer

Steven Smolski

PRENTICE
HALL
PTR

Prentice Hall Professional Technical Reference

Upper Saddle River, NJ · Boston· Indianapolis · San Francisco

New York · Toronto · Montreal · London · Munich · Paris · Madrid

Capetown · Sydney · Tokyo · Singapore · Mexico City

Many of the designations used by manufacturers and sellers to distinguish their products are claimed as trademarks. Where those designations appear in this book, and the publisher was aware of a trademark claim, the designations have been printed with initial capital letters or in all capitals.

The authors and publisher have taken care in the preparation of this book, but make no expressed or implied warranty of any kind and assume no responsibility for errors or omissions. No liability is assumed for incidental or consequential damages in connection with or arising out of the use of the information or programs contained herein.

The publisher offers excellent discounts on this book when ordered in quantity for bulk purchases or special sales, which may include electronic versions and/or custom covers and content particular to your business, training goals, marketing focus, and branding interests. For more information, please contact:

U. S. Corporate and Government Sales
(800) 382-3419
corpsales@pearsontechgroup.com

For sales outside the U. S., please contact:

International Sales
international@pearsoned.com

Visit us on the Web: www.phptr.com

Library of Congress Cataloging-in-Publication Data:

Salzberg Rodriguez, Claudia.

  The Linux Kernel primer : a top-down approach for x86 and PowerPC architectures / Claudia Salzberg Rodriguez, Gordon Fischer, Steven Smolski.
      p. cm.
  ISBN 0-13-118163-7 (pbk. : alk. paper) 1. Linux. 2. Operating systems (Computers) I. Fischer, Gordon.
II. Smolski, Steven. III. Title.
  QA76.76.O63R633 2005
  005.4'32—dc22

2005016702

ISBN 0-13-118163-7
Text printed in the United States on recycled paper at R.R. Donnelly in Crawfordsville, IN.
First printing, September 2005

To my parents, Pablo & Maria, por ser trigo, escudo, viento y bandera.
—Claudia Salzberg Rodriguez

To Lisa,

To Jan & Hart.

—Gordon Fischer

To my dear friend Wes, whose wisdom and friendship I will cherish forever.
—Steven Smolski

Contents

Foreword

Here there be dragons. Medieval mapmakers wrote that about unknown or dangerous places, and that is likely the feeling you get the first time you type:

```
cd /usr/src/linux ; ls
```

"Where do I start?" you wonder. "What exactly am I looking at? How does it all hang together and actually work?"

Modern, full-featured operating systems are big and complex. The number of subsystems is large, and their interactions are many and often subtle. And while it's great that you *have* the Linux kernel source code (more about that in a moment), knowing where to start, what to look at, and in what order, is far from self-evident.

That is the purpose of this book. Step by step, you will learn about the different kernel components, how they work, and how they relate to each other. The authors are intimately familiar with the kernel, and this knowledge shows through; by the end of the book, you and the kernel will at least be good friends, with the prospect of a deeper relationship ahead of you.

The Linux kernel is "Free" (as in freedom) Software. In *The Free Software Definition*,[1] Richard Stallman defines the freedoms that make software Free (with a capital F). Freedom 0 is the freedom to run the software. This is the most fundamental freedom. But immediately after that is Freedom 1, the freedom to study how a program works. This freedom is often overlooked. However, it is very important, because one of the best ways to learn how to do something is by watching other people do it. In the software world, that means reading other peoples' programs and

---

[1] http://www.gnu.org/philosophy/free-sw.html

seeing what they did well as well as what they did poorly. The freedoms of the GPL are, at least in my opinion, one of the most fundamental reasons that GNU/Linux systems have become such an important force in modern computing. Those freedoms benefit you every moment you use your GNU/Linux system, and it's a good idea to stop and think about that every once in awhile.

With this book, we take advantage of Freedom 1 to give you the opportunity to study the Linux kernel source code in depth. You will see things that are done well, and other things that are done, shall we say, *less well*. But because of Freedom 1, *you will see it all*, and you will be able to learn from it.

And that brings me to the *Prentice Hall Open Source Software Development Series*, of which this book is one of the first members. The idea for the series developed from the principle that reading programs is one of the best ways to learn. Today, the world is blessed with an abundance of Free and Open Source software—whose source code is just waiting (maybe even eager!) to be read, understood, and appreciated. The aim of the series is to be your guide up the software development learning curve, so to speak, and to help you learn by showing you as much real code as possible.

I sincerely hope that you will enjoy this book and learn a lot. I also hope that you will be inspired to carve out your own niche in the Free Software and Open Source worlds, which is definitely the most enjoyable way to participate in them.

Have fun!

Arnold Robbins
Series Editor

Acknowledgments

We would like to thank the many people without whom this book would not have been possible.

Claudia Salzberg Rodriguez: I would like to note that it is oftentimes difficult, when faced with a finite amount of space in which to acknowledge people, to distinguish the top contributors to your current and well-defined accomplishment from the mass of humanity which has, in countless and innumerable ways, contributed to you being capable of this accomplishment. That being said, I would like to thank all the contributors to the Linux kernel for all the hard work and dedication that has gone into developing this operating system into what it has become—for love of the game. My deepest appreciation goes out to the many key teachers and mentors along the way for awakening and fostering the insatiable curiosity for how things work and for teaching me how to learn. I would also like to thank my family for their constant love, support, and for maintaining their enthusiasm well past the point where mine was exhausted. Finally, I wish to thank Jose Raul, for graciously handling the demands on my time and for consistently finding the way to rekindle inspiration that insisted on giving out.

Gordon Fischer: I would like to thank all the programmers who patiently explained to me the intricacies of the Linux kernel when I was but a n00b. I would also like to thank Grady and Underworld for providing excellent coding music.

We would all like to thank our superb editor, Mark L. Taub, for knowing what was necessary to make the book better every step of the way and for leading us in that direction. Thank you for being constantly and simultaneously reasonable, understanding, demanding, and vastly accessible throughout the writing of this book.

We would also like to thank Jim Markham and Erica Jamison. Jim Markham we thank for his early editorial comments that served us so well throughout the rest of the writing of the manuscript. Erica Jamison we thank for providing us with editorial feedback during the last version of the manuscript.

Our appreciation flows out to our reviewers who spent so many hours reading and making suggestions that made the book better. Thank you for your keen eyes and insightful comments; your suggestions and comments were invaluable. The reviewers are (in alphabetical order) Alessio Gaspar, Mel Gorman, Benjamin Herrenschmidt, Ron McCarty, Chet Ramey, Eric Raymond, Arnold Robbins, and Peter Salus.

We would like to thank Kayla Dugger for driving us through the copyediting and proofreading process with unwavering good cheer, and Ginny Bess for her hawk-eyed copyedit. A special thanks goes to the army of people behind the scenes of the copyediting, proofreading, layout, marketing, and printing who we did not get to meet personally for making this book possible.

About the Authors

Claudia Salzberg Rodriguez works in IBM's Linux Technology Center, developing the kernel and associated programming tools. A Linux systems programmer for over five years, she has worked with Linux for Intel and PPC on platforms ranging from embedded to high-performance systems.

Gordon Fischer has written Linux and UNIX device drivers for many low-level devices, and has used Linux kernels in diverse enterprise settings across both Intel and PPC platforms.

Steve Smolski has been in the semiconductor business for 26 years. He has worked in the manufacturing, testing, and development of memory, processors, and ASICS; has written applications and drivers for Linux, AIX, and Windows; and has embedded operating systems.

Preface

Technology in general and computers in specific have a magical allure that seems to consume those who would approach them. Developments in technology push established boundaries and force the re-evaluation of troublesome concepts previously laid to rest. The Linux operating system has been a large contributor to a torrent of notable shifts in industry and the way business is done. By its adoption of the GNU Public License and its interactions with GNU software, it has served as a cornerstone to the various debates that surround open source, free software, and the concept of the development community. Linux is an extremely successful example of how powerful an open source operating system can be, and how the magic of its underpinnings can hold programmers from all corners of the world spellbound.

The use of Linux is something that is increasingly accessible to most computer users. With multiple distributions, community support, and industry backing, the use of Linux has also found safe harbor in universities, industrial applications, and the homes of millions of users.

Increased need in support and for new functionality follow at the heels of this upsurge in use. In turn, more and more programmers are finding themselves interested in the internals of the Linux kernel as the number of architectures and devices that demand support are added to the already vast (and rapidly growing) arsenal.

The porting of the Linux kernel to the Power architecture has contributed to the operating system's blossoming among high-end servers and embedded systems. The need for understanding how Linux runs on the Power architecture

has grown, with companies now purchasing PowerPC-based systems intended to run Linux.

Intended Audience

This book is intended for the budding and veteran systems programmer, the Linux enthusiast, and the application programmer eager to have a better understanding of what makes his programs work the way they do. Anyone who has knowledge of C, familiarity with basic Linux user fundamentals, and wants to know how Linux works should find this book provides him with the basic concepts necessary to build this understanding—it is intended to be a primer for understanding how the Linux kernel works.

Whether your experience with Linux has been logging in and writing small programs to run on Linux, or you are an established systems programmer seeking to understand particularities of one of the subsystems, this book provides you with the information you are looking for.

Organization of Material

This book is divided into three parts, each of which provides the reader with knowledge necessary to succeed in the study of Linux internals.

Part I provides the necessary tools and understanding to tackle the exploration of the kernel internals:

Chapter 1, "Overview," provides a history of Linux and UNIX, a listing of the many distributions, and a short overview of the various kernel subsystems from a user space perspective.

Chapter 2, "Exploration Toolkit," provides a description of the data structures and language usage commonly found throughout the Linux kernel, an introduction to assembly for x86 and PowerPC architectures, and a summary of tools and utilities used to get the information needed to understand kernel internals.

Part II introduces the reader to the basic concepts in each kernel subsystem and to trace the code that executes the subsystem functionality:

Chapter 3, "Processes: The Principal Model of Execution," covers the implementation of the process model. We explain how processes come to be and discuss the flow of control of a user space process into kernel space and back. We also discuss how processes are implemented in the kernel and discuss all data structures associated with process execution. This chapter also covers interrupts and exceptions, how these hardware mechanisms occur in each of the architectures, and how they interact with the Linux kernel.

Chapter 4, "Memory Management," describes how the Linux kernel tracks and manages available memory among various user space processes and the kernel. This chapter describes the way in which the kernel categorizes memory and how it decides to allocate and deallocate memory. It also describes in detail the mechanism of the page fault and how it is executed in the hardware.

Chapter 5, "Input/Output," describes how the processor interacts with other devices, and how the kernel interfaces and controls these interactions. This chapter also covers various kinds of devices and their implementation in the kernel.

Chapter 6, "Filesystems," provides an overview of how files and directories are implemented in the kernel. This chapter introduces the virtual filesystem, the layer of abstraction used to support multiple filesystems. This chapter also traces the execution of file-related operations such as open and close.

Chapter 7, "Scheduling and Kernel Synchronization," describes the operation of the scheduler, which allows multiple processes to run as though they are the only process in the system. This chapter covers in detail how the kernel selects which task to execute and how it interfaces with the hardware to switch from one process to another. This chapter also describes what kernel preemption is and how it is executed. Finally, it describes how the system clock works and its use by the kernel to keep time.

Chapter 8, "Booting the Kernel," describes what happens from Power On to Power Off. It traces how the various processors handle the loading of the kernel, including a description of BIOS, Open Firmware, and bootloaders. This chapter then goes through the linear order in kernel bringup and initialization, covering all the subsystems discussed in previous chapters.

Part III deals with a more hands-on approach to building and interacting with the Linux kernel:

Chapter 9, "Building the Linux Kernel," covers the toolchain necessary to build the kernel and the format of the object files executed. It also describes in detail how the Kernel Source Build system operates and how to add configuration options into the kernel build system.

Chapter 10, "Adding Your Code to the Kernel," describes the operation of /dev/random, which is seen in all Linux systems. As it traces the device, the chapter touches on previously described concepts from a more practical perspective. It then covers how to implement your own device in the kernel.

Our Approach

This book introduces the reader to the concepts necessary to understand the kernel. We follow a top-down approach in the following two ways:

First, we associate the kernel workings with the execution of user space operations the reader may be more familiar with and strive to explain the kernel workings in association with this. When possible, we begin with a user space example and trace the execution of the code down into the kernel. It is not always possible to follow this tracing straight down since the subsystem data types and substructures need to be introduced before the explanation of how it works can take place. In these cases, we tie in explanations of the kernel subsystem with specific examples of how it relates to a user space program. The intent is twofold: to highlight the layering seen in the kernel as it interfaces with user space on one side and the hardware on the other, and to explain workings of the subsystem by tracing the code and following the order of events as they occur. We believe this will help the reader get a sense of how the kernel workings fit in with what he knows, and will provide him with a framed reference for how a particular functionality associates to the rest of the operating system.

Second, we use the top-down perspective to view the data structures central to the operation of the subsystem and see how they relate to the execution of the system's management. We strive to delineate structures central to the subsystem operation and to keep focus on them as we follow the operation of the subsystem.

Conventions

Throughout this book, you will see listings of the source code. The top-right corner will hold the location of the source file with respect to the root of the source code tree. The listings are shown in this font. Line numbers are provided for the code commentary that usually follows. As we explain the kernel subsystem and how it works, we will continually refer to the source code and explain it.

Command-line options, function names, function output, and variable names are distinguished by `this font`.

Bold type is used whenever a new concept is introduced.

Chapter 1

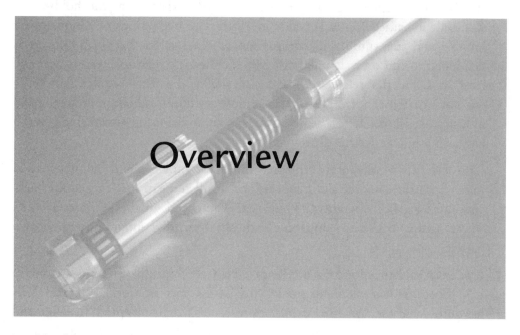

Overview

In this chapter

L inux is an operating system that came into existence as the hobby of a student named Linus Torvalds in 1991. The beginnings of Linux appear humble and unassuming in comparison to what it has become. Linux was developed to run on machines with x86 architecture microprocessors with AT hard disks. The first release sported a bash shell and a gcc compiler. Portability was not a design concern at that time, nor was widespread use in academia and industry its vision. There was no business plan or vision statement. However, it has been available for free from day one.

Linux became a collaborative project under the guidance and maintenance of Linus from the early days of beta versions. It filled a gap that existed for hackers wanting a free operating system that would run on the x86 architecture. These hackers began to contribute code that provided support for their own particular needs.

It is often said that Linux is a type of UNIX. Technically, Linux is a clone of UNIX because it implements the POSIX UNIX Specification P1003.0. UNIX has dominated the non-Intel workstation scene since its inception in 1969, and it is highly regarded as a powerful and elegant operating system. Relegated to high-performance workstations, UNIX was only available at research, academic, and development institutions. Linux brought the capabilities of a UNIX system to the Intel personal computer and into the homes of its users. Today, Linux sees widespread use in industry and academia, and it supports numerous architectures, such as PowerPC.

This chapter provides a bird's eye view of the concepts that surround Linux. It takes you through an overview of the components and features of the kernel and introduces some of the features that make Linux so appealing. To understand the concepts of the Linux kernel, you need to have a basic understanding of its intended purpose.

1.1 History of UNIX

We mentioned that Linux is a type of UNIX. Although Linux did not develop directly from an existing UNIX, the fact that it implements common UNIX standards makes the history of UNIX relevant to our discussion.

MULTiplexed Information and Computing Service (MULTICS), which is considered the precursor of the UNIX operating systems, came about from a joint venture between MIT, Bell Laboratories, and the General Electric Company (GEC), which was involved in the computer-manufacturing business at that time. The development of MULTICS was born of the desire to introduce a machine to support numerous timesharing users. At the time of this joint venture in 1965, operating systems, although capable of **multiprogramming** (timesharing between jobs), were batch systems that supported only a single user. The response time between a user submitting a job and getting back the output was in the order of hours. The goal behind MULTICS was to create an operating system that allowed **multiuser timesharing** that provided each user access to his own terminal. Although Bell Labs and General Electric eventually abandoned the project, MULTICS eventually ran in production settings in numerous places.

UNIX development began with the porting of a stripped-down version of MULTICS in an effort to develop an operating system to run in the PDP-7 minicomputer that would support a new filesystem. The new filesystem was the first version of the UNIX filesystem. This operating system, developed by Ken Thompson, supported two users and had a command interpreter and programs that allowed file manipulation for the new filesystem. In 1970, UNIX was ported to the PDP-11 and updated to support more users. This was technically the first edition of UNIX.

In 1973, for the release of the fourth edition of UNIX, Ken Thompson and Dennis Ritchie rewrote UNIX in C (a language then recently developed by Ritchie). This moved the operating system away from pure assembly and opened the doors to the portability of the operating system. Take a moment to consider the pivotal nature of this decision. Until then, operating systems were entirely entrenched with the system's architecture specifications because assembly language is extremely particular and not easily ported to other architectures. The rewrite of UNIX in C was the first step toward a more portable (and readable) operating system, a step that contributed to UNIX's sudden rise in popularity.

1974 marked the beginning of a boost in popularity of UNIX among universities. Academics began to collaborate with the UNIX systems group at Bell Laboratories to produce the fifth edition with many new innovations. This version was available free of cost and with source code to universities for educational purposes. In 1979, after many innovations, code cleanups, and an effort to improve portability, the seventh edition (V7) of the UNIX operating system came about. This version contained a C compiler and a command interpreter known as the Bourne shell.

The 1980s brought the advent of the personal computer. The workstation was now within the reach of businesses and universities. A number of UNIX variants were then developed from the seventh edition. These include Berkley UNIX (BSD), which was developed at the University of California at Berkley, and the AT&T UNIX System III and System V. Each version was then developed into other systems, such as NetBSD and OpenBSD (variants of BSD), and AIX (IBM's variant of System V). In fact, all commercial variants of UNIX are derived from System V or BSD.

Linux was introduced in 1991 at a time when UNIX was extremely popular but not available for the PC. The cost of UNIX was prohibitive and not really available to a user unless he was affiliated with a university. Linux was first implemented as an extension of an operating system called Minix (a small operating system written by Andrew Tanenbaum for educational purposes).

In the following years, the Linux kernel, combined with system software provided by the Free Software Foundation's (FSF) GNU project, made Linux[1] develop into a sufficiently solid system that attracted attention beyond the scope of the contributing hackers. In 1994, version 1.0 of Linux was released. From then on, Linux has grown vastly, generating a demand for the distribution of Linux in mass quantities and to an increasing number of universities, corporations, and individual users that require support on various architectures.

1.2   Standards and Common Interfaces

Common standards bridge the gaps between the different types of UNIX. The user's decision of what variant of UNIX to use impacts its portability and, therefore, its potential market. If you are a program developer, clearly, the market for your program is limited to the people who use the same system you developed on unless you take the trouble to port it. Standards come about from the need for a specification of a common programming interface that would facilitate having code developed on

---

[1]   Linux is also referred to as GNU/Linux in order to credit the component of system software provided by the FSF's GNU project.

one operating system run on another with minimal or no patching. Various standards organizations have set out to define specifications for UNIX. POSIX, formed by the Institute of Electronic Engineers (IEEE), is a standard for a portable operating system for computer environments with which Linux aims to be compliant.

1.3   Free Software and Open Source

Linux is one of the most successful examples of open-source software. Open-source software is software whose source code is freely available such that anyone can modify, read, and redistribute it. This stands in contrast to the closed-source software distributed only in binary form.

Open source allows a user to develop the software at will to suit his own needs. Depending on the license, certain restrictions apply to the code. The benefit of this is that users are never limited by what has been developed by others because they can freely alter the code to suit their needs. Linux provides an operating system that allows anyone to develop and contribute to it. This caused a fairly rapid evolution of Linux as the rate of involvement, whether in development, testing, or documentation, is staggering.

Various open-source licenses exist: In particular, Linux is licensed under the GNU General Public License (GPL) version 2. A copy of the license can be found at the root of the source code in a file called COPYING. If you plan on hacking the Linux kernel, it is a good idea to become familiar with the terms of this license so that you know what the legal fate of your contribution will be.

There are two main camps around the conveyance of free and open-source software. The Free Software Foundation and the open-source groups differ in ideology. The Free Software Foundation, which is the older of the two groups, holds the ideology that the word free should be applied to software in much the same way that the word free is applied to speech. The open-source group views free and open-source software as a different methodology on par with proprietary software. For more information, go to http://www.fsf.org and http://www.opensource.org.

1.4   A Quick Survey of Linux Distributions

We mentioned that the Linux kernel is only part of what is usually referred to as "Linux." A Linux distribution is a combination of the Linux kernel, tools, window managers, and many other applications. Many of the system programs used in Linux are developed and maintained by the FSF GNU project. With the rise in Linux's demand and popularity, the packaging of the kernel with these and other tools has becoming a significant and lucrative undertaking. Groups of people and corporations take on the mission of providing a particular distribution of Linux in keeping with a particular set of objectives. Without getting into too much detail, we review the major Linux distributions as of this writing. New Linux distributions continue to be released.

Most Linux distributions organize the tools and applications into groups of header and executable files. These groupings are called packages and are the major advantage of using a Linux distribution as opposed to downloading header files and compiling everything from source. Referring to the GPL, the license gives the freedom to charge for added value to the open-source software, such as these services provided in the code's redistribution.

1.4.1   Debian

Debian[2] is a GNU/Linux operating system. Like other distributions, the majority of applications and tools come from GNU software and the Linux kernel. Debian has one of the better package-management systems, *apt* (advanced packaging tool). The major drawback of Debian is in the initial installation procedure, which seems to cause confusion among novice Linux users. Debian is not tied to a corporation and is developed by a community of volunteers.

1.4.2   Red Hat/Fedora

Red Hat[3] (the company) is a major player in the open-source software-development arena. Red Hat Linux was the company's Linux distribution until recently (2002–2003) when it replaced its sole offering with two separate distributions Red Hat Enterprise Linux and the Fedora Core. Red Hat Enterprise Linux is aimed at business, government, or other industries that require a stable and supported Linux environment. The Fedora Core is targeted to individual users and enthusiasts. The major difference between the two distributions is stability versus

---

[2] http://www.debian.org.

[3] http://www.redhat.com.

features. Fedora will have newer, less stable code included in the distribution than Red Hat Enterprise. Red Hat appears to be the Linux enterprise version of choice in America.

1.4.3   Mandriva

Mandriva Linux[4] (formerly Mandrake Linux) originated as an easier-to-install version of Red Hat Linux, but has since diverged into a separate distribution that targets the individual Linux user. The major features of Mandriva Linux are easy system configuration and setup.

1.4.4   SUSE

SUSE Linux[5] is another major player in the Linux arena. SUSE targets business, government, industry, and individual users. The major advantage of SUSE is its installation and administration tool *Yast2*. SUSE appears to be the Linux enterprise version of choice in Europe.

1.4.5   Gentoo

Gentoo[6] is the new Linux distribution on the block, and it has been winning lots of accolades. The major difference with Gentoo Linux is that all the packages are compiled from source for the specific configuration of your machine. This is done via the Gentoo portage system.

1.4.6   Yellow Dog

Yellow Dog Linux[7] is one of the major players in PPC-based Linux distributions. Although a number of the recently described distributions work on PPC, their emphasis is on i386 versions of Linux. Yellow Dog Linux is most similar to Red Hat

---

[4] http://www.mandriva.com/.

[5] http://www.novell.com/linux/suse/.

[6] http://www.gentoo.org/.

[7] http://www.yellowdoglinux.com/.

Linux but with extended development to support the PPC platform in general and Apple-based hardware specifically.

1.4.7   Other Distros

Linux users can be passionate about their distribution of choice, and there are many out there. Slackware is a classic, MontaVista is great for embedded and, of course, you can roll your own distribution. For further reading on the variety of Linux distributions, I recommend the Wikipedia entry at `http://en.wikipedia.org/` `wiki/Category:Linux_distributions`.

This likely contains the most up-to-date information and, if not, links to further information on the Web.

1.5   Kernel Release Information

As with any software project, understanding the project's versioning scheme is a key element in your involvement as a contributor. Prior to Linux kernel 2.6, the development community followed a fairly simple release and development tree methodology. The even-number releases (2.2, 2.4, and 2.6) were considered stable branches. The only code that was accepted into stable branches was code that would fix existing errors. Development would continue in the development tree that was marked by odd numbers (2.1, 2.3, and 2.5). Eventually, the development tree would be deemed complete enough to take most of it and release a new stable tree.

In mid 2004, a change occurred with the standard release cycle: Code that might normally go into a development tree is being included in the stable 2.6 tree. Specifically, "...the mainline kernel will be the fastest and most feature-rich kernel around, but not, necessarily, the most stable. Final stabilization is to be done by distributors (as happens now, really), but the distributors are expected to merge their patches quickly" [Jonathan Corbet via `http://kerneltrap.org/node/view/3513`].

As this is a relatively new development, only time will tell whether the release cycle will be changed significantly in the long run.

1.6   Linux on Power

Linux on Power (Linux systems running on a Power or PowerPC processor) has witnessed a spectacular rise in demand and popularity. An increase in the purchase of PowerPC-based systems with the intention of running Linux on them can be seen among businesses and corporations. The reason for the increase in purchase of PowerPC microprocessors is largely because of the fact that they provide an extremely scalable architecture that addresses a wide range of needs.

The PowerPC architecture has made its presence felt in the embedded market where AMCC PowerPC and Motorola PowerPC deliver 32-bit system-on-chip (SOC) integrated products. These SOCs encompass the processor along with built-in clocks, memory, busses, controllers, and peripherals.

The companies who license PowerPC include AMCC, IBM, and Motorola. Although these three companies develop their chips independently, the chips share a common instruction set and are therefore compatible.

Linux is running on PowerPC-based game consoles, mainframes, and desktops around the world. The rapid expansion of Linux on another increasingly main-stream architecture has come about from the combined efforts of open-source ini-tiatives, such as `http://www.penguinppc.org` and private enterprise initiatives, including the Linux Technology Center at IBM.

With the growing popularity of Linux on this platform, we have undertaken to explore how Linux interfaces and makes use of PowerPC functionality.

Numerous sites contain helpful information related to Linux on Power, and we refer to them as we progress through our explanations. `http://www.penguinppc.org` is where the Linux PPC port is tracked and where the PowerPC developer commu-nity follows Linux on Power news.

1.7   What Is an Operating System?

We now look at general operating system concepts, basic Linux usability and fea-tures, and how they tie together. This section overviews the concepts we cover in more detail in future chapters. If you are familiar with these concepts, you can skip this section and dive right into Chapter 2, "Exploration Toolkit."

The operating system is what turns your hardware into a usable computer. It is in charge of managing the resources provided by your system's particular hardware components and of providing a base for application programs to be developed on and executed. If there were no operating system, each program would have to include drivers for all the hardware it was interested in using, which could prove prohibitive to application programmers.

The anatomy of an operating system depends on its type. Linux and most UNIX variants are **monolithic systems**. When we say a system is monolithic, we do not necessarily mean it is huge (although, in most cases, this second interpretation might well apply). Rather, we mean that it is composed of a single unit—a single object file. The operating system structure is defined by a number of procedures that are compiled and linked together. How the procedures interrelate defines the internal structure of a monolithic system.

In Linux, we have **kernel space** and **user space** as two distinct portions of the operating system. A user associates with the operating system by way of user space where he will develop and/or use application programs. User space does not access the kernel (and hence, the hardware resources) directly but by way of system calls—the outermost layer of procedures defined by the kernel. Kernel space is where the hardware-management functionality takes place. Within the kernel, the system call procedures call on other procedures that are not available to user space to manipulate finer grain functionality.

The subset of procedures that is not visible to user space is made up in part by functions from individual device drivers and by kernel subsystem functions. Device drivers also provide well-defined interface functions for system call or kernel subsystem access. Figure 1.1 shows the structure of Linux.

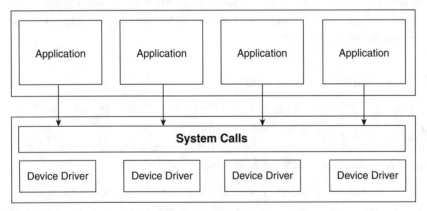

FIGURE 1.1
Linux Architecture Perspective

Linux also sports dynamically loadable device drivers, breaking one of the main drawbacks inherent in monolithic operating systems. Dynamically loadable device drivers allow the systems programmer to incorporate system code into the kernel without having to compile his code into the kernel image. Doing so implies a lengthy wait (depending on your system capabilities) and a reboot, which greatly increases the time a systems programmer spends in developing his code. With dynamically loadable device drivers, the systems programmer can load and unload his device driver in real time without needing to recompile the entire kernel and bring down the system.

Throughout this book, we explain these different "parts" of Linux. When possible, we follow a top-down approach, starting with an example application program and tracing its execution path down through system calls and subsystem functions. This way, you can associate the more familiar user space functionality with the kernel components that support it.

1.8 Kernel Organization

Linux supports numerous architectures—this means that it can be run on many types of processors, which include alpha, arm, i386, ia64, ppc, ppc64, and s390x. The Linux source code is packaged to include support for all these architectures. Most of the source code is written in C and is hardware independent. A portion of the code is heavily hardware dependent and is written in a mix of C and assembly for the particular architecture. The heavily machine-dependent portion is wrapped by a long list of system calls that serve as an interface. As you read this book, you get a chance to see that the architecture-dependent portions of the code are generally involved with system initialization and bootstrapping, exception vector handling, address translation, and device I/O.

1.9 Overview of the Linux Kernel

There are various components to the Linux kernel. Throughout this book, we use the word *component* and *subsystem* interchangeably to refer to these categorical and functional differentiators of the kernel functions.

In the following sections, we discuss some of those components and how they are implemented in the Linux kernel. We also cover some key features of the operating system that provide insight into how things are implemented in the kernel. We break up the components into filesystem, processes, scheduler, and device drivers. Although this is not intended to be a comprehensive list, it provides a reference for the rest of this book.

1.9.1   User Interface

Users communicate with the system by way of programs. A user first logs in to the system through a **terminal** or a **virtual terminal**. In Linux, a program, called **mingetty** for virtual terminals or **agetty** for serial terminals, monitors the inactive terminal waiting for users to notify that they want to log in. To do this, they enter their account name, and the getty program proceeds to call the **login** program, which prompts for a password, accesses a list of names and passwords for authentication, and allows them into the system if there is a match, or exits and terminates the process if there is no match. The getty programs are all **respawned** once terminated, which means they restart if the process ever exits.

Once authenticated in the system, users need a way to tell the system what they want to do. If the user is authenticated successfully, the login program executes a shell. Although technically not part of the operating system, the shell is the primary user interface to the operating system. A shell is a command interpreter and consists of a listening process. The listening process (one that blocks until the condition of receiving input is met) then interprets and executes the requests typed in by the user. The shell is one of the programs found in the top layer of Figure 1.1.

The shell displays a command prompt (which is generally configurable, depending on the shell) and waits for user input. A user can then interact with the system's devices and programs by entering them using a syntax defined by the shell.

The programs a user can call are executable files stored within the filesystem that the user can execute. The execution of these requests is initiated by the shell spawning a child process. The child process might then make system call accesses. After the system call returns and the child process terminates, the shell can go back to listen for user requests.

1.9.2   User Identification

A user logs in with a unique account name. However, he is also associated with a unique **user ID (UID)**. The kernel uses this UID to validate the user's permissions with respect to file accesses. When a user logs in, he is granted access to his **home directory**, which is where he can create, modify, and destroy files. It is important in a multiuser system, such as Linux, to associate users with access permission and/or restrictions to prevent users from interfering with the activity of other users and accessing their data. The **superuser** or **root** is a special user with unrestricted permissions; this user's UID is 0.

A user is also a member of one or more groups, each of which has its own unique **group ID (GID)**. When a user is created, he is automatically a member of a group whose name is identical to his username. A user can also be manually added to other groups that have been defined by the system administrator.

A file or a program (an executable file) is associated with permissions as they apply to users and groups. Any particular user can determine who is allowed to access his files and who is not. A file will be associated with a particular UID and a particular GID.

1.9.3   Files and Filesystems

A **filesystem** provides a method for the storage and organization of data. Linux supports the concept of the **file** as a device-independent sequence of bytes. By means of this abstraction, a user can access a file regardless of what device (for example, hard disk, tape drive, disk drive) stores it. Files are grouped inside a container called a **directory**. Because directories can be nested in each other (which means that a directory can contain another directory), the filesystem structure is that of a hierarchical tree. The **root** of the tree is the top-most node under which all other directories and files are stored. It is identified by a forward slash (/). A filesystem is stored in a hard-drive **partition**, or unit of storage.

1.9.3.1   Directories, Files, and Pathnames

Every file in a tree has a pathname that indicates its name and location. A file also has the directory to which it belongs. A pathname that takes the **current working** directory, or the directory the user is located in, as its root is called a **relative path-name**, because the file is named *relative* to the current working directory. An **absolute pathname** is a pathname that is taken from the root of the filesystem (for example, a pathname that starts with a /). In Figure 1.2, the absolute pathname of user paul's file.c is /home/paul/src/file.c. If we are located inside paul's home directory, the relative pathname is simply src/file.c.

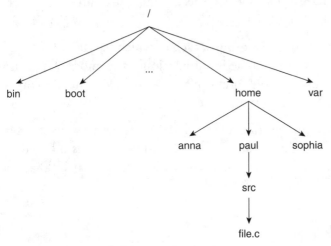

FIGURE 1.2
Hierarchical File Structure

The concepts of absolute versus relative pathnames come into play because the kernel associates processes with the current working directory and with a root direc-tory. The current working directory is the directory from which the process was called and is identified by a . (pronounced "dot"). As an aside, the parent directory is the directory that contains the working directory and is identified by a .. (pro-nounced "dot dot"). Recall that when a user logs in, she is "located" in her home directory. If Anna tells the shell to execute a particular program, such as ls, as soon as she logs in, the process that executes ls has /home/anna as its current working directory (whose parent directory is /home) and / will be its root directory. The root is always its own parent.

1.9.3.2 Filesystem Mounting

In Linux, as in all UNIX-like systems, a filesystem is only accessible if it has been mounted. A filesystem is mounted with the **mount** system call and is unmounted with the **umount** system call. A filesystem is mounted on a mount point, which is a directory used as the root access to the mounted filesystem. A directory mount point should be empty. Any files originally located in the directory used as a mount point are inaccessible after the filesystem is mounted and remains so until the filesystem is unmounted. The /etc/mtab file holds the table of mounted filesystems while **/etc/fstab** holds the filesystem table, which is a table listing all the system's filesystems and their attributes. /etc/mtab lists the device of the mounted filesystem and associates it with its mount point and any options with which it was mounted.[8]

1.9.3.3 File Protection and Access Rights

Files have access permissions to provide some degree of privacy and security. **Access rights** or permissions are stored as they apply to three distinct categories of users: the user himself, a designated group, and everyone else. The three types of users can be granted varying access rights as applied to the three types of access to a file: read, write, and execute. When we execute a file listing with an ls -al, we get a view of the file permissions:

```
lkp :~# ls -al /home/sophia
drwxr-xr-x 22 sophia sophia     4096 Mar 14 15:13 .
drwxr-xr-x 24 root   root     4096 Mar 7 18:47 ..
drwxrwx--- 3 sophia department  4096 Mar 4 08:37 sources
```

The first entry lists the access permissions of sophia's home directory. According to this, she has granted everyone the ability to enter her home directory but not to edit it. She herself has read, write, and execute permission.[9] The second entry indicates the access rights of the parent directory /home. /home is owned by root but it allows everyone to read and execute. In sophia's home directory, she has a directory called sources, which she has granted read, write, and execute permissions to herself, members of the group called department, and no permissions to anyone else.

---

[8]   The options are passed as parameters to the mount system call.

[9]   Execute permission, as applied to a directory, indicates that a user can enter it. Execute permission as applied to a file indicates that it can be run and is used only on executable files.

1.9.3.4   File Modes

In addition to access rights, a file has three additional modes: **sticky**, **suid**, and **sgid**. Let's look at each mode more closely.

sticky

A file with the sticky bit enabled has a "t" in the last character of the mode field (for example, `-rwx-----t`). Back in the day when disk accesses were slower than they are today, when memory was not as large, and when demand-based methodologies hadn't been conceived,[10] an executable file could have the sticky bit enabled and ensure that the kernel would keep it in memory despite its state of execution. When applied to a program that was heavily used, this could increase performance by reducing the amount of time spent accessing the file's information from disk.

When the sticky bit is enabled in a directory, it prevents the removal or renaming of files from users who have write permission in that directory (with exception of root and the owner of the file).

suid

An executable with the `suid` bit set has an "s" where the "x" character goes for the user-permission bits (for example, `-rws------`). When a user executes an executable file, the process is associated with the user who called it. If an executable has the `suid` bit set, the process inherits the UID of the file owner and thus access to its set of access rights. This introduces the concepts of the **real user ID** as opposed to the **effective user ID**. As we soon see when we look at processes in the "Processes" section, a process' real UID corresponds to that of the user that started the process. The effective UID is often the same as the real UID unless the `setuid` bit was set in the file. In that case, the effective UID holds the UID of the file owner.

`suid` has been exploited by hackers who call executable files owned by root with the `suid` bit set and redirect the program operations to execute instructions that they would otherwise not be allowed to execute with root permissions.

sgid

An executable with the `sgid` bit set has an "s" where the "x" character goes for the group permission bits (for example, `-rwxrws---`). The `sgid` bit acts just like

---

[10] This refers to techniques that exploit the principle of locality with respect to loaded program chunks. We see more of this in detail in Chapter 4.

the `suid` bit but as applied to the group. A process also has a **real group ID** and an **effective group ID** that holds the GID of the user and the GID of the file group, respectively.

1.9.3.5   File Metadata

File metadata is all the information about a file that does not include its content. For example, metadata includes the type of file, the size of the file, the UID of the file owner, the access rights, and so on. As we soon see, some file types (devices, pipes, and sockets) contain no data, only metadata. All file metadata, with the exception of the filename, is stored in an **inode** or **index node**. An inode is a block of information, and every file has its own inode. A **file descriptor** is an internal kernel data structure that manages the file data. File descriptors are obtained when a process accesses a file.

1.9.3.6   Types of Files

UNIX-like systems have various file types.

Regular File

A regular file is identified by a dash in the first character of the mode field (for example, `-rw-rw-rw-`). A regular file can contain ASCII data or binary data if it is an executable file. The kernel does not care what type of data is stored in a file and thus makes no distinctions between them. User programs, however, might care. Regular files have their data stored in zero or more data blocks.[11]

Directory

A directory file is identified by a "d" in the first character of the `mode` field (for example, `drwx------`). A directory is a file that holds associations between filenames and the file inodes. A directory consists of a table of entries, each pertaining to a file that it contains. `ls -ai` lists all the contents of a directory and the ID of its associated inode.

Block Devices

A block device is identified by a "b" in the first character of the `mode` field (for example, `brw------`). These files represent a hardware device on which I/O

---

[11] An empty file has zero data blocks.

is performed in discretely sized blocks in powers of 2. Block devices include disk and tape drives and are accessed through the **/dev** directory in the filesystem.[12] Disk accesses can be time consuming; therefore, data transfer for block devices is performed by the kernel's **buffer cache**, which is a method of storing data temporarily to reduce the number of costly disk accesses. At certain intervals, the kernel looks at the data in the buffer cache that has been updated and synchronizes it with the disk. This provides great increases in performance; however, a computer crash can result in loss of the buffered data if it had not yet been written to disk. Synchronization with the disk drive can be forced with a call to the **sync**, **fsync**, or **fdatasync** system calls, which take care of writing buffered data to disk. A block device does not use any data blocks because it stores no data. Only an inode is required to hold its information.

Character Devices

A character device is identified by a "c" in the first character of the mode field (for example, **crw-------**). These files represent a hardware device that is not block structured and on which I/O occurs in streams of bytes and is transferred directly between the device driver and the requesting process. These devices include terminals and serial devices and are accessed through the /dev directory in the filesystem. **Pseudo devices** or device drivers that do not represent hardware but instead perform some unrelated kernel side function can also be character devices. These devices are also known as **raw** devices because of the fact that there is no intermediary cache to hold the data. Similar to a block device, a character device does not use any data blocks because it stores no data. Only an inode is required to hold its information.

Link

A link device is identified by an "l" in the first character of the mode field (for example, **lrw-------**). A link is a pointer to a file. This type of file allows there to be multiple references to a particular file while only one copy of the file and its data actually exists in the filesystem. There are two types of links: **hard link** and **symbolic, or soft, link**. Both are created through a call to **ln**. A hard link has limitations that are absent in the symbolic link. These include being limited to linking files within the same filesystem, being unable to link to directories, and being

---

[12] The mount system call requires a block file.

unable to link to non-existing files. Links reflect the permissions of the file to which it is pointing.

Named Pipes

A pipe file is identified by a "p" in the first character of the `mode` field (for example, `prw-------`). A pipe is a file that facilitates communication between programs by acting as data pipes; data is written into them by one program and read by another. The pipe essentially buffers its input data from the first process. Named pipes are also known as FIFOs because they relay the information to the reading program in a first in, first out basis. Much like the device files, no data blocks are used by pipe files, only the inode.

Sockets

A socket is identified by an "s" in the first character of the mode field (for example, `srw-------`). Sockets are special files that also facilitate communication between two processes. One difference between pipes and sockets is that sockets can facilitate communication between processes on different computers connected by a network. Socket files are also not associated with any data blocks. Because this book does not cover networking, we do not go over the internals of sockets.

1.9.3.7   Types of Filesystems

Linux filesystems support an interface that allows various filesystem types to coexist. A filesystem type is determined by the way the block data is broken down and manipulated in the physical device and by the type of physical device. Some examples of types of filesystems include network mounted, such as NFS, and disk based, such as ext3, which is one of the Linux default filesystems. Some special filesystems, such as `/proc`, provide access to kernel data and address space.

1.9.3.8   File Control

When a file is accessed in Linux, control passes through a number of stages. First, the program that wants to access the file makes a system call, such as `open()`, `read()`, or `write()`. Control then passes to the kernel that executes the system call. There is a high-level abstraction of a filesystem called VFS, which determines what type of specific filesystem (for example, `ext2`, `minix`, and `msdos`) the file exists upon, and control is then passed to the appropriate filesystem driver.

The filesystem driver handles the management of the file upon a given logical device. A hard drive could have `msdos` and `ext2` partitions. The filesystem driver knows how to interpret the data stored on the device and keeps track of all the metadata associated with a file. Thus, the filesystem driver stores the actual file data and incidental information such as the timestamp, group and user modes, and file permissions (`read`/`write`/`execute`).

The filesystem driver then calls a lower-level device driver that handles the actual reading of the data off of the device. This lower-level driver knows about blocks, sectors, and all the hardware information that is necessary to take a chunk of data and store it on the device. The lower-level driver passes the information up to the filesystem driver, which interprets and formats the raw data and passes the information to the VFS, which finally transfers the data back to the originating program.

1.9.4   Processes

If we consider the operating system to be a framework that developers can build upon, we can consider processes to be the basic unit of activity undertaken and managed by this framework. More specifically, a process is a program that is in execution. A single program can be executed multiple times so there might be more than one process associated with a particular program.

The concept of processes became significant with the introduction of multiuser systems in the 1960s. Consider a single-user operating system where the CPU executes only a single process. In this case, no other program can be executed until the currently running process is complete. When multiple users are introduced (or if we want the ability to perform multiple tasks concurrently), we need to define a way to switch between the tasks.

The process model makes the execution of multiple tasks possible by defining **execution contexts**. In Linux, each process operates as though it were the only process. The operating system then manages these contexts by assigning the processor to work on one or the other according to a predefined set of rules. The **scheduler** defines and executes these rules. The scheduler tracks the length of time the process has run and switches it off to ensure that no one process hogs the CPU.

The execution context consists of all the parts associated with the program such as its data (and the memory address space it can access), its registers, its stack and stack pointer, and the program counter value. Except for the data and the memory addressing, the rest of the components of a process are transparent to the programmer. However, the operating system needs to manage the stack, stack pointer, program counter, and machine registers. In a multiprocess system, the operating system must also be responsible for the **context switch** between processes and the management of system resources that processes contend for.

1.9.4.1   Process Creation and Control

A process is created from another process with a call to the **fork() system call**. When a process calls fork(), we say that the process **spawned** a new process, or that it **forked**. The new process is considered the **child process** and the original process is considered the **parent process**. All processes have a parent, with the exception of the init process. All processes are spawned from the first process, **init**, which comes about during the bootstrapping phase. This is discussed further in the next section.

As a result of this child/parent model, a system has a process tree that can define the relationships between all the running processes. Figure 1.3 illustrates a process tree.

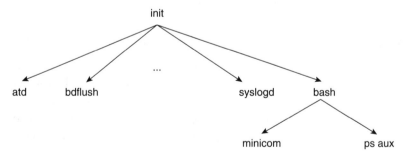

FIGURE 1.3
Process Tree

When a child process is created, the parent process might want to know when it is finished. The **wait() system call** is used to pause the parent process until its child has exited.

A process can also replace itself with another process. This is done, for example, by the `mingetty()` functions previously described. When a user requests access into the system, the `mingetty()` function requests his username and then replaces itself with a process executing `login()` to which it passes the username parameter. This replacement is done with a call to one of the **exec() system calls.**

1.9.4.2   Process IDs

Every process has a unique identifier know as the **process ID (PID)**. A PID is a non-negative integer. Process IDs are handed out in incrementing sequential order as processes are created. When the maximum PID value is hit, the values wrap and PIDs are handed out starting at the lowest available number greater than 1. There are two special processes: **process 0** and **process 1**. Process 0 is the process that is responsible for system initialization and for spawning off process 1, which is also known as the **init** process. All processes in a running Linux system are descendants of process 1. After process 0 executes, the `init` process becomes the idle cycle. Chapter 8, "Booting the Kernel," discusses this process in "The Beginning: start_kernel()" section.

Two system calls are used to identify processes. The `getpid()` system call retrieves the PID of the current process, and the `getppid()` system call retrieves the PID of the process' parent.

1.9.4.3   Process Groups

A process can be a member of a process group by sharing the same **group ID**. A process group facilitates associating a set of processes. This is something you might want to do, for example, if you want to ensure that otherwise unrelated processes receive a `kill` signal at the same time. The process whose PID is identical to the group ID is considered the group leader. Process group IDs can be manipulated by calling the `getpgid()` and `setpgid()` system calls, which retrieve and set the process group ID of the indicated process, respectively.

1.9.4.4   Process States

Processes can be in different states depending on the scheduler and the availability of system resources for which the process contends. A process might be in a **runnable** state if it is currently being executed or in a **run queue**, which is a structure that holds references to processes that are in line to be executed. A process can be **sleeping** if it is waiting for a resource or has yielded to anther process, **dead** if it has been killed, and **defunct** or **zombie** if a process has exited before its parent was able to call `wait()` on it.

1.9.4.5   Process Descriptor

Each process has a process descriptor that contains all the information describing it. The process descriptor contains such information as the process state, the PID, the command used to start it, and so on. This information can be displayed with a call to **ps** (process status). A call to ps might yield something like this:

```
lkp:~#ps aux | more
USER PID TTY STAT COMMAND
root   1  ?     S  init [3]
root   2  ?     SN [ksoftirqd/0]
...
root  10  ?     S< [aio/0]
...
root  2026 ?    Ss /sbin/syslogd -a /var/lib/ntp/dev/log
root  2029 ?    Ss /sbin/klogd -c 1 -2 -x
...
root  3324 tty2   Ss+ /sbin/mingetty tty2
root  3325 tty3   Ss+ /sbin/mingetty tty3
root  3326 tty4   Ss+ /sbin/mingetty tty4
root  3327 tty5   Ss+ /sbin/mingetty tty5
root  3328 tty6   Ss+ /sbin/mingetty tty6
root  3329 ttyS0   Ss+ /sbin/agetty –L 9600 ttyS0 vt102
root  14914 ?    Ss sshd: root@pts/0
...
root  14917 pts/0   Ss –bash
root  17682 pts/0   R+ ps aux
root  17683 pts/0   R+ more
```

The list of process information shows the process with PID 1 to be the `init` process. This list also shows the `mingetty()` and `agetty()` programs listening in on the virtual and serial terminals, respectively. Notice how they are all children of the previous one. Finally, the list shows the bash session on which the `ps aux | more` command was issued. Notice that the | used to indicate a pipe is not a process in itself. Recall that we said pipes facilitate communication between processes. The two processes are `ps aux` and `more`.

As you can see, the STAT column indicates the state of the process, with S referring to sleeping processes and R to running or runnable processes.

1.9.4.6 Process Priority

In single-processor computers, we can have only one process executing at a time. Processes are assigned priorities as they contend with each other for execution time. This priority is dynamically altered by the kernel based on how much a process has run and what its priority has been until that moment. A process is allotted a **timeslice** to execute after which it is swapped out for another process by the scheduler, as we describe next.

Higher priority processes are executed first and more often. The user can set a process priority with a call to **nice()**. This call refers to the niceness of a process toward another, meaning how much the process is willing to yield. A high priority has a negative value, whereas a low priority has a positive value. The higher the value we pass nice, the more we are willing to yield to another process.

1.9.5 System Calls

System calls are the main mechanism by which user programs communicate with the kernel. Systems calls are generally wrapped inside library calls that manage the setup of the registers and data that each system call needs before executing. The user programs then link in the library with the appropriate routines to make the kernel request.

System calls generally apply to specific subsystems. This means that a user space program can interact with any particular kernel subsystem by means of these system calls. For example, files have file-handling system calls, and processes have process-specific system calls. Throughout this book, we identify the system calls associated with particular kernel subsystems. For example, when we talk about filesystems, we look at the read(), write(), open(), and close() system calls. This provides you with a view of how filesystems are implemented and managed within the kernel.

1.9.6 Linux Scheduler

The Linux scheduler handles the task of moving control from one process to another. With the inclusion of kernel pre-emption in Linux 2.6, any process, including the kernel, can be interrupted at nearly any time and control passed to a new process.

For example, when an interrupt occurs, Linux must stop executing the current process and handle the interrupt. In addition, a multitasking operating system, such as Linux, ensures that no one process hogs the CPU for an extended time. The scheduler handles both of these tasks: On one hand, it swaps the current process with a new process; on the other hand, it keeps track of processes' usage of the CPU and indicates that they be swapped if they have run too long.

How the Linux scheduler determines which process to give control of the CPU is explained in depth in Chapter 7, "Scheduling and Kernel Synchronization"; however, a quick summary is that the scheduler determines priority based on past performance (how much CPU the process has used before) and on the criticality of the process (interrupts are more critical than the log system).

The Linux scheduler also manages how processes execute on multiprocessor machines (SMP). There are some interesting features for load balancing across multiple CPUs as well as the ability to tie processes to a specific CPU. That being said, the basic scheduling functionality operates identically across CPUs.

1.9.7   Linux Device Drivers

Device drivers are how the kernel interfaces with hard disks, memory, sound cards, Ethernet cards, and many other input and output devices.

The Linux kernel usually includes a number of these drivers in a default installation; Linux wouldn't be of much use if you couldn't enter any data via your keyboard. Device drivers are encapsulated in a module. Although Linux is a monolithic kernel, it achieves a high degree of modularization by allowing each device driver to be dynamically loaded. Thus, a default kernel can be kept relatively small and slowly extended based upon the actual configuration of the system on which Linux runs.

In the 2.6 Linux kernel, device drivers have two major ways of displaying their status to a user of the system: the /proc and /sys filesystems. In a nutshell, /proc is usually used to debug and monitor devices and /sys is used to change settings. For example, if you have an RF tuner on an embedded Linux device, the default tuner frequency could be visible, and possibly changeable, under the devices entry in sysfs.

In Chapters 5, "Input/Output," and 10, "Adding Your Code to the Kernel," we closely look at device drivers for both character and block devices. More specifically, we tour the /dev/random device driver and see how it gathers entropy information from other devices on the Linux system.

1.10 Portability and Architecture Dependence

As we explore the internals of the Linux kernel, more often than not, we find ourselves discussing some aspect of the underlying hardware or *architecture*. After all, the Linux kernel is a large lump of software running on a specific kind of processor, and as such, it must have intimate knowledge of that processor's (or processors') instruction set and capabilities. This however, does not require every kernel or system programmer to be an expert on the host microprocessor, but a good idea of how the kernel code is constructed or *layered* will go a long way to help debug some of the stickier problems one will come across.

The Linux kernel is crafted in such a way as to minimize how much of its code is directly dependent on the underlying hardware. When interaction with the hardware *is* required, appropriate libraries have been brought in at compile time to execute that particular function on a given architecture. For example, when the kernel wants to make a context switch, it calls the function **switch_to()**. Because the kernel has been compiled for a given architecture (for example, PowerPC or x86), it linked in (at compile time) the appropriate include files include/asm-ppc/system.h or include/asm-i386/system.h in which the architecture-dependent definition of switch_to() resides. At boot time, the architecture-dependent initialization code makes calls to Firmware or BIOS (BIOS is the system startup software which is covered in Chapter 9, "Building the Linux Kernel").

Depending on the target architecture, a different layer of software is brought in to interface with the hardware. Above this layer, the kernel code is oblivious to the underlying hardware.

For this reason, the Linux kernel is said to be *portable* across different architectures. Limitations arise when drivers have not been ported, either because the hardware they are bound to is not available for a certain architecture or because there has not been enough demand for a port. To create a device driver, the programmer must have a register-level specification for a given piece of hardware. Not all manufacturers are willing to furnish this document because of the proprietary nature of their hardware. This, too, indirectly limits the portability of Linux across architectures.

Summary

This chapter gave a brief overview and introduction to the topics that will be touched on in more detail. We have also mentioned some of the features that have made Linux so popular, as well as some of the issues surrounding this operating system. The following chapter goes over some basic tools you need to effectively explore the Linux kernel.

Exercises

1. What is the difference between a UNIX system and a UNIX clone?

2. What does the term "Linux on Power" refer to?

3. What is user space? What is kernel space?

4. What is the interface to kernel functionality for user space programs?

5. What is the relationship between a user's UID and a username?

6. List the ways in which files are associated with users.

7. List the various types of files supported by Linux.

8. Is the shell part of the operating system?

9. Why do we have both file protection and file modes?

10. List the kind of information you would expect to find in a structure holding file metadata.

11. What is the basic difference between a character and a block device?

12. What is the subcomponent of the Linux kernel that allows it to be a multiprocess system?

13. How does a process become the parent of another process?

14. In this chapter, we introduced two kinds of hierarchical trees: file trees and process trees. What do they have in common? How do they differ?

15. Is a process ID associated with a user ID?

16. What is the use of assigning process priorities? Should all users be able to alter the priority values? Why or why not?

17. Are device drivers used solely for adding hardware support?

18. What helps make Linux portable across different architectures?

Chapter 2

Exploration Toolkit

In this chapter

This chapter overviews common Linux coding constructs and describes a number of methods to interface with the kernel. We start by looking at common Linux datatypes used for efficient storage and retrieval of information, coding methods, and basic assembly language. This provides a foundation for the more detailed kernel analysis in the later chapters. We then describe how Linux compiles and links the source code into executable code. This is useful for understanding cross-platform code and nicely introduces the GNU toolset. This is followed by an outline of a number of methods to gather information from the Linux kernel. We range from analyzing source and executable code to inserting debugging statements within the Linux kernel. This chapter closes with a "grab bag" of observations and comments on other regularly encountered Linux conventions.[1]

2.1 Common Kernel Datatypes

The Linux kernel has many objects and structures of which to keep track. Examples include memory pages, processes, and interrupts. A timely way to reference one of these objects among many is a major concern if the operating system is run efficiently. Linux uses linked lists and binary search trees (along with a set of helper routines) to first group these objects into a single container and, second, to find a single element in an efficient manner.

2.1.1 Linked Lists

Linked lists are common datatypes in computer science and are used throughout the Linux kernel. Linked lists are often implemented as circular doubly linked lists within the Linux kernel. (See Figure 2.1.) Thus, given any node in a list, we can go to the next or previous node. All the code for linked lists can be viewed in `include/linux/list.h`. This section deals with the major features of linked lists.

---

[1] We do not yet delve into the kernel internals. At this point, we summarize the tools and concepts necessary to navigate through the kernel code. If you are a more experienced kernel hacker, you can skip this section and jump right into the kernel internals, which begins in Chapter 3, "Processes: The Principal Model of Execution."

A linked list is initialized by using the `LIST_HEAD` and `INIT_ LIST_HEAD` macros:

```
------------------------------------------------------------------------
include/linux/list.h
27
28 struct list_head {
29   struct list_head *next, *prev;
30 };
31
32 #define LIST_HEAD_INIT(name) { &(name), &(name) }
33
34 #define LIST_HEAD(name) \
35   struct list_head name = LIST_HEAD_INIT(name)
36
37 #define INIT_LIST_HEAD(ptr) do { \
38   (ptr)->next = (ptr); (ptr)->prev = (ptr); \
39 } while (0)
------------------------------------------------------------------------
```

Line 34

The `LIST_HEAD` macro creates the linked list head specified by `name`.

Line 37

The `INIT_LIST_HEAD` macro initializes the previous and next pointers within the structure to reference the head itself. After both of these calls, `name` contains an empty doubly linked list.[2]

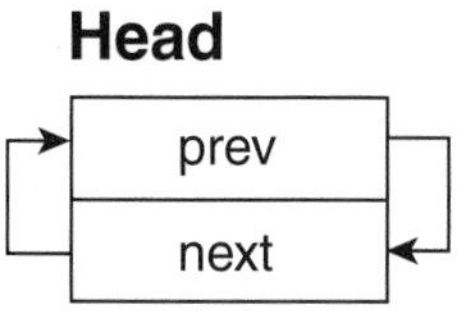

Head

FIGURE 2.1
Linked List After the INIT_LIST_HEAD Macro Is Called

---

[2]   An empty list is defined as one whose `head->next` field points to the list's head element.

Simple stacks and queues can be implemented by the `list_add()` or `list_add_tail()` functions, respectively. A good example of this being used is in the work queue code:

```
------------------------------------------------------------------------
kernel/workqueue.c
330 list_add(&wq->list, &workqueues);
------------------------------------------------------------------------
```

The kernel adds `wq->list` to the system-wide list of work queues, `workqueues`. `workqueues` is thus a stack of queues.

Similarly, the following code adds `work->entry` to the end of the list `cwq->worklist`. `cwq->worklist` is thus being treated as a queue:

```
------------------------------------------------------------------------
kernel/workqueue.c
84 list_add_tail(&work->entry, &cwq->worklist);
------------------------------------------------------------------------
```

When deleting an element from a list, **`list_del()`** is used. `list_del()` takes the list entry as a parameter and deletes the element simply by modifying the entry's next and previous nodes to point to each other. For example, when a work queue is destroyed, the following code removes the work queue from the system-wide list of work queues:

```
------------------------------------------------------------------------
kernel/workqueue.c
382 list_del(&wq->list);
------------------------------------------------------------------------
```

One extremely useful macro in `include/linux/list.h` is the **`list_for_each_entry`** macro:

```
------------------------------------------------------------------------
include/linux/list.h
349 /**
350 * list_for_each_entry -  iterate over list of given type
351 * @pos:  the type * to use as a loop counter.
352 * @head:  the head for your list.
353 * @member:  the name of the list_struct within the struct.
354 */
355 #define list_for_each_entry(pos, head, member)
356    for (pos = list_entry((head)->next, typeof(*pos), member),
357       prefetch(pos->member.next);
358    &pos->member != (head);
359    pos = list_entry(pos->member.next, typeof(*pos), member),
360       prefetch(pos->member.next))
------------------------------------------------------------------------
```

This function iterates over a list and operates on each member within the list. For example, when a CPU comes online, it wakes a process for each work queue:

```
kernel/workqueue.c
59 struct workqueue_struct {
60   struct cpu_workqueue_struct cpu_wq[NR_CPUS];
61   const char *name;
62   struct list_head list; /* Empty if single thread */
63 };
   ...
466   case CPU_ONLINE:
467     /* Kick off worker threads. */
468     list_for_each_entry(wq, &workqueues, list)
469       wake_up_process(wq->cpu_wq[hotcpu].thread);
470     break;
```

The macro expands and uses the `list_head` list within the `workqueue_struct` wq to traverse the list whose head is at work queues. If this looks a bit confusing remember that we do not need to know what list we're a member of in order to traverse it. We know we've reached the end of the list when the value of the current entry's next pointer is equal to the list's head.[3] See Figure 2.2 for an illustration of a work queue list.

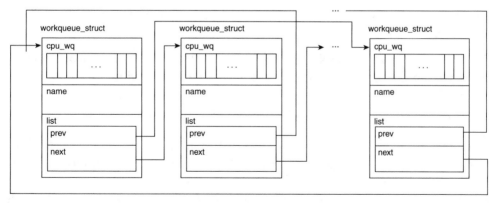

FIGURE 2.2
Work Queue List

---

[3] We could also use `list_for_each_entry_reverse()` to traverse the list backward.

A further refinement of the linked list is an implementation where the head of the list has only a single pointer to the first element. This contrasts the double pointer head discussed in the previous section. Used in hash tables (which are introduced in Chapter 4, "Memory Management"), the single pointer head does not have a back pointer to reference the tail element of the list. This is thought to be less wasteful of memory because the tail pointer is not generally used in a hash search:

```
------------------------------------------------------------------------
include/linux/list.h
484   struct hlist_head {
485     struct hlist_node *first;
486   };

488   struct hlist_node {
489     struct hlist_node *next, **pprev;
490   };

492   #define HLIST_HEAD_INIT { .first = NULL }
493   #define HLIST_HEAD(name) struct hlist_head name = { .first = NULL }
------------------------------------------------------------------------
```

Line 492

The `HLIST_HEAD_INIT` macro sets the pointer `first` to the `NULL` pointer.

Line 493

The `HLIST_HEAD` macro creates the linked list by name and sets the pointer `first` to the `NULL` pointer.

These list constructs are used throughout the Linux kernel code in work queues, as we've seen in the scheduler, the timer, and the module-handling routines.

2.1.2   Searching

The previous section explored grouping elements in a list. An ordered list of elements is sorted based on a key value within each element (for example, each element having a key value greater than the previous element). If we want to find a particular element (based on its key), we start at the head and increment through the list, comparing the value of its key with the value we were searching for. If the value was not equal, we move on to the next element until we find the matching key. In this example, the time it takes to find a given element in the list is directly proportional to the value of the key. In other words, this *linear* search takes longer as more elements are added to the list.

Big-O

For a searching algorithm, **big-O** notation is the theoretical measure of the execution of an algorithm usually in time needed to find a given key. It represents the worst-case search time for a given number (**n**) elements. The big-O notation for a linear search is O(n/2), which indicates that, on average, half of the list is searched to find a given key.

Source: National Institute of Standards and Technology (www.nist.gov).

   With large lists of elements, faster methods of storing and locating a given piece of data are required if the operating system is to be prevented from grinding to a halt. Although many methods (and their derivatives) exist, the other major data structure Linux uses for storage is the *tree*.

2.1.3   Trees

   Used in Linux memory management, the tree allows for efficient access and manipulation of data. In this case, efficiency is measured in how fast we can store and retrieve a single piece of data among many. Basic trees, and specifically red black trees, are presented in this section and, for the specific Linux implementation and helper routines, see Chapter 6, "Filesystems." Rooted trees in computer science consist of *nodes* and *edges* (see Figure 2.3). The node represents the data element and the edges are the paths between the nodes. The first, or top, node in a rooted tree is the *root* node. Relationships between nodes are expressed as *parent*, *child*, and *sibling*, where each child has exactly one parent (except the root), each parent has one or more children, and siblings have the same parent. A node with no children is termed as a *leaf*. The *height* of a tree is the number of edges from the root to the most distant leaf. Each row of descendants across the tree is termed as a *level*. In Figure 2.3, **b** and **c** are one level below **a**, and **d**, **e**, and **f** are two levels below **a**. When looking at the data elements of a given set of siblings, *ordered* trees have the *left*-most sibling being the lowest value ascending in order to the *right*-most sibling. Trees are generally implemented as linked lists or arrays and the process of moving through a tree is called *traversing* the tree.

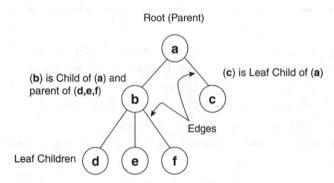

Root (Parent)

(b) is Child of **(a)** and
parent of **(d,e,f)**

(c) is Leaf Child of **(a)**

Edges

Leaf Children

FIGURE 2.3
Rooted Tree

2.1.3.1 Binary Trees

Previously, we looked at finding a key using a linear search, comparing our key with each iteration. What if we could rule out half of the ordered list with every comparison?

A *binary tree*, unlike a linked list, is a hierarchical, rather than linear, data structure. In the binary tree, each element or node points to a left or right child node, and in turn, each child points to a left or right child, and so on. The main rule for ordering the nodes is that the child on the left has a key value less than the parent, and the child on the right has a value equal to or greater than the parent. As a result of this rule, we know that for a key value in a given node, the left child and all its descendants have a key value less than that given node and the right child and all its descendants have a key value greater than or equal to the given node.

When storing data in a binary tree, we reduce the amount of data to be searched by half during each iteration. In big-O notation, this yields a performance (with respect to the number of items searched) of $O \log(n)$. Compare this to the linear search big-O of $O(n/2)$.

The algorithm used to traverse a binary tree is simple and hints of a recursive implementation because, at every node, we compare our key value and either descend left or right into the tree. The following is a discussion on the implementation, helper functions, and types of binary trees.

As just mentioned, a node in a binary tree can have one left child, one right child, a left and right child, or no children. The rule for an ordered binary tree is that for a given node value (**x**), the left child (and all its descendants) have values less than **x** and the right child (and all its descendants) have values greater than **x**. Following this rule, if an ordered set of values were inserted into a binary tree, it would end up being a linear list, resulting in a relatively slow linear search for a given value. For example, if we were to create a binary tree with the values [0,1,2,3,4,5,6], 0 would become the root; 1, being greater than 0, would become the right child; 2, being greater than 1, would become its right child; 3 would become the right child of 2; and so on.

A *height-balanced* binary tree is where no leaf is some number farther from the root than any other. As nodes are added to the binary tree, it needs to be rebalanced for efficient searching; this is accomplished through *rotation*. If, after an insertion, a given node (**e**), has a left child with descendants that are two levels greater than any other leaf, we must right-rotate node **e**. As shown in Figure 2.4, **e** becomes the parent of **h**, and the right child of **e** becomes the left child of **h**. If rebalancing is done after each insertion, we are guaranteed that we need at most one rotation. This rule of balance (no child shall have a leaf distance greater than one) is known as an AVL-tree (after G. M. Adelson-Velskii and E. M. Landis).

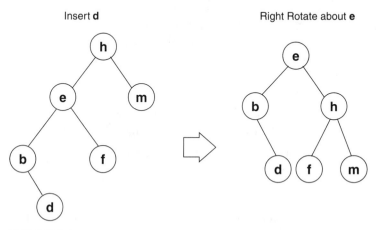

FIGURE 2.4
Right Rotation

2.1.3.2 Red Black Trees

The red black tree used in Linux memory management is similar to an AVL tree. A red black tree is a balanced binary tree in which each node has a red or black color attribute.

Here are the rules for a red black tree:

- All nodes are either red or black.

- If a node is red, both its children are black.

- All leaf nodes are black.

- When traversing from the root node to a leaf, each path contains the same number of black nodes.

Both AVL and red black trees have a big-O of **O log(n)**, and depending on the data being inserted (sorted/unsorted) and searched, each can have their strong points. (Several papers on performance of binary search trees [BSTs] are readily available on the Web and make for interesting reading.)

As previously mentioned, many other data structures and associated search algorithms are used in computer science. This section's goal was to assist you in your exploration by introducing the concepts of the common structures used for organizing data in the Linux kernel. Having a basic understanding of the list and tree structures help you understand the more complex operations, such as memory management and queues, which are discussed in later chapters.

2.2 Assembly

Linux is an operating system. As such, sections of it are closely bound to the processor on which it is running. The Linux authors have done a great job of keeping the processor- (or architecture-) specific code to a minimum, striving for the maximum reuse of code across all the supported architectures. In this section, we look at the following:

- How the same C function is implemented in x86 and PowerPC architectures.

- The use of macros and inline assembly code.

This section's goal is to cover enough of the basics so you can trace through the architecture-specific kernel code having enough understanding so as not to get lost.

We leave advanced assembly-language programming to other books. We also cover some of the trickiest architecture-specific code: inline assembler.

To discuss freely PPC and x86 assembly languages, let's look at the architectures of each processor.

2.2.1 PowerPC

The PowerPC is a **Reduced Instruction Set Computing (RISC)** architecture. The goal of RISC architecture is to improve performance by having a simple instruction set that executes in as few processor cycles as possible. Because they take advantage of the parallel instruction (superscalar) attributes of the hardware, some of these instructions, as we soon see, are far from simple. IBM, Motorola, and Apple jointly defined the PowerPC architecture. Table 2.1 lists the user set of registers for the PowerPC.

TABLE 2.1
PowerPC User Register Set

Register Name	Width for Arch.		Function	Number of Regs
	32 Bit	64 Bit		
CR	32	32	Condition register	1
LR	32	64	Link register	1
CTR	32	64	Count register	1
GPR[0..31]	32	64	General-purpose register	32
XER	32	64	Fixed-point exception register	1
FPR[0..31]	64	64	Floating-point register	32
FPSCR	32	64	Floating-point status control register	1

Table 2.2 illustrates the Application Binary Interface usage of the general and floating-point registers. Volatile registers are for use any time, dedicated registers have specific assigned uses, and non-volatile registers can be used but must be preserved across function calls.

Application Binary Interface (ABI)

An **ABI** is a set of conventions that allows a linker to combine separately compiled modules into one unit without recompilation, such as calling conventions, machine interface, and operating-system interface. Among other things, an ABI defines the binary interface between these units. Several PowerPC ABI variations are in existence. They are often related to the target operating system and/or hardware. These variations or *supplements* are documents based on the *UNIX System V Application Binary Interface*, originally from AT&T and later from the Santa Cruz Operation (SCO). The benefits of conforming to an ABI are that it allows linking object files compiled by different compilers.

TABLE 2.2
ABI Register Usage

Register	Type	Use
r0	Volatile	Prologue/epilogue, language specific
r1	Dedicated	Stack pointer
r2	Dedicated	TOC
r3-r4	Volatile	Parameter passing, in/out
r5-r10	Volatile	Parameter passing
r11	Volatile	Environment pointer
r12	Volatile	Exception handling
r13	Non-volatile	Must be preserved across calls
r14-r31	Non-volatile	Must be preserved across calls
f0	Volatile	Scratch
f1	Volatile	1st FP parm, 1st FP scalar return
f2-f4	Volatile	2nd–4th FP parm, FP scalar return
f5-f13	Volatile	5th–13th FP parm
f14-f31	Non-volatile	Must be preserved across calls

The 32-bit PowerPC architecture uses instructions that are 4 bytes long and word aligned. It operates on byte, half-word, word, and double-word accesses. Instructions are categorized into branch, fixed-point, and floating-point.

2.2.1.1   Branch Instructions

The **condition register (CR)** is integral to all branch operations. It is broken down into eight 4-bit fields that can be set explicitly by a move instruction, implicitly, as the result of an instruction, or most common, as the result of a compare instruction.

The **link register (LR)** is used by certain forms of the branch instruction to provide the target address and the return address after a branch.

The **count register (CTR)** holds a loop count decremented by specific branch instructions. The CTR can also hold the target address for certain branch instructions.

In addition to the CTR and LR above, PowerPC branch instructions can jump to a relative or absolute address. Using Extended Mnemonics, there are many forms of conditional branches along with the unconditional branch.

2.2.1.2   Fixed-Point Instructions

The PPC has no computational instructions that modify storage. All work must be brought into one or more of the 32 general-purpose registers (GPRs). Storage access instructions access byte, half-word, word, and double-word data in Big Endian ordering. With Extended Mnemonics, there are many load, store, arithmetic, and logical fixed-point instructions, as well as special instructions to move to/from system registers.

2.2.1.3   Floating-Point Instructions

Floating-point instructions can be broken down into two categories: computational, which includes arithmetic, rounding, conversion, and comparison; and non-computational, which includes move to/from storage or another register. There are 32 general-purpose floating-point registers; each can contain data in double-precision floating-point format.

Big Endian/Little Endian

In processor architecture, **Endianness** refers to byte ordering and operations. The PowerPC is said to be Big Endian, that is, the most significant byte is at the lower address and the least significant byte is 3 bytes later (for 32-bit words). Little Endian, adopted by the x86 architecture, is just the opposite. The least-significant byte is at the lower address and the most significant is 3 bytes later. Let's examine the representation of 0x12345678 (see Figure 2.5):

Big Endian 32-Bit Byte Ordering (PPC)

12	34	56	78
0 7 8 15 16 23 24 31			

Little Endian 32-Bit Byte Ordering (x86)

78	56	34	12
0 7 8 15 16 23 24 31			

FIGURE 2.5
Big and Little Endian Byte Ordering

Discussion on which system is better is beyond the scope of this book, but it is important to know which system you are working with when writing and debugging code. An example pitfall to Endianness is writing a device driver using one architecture for a PCI device based on the other.

The terms Big Endian and Little Endian originate from Jonathan Swift's *Gulliver's Travels*. In the story, Gulliver comes to find two nations at war over which way to eat a boiled egg—from the big end or the little end.

2.2.2   x86

The x86 architecture is a **Complex Instruction Set Computing (CISC)** architecture. Instructions are variable length, depending on their function. Three kinds of registers exist in the Pentium class x86 architecture: general purpose, segment, and status/control. The basic user set is as follows.

Here are the eight general-purpose registers and their conventional uses:

- **EAX**. General purpose accumulator
- **EBX**. Pointer to data

- **ECX**. Counter for loop operations
- **EDX**. I/O pointer
- **ESI**. Pointer to data in DS segment
- **EDI**. Pointer to data in ES segment
- **ESP**. Stack pointer
- **EBP**. Pointer to data on the stack

These six segment registers are used in *real* mode addressing where memory is accessed in blocks. A given byte of memory is then referenced by an *offset* from this segment (for example, ES:EDI references memory in the ES (extra segment) with an offset of the value in the EDI):

- **CS**. Code segment
- **SS**. Stack segment
- **ES, DS, FS, GS**. Data segment

The EFLAGS register indicates processor status after each instruction. This can hold results such as **zero, overflow**, or **carry**. The EIP is a dedicated pointer register that indicates an offset to the current instruction to the processor. This is generally used with the code segment register to form a complete address (for example, CS:EIP):

- **EFLAGS**. Status, control, and system flags
- **EIP**. The instruction pointer, contains an offset from CS

Data ordering in x86 architecture is in Little Endian. Memory access is in byte (8 bit), word (16 bit), double word (32 bit), and quad word (64 bit). Address translation (and its associated registers) is discussed in Chapter 4, but for this section, it should be enough to know the usual registers for code and data instructions in the x86 architecture can be broken down into three categories: **control, arithmetic**, and **data**.

2.2.2.1 Control Instructions

Control instructions, similar to branch instructions in PPC, alter program flow. The x86 architecture uses various "jump" instructions and labels to selectively execute code based on the values in the EFLAGS register. Although many variations exist, Table 2.3 has some of the most common uses. The **condition codes** are set according to the outcome of certain instructions. For example, when the **cmp** (compare) instruction evaluates two integer operands, it modifies the following flags in the EFLAGS register: **OF** (overflow), **SF** (sine flag), **ZF** (zero flag), **PF** (parity flag), and **CF** (carry flag). Thus, if the **cmp** instruction evaluated two equal operands, the zero flag would be set.

TABLE 2.3
Common Forms of the Jump Instruction

Instruction	Function	EFLAGS Condition Codes
je	Jump if equal	ZF=1
jg	Jump if greater	ZF=0 and SF=OF
jge	Jump if greater or equal	SF=OF
jl	Jump if less	SF!=OF
jle	Jump if less or equal	ZF=1
jmp	Unconditional jump	unconditional

In x86 assembly code, labels consist of a unique name followed by a colon. Labels can be used anywhere in an assembly program and have the same address as the line of code immediately following it. The following code uses a conditional jump and a label:

```
100    pop eax
101 loop2:
102    pop ebx
103    cmp eax, ebx
104    jge loop2
```

Line 100

Get the value from the top of the stack and put it in eax.

Line 101

This is the label named loop2.

Line 102

Get the value from the top of the stack and put it in ebx.

Line 103

Compare the values in eax and ebx.

Line 104

Jump if **eax** is greater than or equal to ebx.

Another method of transferring program control is with the **call** and **ret** instructions. Referring to the following line of assembly code:

```
call my_routine
```

The call instruction transfers program control to the label my_routine, while pushing the address of the instruction immediately following the call instruction on the stack. The ret instruction (executed from within my_routine) then pops the return address and jumps to that location.

2.2.2.2   Arithmetic Instructions

Popular arithmetic instructions include **add**, **sub**, **imul** (integer multiply), **idiv** (integer divide), and the logical operators **and**, **or**, **not**, and **xor**.

x86 floating-point instructions and their associated registers move beyond the scope of this book. Recent extensions to Intel and AMD architectures, such as **MMX, SSE, 3DNow, SIMD,** and **SSE2/3,** greatly enhance math-intensive applications, such as graphics and audio. You are directed to the programming manuals for their respective architectures.

2.2.2.3   Data Instructions

Data can be moved between registers, between registers and memory, and from a constant to a register or memory, but not from one memory location to another. Examples of these are as follows:

```
100   mov eax,ebx
101   mov eax,WORD PTR[data3]
102   mov BYTE PTR[char1],al
103   mov eax,0xbeef
104   mov WORD PTR [my_data],0xbeef
```

Line 100

Move 32 bits of data from `ebx` to `eax`.

Line 101

Move 32 bits of data from memory variable `data3` to `eax`.

Line 102

Move 8 bits of data from memory variable `char1` to `al`.

Line 103

Move the constant value `0xbeef` to `eax`.

Line 104

Move the constant value `0xbeef` to the memory variable `my_data`.

As seen in previous examples, **push**, **pop**, and the long versions **pushl** and **popl** move data to and from the stack (pointed to by `SS:ESP`). Similar to the `mov` instruction, the `push` and `pop` operations can be used with registers, data, and constants.

2.3   Assembly Language Example

We can now create a simple program to see how the different architectures produce assembly language for the same C code. For this experiment, we use the `gcc` compiler that came with Red Hat 9 and the `gcc` cross compiler for PowerPC. We present the C program and then, for comparison, the x86 code and the PPC code.

It might startle you to see how much assembly code is generated with just a few lines of C. Because we are just compiling from C to assembler, we are not linking in any environment code, such as the C runtime libraries or local stack creation/destruction, so the size is much smaller than an actual ELF executable.

Note that with assembler, you are closest to seeing exactly what the processor is fetching from cycle to cycle. Another way to look at it is that you have complete control of your code and the system. It is important to mention that even though instructions are fetched from memory in order, they might not always be executed in exactly the same order read in. Some architectures order load and store operations separately.

Here is the example C code:

```
--------------------------------------------------------------------
count.c
1 int main()
2 {
3  int i,j=0;
4
5  for(i=0;i<8;i++)
6  j=j+i;
7
8  return 0;
9 }
--------------------------------------------------------------------
```

Line 1

This is the function definition `main`.

Line 3

This line initializes the local variables `i` and `j` to 0.

Line 5

The `for` loop: While `i` takes values from 0 to 7, set `j` equal to `j` plus `i`.

Line 8

The return marks the jump back to the calling program.

2.3.1   x86 Assembly Example

Here is the code generated for x86 by entering `gcc -S count.c` on the command line. Upon entering the code, the base of the stack is pointed to by `ss:ebp`. The code is produced in "AT&T" format, in which registers are prefixed with a `%` and constants are prefixed with a `$`. The assembly instruction samples previously provided in this section should have prepared you for this simple program, but one variant of indirect addressing should be discussed before we go further.

When referencing a location in memory (for example, stack), the assembler uses a specific syntax for indexed addressing. By putting a base register in parentheses and an index (or offset) just outside the parentheses, the effective address is found by adding the index to the value in the register. For example, if `%ebp` was assigned the value 20, the effective address of `-8(%ebp)` would be $(-8) + (20) = 12$:

```
-----------------------------------------------------------------------
count.s
1  .file  "count.c"
2  .version  "01.01"
3  gcc2_compiled.:
4  .text
5  .align 4
6  .globl main
7  .type  main,@function
8 main:
   #create a local memory area of 8 bytes for i and j.
9  pushl  %ebp
10  movl  %esp, %ebp
11  subl  $8, %esp

   #initialize i (ebp-4) and j (ebp-8) to zero.
12  movl  $0, -8(%ebp)
13  movl  $0, -4(%ebp)
14  .p2align 2
15 .L3:

#This is the for-loop test
16  cmpl  $7, -4(%ebp)
17  jle  .L6
18  jmp  .L4
19  .p2align 2
20 .L6:

#This is the body of the for-loop
21  movl  -4(%ebp), %eax
22  leal  -8(%ebp), %edx
23  addl  %eax, (%edx)
24  leal  -4(%ebp), %eax
25  incl  (%eax)
26  jmp  .L3
27  .p2align 2
28 .L4:

   #Setup to exit the function
29  movl  $0, %eax    30  leave     31  ret
-----------------------------------------------------------------------
```

Line 9

Push stack base pointer onto the stack.

Line 10

Move the stack pointer into the base pointer.

Line 11

Get 8 bytes of stack mem starting at ebp.

Line 12

Move 0 into address ebp-8 (j).

Line 13

Move 0 into address ebp-4 (i).

Line 14

This is an assembler directive that indicates the instruction should be half-word aligned.

Line 15

This is an assembler-created label called .L3.

Line 16

This instruction compares the value of i to 7.

Line 17

Jump to label .L6 if -4(%ebp) is less than or equal to 7.

Line 18

Otherwise, jump to label .L4.

Line 19

Align.

Line 20

Label .L6.

Line 21

Move i into eax.

Line 22

Load the address of j into edx.

Line 23

Add i to the address pointed to by edx (j).

Line 24

Move the new value of i into eax.

Line 25

Increment i.

Line 26

Jump back to the for loop test.

Line 27

Align as described in Line 14 code commentary.

Line 28

Label .L4.

Line 29

Set the return code in eax.

Line 30

Release the local memory area.

Line 31

Pop any variable off stack, pop the return address, and jump back to the caller.

2.3.2 PowerPC Assembly Example

The following is the resulting PPC assembly code for the C program. If you are familiar with assembly language (and acronyms), the function of many PPC instructions is clear. There are, however, several derivative forms of the basic instructions that we must discuss here:

- **stwu RS, D(RA)** (**Store Word with Update**). This instruction takes the value in (GPR) register RS and stores it into the effective address formed by RA+D. The (GPR) register RA is then *updated* with this new effective address.

- **li RT, RS, SI** (**Load Immediate**). This is an extended mnemonic for a fixed-point load instruction. It is equivalent to adding RT, RS, S1, where the sum of (GPR) RS and S1, the 16-bit 2s complement integer is stored in RT. If RS is (GPR) R0, the value SI is stored in RT. Note that the value being only 16 bit has to do with the fact that the opcode, registers, and value must all be encoded into a 32-bit instruction.

- **lwz RT, D(RA)** (**Load Word and Zero**). This instruction forms an effective address as in stwu and loads a word of data from memory into (GPR) RT. The "and Zero" indicates that the upper 32 bits of the calculated effective address are set to 0 if this is a 64-bit implementation running in 32-bit mode. (See the *PowerPC Architecture Book I* for more on implementations.)

- **blr** (**Branch to Link Register**). This instruction is an unconditional branch to the 32-bit address in the link register. When calling a function, the caller puts the return address into the link register. Similar to the x86 ret instruction, blr is the common method of returning from a function.

The following code was generated by entering gcc -S count.c on the command line:

```
----------------------------------------------------------------
countppc.s
1  .file  "count.c"
2  .section  ".text"
3  .align 2
4  .globl main
5  .type  main,@function
6 main:
#Create 32 byte memory area from stack space and initialize i and j.
7  stwu 1,-32(1)  #Store stack ptr (r1) 32 bytes into the stack
8  stw 31,28(1)  #Store word r31 into lower end of memory area
9  mr 31,1  #Move contents of r1 into r31
10  li 0,0  #Load 0 into r0
11  stw 0,12(31)  #Store word r0 into effective address 12(r31), var j
```

```
12  li 0,0    #Load 0 into r0
13  stw 0,8(31)  #Store word r0 into effective address 8(r31) , var i
14  .L2:
#For-loop test
15  lwz 0,8(31)   #Load i into r0
16  cmpwi 0,0,7   #Compare word immediate r0 with integer value 7
17  ble 0,.L5  #Branch if less than or equal to label .L5
18  b .L3    #Branch unconditional to label .L3
19  .L5:
#The body of the for-loop
20  lwz 9,12(31)  #Load j into r9
21  lwz 0,8(31)  #Load i into r0
22  add 0,9,0  #Add r0 to r9 and put result in r0
23  stw 0,12(31)  #Store r0 into j
24  lwz 9,8(31)  #load i into r9
25  addi 0,9,1  #Add 1 to r9 and store in r0
26  stw 0,8(31)  #Store r0 into i
27  b .L2
28  .L3:
29  li 0,0   #Load 0 into r0
30  mr 3,0   #move r0 to r3
31  lwz 11,0(1)  #load r1 into r11
32  lwz 31,-4(11)  #Restore r31
33  mr 1,11   #Restore r1
34  blr   #Branch to Link Register contents
```

Line 7

Store stack ptr (r1) 32 bytes into the stack.

Line 8

Store word r31 into the lower end of the memory area.

Line 9

Move the contents of r1 into r31.

Line 10

Load 0 into r0.

Line 11

Store word r0 into effective address 12(r31), var j.

Line 12

Load 0 into r0.

Line 13

Store word `r0` into effective address `8(r31)`, `var i`.

Line 14

Label `.L2:`.

Line 15

Load `i` into `r0`.

Line 16

Compare word immediate `r0` with integer value `7`.

Line 17

Branch to label `.L5` if `r0` is less than or equal to `7`.

Line 18

Branch unconditional to label `.L3`.

Line 19

Label `.L5:`.

Line 20

Load `j` into `r9`.

Line 21

Load `i` into `r0`.

Line 22

Add `r0` to `r9` and put the result in `r0`.

Line 23

Store `r0` into `j`.

Line 24

Load `i` into `r9`.

Line 25

Add 1 to r9 and store in r0.

Line 26

Store r0 into i.

Line 27

This is an unconditional branch to label .L2.

Line 28

Label .L3:.

Line 29

Load 0 into r0.

Line 30

Move r0 to r3.

Line 31

Load r1 into r11.

Line 32

Restore r31.

Line 33

Restore r1.

Line 34

This is an unconditional branch to the location indicated by Link Register contents.

Contrasting the two assembler files, they have nearly the same number of lines. Upon further inspection, you can see that the RISC (PPC) processor is characteristically using many load and store instructions while the CISC (x86) tends to use the mov instruction more often.

2.4   Inline Assembly

Another form of coding allowed with the gcc compiler is the ability to do **inline assembly** code. As its name implies, inline assembly does not require a call to a separately compiled assembler program. By using certain constructs, we can tell the compiler that code blocks are to be assembled rather than compiled. Although this makes for an architecture-specific file, the readability and efficiency of a C function can be greatly increased.

Here is the inline assembler construct:

```
1   asm (assembler instruction(s)
2    : output operands    (optional)
3    : input operands     (optional)
4    : clobbered registers (optional)
5   );
```

For example, in its most basic form,

```
asm ("movl %eax, %ebx");
```

could also be written as

```
asm ("movl %eax, %ebx" :::);
```

We would be lying to the compiler because we are indeed clobbering ebx. Read on.

What makes this form of inline assembly so versatile is the ability to take in C expressions, modify them, and return them to the program, all the while making sure that the compiler is aware of our changes. Let's further explore the passing of parameters.

2.4.1   Ouput Operands

On line 2, following the colon, the output operands are a list of C expressions in parentheses preceded by a "constraint." For output operands, the constraint usually has the = modifier, which indicates that this is write-only. The & modifier shows that this is an "early clobber" operand, which means that this operand is clobbered before the instruction is finished using it. Each operand is separated by a comma.

2.4.2   Input Operands

The input operands on line 3 follow the same syntax as the output operands except for the write-only modifier.

2.4.3   Clobbered Registers (or Clobber List)

In our assembly statements, we can modify various registers and memory. For gcc to know that these items have been modified, we list them here.

2.4.4   Parameter Numbering

Each parameter is given a positional number starting with 0. For example, if we have one output parameter and two input parameters, %0 references the output parameter and %1 and %2 reference the input parameters.

2.4.5   Constraints

Constraints indicate how an operand can be used. The GNU documentation has the complete listing of *simple* constraints and *machine* constraints. Table 2.4 lists the most common constraints for the x86.

TABLE 2.4
Simple and Machine Constraints for x86

Constraint	Function
a	eax register.
b	ebx register.
c	ecx register.
d	edx register.
S	esi register.
D	edi register.
I	Constant value (0…31).
q	Dynamically allocates a register from eax, ebx, ecx, edx.
r	Same as q + esi, edi.
m	Memory location.
A	Same as a + b. eax and ebx are allocated together to form a 64-bit register.

2.4.6 asm

In practice (especially in the Linux kernel), the keyword **asm** might cause errors at compile time because of other constructs of the same name. You often see this expression written as __asm__, which has the same meaning.

2.4.7 __volatile__

Another commonly used modifier is **__volatile__**. This modifier is important to assembly code. It tells the compiler not to optimize the inline assembly routine. Often, with hardware-level software, the compiler thinks we are being redundant and wasteful and attempts to rewrite our code to be as efficient as possible. This is useful for application-level programming, but at the hardware level, it can be counterproductive.

For example, say we are writing to a memory-mapped register represented by the **reg** variable. Next, we initiate some action that requires us to poll reg. The compiler simply sees this as consecutive reads to the same memory location and eliminates the apparent redundancy. Using __volatile__, the compiler now knows not to optimize accesses using this variable. Likewise, when you see asm volatile (...) in a block of inline assembler code, the compiler should not optimize this block.

Now that we have the basics of assembly and gcc inline assembly, we can turn our attention to some actual inline assembly code. Using what we just learned, we first explore a simple example and then a slightly more complex code block.

Here's the first code example in which we pass variables to an inline block of code:

```
6  int foo(void)
7  {
8  int ee = 0x4000, ce = 0x8000, reg;
9  __asm__ __volatile__("movl %1, %%eax";
10    "movl %2, %%ebx";
11    "call setbits"  ;
12    "movl %%eax, %0"
13    : "=r" (reg)   // reg [param %0] is output
14    : "r" (ce), "r"(ee) // ce [param %1], ee [param %2] are inputs
15    : "%eax" , "%ebx"   // %eax and % ebx got clobbered
16    )
17  printf("reg=%x",reg);
18 }
```

Line 6

This line is the beginning of the C routine.

Line 8

ee, ce, and `req` are local variables that will be passed as parameters to the inline assembler.

Line 9

This line is the beginning of the inline assembler routine. Move `ce` into `eax`.

Line 10

Move `ee` into `ebx`.

Line 11

Call some function from assembler.

Line 12

Return value in `eax`, and copy it to `reg`.

Line 13

This line holds the output parameter list. The parm `reg` is write only.

Line 14

This line is the input parameter list. The parms `ce` and `ee` are register variables.

Line 15

This line is the clobber list. The regs `eax` and `ebx` are changed by this routine. The compiler knows not to use the values after this routine.

Line 16

This line marks the end of the inline assembler routine.

This second example uses the `switch_to()` function from `include/asm-i386/system.h`. This function is the heart of the Linux context switch. We explore only the mechanics of its inline assembly in this chapter. Chapter 9, "Building the Linux Kernel," covers how `switch_to()` is used:

```
-----------------------------------------------------------------------
include/asm-i386/system.h
012  extern struct task_struct * FASTCALL(__switch_to(struct task_struct *prev,
struct task_struct *next));
...
015  #define switch_to(prev,next,last) do {
016    unsigned long esi,edi;
017    asm volatile("pushfl\n\t"
018    "pushl %%ebp\n\t"
019    "movl %%esp,%0\n\t"   /* save ESP */
020    "movl %5,%%esp\n\t"   /* restore ESP */
021    "movl $1f,%1\n\t"     /* save EIP */
022    "pushl %6\n\t"        /* restore EIP */
023    "jmp __switch_to\n"
023    "1:\t"
024    "popl %%ebp\n\t"
025    "popfl"
026    :"=m" (prev->thread.esp),"=m" (prev->thread.eip),
027    "=a" (last),"=S" (esi),"=D" (edi)
028    :"m" (next->thread.esp),"m" (next->thread.eip),
029    "2" (prev), "d" (next));
030  } while (0)
-----------------------------------------------------------------------
```

Line 12

FASTCALL tells the compiler to pass parameters in `registers`.

The `asmlinkage` tag tells the compiler to pass parameters on the `stack`.

Line 15

do { statements...} while(0) is a coding method to allow a macro to appear more like a function to the compiler. In this case, it allows the use of local variables.

Line 16

Don't be confused; these are just local variable names.

Line 17

This is the inline assembler; do not optimize.

Line 23

Parameter 1 is used as a return address.

Lines 17–24

\n\t has to do with the compiler/assembler interface. Each assembler instruction should be on its own line.

Line 26

`prev->thread.esp` and `prev->thread.eip` are the output parameters:

```
[ %0]= (prev->thread.esp), is write-only memory
[%1]= (prev->thread.eip), is write-only memory
```

Line 27

`[%2]=(last)` is write only to register `eax`:

```
[%3]=(esi), is write-only to register esi
[%4]=(edi), is write-only to register edi
```

Line 28

Here are the input parameters:

```
[%5]=  (next->thread.esp), is memory
[%6]= (next->thread.eip), is memory
```

Line 29

`[%7]= (prev)`, reuse parameter "2" (register `eax`) as an input:

```
[%8]= (next), is an input assigned to register edx.
```

Note that there is no clobber list.

The inline assembler for PowerPC is nearly identical in construct to x86. The simple constraints, such as "m" and "r," are used along with a PowerPC set of machine constraints. Here is a routine to exchange a 32-bit pointer. Note how similar the inline assembler syntax is to x86:

```
-----------------------------------------------------------------
include/asm-ppc/system.h
103  static __inline__ unsigned long
104  xchg_u32(volatile void *p, unsigned long val)
105  {
```

```
106   unsigned long prev;
107
108    __asm__ __volatile__ ("\n\
109  1:  lwarx  %0,0,%2 \n"
110
111  "  stwcx.  %3,0,%2 \n\
112    bne-  1b"
113    : "=&r" (prev), "=m" (*(volatile unsigned long *)p)
114    : "r" (p), "r" (val), "m" (*(volatile unsigned long *)p)
115    : "cc", "memory");
116
117    return prev;
118  }
```

Line 103

This subroutine is expanded in place; it will not be called.

Line 104

Routine names with parameters p and val.

Line 106

This is the local variable prev.

Line 108

This is the inline assembler. Do not optimize.

Lines 109–111

lwarx, along with stwcx, form an "atomic swap." lwarx loads a word from memory and "reserves" the address for a subsequent store from stwcx.

Line 112

Branch if not equal to label 1 (b = backward).

Line 113

Here are the output operands:

```
[%0]= (prev), write-only, early clobber
[%1]= (*(volatile unsigned long *)p), write-only memory operand
```

Line 114

Here are the input operands:

```
[%2]= (p), register operand
[%3]= (val), register operand
[%4]= (*(volatile unsigned long *)p), memory operand
```

Line 115

Here are the clobber operands:

```
[%5]= Condition code register is altered
[%6]= memory is clobbered
```

This closes our discussion on assembly language and how the Linux 2.6 kernel uses it. We have seen how the PPC and x86 architectures differ and how general ASM programming techniques are used regardless of platform. We now turn our attention to the programming language C, in which the majority of the Linux kernel is written, and examine some common problems programmers encounter when using C.

2.5   Quirky C Language Usage

Within the Linux kernel are a number of conventions that can require lots of searching and reading to discover their ultimate meaning and intent. This section clarifies some of the obscure or misleading usage of C, with a specific focus on common C conventions that are used throughout the 2.6 Linux kernel.

2.5.1   asmlinkage

asmlinkage tells the compiler to pass parameters on the local stack. This is related to the FASTCALL macro, which resolves to tell the (architecture-specific) compiler to pass parameters in the general-purpose registers. Here are the macros from include/asm/linkage.h:

```
-----------------------------------------------------------------
include/asm/linkage.h
4  #define asmlinkage CPP_ASMLINKAGE __attribute__((regparm(0)))
5  #define FASTCALL(x)  x __attribute__((regparm(3)))
6  #define fastcall  __attribute__((regparm(3)))
-----------------------------------------------------------------
```

An example of `asmlinkage` is as follows:

```
asmlinkage long sys_gettimeofday(struct timeval __user *tv, struct timezone
__user *tz)
```

2.5.2   UL

UL is commonly appended to the end of a numerical constant to mark an "unsigned long." UL (or L for long) is necessary because it tells the compiler to treat the value as a long value. This prevents certain architectures from overflowing the bounds of their datatypes. For example, a 16-bit integer can represent numbers between −32,768 and +32,767; an unsigned integer can represent numbers up to 65,535. Using UL allows you to write architecturally independent code for large numbers or long bitmasks.

Some kernel code examples include the following:

```
-----------------------------------------------------------------------
include/linux/hash.h
18   #define GOLDEN_RATIO_PRIME 0x9e370001UL
-----------------------------------------------------------------------

include/linux/kernel.h
23   #define ULONG_MAX   (~0UL)
-----------------------------------------------------------------------

include/linux/slab.h
39   #define SLAB_POISON    0x00000800UL /* Poison objects */
-----------------------------------------------------------------------
```

2.5.3   inline

The **inline** keyword is intended to optimize the execution of functions by integrating the code of the function into the code of its callers. The Linux kernel uses mainly inline functions that are also declared as static. A "static inline" function results in the compiler attempting to incorporate the function's code into all its callers and, if possible, it discards the assembly code of the function. Occasionally, the compiler cannot discard the assembly code (in the case of recursion), but for the most part, functions declared as static inline are directly incorporated into the callers.

The point of this incorporation is to eliminate any overhead from having a function call. The #define statement can also eliminate function call overhead and is typically used for portability across compilers and within embedded systems.

So, why not always use inline? The drawback to using inline is an increased binary image and, possibly, a slow down when accessing the CPU's cache.

2.5.4   const and volatile

These two keywords are the bane of many an emerging programmer. The const keyword must not be thought of as *constant*, but rather *read only*. For example, *const int *x* is a pointer to a const integer. Thus, the pointer can be changed but the integer cannot. However, *int const *x* is a const pointer to an integer, and the integer can change but the pointer cannot. Here is an example of const:

```
----------------------------------------------------------------
include/asm-i386/processor.h
628  static inline void prefetch(const void *x)
629  {
630    __asm__ __volatile__ ("dcbt 0,%0" : : "r" (x));
631  }
----------------------------------------------------------------
```

The volatile keyword marks variables that could change without warning. volatile informs the compiler that it needs to reload the marked variable every time it encounters it rather than storing and accessing a copy. Some good examples of variables that should be marked as volatile are ones that deal with interrupts, hardware registers, or variables that are shared between concurrent processes. Here is an example of how volatile is used:

```
----------------------------------------------------------------
include/linux/spinlock.h
51  typedef struct {
...
volatile unsigned int lock;
...
58  } spinlock_t;
----------------------------------------------------------------
```

Given that const should be interpreted as read only, we see that certain variables can be both const and volatile (for example, a variable holding the contents of a read-only hardware register that changes regularly).

This quick overview puts the prospective Linux kernel hacker on the right track for reading through the kernel sources.

2.6   A Quick Tour of Kernel Exploration Tools

After successfully compiling and building your Linux kernel, you might want to peer into its internals before, after, or even during its operation. This section quickly overviews the tools commonly used to explore various files in the Linux kernel.

2.6.1   objdump/readelf

The **objdump** and **readelf** utilities display any of the information within object files (for objdump), or within ELF files (for readelf). Through command-line arguments, you can use the command to look at the headers, size, or architecture of a given object file. For example, here is a dump of the ELF header for a simple C program (a.out) using the -h flag of readelf:

```
Lwp> readelf -h a.out
ELF Header:
 Magic: 7f 45 4c 46 01 01 01 00 00 00 00 00 00 00 00 00
 Class:          ELF32
 Data:           2's complement, little endian
 Version:          1 (current)
 OS/ABI:          UNIX - System V
 ABI Version:          0
 Type:          EXEC (Executable file)
 Machine:          Intel 80386
 Version:          0x1
 Entry point address:      0x8048310
 Start of program headers:    52 (bytes into file)
 Start of section headers:    10596 (bytes into file)
 Flags:          0x0
 Size of this header:    52 (bytes)
 Size of program headers:    32 (bytes)
 Number of program headers:    6
 Size of section headers:    40 (bytes)
 Number of section headers:    29
 Section header string table index: 26
```

Here is a dump of the program headers using the -l flag of readelf:

```
Lwp> readelf -l a.out
Elf file type is EXEC (Executable file)
Entry point 0x8048310
There are 6 program headers, starting at offset 52
Program Headers:
 Type   Offset VirtAddr PhysAddr FileSiz MemSiz Flg Align
 PHDR   0x000034 0x08048034 0x08048034 0x000c0 0x000c0 R E 0x4
```

```
INTERP     0x0000f4 0x080480f4 0x080480f4 0x00013 0x00013 R 0x1
 [Requesting program interpreter: /lib/ld-linux.so.2]
LOAD     0x000000 0x08048000 0x08048000 0x00498 0x00498 R E 0x1000
LOAD     0x000498 0x08049498 0x08049498 0x00108 0x00120 RW 0x1000
DYNAMIC  0x0004ac 0x080494ac 0x080494ac 0x000c8 0x000c8 RW 0x4
NOTE     0x000108 0x08048108 0x08048108 0x00020 0x00020 R 0x4
Section to Segment mapping:
Segment Sections...
 00
 01   .interp
 02   .interp .note.ABI-tag .hash .dynsym .dynstr .gnu.version .gnu.version_r
.rel.dyn .rel.plt .init .plt .text .fini .rodata
 03   .data .eh_frame .dynamic .ctors .dtors .got .bss
 04   .dynamic
 05   .note.ABI-tag
```

2.6.2   hexdump

The **hexdump** command displays the contents of a given file in hexadecimal, ASCII, or octal format. (Note that, on older versions of Linux, od (octal dump) was also used. Most systems now use hexdump instead.)

For example, to look at the first 64 bytes of the ELF file a.out in hex, you could type the following:

```
Lwp>   hexdump -x -n 64 a.out

0000000 457f 464c 0101 0001 0000 0000 0000 0000
0000010 0002 0003 0001 0000 8310 0804 0034 0000
0000020 2964 0000 0000 0000 0034 0020 0006 0028
0000030 001d 001a 0006 0000 0034 0000 8034 0804
0000040
```

Note the (byte-swapped) ELF header magic number at address 0x0000000.

This is extremely useful in debugging activities; when a hardware device dumps its state to a file, a normal text editor usually interprets the file as containing numerous control characters. hexdump allows you to peek at what is actually contained in the file without intervening editor translation. hexedit is an editor that enables you to directly modify the files without translating the contents into ASCII (or Unicode).

2.6.3   nm

The **nm** utility lists the symbols that reside within a specified object file. It displays the symbols value, type, and name. This utility is not as useful as other utilities, but it can be helpful when debugging library files.

2.6.4   objcopy

Use the **objcopy** command when you want to copy an object file but omit or change certain aspects of it. A common use of objcopy is to strip debugging symbols from a tested and working object file. This results in a reduced object file size and is routinely done on embedded systems.

2.6.5   ar

The **ar** (or **archive**) command helps maintain the indexed libraries that the linker uses. The ar command combines one or more object files into one library. It can also separate object files from a single library. The ar command is more likely to be seen in a Make file. It is often used to combine commonly used functions into a single library file. For example, you might have a routine that parses a command file and extracts certain data or a call to extract information from a specific register in the hardware. These routines might be needed by several executable programs. Archiving these routines into a single library file allows for better version control by having a central location.

2.7   Kernel Speak: Listening to Kernel Messages

When your Linux system is up and running, the kernel itself logs messages and provides information about its status throughout its operation. This section gives a few of the most common ways the Linux kernel speaks to an end user.

2.7.1   printk()

One of the most basic kernel messaging systems is the **printk()** function. The kernel uses printk() as opposed to printf() because the standard C library is not linked to the kernel. printk() uses the same interface as printf() does and displays up to 1,024 characters to the console. The printk() function operates by trying to grab the console semaphore, place the output into the console's log buffer, and then call the console driver to flush the buffer. If printk() cannot grab the console semaphore, it places the output into the log buffer and relies on the process that has the console semaphore to flush the buffer. The log-buffer lock is taken before printk() places any data into the log buffer, so concurrent calls to printk() do not trample each other. If the console semaphore is being held, numerous calls to `printk()` can occur before the log buffer is flushed. So, do not rely on `printk()` statements to indicate any program timing.

2.7.2 dmesg

The Linux kernel stores its logs, or messages, in a variety of ways. `sysklogd()` is a combination of `syslogd()` and `klogd()`. (More in-depth information can be found in the man page of these commands, but we can quickly summarize the system.) The Linux kernel sends its messages through `klogd()`, which tags them with appropriate warning levels, and all levels of messages are placed in `/proc/kmsg`. **dmesg** is a command-line tool to display the buffer stored in `/proc/kmsg` and, optionally, filter the buffer based on the message level.

2.7.3 /var/log/messages

This location on a Linux system is where a majority of logged system messages reside. The `syslogd()` program reads information in `/etc/syslogd.conf` for specific locations on where to store received messages. Depending on the entries in `syslogd.conf`, which can vary among Linux distributions, log messages can be stored in numerous files. However, **/var/log/messages** is usually the standard location.

2.8   Miscellaneous Quirks

This section serves as a catch-all for quirks that plagued the authors when they began to traipse through the kernel code. We include them here to give you an edge on Linux internals.

2.8.1   __init

The **__init** macro tells the compiler that the associate function or variable is used only upon initialization. The compiler places all code marked with __init into a special memory section that is freed after the initialization phase ends:

```
--------------------------------------------------------------------
drivers/char/random.c
 679 static int __init batch_entropy_init(int size, struct entropy_store *r)
--------------------------------------------------------------------
```

As an example, the random device driver initializes a pool of entropy upon being loaded. While the driver is loaded, different functions are used to increase or decrease the size of the entropy pool. This practice of device driver initialization being marked with __init is common, if not a standard.

Similarly, if there is data that is used only during initialization, the data needs to be marked with **__initdata**. Here, we can see how __initdata is used in the ESP device driver:

```
------------------------------------------------------------------
drivers/char/esp.c
107 static char serial_name[] __initdata = "ESP serial driver";
108 static char serial_version[] __initdata = "2.2";
------------------------------------------------------------------
```

Also, the **__exit** and **__exitdata** macros are to be used only in the exit or shutdown routines. These are commonly used when a device driver is unregistered.

2.8.2   likely() and unlikely()

likely() and **unlikely()** are macros that Linux kernel developers use to give hints to the compiler and chipset. Modern CPUs have extensive branch-prediction heuristics that attempt to predict incoming commands in order to optimize speed. The likely() and unlikely() macros allow the developer to tell the CPU, through the compiler, that certain sections of code are likely, and thus should be predicted, or unlikely, so they shouldn't be predicted.

The importance of branch prediction can be seen with some understanding of instruction *pipelining*. Modern processors do anticipatory fetching—that is, they anticipate the next few instructions that will be executed and load them into the processor. Within the processor, these instructions are examined and dispatched to the various units within the processor (integer, floating point, and so on) depending on how they can best be executed. Some instructions might be stalled in the processor, waiting for an intermediate result from a previous instruction. Now, imagine in the instruction stream, a branch instruction is loaded. The processor now has two instruction streams from which to continue its prefetching. If the processor often chooses poorly, it spends too much time reloading the pipeline of instructions that need execution. What if the processor had a *hint* of which way the branch was going to go? A simple method of branch prediction, in some architectures, is to examine the target address of the branch. If the value is previous to the current address, there's a good chance that this branch is at the end of a loop construct where it loops back many times and only falls through once.

Software is allowed to override the architectural branch prediction with special mnemonics. This ability is surfaced by the compiler by the **`__builtin_expect()`** function, which is the foundation of the `likely()` and `unlikely()` macros.

As previously mentioned, branch prediction and processor pipelining is complicated and beyond the scope of this book, but the ability to "tune" the code where we think we can make a difference is always a performance plus. Consider the following code block:

```
------------------------------------------------------------------------
kernel/time.c
 90 asmlinkage long sys_gettimeofday(struct timeval __user *tv, struct timezone
__user *tz)
 91 {
 92   if (likely(tv != NULL)) {
 93     struct timeval ktv;
 94     do_gettimeofday(&ktv);
 95     if (copy_to_user(tv, &ktv, sizeof(ktv)))
 96       return -EFAULT;
 97   }
 98   if (unlikely(tz != NULL)) {
 99     if (copy_to_user(tz, &sys_tz, sizeof(sys_tz)))
100       return -EFAULT;
101   }
102   return 0;
103 }
------------------------------------------------------------------------
```

In this code, we see that a syscall to get the time of day is likely to have a `timeval` structure that is not null (lines 92–96). If it were null, we couldn't fill in the requested time of day! It is also unlikely that the timezone is not null (lines 98–100). To put it another way, the caller rarely asks for the timezone and usually asks for the time.

The specific implementation of `likely()` and `unlikely()` are specified as follows:[4]

```
------------------------------------------------------------------------
include/linux/compiler.h
 45 #define likely(x)   __builtin_expect(!!(x), 1)
 46 #define unlikely(x)   __builtin_expect(!!(x), 0)
------------------------------------------------------------------------
```

---

[4] `__builtin_expect()`, as seen in the code excerpt, is nulled before GCC 2.96, because there was no way to influence branch prediction before that release of GCC.

2.8.3   IS_ERR and PTR_ERR

The **IS_ERR** macro encodes a negative error number into a pointer, while the **PTR_ERR** macro retrieves the error number from the pointer.

Both macros are defined in `include/linux/err.h`.

2.8.4   Notifier Chains

The notifier-chain mechanism is provided for the kernel to register its interest in being informed regarding the occurrence of variable asynchronous events. This generic interface extends its usability to all subsystems or components of the kernel.

A **notifier chain** is a simply linked list of **notifier_block** objects:

```
-------------------------------------------------------------------
include/linux/notifier.h
14 struct notifier_block
15 {
16 int(*notifier_call)(struct notifier_block *self, unsigned long, void *);
17 struct notifier_block *next;
18 int priority;
19 };
-------------------------------------------------------------------
```

`notifier_block` contains a pointer to a function (**notifier_call**) to be called when the event comes to pass. This function's parameters include a pointer to the `notifier_block` holding the information, a value corresponding to event codes or flags, and a pointer to a datatype specific to the subsystem.

The `notifier_block` struct also contains a pointer to the next `notifier_block` in the chain and a priority declaration.

The routines **notifier_chain_register()** and **notifier_chain_unregister()** register or unregister a `notifier_block` object in a specific notifier chain.

Summary

This chapter exposed you to enough background to begin exploring the Linux kernel. Two methods of dynamic storage were introduced: the linked list and the binary search tree. Having a basic understanding of these structures helps you when, among many other topics, processes and paging are discussed. We then introduced the basics of assembly language to assist you in exploring or debugging down to the machine level and, focusing on an inline assembler, we showed the hybrid of C and assembler within the same function. We end this chapter with a discussion of various commands and functions that are necessary to study various aspects of the kernel.

Project: Hellomod

This section introduces the basic concepts necessary to understand other Linux concepts and structures discussed later in the book. Our projects center on the creation of a loadable module using the new 2.6 driver architecture and building on that module for subsequent projects. Because device drivers can quickly become complex; our goal here is only to introduce the basic constructs of a Linux module. We will be developing on this driver in later projects. This module runs in both PPC and x86.

Step 1: Writing the Linux Module Skeleton

The first module we write is the basic "hello world" character device driver. First, we look at the basic code for the module, and then show how to compile with the new 2.6 `Makefile` system (this is discussed in detail in Chapter 9), and finally, we attach and remove our module to the kernel using the `insmod` and `rmmod` commands respectively:[5]

```
-----------------------------------------------------------------
hellomod.c
001
// hello world driver for Linux 2.6

004   #include <linux/module.h>
005   #include <linux/kernel.h>
006   #include <linux/init.h>
007   #MODULE_LICENCE("GPL"); //get rid of taint message

009   static int __init lkp_init( void )
{
  printk("<1>Hello,World! from the kernel space...\n");
  return 0;
013  }

015   static void __exit lkp_cleanup( void )
{
  printk("<1>Goodbye, World! leaving kernel space...\n");
018  }
```

_____

[5] Be sure to have module unloading enabled in your configuration.

```
020   module_init(lkp_init);
021   module_exit(lkp_cleanup);
```

Line 4

All modules use the `module.h` header file and must be included.

Line 5

The `kernel.h` header file contains often used kernel functions.

Line 6

The `init.h` header file contains the `__init` and `__exit` macros. These macros allow kernel memory to be freed up. A quick read of the code and comments in this file are recommended.

Line 7

To warn of a possible non-GNU public license, several macros were developed starting in the 2.4 kernel. (For more information, see `modules.h`.)

Lines 9–12

This is our module initialization function. This function should, for example, contain code to build and initialize structures. On line 11, we are able to send out a message from the kernel with `printk()`. More on where we read this message when we load our module.

Lines 15–18

This is our module exit or cleanup function. Here, we would do any housekeeping associated with our driver being terminated.

Line 20

This is the driver initialization entry point. The kernel calls here at boot time for a built-in module or at insertion-time for a loadable module.

Line 21

For a loadable module, the kernel calls the `cleanup_module()` function. For a built-in module, this has no effect.

We can have only one initialization (`module_init`) point and one cleanup
·(`module_exit`) point in our driver. These functions are what the kernel is looking
for when we load and unload our module.

Step 2: Compiling the Module

If you are used to the older methods of building kernel modules (for example,
those that started with `#define MODULE`), the new method is quite a change. For
those whose 2.6 modules are their first, this might seem rather simple. The basic
`Makefile` for our single module is as follows:

Makefile

```
002 # Makefile for Linux Kernel Primer module skeleton (2.6.7)



006   obj-m += hellomod.o
```

Notice that we specify to the build system that this be compiled as a loadable
module. The command-line invocation of this `Makefile` wrapped in a bash script
called `doit` is as follows:

```
----------------------------------------------------------------------------doit
001 make -C /usr/src/linux-2.6.7 SUBDIRS=$PWD modules
----------------------------------------------------------------------------
```

Line 1

The `-C` option tells `make` to change to the Linux source directory (in our case,
`/usr/src/linux-2.6.7`) before reading the `Makefiles` or doing anything else.

Upon executing `./doit`, you should get similar to the following output:

```
Lkp# ./doit
make: Entering directory '/usr/src/linux-2.6.7'
  CC [M]  /mysource/hellomod.o
  Building modules, stage 2
  MODPOST
  CC  /mysource/hellomod.o
  LD [M]  /mysource/hellomod.ko
  make: Leaving directory '/usr/src/linux-2.6.7'
  lkp# _
```

For those who have compiled or created Linux modules with earlier Linux versions, notice that we now have a linking step `LD` and that our output module is `hellomod.ko`.

Step 3: Running the Code

We are now ready to insert our new module into the kernel. We do this using the `insmod` command, as follows:

```
lkp# insmod hellomod.ko
```

To check that the module was inserted properly, you can use the `lsmod` command, as follows:

```
lkp# lsmod
Module      Size  Used  by
hellomod    2696  0
lkp#
```

The output of our module is generated by `printk()`. This function prints to the system file `/var/log/messages` by default. To quickly view this, type the following:

```
lkp# tail /var/log/messages
```

This prints the last 10 lines of the log file. You should see our initialization message:

```
...
...
Mar  6 10:35:55  lkp1  kernel: Hello,World! from the kernel space...
```

To remove our module (and see our exit message), use the `rmmod` command followed by the module name as seen from the `insmod` command. For our program, this would look like the following:

```
lkp# rmmod hellomod
```

Again, your output should go to the log file and look like the following:

```
...
...
Mar  6 12:00:05  lkp1  kernel: Hello,World! from the kernel space...
```

Depending on how your X-system is configured or if you are at a basic command line, the `printk` output should go to your console, as well as the log file. In our next project, we touch on this again when we look at system task variables.

Exercises

1. Describe how hash tables are implemented in the Linux kernel.

2. A structure that is a member of a doubly linked list will have a `list_head` structure. Before the adoption of the `list_head` structure in the kernel, the structure would have the fields `prev` and `next` pointing to other like structures. What is the purpose of creating a structure solely to hold the `prev` and `next` pointers?

3. What is inline assembly and why would you want to use it?

4. Assume you write a device driver that accesses the serial port registers. Would you mark these addresses volatile? Why or why not?

5. Given what `__init` does, what types of functions would you expect to use this macro?

Chapter 3

Processes: The Principal Model of Execution

In this chapter

The term **process**, defined here as the basic unit of execution of a program, is perhaps the most important concept to understand when learning how an operating system works. It is essential to understand the difference between a program and a process. Therefore, we refer to a *program* as an executable file that contains a set of functions, and we refer to a *process* as a single instantiation of a particular program. A process is the unit of operation that uses resources provided by the hardware and executes according to the orders of the program it instantiates. The operating system facilitates and manages the system's resources as the process requires.

Computers do many things. Processes can perform tasks ranging from executing user commands and managing system resources to accessing hardware. In part, a process is defined by the set of instructions it is to execute, the contents of the registers and program counter when the program is in execution, and its **state**.

A process, like any dynamic entity, goes through various states. In fact, a process has a lifecycle: After a process is created, it lives for a variable time span during which it goes through a number of state changes and then dies. Figure 3.1 shows the process lifecycle from a high-level view.

When a Linux system is powered on, the number of processes it will need is undetermined. Processes need to be created and destroyed when they are needed.

A process is created by a previously existing process with a call to fork(). Forked processes are referred to as the **child processes**, and the process that creates them is referred to as the **parent process**. The child and parent processes continue to run in parallel. If the parent continues to spawn more child processes, these processes are **sibling processes** to the original child. The children may in turn spawn off child processes of their own. This creates a hierarchical relationship among processes that define their relationship.

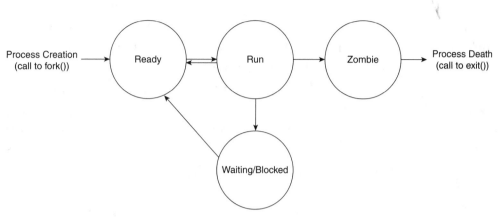

FIGURE 3.1
Process Lifecycle

After a process is created, it is ready to become the **running process**. This means that the kernel has set up all the structures and acquired all the necessary information for the CPU to execute the process. When a process is prepared to become the running process but has not been selected to run, it is in a **ready** state. After the task becomes the running process, it can

- Be "deselected" and set back to the ready state by the scheduler.

- Be interrupted and placed in a waiting or **blocked** state.

- Become a **zombie** on its way to process death. Process death is reached by a call to exit().

This chapter looks closely at all these states and transitions. The **scheduler** handles the selection and deselection of processes to be executed by the CPU. Chapter 7, "Scheduling and Kernel Synchronization," covers the scheduler in great detail.

A program contains a number of components that are laid out in memory and accessed by the process that executes the program. This includes a **text segment**, which holds the instructions that are executed by the CPU; the **data segments**, which hold all the data variables manipulated by the process; the **stack**, which holds automatic variables and function data; and a **heap**, which holds dynamic memory allocations. When a process is created, the child process receives a copy of the parent's data space, heap, stack, and **process descriptor**. The next section provides a more detailed description of the Linux process descriptor.

There are many ways to explain a process. The approach we take is to start with a high-level view of the execution of a process and follow it into the kernel, periodically explaining the kernel support structures that sustain it.

As programmers, we are familiar with writing, compiling, and executing programs. But how does this tie into a process? We discuss an example program throughout this chapter that we will follow from its creation through its performance of some key tasks. In our case, the Bash shell process will create the process that instantiates our program; in turn, our program instantiates another child process.

Before we proceed to the discussion of processes, a few naming conventions need to be clarified. Often, we use the word *process* and the word *task* to refer to the same thing. When we refer to the *running process*, we refer to the process that the CPU is currently executing.

User Mode Versus Kernel Mode

What do we mean when we say a program is running in user mode or kernel mode? In a process' lifespan, it executes either its own code or kernel code. Code is considered kernel code when a system call is made, an exception occurs, or an interrupt comes through (and we are executing in the interrupt handler). Any code a process uses that is not a system call is considered user mode code and, hence, the process is running in user mode and is subject to processor-imposed restrictions. If the process is in the middle of executing a system call, we say that it is running in kernel mode. From a hardware point of view, kernel code on the Intel processors is said to be running at *ring 0* and on the PowerPC, it is said to be running in *supervisor mode*.

3.1 Introducing Our Program

This section introduces the sample program called create_process. This example C program illustrates the various states a process can go through, the system calls (which generate the transitions between these states), and the manipulation of the kernel objects that support the execution of processes. The idea is to reach an understanding of how a program is instantiated into a process and how an operating system handles a process.

```
------------------------------------------------------------------
create_process.c
1    #include <stdio.h>
2    #include <sys/types.h>
3    #include <sys/stat.h>
4    #include <fcntl.h>
5
6    int main(int argc, char *argv[])
7    {
8      int fd;
9      int pid;
11
12     pid = fork();
13     if (pid == 0)
14     {
15        execle("/bin/ls", NULL);
16        exit(2);
17     }
18
19     if(waitpid(pid) < 0)
20        printf("wait error\n");
21
22     pid = fork();
23     if (pid == 0){
24        fd=open("Chapter_03.txt", O_RDONLY);
25        close(fd);
26     }
27
28     if(waitpid(pid)<0)
29        printf("wait error\n");
30
31
32     exit(0);
33   }
------------------------------------------------------------------
```

This program defines a **context of execution**, which includes information regarding resources needed to fulfill the requirements that the program defines. For example, at any moment, a CPU executes exactly one instruction that it has just fetched from memory.[1] However, this instruction would not make sense if a **context** did not surround it to keep track of how the instruction referenced relates to the logic of the program. A process has a context that is composed of values held in the program counter, registers, memory, and files (or hardware accessed).

This program is compiled and linked to create an executable file that holds all the information required to execute this program. Chapter 9, "Building the Linux

---

[1]   Recall the text segment that was previously mentioned.

Kernel," details the partitioning of the address space of the program and how it relates to the information referred to by the program when we discuss process images and binary formats.

A process contains a number of characteristics that can describe the process as being unique from other processes. The characteristics necessary for process management are kept in a single data type, which is referred to as a **process descriptor**. We need to look at the process descriptor before we delve into the details of process management.

3.2   Process Descriptor

In the kernel, the process descriptor is a structure called `task_struct`, which keeps track of process attributes and information. All kernel information regarding a process is found there. Throughout a process' lifecycle, a process interacts with many aspects of the kernel, such as memory management and scheduling. The process descriptor keeps track of information regarding these interactions, as well as the standard UNIX process attributes. The kernel stores all the process descriptors in a circular doubly linked list called the **task_list**. The kernel also keeps a reference to the currently running process' `task_struct` by means of the global variable **current**. (We refer to current throughout this book to indicate the process descriptor of the currently running process.)

A process may be comprised of one or more threads. Each thread has a `task_struct` associated with it, including a unique thread ID. Threads in a common process share the same memory address space.

The following categories describe some of the types of things a process descriptor must keep track of during a process' lifespan:

- Process attributes
- Process relationships
- Process memory space
- File management
- Signal management
- Process credentials

- Resource limits

- Scheduling related fields

We now closely look at the fields in the `task_struct` structure. This section describes what they do and refers to the actual processing with which the field is involved. Although many of the fields are used for activities related to the aforementioned categories, some are beyond the scope of this book. The `task_struct` structure is defined in `include/linux/sched.h`:

```
-----------------------------------------------------------------------
include/linux/sched.h
384   struct task_struct {
385      volatile long state;
386      struct thread_info *thread_info;
387      atomic_t usage;
388      unsigned long flags;
389      unsigned long ptrace;
390
391      int lock_depth;
392
393      int prio, static_prio;
394      struct list_head run_list;
395      prio_array_t *array;
396
397      unsigned long sleep_avg;
398      long interactive_credit;
399      unsigned long long timestamp;
400      int activated;
401
302      unsigned long policy;
403      cpumask_t cpus_allowed;
404      unsigned int time_slice, first_time_slice;
405
406      struct list_head tasks;
407      struct list_head ptrace_children;
408      struct list_head ptrace_list;
409
410      struct mm_struct *mm, *active_mm;
...
413      struct linux_binfmt *binfmt;
414      int exit_code, exit_signal;
415      int pdeath_signal;
...
419      pid_t pid;
420      pid_t tgid;
...
426      struct task_struct *real_parent;
427      struct task_struct *parent;
428      struct list_head children;
```

```
429      struct list_head sibling;
430      struct task_struct *group_leader;
...
433      struct pid_link pids[PIDTYPE_MAX];
434
435      wait_queue_head_t wait_chldexit;
436      struct completion *vfork_done;
437      int __user *set_child_tid;
438      int __user *clear_child_tid;
439
440      unsigned long rt_priority;
441      unsigned long it_real_value, it_prof_value, it_virt_value;
442      unsigned long it_real_incr, it_prof_incr, it_virt_incr;
443      struct timer_list real_timer;
444      unsigned long utime, stime, cutime, cstime;
445      unsigned long nvcsw, nivcsw, cnvcsw, cnivcsw;
446      u64 start_time;
...
450      uid_t uid,euid,suid,fsuid;
451      gid_t gid,egid,sgid,fsgid;
452      struct group_info *group_info;
453      kernel_cap_t cap_effective, cap_inheritable, cap_permitted;
454      int keep_capabilities:1;
455      struct user_struct *user;
...
457      struct rlimit rlim[RLIM_NLIMITS];
458      unsigned short used_math;
459      char comm[16];
...
461      int link_count, total_link_count;
...
467      struct fs_struct *fs;
...
469      struct files_struct *files;
...
509      unsigned long ptrace_message;
510      siginfo_t *last_siginfo;
...
516    };
```

3.2.1   Process Attribute–Related Fields

The process attribute category is a catch-all category we defined for task characteristics related to the state and identification of a task. Examining these fields' values at any time gives the kernel hacker an idea of the current status of a process.
Figure 3.2 illustrates the process attribute–related fields of the task_struct.

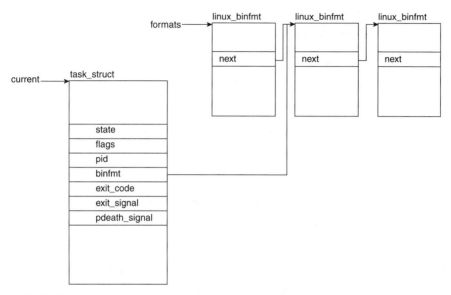

FIGURE 3.2
Process Attribute–Related Fields

3.2.1.1 state

The `state` field keeps track of the state a process finds itself in during its execution lifecycle. Possible values it can hold are `TASK_RUNNING`, `TASK_INTERRUPTIBLE`, `TASK_UNINTERRUPTIBLE`, `TASK_ZOMBIE`, `TASK_STOPPED`, and `TASK_DEAD` (see the "Process Lifespan" section in this chapter for more detail).

3.2.1.2 pid

In Linux, each process has a unique **process identifier** (`pid`). This `pid` is stored in the `task_struct` as a type `pid_t`. Although this type can be traced back to an integer type, the default maximum value of a `pid` is 32,768 (the value pertaining to a short int).

3.2.1.3 flags

Flags define special attributes that belong to the task. Per process flags are defined in `include/linux/sched.h` and include those flags listed in Table 3.1. The flag's value provides the kernel hacker with more information regarding what the task is undergoing.

TABLE 3.1
Selected task_struct Flag's Field Values

Flag Name	When Set
PF_STARTING	Set when the process is being created.
PF_EXITING	Set during the call to do_exit().
PF_DEAD	Set during the call to exit_notify() in the process of exiting. At this point, the state of the process is either TASK_ZOMBIE or TASK_DEAD.
PF_FORKNOEXEC	The parent upon forking sets this flag.

3.2.1.4   binfmt

Linux supports a number of executable formats. An executable format is what defines the structure of how your program code is to be loaded into memory. Figure 3.2 illustrates the association between the task_struct and the linux_binfmt struct, the structure that contains all the information related to a particular binary format (see Chapter 9 for more detail).

3.2.1.5   exit_code and exit_signal

The exit_code and exit_signal fields hold a task's exit value and the terminating signal (if one was used). This is the way a child's exit value is passed to its parent.

3.2.1.6   pdeath_signal

pdeath_signal is a signal sent upon the parent's death.

3.2.1.7   comm

A process is often created by means of a command-line call to an executable. The comm field holds the name of the executable as it is called on the command line.

3.2.1.8   ptrace

ptrace is set when the ptrace() system call is called on the process for performance measurements. Possible ptrace() flags are defined in include/linux/ptrace.h.

3.2.2   Scheduling Related Fields

A process operates as though it has its own virtual CPU. However, in reality, it shares the CPU with other processes. To sustain the switching between process executions, each process closely interrelates with the scheduler (see Chapter 7 for more detail).

However, to understand some of these fields, you need to understand a few basic scheduling concepts. When more than one process is ready to run, the scheduler decides which one runs first and for how long. The scheduler achieves fairness and efficiency by allotting each process a **timeslice** and a **priority**. The timeslice defines the amount of time the process is allowed to execute before it is switched off for another process. The priority of a process is a value that defines the relative order in which it will be allowed to be executed with respect to other waiting processes—the higher the priority, the sooner it is scheduled to run. The fields shown in Figure 3.3 keep track of the values necessary for scheduling purposes.

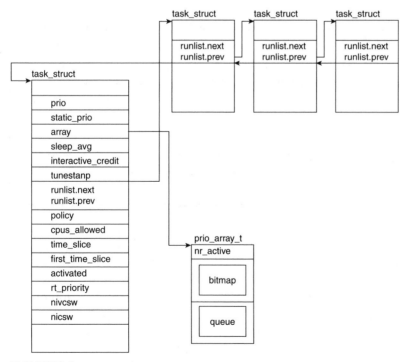

FIGURE 3.3
Scheduling Related Fields

3.2.2.1 prio

In Chapter 7, we see that the dynamic priority of a process is a value that depends on the processes' scheduling history and the specified nice value. (See the following sidebar for more information about nice values.) It is updated at sleep time, which is when the process is not being executed and when timeslice is used up. This value, prio, is related to the value of the static_prio field described next. The prio field holds +/- 5 of the value of static_prio, depending on the process' history; it will get a +5 bonus if it has slept a lot and a -5 handicap if it has been a processing hog and used up its timeslice.

3.2.2.2 static_prio

static_prio is equivalent to the nice value. The default value of static_prio is MAX_PRIO-20. In our kernel, MAX_PRIO defaults to 140.

Nice

The nice() system call allows a user to modify the static scheduling priority of a process. The nice value can range from −20 to 19. The nice() function then calls set_user_nice() to set the static_prio field of the task_struct. The static_prio value is computed from the nice value by way of the PRIO_TO_NICE macro. Likewise, the nice value is computed from the static_prio value by means of a call to NICE_TO_PRIO.

```
-----------------------------------kernel/sched.c
#define NICE_TO_PRIO(nice)  (MAX_RT_PRIO + nice + 20)
#define PRIO_TO_NICE(prio)  ((prio - MAX_RT_PRIO - 20)
-------------------------------------------------
```

3.2.2.3 run_list

The run_list field points to the runqueue. A runqueue holds a list of all the processes to run. See the "Basic Structure" section for more information on the runqueue struct.

3.2.2.4   array

The `array` field points to the priority array of a `runqueue`. The "Keeping Track of Processes: Basic Scheduler Construction" section in this chapter explains this array in detail.

3.2.2.5   sleep_avg

The `sleep_avg` field is used to calculate the effective priority of the task, which is the average amount of clock ticks the task has spent sleeping.

3.2.2.6   timestamp

The `timestamp` field is used to calculate the `sleep_avg` for when a task sleeps or yields.

3.2.2.7   interactive_credit

The `interactive_credit` field is used along with the `sleep_avg` and activated fields to calculate `sleep_avg`.

3.2.2.8   policy

The `policy` determines the type of process (for example, time sharing or real time). The type of a process heavily influences the priority scheduling. For more information on this field, see Chapter 7.

3.2.2.9   cpus_allowed

The `cpus_allowed` field specifies which CPUs might handle a task. This is one way in which we can specify which CPU a particular task can run on when in a multiprocessor system.

3.2.2.10   time_slice

The `time_slice` field defines the maximum amount of time the task is allowed to run.

3.2.2.11   first_time_slice

The first_time_slice field is repeatedly set to 0 and keeps track of the scheduling time.

3.2.2.12   activated

The activated field keeps track of the incrementing and decrementing of sleep averages. If an uninterruptible task gets woken, this field gets set to -1.

3.2.2.13   rt_priority

rt_priority is a static value that can only be updated through schedule(). This value is necessary to support real-time tasks.

3.2.2.14   nivcsw and nvcsw

Different kinds of context switches exist. The kernel keeps track of these for profiling reasons. A global switch count gets set to one of the four different context switch counts, depending on the kind of transition involved in the context switch (see Chapter 7 for more information on context switch). These are the counters for the basic context switch:

- The nivcsw field (**number of involuntary context switches**) keeps count of kernel preemptions applied on the task. It gets incremented only upon a task's return from a kernel preemption where the switch count is set to nivcsw.

- The nvcsw field (**number of voluntary context switches**) keeps count of context switches that are not based on kernel preemption. The switch count gets set to nvcsw if the previous state was not an active preemption.

3.2.3   Process Relations–Related Fields

The following fields of the task_struct are those related to process relationships. Each task or process p has a parent that created it. Process p can also create processes and, therefore, might have children. Because p's parent could have created more than one process, it is possible that process p might have siblings. Figure 3.4 illustrates how the task_structs of all these processes relate.

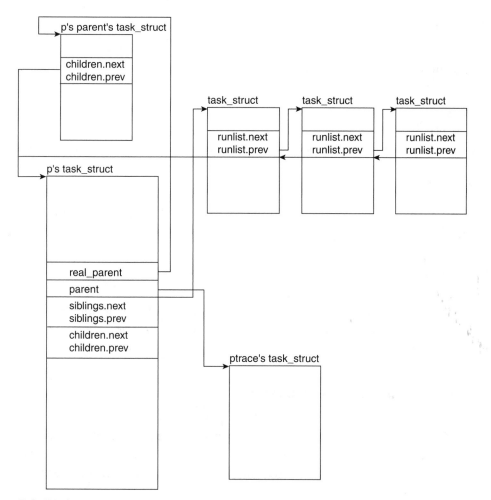

FIGURE 3.4
Process Relations–Related Fields

3.2.3.1 real_parent

real_parent points to the current process' parent's description. It will point to the process descriptor of init() if the original parent of our current process has been destroyed. In previous kernels, this was known as p_opptr.

3.2.3.2   parent

`parent` is a pointer to the descriptor of the parent process. In Figure 3.4, we see that this points to the `ptrace task_struct`. When `ptrace` is run on a process, the parent field of `task_struct` points to the `ptrace` process.

3.2.3.3   children

`children` is the `struct` that points to the list of our current process' children.

3.2.3.4   sibling

`sibling` is the `struct` that points to the list of the current process' siblings.

3.2.3.5   group_leader

A process can be a member of a group of processes, and each group has one process defined as the group leader. If our process is a member of a group, group_leader is a pointer to the descriptor of the leader of that group. A group leader generally owns the `tty` from which the process was created, called the **controlling terminal.**

3.2.4   Process Credentials–Related Fields

In multiuser systems, it is necessary to distinguish among processes that are created by different users. This is necessary for the security and protection of user data. To this end, each process has credentials that help the system determine what it can and cannot access. Figure 3.5 illustrates the fields in the task_struct related to process credentials.

3.2.4.1   uid and gid

The `uid` field holds the user ID number of the user who created the process. This field is used for protection and security purposes. Likewise, the `gid` field holds the group ID of the group who owns the process. A `uid` or `gid` of 0 corresponds to the root user and group.

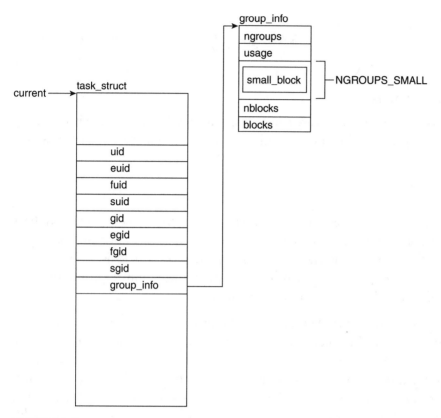

FIGURE 3.5
Process Credentials–Related Fields

3.2.4.2   euid and egid

The effective user ID usually holds the same value as the user ID field. This changes if the executed program has the set UID (SUID) bit on. In this case, the effective user ID is that of the owner of the program file. Generally, this is used to allow any user to run a particular program with the same permissions as another user (for example, root). The effective group ID works in much the same way, holding a value different from the gid field only if the set group ID (SGID) bit is on.

3.2.4.3   suid and sgid

suid (saved user ID) and sgid (saved group ID) are used in the setuid() system calls.

3.2.4.4   fsuid and fsgid

The fsuid and fsgid values are checked specifically for filesystem checks. They generally hold the same values as uid and gid except for when a setuid() system call is made.

3.2.4.5   group_info

In Linux, a user may be part of more than one group. These groups may have varying permissions with respect to system and data accesses. For this reason, the processes need to inherit this credential. The group_info field is a pointer to a structure of type group_info, which holds all the information regarding the various groups of which the process can be a member.

The group_info structure allows a process to associate with a number of groups that is bound by available memory. In Figure 3.5, you can see that a field of group_info called small_block is an array of NGROUPS_SMALL (in our case, 32) gid_t units. If a task belongs to more than 32 groups, the kernel can allocate **blocks** or pages that hold the necessary number of gid_ts beyond NGROUPS_SMALL. The field nblocks holds the number of blocks allocated, while ngroups holds the value of units in the small_block array that hold a gid_t value.

3.2.5   Process Capabilities-Related Fields

Traditionally, UNIX systems offer process-related protection of certain accesses and actions by defining any given process as privileged (super user or UID = 0) or unprivileged (any other process). In Linux, capabilities were introduced to partition the activities previously available only to the superuser; that is, capabilities are individual "privileges" that may be conferred upon a process independently of each other and of its UID. In this manner, particular processes can be given permission to perform particular administrative tasks without necessarily getting all the privileges or having to be owned by the superuser. A capability is thus defined as a given administrative operation. Figure 3.6 shows the fields that are related to process capabilities.

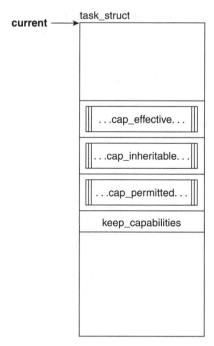

FIGURE 3.6
Process Capabilities–Related Fields

3.2.5.1   cap_effective, cap_inheritable, cap_permitted, and keep_capabilities

The structure used to support the capabilities model is defined in include/linux/security.h as an unsigned 32-bit value. Each 32-bit mask corresponds to a capability set; each capability is assigned a bit in each of:

- **cap_effective**. The capabilities that can be currently used by the process.

- **cap_inheritable**. The capabilities that are passed through a call to execve.

- **cap_permitted**. The capabilities that can be made either effective or inheritable.

One way to understand the distinction between these three types is to consider the permitted capabilities to be similar to a trivialized gene pool made available by one's parents. Of the genetic qualities made available by one's parents, we can display a subset of them (effective qualities) and/or pass them on (inheritable). Permitted capabilities constitute more of a potentiality whereas effective capabilities are an actuality.

Therefore, `cap_effective` and `cap_inheritable` are always subsets of `cap_permitted`.

- **keep_capabilities**. Keeps track of whether the process will drop or maintain its capabilities on a call to `setuid()`.

Table 3.2 lists some of the supported capabilities that are defined in `include/linux/capability.h`.

TABLE 3.2
Selected Capabilities

Capability	Description
CAP_CHOWN	Ignores the restrictions imposed by `chown()`
CAP_FOWNER	Ignores file-permission restrictions
CAP_FSETID	Ignores `setuid` and `setgid` restrictions on files
CAP_KILL	Ignores `ruid` and `euids` when sending signals
CAP_SETGID	Ignores group-related permissions checks
CAP_SETUID	Ignores `uid`-related permissions checks
CAP_SETCAP	Allows a process to set its capabilities

The kernel checks if a particular capability is set with a call to `capable()` passing as a parameter the capability variable. Generally, the function checks to see whether the capability bit is set in the `cap_effective` set; if so, it sets `current->flags` to `PF_SUPERPRIV`, which indicates that the capability is granted. The function returns a 1 if the capability is granted and 0 if capability is not granted.

Three system calls are associated with the manipulation of capabilities: `capget()`, `capset()`, and `prctl()`. The first two allow a process to get and set its capabilities, while the `prctl()` system call allows manipulation of `current->keep_capabilities`.

3.2.6   Process Limitations–Related Fields

A task uses a number of the resources made available by hardware and the scheduler. To keep track of how they are used and any limitations that might be applied to a process, we have the following fields.

3.2.6.1   rlim

The rlim field holds an array that provides for resource control and accounting by maintaining resource limit values. Figure 3.7 illustrates the rlim field of the task_struct.

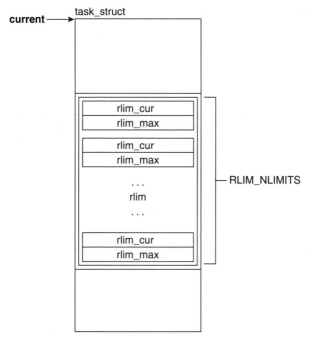

FIGURE 3.7
task_struct Resource Limits

Linux recognizes the need to limit the amount of certain resources that a process is allowed to use. Because the kinds and amounts of resources processes might use varies from process to process, it is necessary to keep this information on a per process basis. What better place than to keep a reference to it in the process descriptor?

The `rlimit` descriptor (`include/linux/resource.h`) has the fields `rlim_cur` and `rlim_max`, which are the current and maximum limits that apply to that resource. The limit "units" vary by the kind of resource to which the structure refers.

```
------------------------------------------------------------------------
include/linux/resource.h
struct rlimit {
    unsigned long    rlim_cur;
    unsigned long    rlim_max;
};
------------------------------------------------------------------------
```

Table 3.3 lists the resources upon which their limits are defined in `include/asm/resource.h`. However, both x86 and PPC have the same resource limits list and default values.

TABLE 3.3
Resource Limits Values

RL Name	Description	Default rlim_cur	Default rlim_max
RLIMIT_CPU	The amount of CPU time in seconds this process may run.	RLIM_INFINITY	RLIM_INFINITY
RLIMIT_FSIZE	The size of a file in 1KB blocks.	RLIM_INFINITY	RLIM_INFINITY
RLIMIT_DATA	The size of the heap in bytes.	RLIM_INFINITY	RLIM_INFINITY
RLIMIT_STACK	The size of the stack in bytes.	_STK_LIM	RLIM_INFINITY
RLIMIT_CORE	The size of the core dump file.	0	RLIM_INFINITY
RLIMIT_RSS	The maximum resident set size (real memory).	RLIM_INFINITY	RLIM_INFINITY
RLIMIT_NPROC	The number of processes owned by this process.	0	0

continues

TABLE 3.3
Continued

RL Name	Description	Default rlim_cur	Default rlim_max
RLIMIT_NOFILE	The number of open files this process may have at one time.	INR_OPEN	INR_OPEN
RLIMIT_MEMLOCK	Physical memory that can be locked (not swapped).	RLIM_INFINITY	RLIM_INFINITY
RLIMIT_AS	Size of process address space in bytes.	RLIM_INFINITY	RLIM_INFINITY
RLIMIT_LOCKS	Number of file locks.	RLIM_INFINITY	RLIM_INFINITY

When a value is set to RLIM_INFINITY, the resource is unlimited for that process.

The current limit (rlim_cur) is a soft limit that can be changed via a call to setrlimit(). The maximum limit is defined by rlim_max and cannot be exceeded by an unprivileged process. The getrlimit() system call returns the value of the resource limits. Both setrlimit() and getrlimit() take as parameters the resource name and a pointer to a structure of type rlimit.

3.2.7   Filesystem- and Address Space–Related Fields

Processes can be heavily involved with files throughout their lifecycle, performing tasks such as opening, closing, reading, and writing. The task_struct has two fields that are associated with file- and filesystem-related data: fs and files (see Chapter 6, "Filesystems," for more detail). The two fields related to address space are active_mm and mm (see Chapter 4, "Memory Management," for more detail on mm_struct). Figure 3.8 shows the filesystem- and address space–related fields of the task_struct.

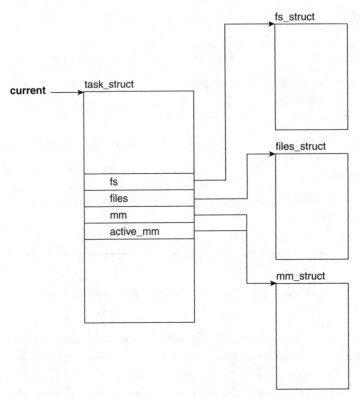

FIGURE 3.8
Filesystem- and Address Space–Related Fields

3.2.7.1   fs

The fs field holds a pointer to filesystem information.

3.2.7.2   files

The files field holds a pointer to the file descriptor table for the task. This file descriptor holds pointers to files (more specifically, to their descriptors) that the task has open.

3.2.7.3   mm

mm points to address-space and memory-management–related information.

3.2.7.4   active_mm

active_mm is a pointer to the most recently accessed address space. Both the mm and active_mm fields start pointing at the same mm_struct.

Evaluating the process descriptor gives us an idea of the type of data that a process is involved with throughout its lifetime. Now, we can look at what happens throughout the lifespan of a process. The following sections explain the various stages and states of a process and go through the sample program line by line to explain what happens in the kernel.

3.3   Process Creation: fork(), vfork(), and clone() System Calls

After the sample code is compiled into a file (in our case, an ELF executable[2]), we call it from the command line. Look at what happens when we press the Return key. We already mentioned that any given process is created by another process. The operating system provides the functionality to do this by means of the fork(), vfork(), and clone() system calls.

The C library provides three functions that issue these three system calls. The prototypes of these functions are declared in <unistd.h>. Figure 3.9 shows how a process that calls fork() executes the system call sys_fork(). This figure describes how kernel code performs the actual process creation. In a similar manner, vfork() calls sys_fork(), and clone() calls sys_clone().

All three of these system calls eventually call do_fork(), which is a kernel function that performs the bulk of the actions related to process creation. You might wonder why three different functions are available to create a process. Each function slightly differs in how it creates a process, and there are specific reasons why one would be chosen over the other.

---

[2] ELF executable is an executable format that Linux supports. Chapter 9 discusses the ELF executable format.

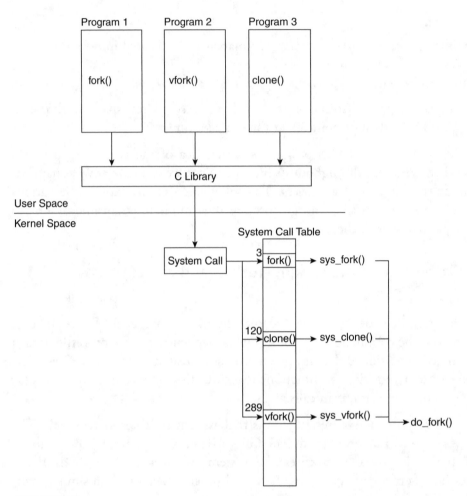

FIGURE 3.9
Process Creation System Calls

When we press Return at the `shell` prompt, the shell creates the new process that executes our program by means of a call to `fork()`. In fact, if we type the command `ls` at the shell and press Return, the pseudocode of the shell at that moment looks something like this:

```
if( (pid = fork()) == 0 )
   execve("foo");
else
   waitpid(pid);
```

We can now look at the functions and trace them down to the system call. Although our program calls fork(), it could just as easily have called vfork() or clone(), which is why we introduced all three functions in this section. The first function we look at is fork(). We delve through the calls fork(), sys_fork(), and do_fork(). We follow that with vfork() and finally look at clone() and trace them down to the do_fork() call.

3.3.1   fork() Function

The fork() function returns twice: once in the parent and once in the child process. If it returns in the child process, fork() returns 0. If it returns in the parent, fork() returns the child's PID. When the fork() function is called, the function places the necessary information in the appropriate registers, including the index into the system call table where the pointer to the system call resides. The processor we are running on determines the registers into which this information is placed.

At this point, if you want to continue the sequential ordering of events, look at the "Interrupts" section in this chapter to see how sys_fork() is called. However, it is not necessary to understand how a new process gets created.

Let's now look at the sys_fork() function. This function does little else than call the do_fork() function. Notice that the sys_fork() function is architecture dependent because it accesses function parameters passed in through the system registers.

```
-----------------------------------------------------------------------
arch/i386/kernel/process.c
asmlinkage int sys_fork(struct pt_regs regs)
{
    return do_fork(SIGCHLD, regs.esp, &regs, 0, NULL, NULL);
}
-----------------------------------------------------------------------
```

```
-------------------------------------------------------------------
arch/ppc/kernel/process.c
int sys_fork(int p1, int p2, int p3, int p4, int p5, int p6,
            struct pt_regs *regs)
{
        CHECK_FULL_REGS(regs);
        return do_fork(SIGCHLD, regs->gpr[1], regs, 0, NULL, NULL);
}
-------------------------------------------------------------------
```

The two architectures take in different parameters to the system call. The structure pt_regs holds information such as the stack pointer. The fact that gpr[1] holds the stack pointer in PPC, whereas %esp[3] holds the stack pointer in x86, is known by convention.

3.3.2 vfork() Function

The vfork() function is similar to the fork() function with the exception that the parent process is blocked until the child calls exit() or exec().

```
sys_vfork()
arch/i386/kernel/process.c
asmlinkage int sys_vfork(struct pt_regs regs)
{
    return do_fork(CLONE_VFORK | CLONE_VM | SIGCHLD, regs.ep, &regs, 0, NULL,
NULL);
}
-------------------------------------------------------------------
arch/ppc/kernel/process.c
int sys_vfork(int p1, int p2, int p3, int p4, int p5, int p6,
            struct pt_regs *regs)
{
        CHECK_FULL_REGS(regs);
        return do_fork(CLONE_VFORK | CLONE_VM | SIGCHLD, regs->gpr[1],
                     regs, 0, NULL, NULL);
}
-------------------------------------------------------------------
```

The only difference between the calls to sys_fork() in sys_vfork() and sys_fork() are the flags that do_fork() is passed. The presence of these flags are used later to determine if the added behavior just described (of blocking the parent) will be executed.

---

[3]   Recall that in code produced in "AT&T" format, registers are prefixed with a %.

3.3.3 clone() Function

The `clone()` library function, unlike `fork()` and `vfork()`, takes in a pointer to a function along with its argument. The child process created by `do_fork()` calls this function as soon as it gets created.

```
------------------------------------------------------------------------
sys_clone()
arch/i386/kernel/process.c
asmlinkage int sys_clone(struct pt_regs regs)
{
 unsigned long clone_flags;
        unsigned long newsp;
        int __user *parent_tidptr, *child_tidptr;

        clone_flags = regs.ebx;
        newsp = regs.ecx;
        parent_tidptr = (int __user *)regs.edx;
        child_tidptr = (int __user *)regs.edi;
        if (!newsp)
                newsp = regs.esp;
        return do_fork(clone_flags & ~CLONE_IDLETASK, newsp, &regs, 0,
parent_tidptr, child_tidptr);
}
------------------------------------------------------------------------


------------------------------------------------------------------------
arch/ppc/kernel/process.c
int sys_clone(unsigned long clone_flags, unsigned long usp,
              int __user *parent_tidp, void __user *child_thread\
ptr,
              int __user *child_tidp, int p6,
              struct pt_regs *regs)
{
        CHECK_FULL_REGS(regs);
        if (usp == 0)
                usp = regs->gpr[1];       /* stack pointer for chi\
ld */
        return do_fork(clone_flags & ~CLONE_IDLETASK, usp, regs,\
 0,
                        parent_tidp, child_tidp);
}
------------------------------------------------------------------------
```

As Table 3.4 shows, the only difference between `fork()`, `vfork()`, and `clone()` is which flags are set in the subsequent calls to `do_fork()`.

TABLE 3.4
Flags Passed to do_fork by fork(), vfork(), and clone()

	fork()	vfork()	clone()
SIGCHLD	X	X	
CLONE_VFORK		X	
CLONE_VM		X	

Finally, we get to `do_fork()`, which performs the real process creation. Recall that up to this point, we only have the parent executing the call to `fork()`, which then enables the system call `sys_fork()`; we still do not have a new process. Our program `foo` still exists as an executable file on disk. It is not running or in memory.

3.3.4   do_fork() Function

We follow the kernel side execution of `do_fork()` line by line as we describe the details behind the creation of a new process.

```
------------------------------------------------------------------
kernel/fork.c
1167   long do_fork(unsigned long clone_flags,
1168       unsigned long stack_start,
1169       struct pt_regs *regs,
1170       unsigned long stack_size,
1171       int __user *parent_tidptr,
1172       int __user *child_tidptr)
1173   {
1174     struct task_struct *p;
1175     int trace = 0;
1176     long pid;
1177
1178     if (unlikely(current->ptrace)) {
1179        trace = fork_traceflag (clone_flags);
1180        if (trace)
1181          clone_flags |= CLONE_PTRACE;
1182     }
1183
1184     p = copy_process(clone_flags, stack_start, regs, stack_size,
parent_tidptr, child_tidptr);
------------------------------------------------------------------
```

Lines 1178–1183

The code begins by verifying if the parent wants the new process ptraced. ptracing references are prevalent within functions dealing with processes. This book explains only the ptrace references at a high level. To determine whether a child can be traced, fork_traceflag() must verify the value of clone_flags. If CLONE_VFORK is set in clone_flags, if SIGCHLD is not to be caught by the parent, or if the current process also has PT_TRACE_FORK set, the child is traced, unless the CLONE_UNTRACED or CLONE_IDLETASK flags have also been set.

Line 1184

This line is where a new process is created and where the values in the registers are copied out. The copy_process() function performs the bulk of the new process space creation and descriptor field definition. However, the start of the new process does not take place until later. The details of copy_process() make more sense when the explanation is scheduler-centric. See the "Keeping Track of Processes: Basic Scheduler Construction" section in this chapter for more detail on what happens here.

```
-----------------------------------------------------------------------
kernel/fork.c
...
1189      pid = IS_ERR(p) ? PTR_ERR(p) : p->pid;
1190
1191      if (!IS_ERR(p)) {
1192          struct completion vfork;
1193
1194          if (clone_flags & CLONE_VFORK) {
1195            p->vfork_done = &vfork;
1196            init_completion(&vfork);
1197          }
1198
1199          if ((p->ptrace & PT_PTRACED) || (clone_flags & CLONE_STOPPED)) {
...
1203              sigaddset(&p->pending.signal, SIGSTOP);
1204              set_tsk_thread_flag(p, TIF_SIGPENDING);
1205          }
...
-----------------------------------------------------------------------
```

Line 1189

This is a check for pointer errors. If we find a pointer error, we return the pointer error without further ado.

Lines 1194–1197

At this point, check if do_fork() was called from vfork(). If it was, enable the wait queue involved with vfork().

Lines 1199–1205

If the parent is being traced or the clone is set to CLONE_STOPPED, the child is issued a SIGSTOP signal upon startup, thus starting in a stopped state.

```
------------------------------------------------------------------
kernel/fork.c
1207      if (!(clone_flags & CLONE_STOPPED)) {
...
1222            wake_up_forked_process(p);
1223      } else {
1224        int cpu = get_cpu();
1225
1226        p->state = TASK_STOPPED;
1227        if (!(clone_flags & CLONE_STOPPED))
1228        wake_up_forked_process(p);    /* do this last */
1229        ++total_forks;
1230
1231        if (unlikely (trace)) {
1232          current->ptrace_message = pid;
1233          ptrace_notify ((trace << 8) | SIGTRAP);
1234        }
1235
1236        if (clone_flags & CLONE_VFORK) {
1237          wait_for_completion(&vfork);
1238          if (unlikely (current->ptrace & PT_TRACE_VFORK_DONE))
1239            ptrace_notify ((PTRACE_EVENT_VFORK_DONE << 8) | SIGTRAP);
1240        } else
...
1248          set_need_resched();
1249      }
1250      return pid;
1251  }
------------------------------------------------------------------
```

Lines 1226–1229

In this block, we set the state of the task to TASK_STOPPED. If the CLONE_STOPPED flag was not set in clone_flags, we wake up the child process; otherwise, we leave it waiting for its wakeup signal.

Lines 1231–1234

If ptracing has been enabled on the parent, we send a notification.

Lines 1236–1239

If this was originally a call to `vfork()`, this is where we set the parent to blocking and send a notification to the trace if enabled. This is implemented by the parent being placed in a wait queue and remaining there in a `TASK_UNINTERRUPTIBLE` state until the child calls `exit()` or `execve()`.

Line 1248

We set `need_resched` in the current task (the parent). This allows the child process to run first.

3.4 Process Lifespan

Now that we have seen how a process is created, we need to look at what happens during the course of its lifespan. During this time, a process can find itself in various states. The transition between these states depends on the actions that the process performs and on the nature of the signals sent to it. Our example program has found itself in the `TASK_INTERRUPTIBLE` state and in `TASK_RUNNING` (its current state).

The first state a process state is set to is `TASK_INTERRUPTIBLE`. This occurs during process creation in the `copy_process()` routine called by `do_fork()`. The second state a process finds itself in is `TASK_RUNNING`, which is set prior to exiting `do_fork()`. These two states are guaranteed in the life of the process. Following those two states, many variables come into play that determine what states the process will find itself in. The last state a process is set to is `TASK_ZOMBIE`, during the call to `do_exit()`. Let's look at the various process states and the manner in which the transitions from one state to the next occur. We point out how our process proceeds from one state to another.

3.4.1 Process States

When a process is running, it means that its context has been loaded into the CPU registers and memory and that the program that defines this context is being executed. At any particular time, a process might be unable to run for a number of reasons. A process might be unable to continue running because it is waiting for input that is not present or the scheduler may have decided it has run the maximum amount of time units allotted and that it must yield to another process. A process is considered ready when it's not running but is able to run (as with the rescheduling) or blocked when waiting for input.

Figure 3.10 shows the abstract process states and underlies the possible Linux task states that correspond to each abstract state. Table 3.5 outlines the four transitions and how it is brought about. Table 3.6 associates the abstract states with the values used in the Linux kernel to identify those states.

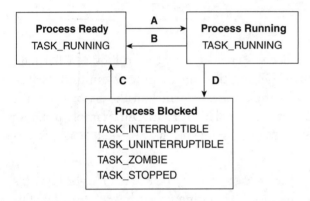

FIGURE 3.10
Process State Transition

TABLE 3.5
Summary of Transitions

Transition	Agent of Transition
Ready to Running (A)	Selected by scheduler
Running to Ready (B)	Timeslice ends (inactive)
	Process yields (active)
Blocked to Ready (C)	Signal comes in
	Resource becomes available
Running to Blocked (D)	Process sleeps or waits on something

TABLE 3.6
Association of Linux Flags with Abstract Process States

Abstract State	Linux Task States
Ready	`TASK_RUNNING`
Running	`TASK_RUNNING`
Blocked	`TASK_INTERRUPTIBLE`
	`TASK_UNINTERRUPTIBLE`
	`TASK_ZOMBIE`
	`TASK_STOPPED`

> NOTE The `set_current_state()` process state can be set if access to the task struct is available by a direct assignment setting such as `current->state= TASK_INTERRUPTIBLE`. A call to `set_current_state(TASK_INTERRUPTIBLE)` will perform the same effect.

3.4.2   Process State Transitions

We now look at the kinds of events that would cause a process to go from one state to another. The abstract process transitions (refer to Table 3.5) include the transition from the ready state to the running state, the transition from the running state to the ready state, the transitions from the blocked state to the ready state, and the transition from the running state to the blocked state. Each transition can translate into more than one transition between different Linux task states. For example, going from blocked to running could translate to going from any one of `TASK_INTERRUPTIBLE`, `TASK_UNINTERRUPTIBLE`, `TASK_ZOMBIE`, or `TASK_STOPPED` to `TASK_RUNNING`. Figure 3.11 and Table 3.7 describe these transitions.

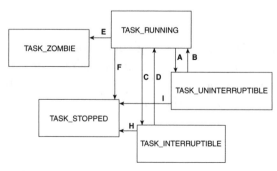

FIGURE 3.11
Task State Transitions

TABLE 3.7
Summary of Task Transitions

Start Linux Task State	End Linux Task State	Agent of Transition
TASK_RUNNING	TASK_UNINTERRUPTIBLE	Process enters wait queue.
TASK_RUNNING	TASK_INTERRUPTIBLE	Process enters wait queue.
TASK_RUNNING	TASK_STOPPED	Process receives SIGSTOP signal or process is being traced.
TASK_RUNNING	TASK_ZOMBIE	Process is killed but parent has not called sys_wait4().
TASK_INTERRUPTIBLE	TASK_STOPPED	During signal receipt.
TASK_UNINTERRUPTIBLE	TASK_STOPPED	During waking up.
TASK_UNINTERRUPTIBLE	TASK_RUNNING	Process has received the resource it was waiting for.
TASK_INTERRUPTIBLE	TASK_RUNNING	Process has received the resource it was waiting for or has been set to running as a result of a signal it received.
TASK_RUNNING	TASK_RUNNING	Moved in and out by the scheduler.

We now explain the various state transitions detailing the Linux task state transitions under the general process transition categories.

3.4.2.1   Ready to Running

The abstract process state transition of "ready to running" does not correspond to an actual Linux task state transition because the state does not actually change (it stays as TASK_RUNNING). However, the process goes from being in a queue of ready to run tasks (or **run queue**) to actually being run by the CPU.

TASK_RUNNING to TASK_RUNNING

Linux does not have a specific state for the task that is currently using the CPU, and the task retains the state of `TASK_RUNNING` even though the task moves out of a queue and its context is now executing. The scheduler selects the task from the run queue. Chapter 7 discusses how the scheduler selects the next task to set to running.

3.4.2.2 Running to Ready

In this situation, the task state does not change even though the task itself undergoes a change. The abstract process state transition helps us understand what is happening. As previously stated, a process goes from running to being ready to run when it transitions from being run by the CPU to being placed in the run queue.

TASK_RUNNING to TASK_RUNNING

Because Linux does not have a separate state for the task whose context is being executed by the CPU, the task does not suffer an explicit Linux task state transition when this occurs and stays in the `TASK_RUNNING` state. The scheduler selects when to switch out a task from being run to being placed in the run queue according to the time it has spent executing and the task's priority (Chapter 7 covers this in detail).

3.4.2.3 Running to Blocked

When a process gets blocked, it can be in one of the following states: `TASK_INTERRUPTIBLE`, `TASK_UNINTERRUPTIBLE`, `TASK_ZOMBIE`, or `TASK_STOPPED`. We now describe how a task gets to be in each of these states from `TASK_RUNNING`, as detailed in Table 3.7.

TASK_RUNNING to TASK_INTERRUPTIBLE

This state is usually called by blocking I/O functions that have to wait on an event or resource. What does it mean for a task to be in the `TASK_INTERRUPTIBLE` state? Simply that it is not on the run queue because it is not ready to run. A task in `TASK_INTERRUPTIBLE` wakes up if its resource becomes available (time or hardware) or if a signal comes in. The completion of the original system call depends on the implementation of the interrupt handler. In the code example, the child process accesses a file that is on disk. The disk driver is in charge of knowing when the device is ready for the data to be accessed. Hence, the driver will have code that looks something like this:

```
while(1)
{
  if(resource_available)
   break();
set_current_state(TASK_INTERRUPTIBLE);
schedule();
}
set_current_state(TASK_RUNNING);
```

The example process enters the `TASK_INTERRUPTIBLE` state at the time it performs the call to `open()`. At this point, it is removed from being the running process by the call to `schedule()`, and another process that the run queue selects becomes the running process. After the resource becomes available, the process breaks out of the loop and sets the process' state to `TASK_RUNNING`, which puts it back on the run queue. It then waits until the scheduler determines that it is the process' turn to run.

The following listing shows the function `interruptible_sleep_on()`, which can set a task in the `TASK_INTERRUPTIBLE` state:

```
------------------------------------------------------------------
kernel/sched.c
2504   void interruptible_sleep_on(wait_queue_head_t *q)
2505   {
2506     SLEEP_ON_VAR
2507
2508     current->state = TASK_INTERRUPTIBLE;
2509
2510     SLEEP_ON_HEAD
2511     schedule();
2512     SLEEP_ON_TAIL
2513   }
------------------------------------------------------------------
```

The `SLEEP_ON_HEAD` and the `SLEEP_ON_TAIL` macros take care of adding and removing the task from the wait queue (see the "Wait Queues" section in this chapter). The `SLEEP_ON_VAR` macro initializes the task's wait queue entry for addition to the wait queue.

TASK_RUNNING to TASK_UNINTERRUPTIBLE

The `TASK_UNINTERRUPTIBLE` state is similar to `TASK_INTERRUPTIBLE` with the exception that processes do not heed signals that come in while it is in kernel mode. This state is also the default state into which a task is set when it is initialized during creation in do_fork(). The sleep_on() function is called to set a task in the TASK_UNINTERRUPTIBLE state.

```
------------------------------------------------------------------
kernel/sched.c
2545  long fastcall __sched sleep_on(wait_queue_head_t *q)
2546  {
2547    SLEEP_ON_VAR
2548
2549    current->state = TASK_UNINTERRUPTIBLE;
2550
2551    SLEEP_ON_HEAD
2552    schedule();
2553    SLEEP_ON_TAIL
2554
2555    return timeout;
2556  }
------------------------------------------------------------------
```

This function sets the task on the wait queue, sets its state, and calls the scheduler.

TASK_RUNNING to TASK_ZOMBIE

A process in the TASK_ZOMBIE state is called a **zombie** process. Each process goes through this state in its lifecycle. The length of time a process stays in this state depends on its parent. To understand this, realize that in UNIX systems, any process may retrieve the exit status of a child process by means of a call to wait() or waitpid() (see the "Parent Notification and sys_wait4()" section). Hence, minimal information needs to be available to the parent, even once the child terminates. It is costly to keep the process alive just because the parent needs to know its state; hence, the zombie state is one in which the process' resources are freed and returned but the process descriptor is retained.

This temporary state is set during a process' call to sys_exit() (see the "Process Termination" section for more information). Processes in this state will never run again. The only state they can go to is the TASK_STOPPED state.

If a task stays in this state for too long, the parent task is not reaping its children. A zombie task cannot be killed because it is not actually alive. This means that no task exists to kill, merely the task descriptor that is waiting to be released.

TASK_RUNNING to TASK_STOPPED

This transition will be seen in two cases. The first case is processes that a debugger or a trace utility is manipulating. The second is if a process receives SIGSTOP or one of the stop signals.

TASK_UNINTERRUPTIBLE or TASK_INTERRUPTIBLE to TASK_STOPPED

TASK_STOPPED manages processes in SMP systems or during signal handling. A process is set to the TASK_STOPPED state when the process receives a wake-up signal or if the kernel specifically needs the process to not respond to anything (as it would if it were set to TASK_INTERRUPTIBLE, for example).

Unlike a task in state TASK_ZOMBIE, a process in state TASK_STOPPED is still able to receive a SIGKILL signal.

3.4.2.4   Blocked to Ready

The transition of a process from blocked to ready occurs upon acquisition of the data or hardware on which the process was waiting. The two Linux-specific transitions that occur under this category are TASK_INTERRUPTIBLE to TASK_RUNNING and TASK_UNINTERRUPTIBLE to TASK_RUNNING.

3.5   Process Termination

A process can terminate voluntarily and explicitly, voluntarily and implicitly, or involuntarily. Voluntary termination can be attained in two ways:

1.   Returning from the main() function (implicit)

2.   Calling exit() (explicit)

Executing a return from the main() function literally translates into a call to exit(). The linker introduces the call to exit() under these circumstances.

Involuntary termination can be attained in three ways:

1.   The process might receive a signal that it cannot handle.

2.   An exception might be raised during its kernel mode execution.

3.   The process might have received the SIGABRT or other termination signal.

The termination of a process is handled differently depending on whether the parent is alive or dead. A process can

• Terminate before its parent

• Terminate after its parent

In the first case, the child is turned into a zombie process until the parent makes the call to wait/waitpid(). In the second case, the child's parent status will have been inherited by the init() process. We see that when any process terminates, the kernel reviews all the active processes and verifies whether the terminating process is parent to any process that is still alive and active. If so, it changes that child's parent PID to 1.

Let's look at the example again and follow it through its demise. The process explicitly calls exit(0). (Note that it could have just as well called _exit(), return(0), or fallen off the end of main with neither call.) The exit() C library function then calls the sys_exit() system call. We can review the following code to see what happens to the process from here onward.

We now look at the functions that terminate a process. As previously mentioned, our process foo calls exit(), which calls the first function we look at, sys_exit(). We delve through the call to sys_exit() and into the details of do_exit().

3.5.1   sys_exit() Function

```
----------------------------------------------------------------------
kernel/exit.c
asmlinkage long sys_exit(int error_code)
{
  do_exit((error_code&0xff)<<8);
}
----------------------------------------------------------------------
```

sys_exit() does not vary between architectures, and its job is fairly straightforward—all it does is call do_exit() and convert the exit code into the format required by the kernel.

3.5.2   do_exit() Function

```
----------------------------------------------------------------------
kernel/exit.c
707  NORET_TYPE void do_exit(long code)
708  {
709    struct task_struct *tsk = current;
710
711    if (unlikely(in_interrupt()))
712     panic("Aiee, killing interrupt handler!");
713    if (unlikely(!tsk->pid))
714     panic("Attempted to kill the idle task!");
715    if (unlikely(tsk->pid == 1))
```

```
716    panic("Attempted to kill init!");
717    if (tsk->io_context)
718      exit_io_context();
719    tsk->flags |= PF_EXITING;
720    del_timer_sync(&tsk->real_timer);
721
722    if (unlikely(in_atomic()))
723      printk(KERN_INFO "note: %s[%d] exited with preempt_count %d\n",
724          current->comm, current->pid,
725          preempt_count());
```

Line 707

The parameter code comprises the exit code that the process returns to its parent.

Lines 711–716

Verify against unlikely, but possible, invalid circumstances. These include the following:

1. Making sure we are not inside an interrupt handler.

2. Ensure we are not the `idle` task (PID0=0) or the `init` task (PID=1). Note that the only time the `init` process is killed is upon system shutdown.

Line 719

Here, we set PF_EXITING in the `flags` field of the processes' task struct. This indicates that the process is shutting down. For example, this is used when creating interval timers for a given process. The process flags are checked to see if this flag is set and thus helps prevent wasteful processing.

```
kernel/exit.c
...
727    profile_exit_task(tsk);
728
729    if (unlikely(current->ptrace & PT_TRACE_EXIT)) {
730      current->ptrace_message = code;
731      ptrace_notify((PTRACE_EVENT_EXIT << 8) | SIGTRAP);
732    }
733
734    acct_process(code);
735    __exit_mm(tsk);
736
737    exit_sem(tsk);
738    __exit_files(tsk);
```

```
739    __exit_fs(tsk);
740    exit_namespace(tsk);
741    exit_thread();
...
```

Lines 729–732

If the process is being ptraced and the PT_TRACE_EXIT flag is set, we pass the exit code and notify the parent process.

Lines 735–742

These lines comprise the cleaning up and reclaiming of resources that the task has been using and will no longer need. __exit_mm() frees the memory allocated to the process and releases the mm_struct associated with this process. exit_sem() disassociates the task from any IPC semaphores. __exit_files() releases any files the task allocated and decrements the file descriptor counts. __exit_fs() releases all file system data.

```
kernel/exit.c
...
744    if (tsk->leader)
745      disassociate_ctty(1);
746
747    module_put(tsk->thread_info->exec_domain->module);
748    if (tsk->binfmt)
749      module_put(tsk->binfmt->module);
...
```

Lines 744–745

If the process is a session leader, it is expected to have a controlling terminal or tty. This function disassociates the task leader from its controlling tty.

Lines 747–749

In these blocks, we decrement the reference counts for the module:

```
kernel/exit.c
...
751    tsk->exit_code = code;
752    exit_notify(tsk);
753
754    if (tsk->exit_signal == -1 && tsk->ptrace == 0)
755      release_task(tsk);
```

```
756
757   schedule();
758   BUG();
759   /* Avoid "noreturn function does return". */
760   for (;;) ;
761 }
...
```

Line 751

Set the task's exit code in the `task_struct` field `exit_code`.

Line 752

Send the `SIGCHLD` signal to parent and set the task state to `TASK_ZOMBIE`. `exit_notify()` notifies the relations of the impending task's death. The parent is informed of the exit code while the task's children have their parent set to the `init` process. The only exception to this is if another existing process exists within the same process group: In this case, the existing process is used as a surrogate parent.

Line 754

If `exit_signal` is -1 (indicating an error) and the process is not being ptraced, the kernel calls on the scheduler to release the process descriptor of this task and to reclaim its timeslice.

Line 757

Yield the processor to a new process. As we see in Chapter 7, the call to `schedule()` will not return. All code past this point catches impossible circumstances or avoids compiler warnings.

3.5.3   Parent Notification and sys_wait4()

When a process is terminated, its parent is notified. Prior to this, the process is in a zombie state where all its resources have been returned to the kernel, but the process descriptor remains. The parent task (for example, the Bash shell) receives the signal `SIGCHLD` that the kernel sends to it when the child process terminates. In the example, the shell calls `wait()` when it wants to be notified. A parent process can ignore the signal by not implementing an interrupt handler and can instead choose to call `wait()` (or `waitpid()`) at any point.

The wait family of functions serves two general roles:

- **Mortician.** Getting task death information.
- **Grave digger.** Getting rid of all traces of a process.

Our parent program can choose to call one of the four functions in the wait family:

- pid_t wait(int *status)
- pid_t waitpid(pid_t pid, int *status, int options)
- pid_t wait3(int *status, int options, struct rusage *rusage)
- pid_t wait4(pid_t pid, int *status, int options, struct rusage *rusage)

Each function will in turn call sys_wait4(), which is where the bulk of the notification occurs.

A process that calls one of the wait functions is blocked until one of its children terminates or returns immediately if the child has terminated (or if the parent is childless). The sys_wait4() function shows us how the kernel manages this notification:

```
--------------------------------------------------------------------
kernel/exit.c
1031  asmlinkage long sys_wait4(pid_t pid,unsigned int * stat_addr,
int options, struct rusage * ru)
1032  {
1033    DECLARE_WAITQUEUE(wait, current);
1034    struct task_struct *tsk;
1035    int flag, retval;
1036
1037    if (options & ~(WNOHANG|WUNTRACED|__WNOTHREAD|__WCLONE|__WALL))
1038      return -EINVAL;
1039
1040    add_wait_queue(&current->wait_chldexit,&wait);
1041  repeat:
1042    flag = 0;
1043    current->state = TASK_INTERRUPTIBLE;
1044    read_lock(&tasklist_lock);
...
--------------------------------------------------------------------
```

Line 1031

The parameters include the PID of the target process, the address in which the exit status of the child should be placed, flags for `sys_wait4()`, and the address in which the resource usage information of the child should be placed.

Lines 1033 and 1040

Declare a wait queue and add the process to it. (This is covered in more detail in the "Wait Queues" section.)

Line 1037–1038

This code mostly checks for error conditions. The function returns a failure code if the system call is passed options that are invalid. In this case, the error EINVAL is returned.

Line 1042

The `flag` variable is set to 0 as an initial value. This variable is changed once the `pid` argument is found to match one of the calling task's children.

Line 1043

This code is where the calling process is set to blocking. The state of the task is moved from TASK_RUNNING to TASK_INTERRUPTIBLE.

```
-----------------------------------------------------------------
kernel/exit.c
...
1045   tsk = current;
1046   do {
1047     struct task_struct *p;
1048     struct list_head *_p;
1049     int ret;
1050
1051     list_for_each(_p,&tsk->children) {
1052       p = list_entry(_p,struct task_struct,sibling);
1053
1054       ret = eligible_child(pid, options, p);
1055       if (!ret)
1056         continue;
1057       flag = 1;
1058       switch (p->state) {
1059       case TASK_STOPPED:
1060         if (!(options & WUNTRACED) &&
```

```
1061          !(p->ptrace & PT_PTRACED))
1062           continue;
1063          retval = wait_task_stopped(p, ret == 2,
1064             stat_addr, ru);
1065          if (retval != 0) /* He released the lock. */
1066             goto end_wait4;
1067          break;
1068        case TASK_ZOMBIE:
...
1072          if (ret == 2)
1073            continue;
1074          retval = wait_task_zombie(p, stat_addr, ru);
1075          if (retval != 0) /* He released the lock. */
1076            goto end_wait4;
1077          break;
1078        }
1079      }
...
1091    tsk = next_thread(tsk);
1092    if (tsk->signal != current->signal)
1093      BUG();
1094  } while (tsk != current);
...
------------------------------------------------------------------------
```

Lines 1046 and 1094

The do while loop iterates once through the loop while looking at itself, then continues while looking at other tasks.

Line 1051

Repeat the action on every process in the task's children list. Remember that this is the parent process that is waiting on its children's exit. The process is currently in TASK_INTERRUPTIBLE and iterating over its children list.

Line 1054

Determine if the pid parameter passed is unreasonable.

Line 1058–1079

Check the state of each of the task's children. Actions are performed only if a child is stopped or if it is a zombie. If a task is sleeping, ready, or running (the remaining states), nothing is done. If a child is in TASK_STOPPED and the

UNTRACED option has been used (which means that the task wasn't stopped because of a process trace), we verify if the status of that child has been reported and return the child's information. If a child is in TASK_ZOMBIE, it is reaped.

```
------------------------------------------------------------------
kernel/exit.c
...
1106    retval = -ECHILD;
1107    end_wait4:
1108    current->state = TASK_RUNNING;
1109    remove_wait_queue(&current->wait_chldexit,&wait);
1110    return retval;
1111    }
------------------------------------------------------------------
```

Line 1106

If we have gotten to this point, the PID specified by the parameter is not a child of the calling process. ECHILD is the error used to notify us of this event.

Line 1107–1111

At this point, the children list has been processed, and any children that needed to be reaped have been reaped. The parent's block is removed and its state is set to TASK_RUNNING once again. Finally, the wait queue is removed.

At this point, you should be familiar with the various stages that a process goes through during its lifecycle, the kernel functions that make all this happen, and the structures the kernel uses to keep track of all this information. Now, we look at how the scheduler manipulates and manages processes to create the effect of a multi-threaded system. We also see in more detail how processes go from one state to another.

3.6   Keeping Track of Processes: Basic Scheduler Construction

Until this point, we kept the concepts of the states and the transitions process-centric. We have not spoken about how the transition is managed, nor have we spoken about the kernel infrastructure, which performs the running and stopping of processes. The scheduler handles all these details. Having finished the exploration of the process lifecycle, we now introduce the basics of the scheduler and how it interacts with the do_fork() function during process creation.

3.6.1 Basic Structure

The scheduler operates on a structure called a **run queue**. There is one run queue per CPU on the system. The core data structures within a run queue are two priority-ordered arrays. One of these contains active tasks and the other contains expired tasks. In general, an active task runs for a set amount of time, the length of its **timeslice** or quantum, and is then inserted into the expired array to wait for more CPU time. When the active array is empty, the scheduler swaps the two arrays by exchanging the active and expired pointers. The scheduler then begins executing tasks on the new active array.

Figure 3.12 illustrates the priority arrays within the run queue. The definition of the priority array structure is as follows:

```
------------------------------------------------------------------------
kernel/sched.c
192  struct prio_array {
193    int nr_active;
194    unsigned long bitmap[BITMAP_SIZE];
195    struct list_head queue[MAX_PRIO];
196  };
------------------------------------------------------------------------
```

The fields of the prio_array struct are as follows:

- **nr_active**. A counter that keeps track of the number of tasks held in the priority array.

- **bitmap**. This keeps track of the priorities within the array. The actual length of bitmap depends on the size of unsigned longs on the system. It will always be enough to store MAX_PRIO bits, but it could be longer.

- **queue**. An array that stores lists of tasks. Each list holds tasks of a certain priority. Thus, queue[0] holds a list of all tasks of priority 0, queue[1] holds a list of all tasks of priority 1, and so on.

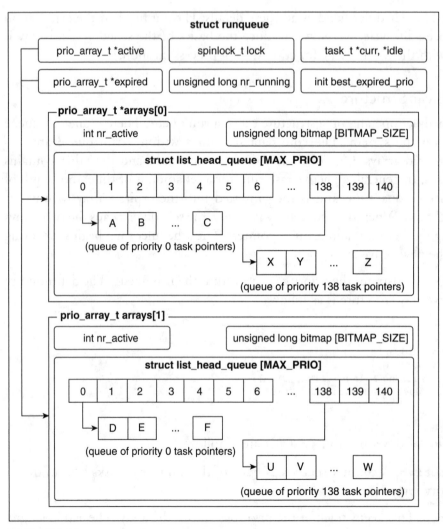

FIGURE 3.12
Priority Arrays in a Run Queue

With this basic understanding of how a run queue is organized, we can now embark on following a task through the scheduler on a single CPU system.

3.6.2 Waking Up from Waiting or Activation

Recall that when a process calls fork(), a new process is made. As previously mentioned, the process calling fork() is called the parent, and the new process is called the child. The newly created process needs to be scheduled for access to the CPU. This occurs via the `do_fork()` function.

Two important lines deal with the scheduler in `do_fork()` related to waking up processes. `copy_process()`, called on line 1184 of `linux/kernel/fork.c`, calls the function `sched_fork()`, which initializes the process for an impending insertion into the scheduler's run queue. `wake_up_forked_process()`, called on line 1222 of `linux/kernel/fork.c`, takes the initialized process and inserts it into the run queue. Initialization and insertion have been separated to allow for the new process to be killed, or otherwise terminated, before being scheduled. The process will only be scheduled if it is created, initialized successfully, and has no pending signals.

3.6.2.1   sched_fork(): Scheduler Initialization for Newly Forked Process

The `sched_fork()` function performs the infrastructure setup the scheduler requires for a newly forked process:

```
------------------------------------------------------------------
kernel/sched.c
719 void sched_fork(task_t *p)
720 {
721     /*
722      * We mark the process as running here, but have not actually
723      * inserted it onto the runqueue yet. This guarantees that
724      * nobody will actually run it, and a signal or other external
725      * event cannot wake it up and insert it on the runqueue either.
726      */
727     p->state = TASK_RUNNING;
728     INIT_LIST_HEAD(&p->run_list);
729     p->array = NULL;
730     spin_lock_init(&p->switch_lock);
------------------------------------------------------------------
```

Line 727

The process is marked as running by setting the `state` attribute in the task structure to `TASK_RUNNING` to ensure that no event can insert it on the run queue and run the process before `do_fork()` and `copy_process()` have verified that the process was created properly. When that verification passes, `do_fork()` adds it to the run queue via `wake_up_forked_process()`.

Line 728–730

The process' `run_list` field is initialized. When the process is activated, its `run_list` field is linked into the queue structure of a priority array in the run queue. The process' `array` field is set to NULL to represent that it is not part of either priority array on a run queue. The next block of `sched_fork()`, lines 731 to 739, deals with kernel preemption. (Refer to Chapter 7 for more information on preemption.)

```
---------------------------------------------------------------------
kernel/sched.c
740    /*
741    * Share the timeslice between parent and child, thus the
742    * total amount of pending timeslices in the system doesn't change,
743    * resulting in more scheduling fairness.
744    */
745    local_irq_disable();
746    p->time_slice = (current->time_slice + 1) >> 1;
747    /*
748    * The remainder of the first timeslice might be recovered by
749    * the parent if the child exits early enough.
750    */
751    p->first_time_slice = 1;
752    current->time_slice >>= 1;
753    p->timestamp = sched_clock();
754    if (!current->time_slice) {
755       /*
756       * This case is rare, it happens when the parent has only
757       * a single jiffy left from its timeslice. Taking the
758       * runqueue lock is not a problem.
759       */
760       current->time_slice = 1;
761       preempt_disable();
762       scheduler_tick(0, 0);
763       local_irq_enable();
764       preempt_enable();
765    } else
766       local_irq_enable();
767 }
---------------------------------------------------------------------
```

Lines 740–753

After disabling local interrupts, we divide the parent's timeslice between the parent and the child using the shift operator. The new process' first timeslice is set to 1 because it hasn't been run yet and its timestamp is initialized to the current time in nanosec units.

Lines 754–767

If the parent's timeslice is 1, the division results in the parent having 0 time left to run. Because the parent was the current process on the scheduler, we need the scheduler to choose a new process. This is done by calling `scheduler_tick()` (on line 762). Preemption is disabled to ensure that the scheduler chooses a new current process without being interrupted. Once all this is done, we enable preemption and restore local interrupts.

At this point, the newly created process has had its scheduler-specific variables initialized and has been given an initial timeslice of half the remaining timeslice of its parent. By forcing a process to sacrifice a portion of the CPU time it's been allocated and giving that time to its child, the kernel prevents processes from seizing large chunks of processor time. If processes were given a set amount of time, a malicious process could spawn many children and quickly become a CPU hog.

After a process has been successfully initialized, and that initialization verified, `do_fork()` calls `wake_up_forked_process()`:

```
------------------------------------------------------------------
kernel/sched.c
922 /*
923 * wake_up_forked_process - wake up a freshly forked process.
924 *
925 * This function will do some initial scheduler statistics housekeeping
926 * that must be done for every newly created process.
927 */
928 void fastcall wake_up_forked_process(task_t * p)
929 {
930   unsigned long flags;
931   runqueue_t *rq = task_rq_lock(current, &flags);
932
933   BUG_ON(p->state != TASK_RUNNING);
934
935   /*
936   * We decrease the sleep average of forking parents
937   * and children as well, to keep max-interactive tasks
938   * from forking tasks that are max-interactive.
939   */
940   current->sleep_avg = JIFFIES_TO_NS(CURRENT_BONUS(current) *
941     PARENT_PENALTY / 100 * MAX_SLEEP_AVG / MAX_BONUS);
942
943   p->sleep_avg = JIFFIES_TO_NS(CURRENT_BONUS(p) *
944     CHILD_PENALTY / 100 * MAX_SLEEP_AVG / MAX_BONUS);
945
946   p->interactive_credit = 0;
947
948   p->prio = effective_prio(p);
949   set_task_cpu(p, smp_processor_id());
950
951   if (unlikely(!current->array))
952     __activate_task(p, rq);
```

```
953   else {
954     p->prio = current->prio;
955     list_add_tail(&p->run_list, &current->run_list);
956     p->array = current->array;
957     p->array->nr_active++;
958     rq->nr_running++;
959   }
960   task_rq_unlock(rq, &flags);
961 }
```

Lines 930–934

The first thing that the scheduler does is lock the run queue structure. Any modifications to the run queue must be made with the lock held. We also throw a bug notice if the process isn't marked as TASK_RUNNING, which it should be thanks to the initialization in sched_fork() (see Line 727 in kernel/sched.c shown previously).

Lines 940–947

The scheduler calculates the sleep average of the parent and child processes. The sleep average is the value of how much time a process spends sleeping compared to how much time it spends running. It is incremented by the amount of time the process slept, and it is decremented on each timer tick while it's running. An interactive, or I/O bound, process spends most of its time waiting for input and normally has a high sleep average. A non-interactive, or CPU-bound, process spends most of its time using the CPU instead of waiting for I/O and has a low sleep average. Because users want to see results of their input, like keyboard strokes or mouse movements, interactive processes are given more scheduling advantages than non-interactive processes. Specifically, the scheduler reinserts an interactive process into the active priority array after its timeslice expires. To prevent an interactive process from creating a non-interactive child process and thereby seizing a disproportionate share of the CPU, these formulas are used to lower the parent and child sleep averages. If the newly forked process is interactive, it soon sleeps enough to regain any scheduling advantages it might have lost.

Line 948

The function effective_prio() modifies the process' static priority. It returns a priority between 100 and 139 (MAX_RT_PRIO to MAX__PRIO-1). The process' static priority can be modified by up to 5 in either direction based on its previous

CPU usage and time spent sleeping, but it always remains in this range. From the command line, we talk about the `nice` value of a process, which can range from +19 to -20 (lowest to highest priority). A `nice` priority of 0 corresponds to a static priority of 120.

Line 749

The process has its CPU attribute set to the current CPU.

Lines 951–960

The overview of this code block is that the new process, or child, copies the scheduling information from its parent, which is **current**, and then inserts itself into the run queue in the appropriate place. We have finished our modifications of the run queue, so we unlock it. The following paragraph and Figure 3.13 discuss this process in more detail.

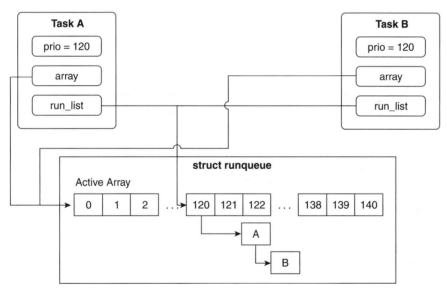

FIGURE 3.13
Run Queue Insertion

The pointer **array** points to a priority array in the run queue. If the current process isn't pointing to a priority array, it means that the current process has finished or is asleep. In that case, the current process' `runlist` field is not in the queue

of the run queue's priority array, which means that the `list_add_tail()`
operation (on line 955) would fail. Instead, we insert the newly created process
using `__activate_task()`, which adds the new process to the queue without
referring to its parent.

In the normal case, when the current process is waiting for CPU time on a run
queue, the process is added to the queue residing at slot `p->prio` in the priority
array. The array that the process was added to has its process counter, `nr_active`,
incremented and the run queue has its process counter, `nr_running`, incremented.
Finally, we unlock the run queue lock.

The case where the current process doesn't point to a priority array on the run
queue is useful in seeing how the scheduler manages the run queue and priority
array attributes.

```
---------------------------------------------------------------------
kernel/sched.c
366 static inline void __activate_task(task_t *p, runqueue_t *rq)
367 {
368    enqueue_task(p, rq->active);
369    rq->nr_running++;
370 }
---------------------------------------------------------------------
```

`__activate_task()` places the given process `p` on to the active priority array on
the run queue `rq` and increments the run queue's `nr_running` field, which is the
counter for total number of processes that are on the run queue.

```
---------------------------------------------------------------------
kernel/sched.c
311 static void enqueue_task(struct task_struct *p, prio_array_t *array)
312 {
313    list_add_tail(&p->run_list, array->queue + p->prio);
314    __set_bit(p->prio, array->bitmap);
315    array->nr_active++;
316    p->array = array;
317 }
---------------------------------------------------------------------
```

Lines 311–312

`enqueue_task()` takes a process `p` and places it on priority array `array`, while
initializing aspects of the priority array.

Line 313

The process' `run_list` is added to the tail of the queue located at `p->prio` in
the priority array.

Line 314

The priority array's bitmap at priority p->prio is set so when the scheduler runs, it can see that there is a process to run at priority p->prio.

Line 315

The priority array's process counter is incremented to reflect the addition of the new process.

Line 316

The process' array pointer is set to the priority array to which it was just added.

To recap, the act of adding a newly forked process is fairly straightforward, even though the code can be confusing because of similar names throughout the scheduler. A process is placed at the end of a list in a run queue's priority array at the slot specified by the process' priority. The process then records the location of the priority array and the list it's located in within its structure.

3.7   Wait Queues

We discussed the process transition between the states of TASK_RUNNING and TASK_INTERRUPTIBLE or TASK_UNINTERRUPTIBLE. Now, we look at another structure that's involved in this transition. When a process is waiting on an external event to occur, it is removed from the run queue and placed on a **wait queue**. Wait queues are doubly linked lists of wait_queue_t structures. The wait_queue_t structure is set up to hold all the information required to keep track of a waiting task. All tasks waiting on a particular external event are placed in a wait queue. The tasks on a given wait queue are woken up, at which point the tasks verify the condition they are waiting for and either resume sleep or remove themselves from the wait queue and set themselves back to TASK_RUNNING. You might recall that sys_wait4() system calls use wait queues when a parent requests status of its forked child. Note that a task waiting for an external event (and therefore is no longer on the run queue[4]) is either in the TASK_INTERRUPTIBLE or TASK_UNINTERRUPTIBLE states.

---

[4]   A task is removed from the run queue once it sleeps and, therefore, yields control to another process.

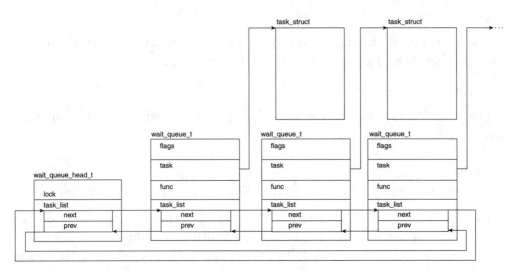

FIGURE 3.14
Wait Queue Structures

A wait queue is a doubly linked list of **wait_queue_t** structures that hold pointers to the process task structures of the processes that are blocking. Each list is
headed up by a **wait_queue_head_t** structure, which marks the head of the list and
holds the spinlock to the list to prevent wait_queue_t additional race conditions.
Figure 3.14 illustrates wait queue implementation. We now look at the
wait_queue_t and the wait_queue_head_t structures:

```
-------------------------------------------------------------------
include/linux/wait.h
19  typedef struct __wait_queue wait_queue_t;
...
23  struct __wait_queue {
24    unsigned int flags;
25  #define WQ_FLAG_EXCLUSIVE  0x01
26    struct task_struct * task;
27    wait_queue_func_t func;
28    struct list_head task_list;
29  };
30
31  struct __wait_queue_head {
32    spinlock_t lock;
33    struct list_head task_list;
34  };
35  typedef struct __wait_queue_head wait_queue_head_t;
-------------------------------------------------------------------
```

The `wait_queue_t` structure is comprised of the following fields:

- **flags**. Can hold the value `WQ_FLAG_EXCLUSIVE`, which is set to 1, or `~WQ_FLAG_EXCLUSIVE`, which would be 0. The `WQ_FLAG_EXCLUSIVE` flag marks this process as an exclusive process. Exclusive and non-exclusive processes are discussed in the next section.

- **task**. The pointer to the task descriptor of the process being placed on the wait queue.

- **func**. A structure holding a function used to wake the task on the wait queue. This field uses as default `default_wake_function()`, which is covered in detail in the section, "Waiting on the Event."

  wait_queue_func_t is defined as follows:

  ```
  ----------------------------------------------------------------
  include/linux/wait.h
  typedef int (*wait_queue_func_t)(wait_queue_t *wait,
  unsigned mode, int sync);
  ----------------------------------------------------------------
  ```

  where `wait` is the pointer to the wait queue, `mode` is either `TASK_INTERRUPTIBLE` or `TASK_UNINTERRUPTIBLE`, and `sync` specifies if the wakeup should be synchronous.

- **task_list**. The structure that holds pointers to the previous and next elements in the wait queue.

The structure `__wait_queue_head` is the head of a wait queue list and is comprised of the following fields:

- **lock**. One lock per list allows the addition and removal of items into the wait queue to be synchronized.

- **task_list**. The structure that points to the first and last elements in the wait queue.

The "Wait Queues" section in Chapter 10, "Adding Your Code to the Kernel," describes an example implementation of a wait queue. In general, the way in which a process puts itself to sleep involves a call to one of the `wait_event*` macros (which is discussed shortly) or by executing the following steps, as in the example shown in Chapter 10:

  1. By declaring the wait queue, the process sleeps on by way of `DECLARE_WAITQUEUE_HEAD`.

2. Adding itself to the wait queue by way of `add_wait_queue()` or `add_wait_queue_exclusive()`.

3. Changing its state to `TASK_INTERRUPTIBLE` or `TASK_UNINTERRUPTIBLE`.

4. Testing for the external event and calling `schedule()`, if it has not occurred yet.

5. After the external event occurs, setting itself to the `TASK_RUNNING` state.

6. Removing itself from the wait queue by calling `remove_wait_queue()`.

The waking up of a process is handled by way of a call to one of the `wake_up` macros. These wake up all processes that belong to a particular wait queue. This places the task in the `TASK_RUNNING` state and places it back on the run queue.

Let's look at what happens when we call the `add_wait_queue()` functions.

3.7.1   Adding to the Wait Queue

Two different functions are used to add sleeping processes into a wait queue: `add_wait_queue()` and `add_wait_queue_exclusive()`. The two functions exist to accommodate the two types of sleeping processes. Non-exclusive waiting processes are those that wait for the return of a condition that is not shared by other waiting processes. Exclusive waiting processes are waiting for a condition that another waiting process might be waiting on, which potentially generates a race condition.

The `add_wait_queue()` function inserts a non-exclusive process into the wait queue. A non-exclusive process is one which will, under any circumstance, be woken up by the kernel when the event it is waiting for comes to fruition. The function sets the `flags` field of the wait queue struct, which represents the sleeping process to 0, sets the wait queue lock to avoid interrupts accessing the same wait queue from generating a race condition, adds the structure to the wait queue list, and restores the lock from the wait queue to make it available to other processes:

```
-------------------------------------------------------------------
kernel/fork.c
93  void add_wait_queue(wait_queue_head_t *q, wait_queue_t * wait)
```

```
94   {
95     unsigned long flags;
96
97     wait->flags &= ~WQ_FLAG_EXCLUSIVE;
98     spin_lock_irqsave(&q->lock, flags);
99     __add_wait_queue(q, wait);
100    spin_unlock_irqrestore(&q->lock, flags);
101  }
```

The `add_wait_queue_exclusive()` function inserts an exclusive process into the wait queue. The function sets the `flags` field of the wait queue struct to 1 and proceeds in much the same manner as `add_wait_queue()` exclusive, with the exception that it adds exclusive processes into the queue from the tail end. This means that in a particular wait queue, the non-exclusive processes are at the front and the exclusive processes are at the end. This comes into play with the order in which the processes in a wait queue are woken up, as we see when we discuss waking up sleeping processes:

----
kernel/fork.c
```
105    void add_wait_queue_exclusive(wait_queue_head_t *q, wait_queue_t * wait)
106    {
107      unsigned long flags;
108
109      wait->flags |= WQ_FLAG_EXCLUSIVE;
110      spin_lock_irqsave(&q->lock, flags);
111      __add_wait_queue_tail(q, wait);
112      spin_unlock_irqrestore(&q->lock, flags);
113    }
```

3.7.2   Waiting on the Event

The `sleep_on()`, `sleep_on_timeout()`, and `interruptible_sleep_on()` interfaces, although still supported in 2.6, will be removed for the 2.7 release. Therefore, we cover only the `wait_event*()` interfaces that are to replace the `sleep_on*()` interfaces.

The `wait_event*()` interfaces include `wait_event()`, `wait_event_interruptible()`, and `wait_event_interruptible_timeout()`. Figure 3.15 shows the function skeleton calling routing.

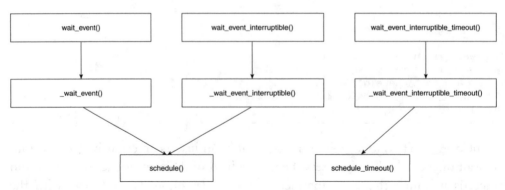

FIGURE 3.15
wait_event*() Call Graph

We go through and describe the interfaces related to `wait_event()` and mention what the differences are with respect to the other two functions. The `wait_event()` interface is a wrapper around the call to `__wait_event()` with an infinite loop that is broken only if the condition being waited upon returns. `wait_event_interruptible_timeout()` passes a third parameter called `ret` of type `int`, which is used to pass the timeout time.

`wait_event_interruptible()` is the only one of the three interfaces that returns a value. This return value is `-ERESTARTSYS` if a signal broke the waiting event, or 0 if the condition was met:

```
------------------------------------------------------------------
include/linux/wait.h
137  #define wait_event(wq, condition)
138  do {
139    if (condition)
140      break;
141    __wait_event(wq, condition);
142  } while (0)
------------------------------------------------------------------
```

The `__wait_event()` interface does all the work around the process state change and the descriptor manipulation:

```
------------------------------------------------------------------
include/linux/wait.h
121  #define __wait_event(wq, condition)
122  do {
123    wait_queue_t __wait;
124    init_waitqueue_entry(&__wait, current);
125
126    add_wait_queue(&wq, &__wait);
```

```
127  for (;;) {
128    set_current_state(TASK_UNINTERRUPTIBLE);
129    if (condition)
130      break;
131    schedule();
132  }
133  current->state = TASK_RUNNING;
134  remove_wait_queue(&wq, &__wait);
135  } while (0)
```

Line 124–126

Initialize the wait queue descriptor for the current process and add the descriptor entry to the wait queue that was passed in. Up to this point, __wait_event_interruptible and __wait_event_interruptible_timeout look identical to __wait_event.

Lines 127–132

This code sets up an infinite loop that will only be broken out of if the condition is met. Before blocking on the condition, we set the state of the process to TASK_INTERRUPTIBLE by using the set_current_state macro. Recall that this macro references the pointer to the current process so we do not need to pass in the process information. Once it blocks, it yields the CPU to the next process by means of a call to the scheduler(). __wait_event_interruptible() differs in one large respect at this point; it sets the state field of the process to TASK_UNINTERRUPTIBLE and waits on a signal_pending call to the current process. __wait_event_interruptible_timeout is much like __wait_event_interruptible except for its call to schedule_timeout() instead of the call to schedule() when calling the scheduler. schedule_timeout takes as a parameter the timeout length passed in to the original wait_event_interruptible_timeout interface.

Lines 133–134

At this point in the code, the condition has been met or, in the case of the other two interfaces, a signal might have been received or the timeout reached. The state field of the process descriptor is now set back to TASK_RUNNING (the scheduler places this in the run queue). Finally, the entry is removed from the wait queue. The remove_wait_queue() function locks the wait queue before removing the entry, and then it restores the lock before returning.

3.7.3   Waking Up

A process must be woken up to verify whether its condition has been met. Note that a process might put itself to sleep, but it cannot wake itself up. Numerous macros can be used to wake_up tasks in a wait queue but only three main "wake_up" functions exist. The macros wake_up, wake_up_nr, wake_up_all, wake_up_interruptible, wake_up_interruptible_nr, and wake_up_interruptible_all all call __wake_up() with different parameters. The macros wake_up_all_sync and wake_up_interruptible_sync both call __wake_up_sync() with different parameters. Finally, the wake_up_locked macro defaults to the __wake_up_locked() function:

```
------------------------------------------------------------------------
include/linux/wait.h
116 extern void FASTCALL(__wake_up(wait_queue_head_t *q, unsigned int mode, int nr));
117 extern void FASTCALL(__wake_up_locked(wait_queue_head_t *q, unsigned int mode));
118 extern void FASTCALL(__wake_up_sync(wait_queue_head_t *q, unsigned int mode, int
 nr));
119
120 #define wake_up(x)      __wake_up((x),TASK_UNINTERRUPTIBLE |
TASK_INTERRUPTIBLE, 1)
121 #define wake_up_nr(x, nr) __wake_up((x),TASK_UNINTERRUPTIBLE |
TASK_INTERRUPTIBLE, nr)
122 #define wake_up_all(x)   __wake_up((x),TASK_UNINTERRUPTIBLE |
TASK_INTERRUPTIBLE, 0)
123 #define wake_up_all_sync(x) __wake_up_sync((x),TASK_UNINTERRUPTIBLE |
TASK_INTERRUPTIBLE, 0)
124 #define wake_up_interruptible(x)   __wake_up((x),TASK_INTERRUPTIBLE, 1)
125 #define wake_up_interruptible_nr(x, nr)   __wake_up((x),TASK_INTERRUPTIBLE, nr)
126 #define wake_up_interruptible_all(x) __wake_up((x),TASK_INTERRUPTIBLE, 0)
127 #define wake_up_locked(x)      __wake_up_locked((x), TASK_UNINTERRUPTIBLE
| TASK_INTERRUPTIBLE)
128 #define wake_up_interruptible_sync(x) __wake_up_sync((x),TASK_INTERRUPTIBLE, 1
129 )
------------------------------------------------------------------------
```

Let's look at __wake_up():

```
------------------------------------------------------------------------
kernel/sched.c
2336  void fastcall __wake_up(wait_queue_head_t *q, unsigned int mode, int
nr_exclusive)
2337  {
2338    unsigned long flags;
2339
2340    spin_lock_irqsave(&q->lock, flags);
2341    __wake_up_common(q, mode, nr_exclusive, 0);
2342    spin_unlock_irqrestore(&q->lock, flags);
2343  }
------------------------------------------------------------------------
```

Line 2336

The parameters passed to __wake_up include q, the pointer to the wait queue; **mode**, the indicator of the type of thread to wake up (this is identified by the state of the thread); and **nr_exclusive**, which indicates whether it's an exclusive or non-exclusive wakeup. An exclusive wakeup (when nr_exclusive = 0) wakes up all the tasks in the wait queue (both exclusive and non-exclusive), whereas a non-exclusive wakeup wakes up all the non-exclusive tasks and only one exclusive task.

Lines 2340, 2342

These lines set and unset the wait queue's spinlock. Set the lock before calling __wake_up_common() to ensure no race condition comes up.

Line 2341

The function __wake_up_common() performs the bulk of the wakeup function:

```
-------------------------------------------------------------------
kernel/sched.c
2313  static void __wake_up_common(wait_queue_head_t *q,
unsigned int mode, int nr_exclusive, int sync)
2314  {
2315    struct list_head *tmp, *next;
2316
2317    list_for_each_safe(tmp, next, &q->task_list) {
2318        wait_queue_t *curr;
2319        unsigned flags;
2320      curr = list_entry(tmp, wait_queue_t, task_list);
2321        flags = curr->flags;
2322        if (curr->func(curr, mode, sync) &&
2323         (flags & WQ_FLAG_EXCLUSIVE) &&
2324         !--nr_exclusive)
2325           break;
2326    }
2327  }
-------------------------------------------------------------------
```

Line 2313

The parameters passed to __wake_up_common are **q**, the pointer to the wait queue; **mode**, the type of thread to wake up; **nr_exclusive**, the type of wakeup previously shown; and **sync**, which states whether the wakeup should be synchronous.

Line 2315

Here, we set temporary pointers for list-entry manipulation.

Line 2317

The `list_for_each_safe` macro scans each item of the wait queue. This is the beginning of our loop.

Line 2320

The `list_entry` macro returns the address of the wait queue structure held by the `tmp` variable.

Line 2322

The `wait_queue_t`'s func field is called. By default, this calls `default_wake_function()`, which is shown here:

```
-------------------------------------------------------------------
kernel/sched.c
2296  int default_wake_function(wait_queue_t *curr, unsigned mode,
int sync)
2297  {
2298    task_t *p = curr->task;
2299    return try_to_wake_up(p, mode, sync);
2300  }
-------------------------------------------------------------------
```

This function calls `try_to_wake_up()` (`kernel/sched.c`) on the task pointed to by the `wait_queue_t` structure. This function performs the bulk of the work of waking up a process, including putting it on the run queue.

Lines 2322–2325

The loop terminates if the process being woken up is the first exclusive process. This makes sense if we realize that all the exclusive processes are queued at the end of the wait queue. After we encounter the first exclusive task in the wait queue all remaining tasks will also be exclusive so we do not want to wake them and we break out of the loop.

3.8 Asynchronous Execution Flow

We mentioned that processes can transition from one state to another by means of interrupts, for instance going from TASK_INTERRUPTIBLE to TASK_RUNNING. One of the ways this is attained is by means of asynchronous execution which includes exceptions and interrupts. We have mentioned that processes move in and out of user and kernel mode. We will now go into a description of how exceptions work and follow it up with an explanation of how interrupts work.

3.8.1 Exceptions

Exceptions, also known as **synchronous interrupts**, are events that occur entirely within the processor's hardware. These events are synchronous to the execution of the processor; that is, they occur not during but after the execution of a code instruction. Examples of processor exceptions include the referencing of a virtual memory location, which is not physically there (known as a **page fault**) and a calculation that results in a divide by 0. The important thing to note with exceptions (sometimes called soft `irqs`) is that they typically happen after an intruction's execution. This differentiates them from external or **asynchronous events**, which are discussed later in Section 3.8.2, "Interrupts."

Most modern processors (the x86 and the PPC included) allow the programmer to initiate an exception by executing certain instructions. These instructions can be thought of as hardware-assisted subroutine calls. An example of this is the **system call**.

3.8.1.1 System Calls

Linux provides user mode programs with entry points into the kernel by which services or hardware access can be requested from the kernel. These entry points are standardized and predefined in the kernel. Many of the C library routines available to user mode programs, such as the `fork()` function in Figure 3.9, bundle code and one or more system calls to accomplish a single function. When a user process calls one of these functions, certain values are placed into the appropriate processor registers and a software interrupt is generated. This software interrupt then calls the kernel entry point. Although not recommended, system calls (syscalls) can also be accessed from kernel code. From where a syscall should be accessed is the source of some discussion because syscalls called from the kernel can have an improvement in performance. This improvement in performance is weighed against the added complexity and maintainability of the code. In this section, we explore the "traditional" syscall implementation where syscalls are called from user space.

Syscalls have the ability to move data between user space and kernel space. Two functions are provided for this purpose: `copy_to_user()` and `copy_from_user()`. As in all kernel programming, validation (of pointers, lengths, descriptors, and permissions) is critical when moving data. These functions have the validation built in. Interestingly, they return the number of bytes *not* transferred.

By its nature, the implementation of the syscall is hardware specific. Traditionally, with Intel architecture, all syscalls have used software interrupt 0x80.[5]

Parameters of the syscall are passed in the general registers with the unique syscall number in %eax. The implementation of the system call on the x86 architecture limits the number of parameters to 5. If more than 5 are required, a pointer to a block of parameters can be passed. Upon execution of the assembler instruction int 0x80, a specific kernel mode routine is called by way of the exception-handling capabilities of the processor. Let's look at an example of how a system call entry is initialized:

```
set_system_gate(SYSCALL_VECTOR,&system_call);
```

This macro creates a user privilege descriptor at entry 128 (SYSCALL_VECTOR), which points to the address of the syscall handler in entry.S (system_call).

As we see in the next section on interrupts, PPC interrupt routines are "anchored" to certain memory locations; the external interrupt handler is anchored to address 0x500, the system timer is anchored to address 0x900, and so on. The system call instruction sc vectors to address 0xc00. Let's explore the code segment from head.S where the handler is set for the PPC system call:

```
------------------------------------------------------------------
arch/ppc/kernel/head.S
484   /* System call */
485   . = 0xc00
486   SystemCall:
487   EXCEPTION_PROLOG
488   EXC_XFER_EE_LITE(0xc00, DoSyscall)
------------------------------------------------------------------
```

Line 485

The anchoring of the address. This line tells the loader that the next instruction is located at address 0xc00. Because labels follow similar rules, the label SystemCall along with the first line of code in the macro EXCEPTION_PROLOG both start at address 0xc00.

---

[5] In an effort to gain in performance with the newer (PIV+) Intel processors, work has been done with the implementation of vsyscalls. vsyscalls are based on calls to user space memory (in particular, a "vsyscall" page) and use the faster sysenter and sysexit instructions (when available) over the traditional int 0x80 call. Similar performance work is also being pursued on many PPC implementations.

Line 488

This macro dispatches the `DoSyscall()` handler.

For both architectures, the syscall number and any parameters are stored in the processor's registers.

When the x86 exception handler processes the `int 0x80`, it indexes into the system call table. The file `arch/i386/kernel/entry.S` contains low-level interrupt handling routines and the system call table, `sys_call_table`. Likewise for the PPC, the syscall low-level routines are in `arch/ppc/kernel/entry.S` and the `sys_call_table` is in `arch/ppc/kernel/misc.S`.

The syscall table is an assembly code implementation of an array in C with 4-byte entries. Each entry is initialized to the address of a function. By convention, we must prepend the name of our function with "`sys_`." Because the position in the table determines the syscall number, we must add the name of our function to the end of the list. Even with different assembly languages, the tables are nearly identical between the architectures. However, the PPC table has only 255 entries at the time of this writing, while the x86 table has 275.

The files `include/asm-i386/unistd.h` and `include/asm-ppc/unistd.h` associate the system calls with their positional numbers in the `sys_call_table`. The "`sys_`" is replaced with a "`__NR_`" in this file. This file also has macros to assist the user program in loading the registers with parameters. (See the assembly programming section in Chapter 2, "Exploration Toolkit," for a crash course in C and assembler variables and inline assembler.)

Let's look at how we would add a system call named `sys_ourcall`. The system call must be added to the `sys_call_table`. The addition of our system call into the x86 `sys_call_table` is shown here:

```
-------------------------------------------------------------------
arch/i386/kernel/entry.S
607   .data
608   ENTRY(sys_call_table)
609   .long sys_restart_syscall /* 0 - old "setup()" system call, used for
restarting*/
...
878   .long sys_tgkill    /* 270 */
879   .long sys_utimes
880   .long sys_fadvise64_64
881   .long sys_ni_syscall   /* sys_vserver */
882   .long sys_ourcall    /* our syscall will be 274 */
883
884   nr_syscalls=(.-sys_call_table)/4
-------------------------------------------------------------------
```

In x86, our system call would be number 274. If we were to add a syscall named `sys_ourcall` in PPC, the entry would be number 255. Here, we show how it would look when we introduce the association of our system call with its positional number into `include/asm-ppc/unistd.h`. `__NR_ourcall` is number-entry number 255 at the end of the table:

```
-------------------------------------------------------------------
include/asm-ppc/unistd.h
/*
 * This file contains the system call numbers.
 */

#define __NR_restart_syscall   0
#define __NR_exit     1
#define __NR_fork     2
...
#define __NR_utimes    271
#define __NR_fadvise64_64   272
#define __NR_vserver   273
#define __NR_ourcall    274

/* #define NR_syscalls 274   this is the old value before our syscall */
#define NR_syscalls 275
-------------------------------------------------------------------
```

The next section discusses interrupts and the hardware involved to alert the kernel to the need for handling them. Where exceptions as a group diverge somewhat is what their handler does in response to being called. Although exceptions travel the same route as interrupts at handling time, exceptions tend to send signals back to the current process rather than work with hardware devices.

3.8.2 Interrupts

Interrupts are asynchronous to the execution of the processor, which means that interrupts can happen in between instructions. The processor receives notification of an interrupt by way of an external signal to one of its pins (INTR or NMI). This signal comes from a hardware device called an **interrupt controller**. Interrupts and interrupt controllers are hardware and system specific. From architecture to architecture, many differences exist in how interrupt controllers are designed. This section touches on the major hardware differences and functions tracing the kernel code from the architecture-independent to the architecture-dependent parts.

An interrupt controller is needed because the processor must be in communication with one of several peripheral devices at any given moment. Older x86 computers used a cascaded pair of Intel 8259 interrupt controllers configured in such a way[6] that the processor was able to discern between 15 discrete interrupt lines (IRQ) (see Figure 3.16). When the interrupt controller has a pending interrupt (for example, when you press a key), it asserts its `INT` line, which is connected to the processor. The processor then acknowledges this signal by asserting its acknowledge line connected to the **INTA** line on the interrupt controller. At this moment, the interrupt controller transfers the IRQ data to the processor. This sequence is known as an **interrupt-acknowledge cycle**.

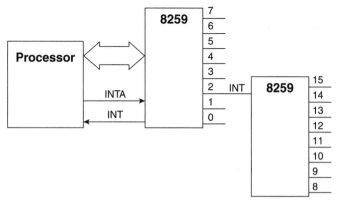

FIGURE 3.16
Cascaded Interrupt Controllers

Newer x86 processors have a local Advanced Programmable Interrupt Controller (APIC). The local APIC (which is built into the processor package) receives interrupt signals from the following:

- Processor's interrupt pins (LINT0, LINT1)

- Internal timer

- Internal performance monitor

- Internal temperature sensor

- Internal APIC error

- Another processor (inter-processor interrupts)

- An external I/O APIC (via an APIC bus on multiprocessor systems)

---

[6]   An IRQ from the first 8259 (usually IRQ2) is connected to the output of the second 8259.

After the APIC receives an interrupt signal, it routes the signal to the processor core (internal to the processor package). The I/O APIC shown in Figure 3.17 is part of a processor chipset and is designed to receive 24 programmable interrupt inputs.

The x86 processors with local APIC can also be configured with 8259 type interrupt controllers instead of the I/O APIC architecture (or the I/O APIC can be configured to interface to an 8259 controller). To find out if a system is using the I/O APIC architecture, enter the following on the command line:

```
lkp:~# cat /proc/interrupts
```

If you see I/O-APIC listed, it is in use. Otherwise, you see XT-PIC, which means it is using the 8259 type architecture.

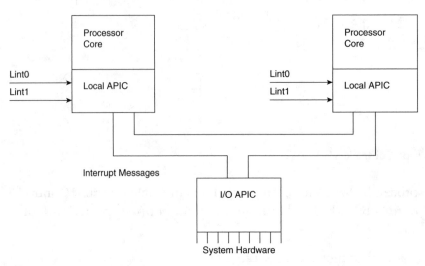

FIGURE 3.17
I/O APIC

The PowerPC interrupt controllers for the Power Mac G4 and G5 are integrated into the Key Largo and K2 I/O controllers. Entering this on the command line:

```
lkp:~# cat /proc/interrupts
```

on a G4 machine yields OpenPIC, which is an Open Programmable Interrupt Controller standard initiated by AMD and Cyrix in 1995 for multiprocessor systems. MPIC is the IBM implementation of OpenPIC, and is used in several of their CHRP designs. Old-world Apple machines had an in-house interrupt controller and, for the 4xx embedded processors, the interrupt controller core is integrated into the ASIC chip.

Now that we have had the necessary discussion of how, why, and when interrupts are delivered to the kernel by the hardware, we can analyze a real-world example of the kernel handling the Hardware System Timer interrupt and expand on where the interrupt is delivered. As we go through the System Timer code, we see that at interrupt time, the hardware-to-software interface is implemented in both the x86 and PPC architectures with jump tables that select the proper handler code for a given interrupt.

Each interrupt of the x86 architecture is assigned a unique number or **vector**. At interrupt time, this vector is used to index into the **Interrupt Descriptor Table (IDT)**. (See the *Intel Programmer's Reference* for the format of the x86 gate descriptor.) The IDT allows the hardware to assist the software with address resolution and privilege checking of handler code at interrupt time. The PPC architecture is somewhat different in that it uses an interrupt table created at compile time to execute the proper interrupt handler. (Later in this section, there is more on the software aspects of initialization and use of the jump tables, when we compare x86 and PPC interrupt handling for the system timer.) The next section discusses interrupt handlers and their implementation. We follow that with a discussion of the system timer as an example of the Linux implementation of interrupts and their associated handlers.

We now talk about the different kinds of interrupt handlers.

3.8.2.1   Interrupt Handlers

Interrupt and exception handlers look much like regular C functions. They may—and often do—call hardware-specific assembly routines. Linux interrupt handlers are broken into a high-performance top half and a low-performance bottom half:

- **Top half.** Must execute as quickly as possible. Top-half handlers, depending on how they are registered, can run with all local (to a given processor) interrupts disabled (a fast handler). Code in a top-half handler needs to be limited to responding directly to the hardware and/or performing time-critical tasks. To remain in the top-half handler for a prolonged period of time could significantly impact system performance. To keep performance high and latency (which is the time it takes to acknowledge a device) low, the *bottom-half* architecture was introduced.

- **Bottom half.** Allows the handler writer to delay the less critical work until the kernel has more time.[7] Remember, the interrupt came in asynchronously with the execution of the system; the kernel might have been doing something more time critical at that moment. With the bottom-half architecture, the handler writer can have the kernel run the less critical handler code at a later time.

Table 3.8 illustrates the four most common methods of bottom-half interrupt handling.

TABLE 3.8
Bottom-Half Interrupt Handling Methods

"Old" bottom halves	These pre-SMP handlers are being phased out because of the fact that only one bottom half can run at a time regardless of the number of processors. This system has been removed in the 2.6 kernel and is mentioned only for reference.
Work queues	The top-half code is said to run in **interrupt context**, which means it is not associated with any process. With no process association, the code cannot sleep or block. Work queues run in **process context** and have the abilities of any kernel thread. Work queues have a rich set of functions for creation, scheduling, canceling, and so on. For more information on work queues, see the "Work Queues and Interrupts" section in Chapter 10.
Softirqs	Softirqs run in interrupt context and are similar to bottom halves except that softirqs of the same type can run on multiple processors simultaneously. Only 32 softirqs are available in the system. The system timer uses softirqs.
Tasklets	Similar to softirqs except that no limit exists. All tasklets are funneled through one softirq, and the same tasklet cannot run simultaneously on multiple processors. The tasklet interface is simpler to use and implement compared to softirqs.

---

[7] Earlier versions of Linux used a top-half/bottom-half handler for the system timer. It has since been rewritten to be a high-performance top half only.

3.8.2.2   IRQ Structures

Three main structures contain all the information related to IRQ's: `irq_desc_t`, `irqaction`, and `hw_interrupt_type`. Figure 3.18 illustrates how they interrelate.

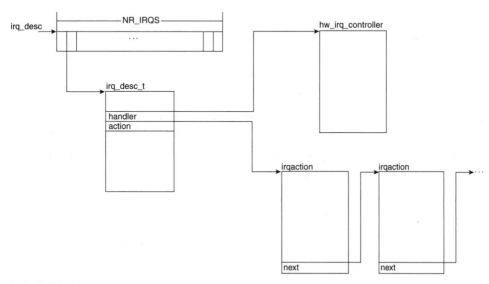

FIGURE 3.18
IRQ Structures

Struct irq_desc_t

The `irq_desc_t` structure is the primary IRQ descriptor. `irq_desc_t` structures are stored in a globally accessible array of size `NR_IRQS` (whose value is architecture dependent) called `irq_desc`.

```
-------------------------------------------------------------------
include/linux/irq.h
60   typedef struct irq_desc {
61     unsigned int status;    /* IRQ status */
62     hw_irq_controller *handler;
63     struct irqaction *action; /* IRQ action list */
64     unsigned int depth;     /* nested irq disables */
65     unsigned int irq_count;  /* For detecting broken interrupts */
66     unsigned int irqs_unhandled;
67     spinlock_t lock;
68   } ____cacheline_aligned irq_desc_t;
69
70   extern irq_desc_t irq_desc [NR_IRQS];
-------------------------------------------------------------------
```

Line 61

The value of the `status` field is determined by setting flags that describe the status of the IRQ line. Table 3.9 shows the flags.

TABLE 3.9
irq_desc_t->field Flags

Flag	Description
IRQ_INPROGRESS	Indicates that we are in the process of executing the handler for that IRQ line.
IRQ_DISABLED	Indicates that the IRQ is disabled by software so that its handler is not executed even if the physical line itself is enabled.
IRQ_PENDING	A middle state that indicates that the occurrence of the interrupt has been acknowledged, but the handler has not been executed.
IRQ_REPLAY	The previous IRQ has not been acknowledged.
IRQ_AUTODETECT	The state the IRQ line is set when being probed.
IRQ_WAITING	Used when probing.
IRQ_LEVEL	The IRQ is level triggered as opposed to edge triggered.
IRQ_MASKED	This flag is unused in the kernel code.
IRQ_PER_CPU	Used to indicate that the IRQ line is local to the CPU calling.

Line 62

The `handler` field is a pointer to the `hw_irq_controller`. The `hw_irq_controller` is a typedef for `hw_interrupt_type` structure, which is the interrupt controller descriptor used to describe low-level hardware.

Line 63

The `action` field holds a pointer to the `irqaction` struct. This structure, described later in more detail, keeps track of the interrupt handler routine to be executed when the IRQ is enabled.

Line 64

The `depth` field is a counter of nested IRQ disables. The `IRQ_DISABLE` flag is cleared only when the value of this field is 0.

Lines 65–66

The `irq_count` field, along with the `irqs_unhandled` field, identifies IRQs that might be stuck. They are used in x86 and PPC64 in the function `note_interrupt()` (`arch/<arch>/kernel/irq.c`).

Line 67

The `lock` field holds the spinlock to the descriptor.

Struct irqaction

The kernel uses the `irqaction` struct to keep track of interrupt handlers and the association with the IRQ. Let's look at the structure and the fields we will view in later sections:

```
-----------------------------------------------------------------------
include/linux/interrupt.h
35   struct irqaction {
36     irqreturn_t (*handler)  (int, void *, struct pt_regs *);
37     unsigned long flags;
38     unsigned long mask;
39     const char *name;
40     void *dev_id;
41     struct irqaction *next;
42   };
-----------------------------------------------------------------------
```

Line 36

The `field` handler is a pointer to the interrupt handler that will be called when the interrupt is encountered.

Line 37

The `flags` field can hold flags such as `SA_INTERRUPT`, which indicates the interrupt handler will run with all interrupts disabled, or `SA_SHIRQ`, which indicates that the handler might share an IRQ line with another handler.

Line 39

The `name` field holds the name of the interrupt being registered.

Struct hw_interrupt_type

The `hw_interrupt_type` or `hw_irq_controller` structure contains all the data related to the system's interrupt controller. First, we look at the structure, and then we look at how it is implemented for a couple of interrupt controllers:

```
------------------------------------------------------------------------
include/linux/irq.h
40   struct hw_interrupt_type {
41     const char * typename;
42     unsigned int (*startup)(unsigned int irq);
43     void (*shutdown)(unsigned int irq);
44     void (*enable)(unsigned int irq);
45     void (*disable)(unsigned int irq);
46     void (*ack)(unsigned int irq);
47     void (*end)(unsigned int irq);
48     void (*set_affinity)(unsigned int irq, cpumask_t dest);
49   };
------------------------------------------------------------------------
```

Line 41

The `typename` holds the name of the Programmable Interrupt Controller (PIC). (PICs are discussed in detail later.)

Lines 42–48

These fields hold pointers to PIC-specific programming functions.

Now, let's look at our PPC controller. In this case, we look at the PowerMac's PIC:

```
------------------------------------------------------------------------
arch/ppc/platforms/pmac_pic.c
170  struct hw_interrupt_type pmac_pic = {
171    " PMAC-PIC ",
172    NULL,
173    NULL,
174    pmac_unmask_irq,
175    pmac_mask_irq,
176    pmac_mask_and_ack_irq,
177    pmac_end_irq,
178    NULL
179  };
------------------------------------------------------------------------
```

As you can see, the name of this PIC is PMAC-PIC, and it has four of the six functions defined. The `pmac_unamsk_irq` and the `pmac_mask_irq` functions enable and disable the IRQ line, respectively. The function `pmac_mask_and_ack_irq` acknowledges that an IRQ has been received, and `pmac_end_irq` takes care of cleaning up when we are done executing the interrupt handler.

```
------------------------------------------------------------------------
arch/i386/kernel/i8259.c
59   static struct hw_interrupt_type i8259A_irq_type = {
60     "XT-PIC",
61     startup_8259A_irq,
62     shutdown_8259A_irq,
63     enable_8259A_irq,
64     disable_8259A_irq,
65     mask_and_ack_8259A,
66     end_8259A_irq,
67     NULL
68   };
------------------------------------------------------------------------
```

The x86 8259 PIC is called XT-PIC, and it defines the first five functions. The first two, `startup_8259A_irq` and `shutdown_8259A_irq`, start up and shut down the actual IRQ line, respectively.

3.8.2.3   An Interrupt Example: System Timer

The system timer is the heartbeat for the operating system. The system timer and its interrupt are initialized during system initialization at boot-up time. The initialization of an interrupt at this time uses interfaces different to those used when an interrupt is registered at runtime. We point out these differences as we go through the example.

As more complex support chips are produced, the kernel designer has gained several options for the source of the system timer. The most common timer implementation for the x86 architecture is the **Programmable Interval Time (PIT)** and, for the PowerPC, it is the **decrementer**.

The x86 architecture has historically implemented the PIT with the Intel 8254 timer. The 8254 is used as a 16-bit down counter—interrupting on terminal count. That is, a value is written to a register and the 8254 decrements this value until it gets to 0. At that moment, it activates an interrupt to the IRQ 0 input on the 8259 interrupt controller, which was previously mentioned in this section.

The system timer implemented in the PowerPC architecture is the decrementer clock, which is a 32-bit down counter that runs at the same frequency as the CPU. Similar to the 8259, it activates an interrupt at its terminal count. Unlike the Intel architecture, the decrementer is built in to the processor.

Every time the system timer counts down and activates an interrupt, it is known as a **tick**. The rate or frequency of this tick is set by the **HZ** variable.

HZ

HZ is a variation on the abbreviation for Hertz (Hz), named for Heinrich Hertz (1857-1894). One of the founders of radio waves, Hertz was able to prove Maxwell's theories on electricity and magnetism by inducing a spark in a wire loop. Marconi then built on these experiments leading to modern radio. In honor of the man and his work the fundamental unit of frequency is named after him; one cycle per second is equal to one Hertz.

HZ is defined in `include/asm-xxx/param.h`. Let's take a look at what these values are in our x86 and PPC.

```
-----------------------------------------------------------------
include/asm-i386/param.h
005  #ifdef __KERNEL__
006  #define HZ          1000           /* internal
kernel timer frequency */
-----------------------------------------------------------------


-----------------------------------------------------------------
include/asm-ppc/param.h
008  #ifdef __KERNEL__
009  #define HZ          100            /* internal
kernel timer frequency */
-----------------------------------------------------------------
```

The value of HZ has been typically 100 across most architectures, but as machines become faster, the tick rate has increased on certain models. Looking at the two main architectures we are using for this book, we can see (above) the default tick rate for both architectures is 1000. The *period* of 1 tick is 1/HZ. Thus the period (or time between interrupts) is 1 millisecond. We can see that as the value of HZ goes up, we get more interrupts in a given amount of time. While this yields better resolution from the timekeeping functions, it is important to note that more of the processor time is spent answering the system timer interrupts in the kernel. Taken to an extreme, this could slow the system response to user mode programs. As with all interrupt handling, finding the right balance is key.

We now begin walking through the code with the initialization of the system timer and its associated interrupts. The handler for the system timer is installed near the end of kernel initialization; we pick up the code segments as `start_kernel()`,

the primary initialization function executed at system boot time, first calls
`trap_init()`, then `init_IRQ()`, and finally `time_init()`:

```
------------------------------------------------------------------
init/main.c
386  asmlinkage void __init start_kernel(void)
387  {
...
413  trap_init();
...
415  init_IRQ();
...
419  time_init();
...
   }
------------------------------------------------------------------
```

Line 413

The macro `trap_init()` initializes the exception entries in the Interrupt
Descriptor Table (IDT) for the x86 architecture running in protected mode. The
IDT is a table set up in memory. The address of the IDT is set in the processor's
IDTR register. Each element of the interrupt descriptor table is one of three gates.
A gate is an x86 protected mode address that consists of a selector, an offset, and a
privilege level. The gate's purpose is to transfer program control. The three types of
gates in the IDT are **system**, where control is transferred to another task; **interrupt**,
where control is passed to an interrupt handler with interrupts disabled; and **trap**,
where control is passed to the interrupt handler with interrupts unchanged.

The PPC is architected to jump to specific addresses, depending on the exception. The function `trap_init()` is a **no-op** for the PPC. Later in this section, as
we continue to follow the system timer code, we will contrast the PPC interrupt
table with the x86 interrupt descriptor table initialized next.

```
------------------------------------------------------------------
arch/i386/kernel/traps.c
900  void __init trap_init(void)
901  {
902  #ifdef CONFIG_EISA
903   if (isa_readl(0x0FFFD9) == 'E'+('I'<<8)+('S'<<16)+('A'<<24)) {
904     EISA_bus = 1;
905   }
906  #endif
907
908  #ifdef CONFIG_X86_LOCAL_APIC
909   init_apic_mappings();
910  #endif
```

```
911
912     set_trap_gate(0,&divide_error);
913     set_intr_gate(1,&debug);
914     set_intr_gate(2,&nmi);
915     set_system_gate(3,&int3);   /* int3-5 can be called from all */
916     set_system_gate(4,&overflow);
917     set_system_gate(5,&bounds);
918     set_trap_gate(6,&invalid_op);
919     set_trap_gate(7,&device_not_available);
920     set_task_gate(8,GDT_ENTRY_DOUBLEFAULT_TSS);
921     set_trap_gate(9,&coprocessor_segment_overrun);
922     set_trap_gate(10,&invalid_TSS);
923     set_trap_gate(11,&segment_not_present);
924     set_trap_gate(12,&stack_segment);
925     set_trap_gate(13,&general_protection);
926     set_intr_gate(14,&page_fault);
927     set_trap_gate(15,&spurious_interrupt_bug);
928     set_trap_gate(16,&coprocessor_error);
929     set_trap_gate(17,&alignment_check);
930  #ifdef CONFIG_X86_MCE
931     set_trap_gate(18,&machine_check);
932  #endif
933     set_trap_gate(19,&simd_coprocessor_error);
934
935     set_system_gate(SYSCALL_VECTOR,&system_call) ;
936
937     /*
938      * default LDT is a single-entry callgate to lcall7 for iBCS
939      * and a callgate to lcall27 for Solaris/x86 binaries
940      */
941     set_call_gate(&default_ldt[0],lcall7);
942     set_call_gate(&default_ldt[4],lcall27);
943
944     /*
945      * Should be a barrier for any external CPU state.
846      */
947     cpu_init();
948
949     trap_init_hook();
950  }
```

Line 902

Look for EISA signature. `isa_readl()` is a helper routine that allows reading the EISA bus by mapping I/O with `ioremap()`.

Lines 908–910

If an Advanced Programmable Interrupt Controller (APIC) exists, add its address to the system fixed address map. See `include/asm-i386/fixmap.h` for "special" system address helper routines; `set_fixmap_nocache()`.`init_apic_mappings()` uses this routine to set the physical address of the APIC.

Lines 912–935

Initialize the IDT with trap gates, system gates, and interrupt gates.

Lines 941–942

These special intersegment call gates support the Intel Binary Compatibility Standard for running other UNIX binaries on Linux.

Line 947

For the currently executing CPU, initialize its tables and registers.

Line 949

Used to initialize system-specific hardware, such as different kinds of APICs. This is a no-op for most x86 platforms.

Line 415

The call to `init_IRQ()` initializes the hardware interrupt controller. Both x86 and PPC architectures have several device implementations. For the x86 architecture, we explore the **i8259** device. For PPC, we explore the code associated with the Power Mac.

The PPC implementation of `init_IRQ()` is in `arch/ppc/kernel/irq.c`. Depending on the particular hardware configuration, `init_IRQ()` calls one of several routines to initialize the PIC. For a Power Mac configuration, the function `pmac_pic_init()` in `arch/ppc/platforms/pmac_pic.c` is called for the G3, G4, and G5 I/O controllers. This is a hardware-specific routine that tries to identify the type of I/O controller and set it up appropriately. In this example, the PIC is part of the I/O controller device. The process for interrupt initialization is similar to x86, with the minor difference being the system timer is not started in the PPC version of `init_IRQ()`, but rather in the `time_init()` function, which is covered later in this section.

The x86 architecture has fewer options for the PIC. As previously discussed, the older systems use the cascaded 8259, while the later systems use the IOAPIC architecture. This code explores the APIC with the emulated 8259 type controllers:

```
--------------------------------------------------------------------
arch/i386/kernel/i8259.c
342  void __init init_ISA_irqs (void)
343  {
344   int i;
345  #ifdef CONFIG_X86_LOCAL_APIC
346   init_bsp_APIC();
347  #endif
348   init_8259A(0);
...
351   for (i = 0; i < NR_IRQS; i++) {
352    irq_desc[i].status = IRQ_DISABLED;
353    irq_desc[i].action = 0;
354    irq_desc[i].depth = 1;
355
356    if (i < 16) {
357     /*
358      * 16 old-style INTA-cycle interrupts:
359      */
360     irq_desc[i].handler = &i8259A_irq_type;
361    } else {
362     /*
363      * 'high' PCI IRQs filled in on demand
364      */
365     irq_desc[i].handler = &no_irq_type;
366    }
367   }
368  }
...
409
410  void __init init_IRQ(void)
411  {
412   int i;
413
414   /* all the set up before the call gates are initialized */
415   pre_intr_init_hook();
...
422   for (i = 0; i < NR_IRQS; i++) {
423    int vector = FIRST_EXTERNAL_VECTOR + i;
424    if (vector != SYSCALL_VECTOR)
425     set_intr_gate(vector, interrupt[i]) ;
426   }
...
431   intr_init_hook();
...
437   setup_timer();
...
  }
--------------------------------------------------------------------
```

Line 410

This is the function entry point called from `start_kernel()`, which is the primary kernel initialization function called at system startup.

Lines 342–348

If the local APIC is available and desired, initialize it and put it in virtual wire mode for use with the 8259. Then, initialize the 8259 device using register I/O in init_8259A(0).

Lines 422–426

On line 424, syscalls are not included in this loop because they were already installed earlier in `trap_init()`. Linux uses an Intel interrupt gate (kernel-initiated code) as the descriptor for interrupts. This is set with the `set_intr_gate()` macro (on line 425). Exceptions use the Intel system gate and trap gate set by the `set_system_gate()` and `set_trap_gate()`, respectively. These macros can be found in `arch/i386/kernel/traps.c`.

Line 431

Set up interrupt handlers for the local APIC (if used) and call `setup_irq()` in `irq.c` for the cascaded 8259.

Line 437

Start the 8253 PIT using register I/O.

Line 419

Now, we follow `time_init()` to install the system timer interrupt handler for both PPC and x86. In PPC, the system timer (abbreviated for the sake of this discussion) initializes the decrementer:

```
-------------------------------------------------------------------
arch/ppc/kernel/time.c
void __init time_init(void)
{
...
317     ppc_md.calibrate_decr();
...
351     set_dec(tb_ticks_per_jiffy);
...
}
-------------------------------------------------------------------
```

Line 317

Figure the proper count for the system HZ value.

Line 351

Set the decrementer to the proper starting count.

The interrupt architecture of the PowerPC and its Linux implementation does not require the installation of the timer interrupt. The decrementer interrupt vector comes in at 0x900. The handler call is hard coded at this location and it is not shared:

```
-----------------------------------------------------------------------
arch/ppc/kernel/head.S
  /* Decrementer */
479  EXCEPTION(0x900, Decrementer, timer_interrupt, EXC_XFER_LITE)
-----------------------------------------------------------------------
```

More detail on the `EXCEPTION` macro for the decrementer is given later in this section. The handler for the decrementer is now ready to be executed when the terminal count is reached.

The following code snippets outline the x86 system timer initialization:

```
-----------------------------------------------------------------------
arch/i386/kernel/time.c
void __init time_init(void)

{
...
340    time_init_hook();
}
-----------------------------------------------------------------------
```

The function `time_init()` flows down to `time_init_hook()`, which is located in the machine-specific setup file `setup.c`:

```
-----------------------------------------------------------------------
arch/i386/machine-default/setup.c
072  static struct irqaction irq0 = { timer_interrupt, SA_INTERRUPT, 0, "timer",
NULL, NULL};
...
081  void __init time_init_hook(void)
082  {
083    setup_irq(0, &irq0);
084  }
-----------------------------------------------------------------------
```

Line 72

We initialize the `irqaction` struct that corresponds to `irq0`.

Lines 81–84

The function call `setup_irq(0, &irq0)` puts the `irqaction` struct containing the handler `timer_interrupt()` on the queue of shared interrupts associated with `irq0`.

This code segment has a similar effect to calling `request_irq()` for the general case handler (those not loaded at kernel initialization time). The initialization code for the timer interrupt took a shortcut to get the handler into `irq_desc[]`. Runtime code uses `disable_irq()`, `enable_irq()`, `request_irq()`, and `free_irq()` in `irq.c`. All these routines are utilities to work with IRQs and touch an `irq_desc` struct at one point.

Interrupt Time

For PowerPC, the decrementer is internal to the processor and has its own interrupt vector at 0x900. This contrasts the x86 architecture where the PIT is an **external interrupt** coming in from the interrupt controller. The PowerPC external controller comes in on vector 0x500. A similar situation would arise in the x86 architecture if the system timer were based on the local APIC.

Tables 3.10 and 3.11 describe the interrupt vector tables of the x86 and PPC architectures, respectively.

TABLE 3.10
x86 Interrupt Vector Table

Vector Number/IRQ	Description
0	Divide error
1	Debug extension
2	NMI interrupt
3	Breakpoint
4	INTO-detected overflow
5	BOUND range exceeded
6	Invalid opcode
7	Device not available
8	Double fault

continues

TABLE 3.10
Continued

Vector Number/IRQ	Description
9	Coprocessor segment overrun (reserved)
10	Invalid task state segment
11	Segment not present
12	Stack fault
13	General protection
14	Page fault
15	(Intel reserved. Do not use.)
16	Floating point error
17	Alignment check
18	Machine check*
19–31	(Intel reserved. Do not use.)
32–255	Maskable interrupts

TABLE 3.11
PPC Offset of Interrupt Vector

Offset (Hex)	Interrupt Type
00000	Reserved
00100	System reset
00200	Machine check
00300	Data storage
00400	Instruction storage
00500	External
00600	Alignment
00700	Program
00800	Floating point unavailable
00900	Decrementer

continues

TABLE 3.11
Continued

Offset (Hex)	Interrupt Type
00A00	Reserved
00B00	Reserved
00C00	System call
00D00	Trace
00E00	Floating point assist
00E10	Reserved
...	...
00FFF	Reserved
01000	Reserved, implementation specific
...	...
02FFF	(End of interrupt vector locations)

Note the similarities between the two architectures. These tables represent the hardware. The software interface to the Intel exception interrupt vector table is the Interrupt Descriptor Table (IDT) that was previously mentioned in this chapter.

As we proceed, we can see how the Intel architecture handles a hardware interrupt by way of an IRQ, to a jump table in entry.s, to a call gate (descriptor), to finally the handler code. Figure 3.19 illustrates this.

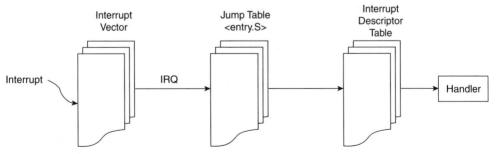

FIGURE 3.19
x86 Interrupt Flow

PowerPC, on the other hand, vectors to specific offsets in memory where the code to jump to the appropriate handler is located. As we see next, the PPC jump table in **head.S** is indexed by way of being fixed in memory. Figure 3.20 illustrates this.

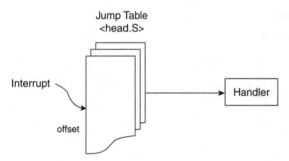

FIGURE 3.20
PPC Interrupt Flow

This should become clearer as we now explore the PPC external (offset 0x500) and timer (offset 0x900) interrupt handlers.

Processing the PowerPC External Interrupt Vector

As previously discussed, the processor jumps to address 0x500 in the event of an external interrupt. Upon further investigation of the EXCEPTION() macro in the file head.S, we can see the following lines of code is linked and loaded such that it is mapped to this memory region at offset 0x500. This architected jump table has the same effect as the x86 IDT:

```
-------------------------------------------------------------------
arch/ppc/kernel/head.S
453    /* External interrupt */
454    EXCEPTION(0x500, HardwareInterrupt, do_IRQ, EXC_XFER_LITE)

The third parameter, do_IRQ(), is called next. Let's take a look at this
function.
arch/ppc/kernel/irq.c
510   void do_IRQ(struct pt_regs *regs)
511   {
512   int irq, first = 1;
513   irq_enter();
...
523   while ((irq = ppc_md.get_irq(regs)) >= 0) {
524    ppc_irq_dispatch_handler(regs, irq);
525    first = 0;
```

```
526  }
527  if (irq != -2 && first)
528   /* That's not SMP safe ... but who cares ? */
529   ppc_spurious_interrupts++;
530  irq_exit();
531  }
```

Lines 513–530

Indicate to the preemption code that we are in a hardware interrupt.

Line 523

Read from the interrupt controller a pending interrupt and convert to an IRQ number (until all interrupts are handled).

Line 524

The `ppc_irq_dispatch_handler()` handles the interrupt. We look at this function in more detail next.

The function `ppc_irq_dispatch_handler()` is nearly identical to the x86 function `do_IRQ()`:

----
arch/ppc/kernel/irq.c
```
428  void ppc_irq_dispatch_handler(struct pt_regs *regs, int irq)
429  {
430  int status;
431  struct irqaction *action;
432  irq_desc_t *desc = irq_desc + irq;
433
434  kstat_this_cpu.irqs[irq]++;
435  spin_lock(&desc->lock);
436  ack_irq(irq);
...
441  status = desc->status & ~(IRQ_REPLAY | IRQ_WAITING);
442  if (!(status & IRQ_PER_CPU))
443   status |= IRQ_PENDING; /* we _want_ to handle it */
...
449   action = NULL;
450   if (likely(!(status & (IRQ_DISABLED | IRQ_INPROGRESS)))) {
451    action = desc->action;
452   if (!action || !action->handler) {
453    ppc_spurious_interrupts++;
454    printk(KERN_DEBUG "Unhandled interrupt %x, disabled\n",irq);
455     /* We can't call disable_irq here, it would deadlock */
456     ++desc->depth;
457     desc->status |= IRQ_DISABLED;
458     mask_irq(irq);
```

```
459     /* This is a real interrupt, we have to eoi it,
460      so we jump to out */
461     goto out;
462     }
463     status &= ~IRQ_PENDING; /* we commit to handling */
464     if (!(status & IRQ_PER_CPU))
465     status |= IRQ_INPROGRESS; /* we are handling it */
466    }
567   desc->status = status;
...
489   for (;;) {
490   spin_unlock(&desc->lock);
491   handle_irq_event(irq, regs, action);
492   spin_lock(&desc->lock);
493
494   if (likely(!(desc->status & IRQ_PENDING)))
495    break;
496   desc->status &= ~IRQ_PENDING;
497   }
498 out:
499   desc->status &= ~IRQ_INPROGRESS;
...
511   }
```

Line 432

Get the IRQ from parameters and gain access to the appropriate `irq_desc`.

Line 435

Acquire the spinlock on the IRQ descriptor in case of concurrent accesses to the same interrupt by different CPUs.

Line 436

Send an acknowledgment to the hardware. The hardware then reacts accordingly, preventing further interrupts of this type from being processed until this one is finished.

Lines 441–443

The flags `IRQ_REPLAY` and `IRQ_WAITING` are cleared. In this case, `IRQ_REPLAY` indicates that the IRQ was dropped earlier and is being resent. `IRQ_WAITING` indicates that the IRQ is being tested. (Both cases are outside the scope of this discussion.) In a uniprocessor system, the `IRQ_PENDING` flag is set, which indicates that we commit to handling the interrupt.

Line 450

This block of code checks for conditions under which we would not process the interrupt. If `IRQ_DISABLED` or `IRQ_INPROGRESS` are set, we can skip over this block of code. The `IRQ_DISABLED` flag is set when we do not want the system to respond to a particular IRQ line being serviced. `IRQ_INPROGRESS` indicates that an interrupt is being serviced by a processor. This is used in the case a second processor in a multiprocessor system tries to raise the same interrupt.

Lines 451–462

Here, we check to see if the handler exists. If it does not, we break out and jump to the "out" label in line 498.

Lines 463–465

At this point, we cleared all three conditions for not servicing the interrupt, so we are committing to doing so. The flag `IRQ_INPROGRESS` is set and the `IRQ_PENDING` flag is cleared, which indicates that the interrupt is being handled.

Lines 489–497

The interrupt is serviced. Before an interrupt is serviced, the spinlock on the interrupt descriptor is released. After the spinlock is released, the routine `handle_irq_event()` is called. This routine executes the interrupt's handler. Once done, the spinlock on the descriptor is acquired once more. If the `IRQ_PENDING` flag has not been set (by another CPU) during the course of the IRQ handling, break out of the loop. Otherwise, service the interrupt again.

Processing the PowerPC System Timer Interrupt

As noted in `timer_init()`, the decrementer is hard coded to 0x900. We can assume the terminal count has been reached and the handler `timer_interrupt()` in `arch/ppc/kernel/time.c` is called at this time:

```
arch/ppc/kernel/head.S
  /* Decrementer */
479  EXCEPTION(0x900, Decrementer, timer_interrupt, EXC_XFER_LITE)
```

Here is the `timer_interrupt()` function.

```
arch/ppc/kernel/time.c
145  void timer_interrupt(struct pt_regs * regs)
146  {
```

```
...
152   if (atomic_read(&ppc_n_lost_interrupts) != 0)
153     do_IRQ(regs);
154
155   irq_enter();
...
159    if (!user_mode(regs))
160      ppc_do_profile(instruction_pointer(regs));
...
165   write_seqlock(&xtime_lock);
166
167    do_timer(regs);
...
189  if (ppc_md.set_rtc_time(xtime.tv_sec+1 + time_offset) == 0)
...
195   write_sequnlock(&xtime_lock);
...
198    set_dec(next_dec);
...
208   irq_exit();
209  }
```

Line 152

  If an interrupt was lost, go back and call the external handler at 0x900.

Line 159

  Do kernel profiling for kernel routing debug.

Lines 165 and 195

  Lock out this block of code.

Line 167

  This code is the same function used in the x86 timer interrupt (coming up next).

Line 189

  Update the RTC.

Line 198

  Restart the decrementer for the next interrupt.

Line 208

  Return from the interrupt.

  The interrupted code now runs as normal until the next interrupt.

Processing the x86 System Timer Interrupt

Upon activation of an interrupt (in our example, the PIT has counted down to 0 and activated IRQ0), the interrupt controller activates an interrupt line going into the processor. The assembly code in entry.S has an entry point that corresponds to each descriptor in the IDT. IRQ0 is the first external interrupt and is vector 32 in the IDT. The code is then ready to jump to entry point 32 in the jump table in entry.S:

```
--------------------------------------------------------------------
arch/i386/kernel/entry.S
385  vector=0
386  ENTRY(irq_entries_start)
387  .rept NR_IRQS
388    ALIGN
389  1:  pushl $vector-256
390    jmp common_interrupt
391  .data
392  .long 1b
393  .text
394  vector=vector+1
395  .endr
396
397    ALIGN
398  common_interrupt:
399    SAVE_ALL
400    call do_IRQ
401    jmp ret_from_intr
--------------------------------------------------------------------
```

This code is a fine piece of assembler magic. The repeat construct .rept (on line 387), and its closing statement (on line 395) create the interrupt jump table at compile time. Notice that as this block of code is repeatedly created, the vector number to be pushed at line 389 is decremented. By pushing the vector, the kernel code now knows what IRQ it is working with at interrupt time.

When we left off the code trace for x86, the code jumps to the proper entry point in the jump table and saves the IRQ on the stack. The code then jumps to the common handler at line 398 and calls do_IRQ() (arch/i386/kernel/irq.c) at line 400. This function is almost identical to ppc_irq_dispatch_handler(), which was described in the section, "Processing the PowerPC External Interrupt Vector" so we will not repeat it here.

Based on the incoming IRQ, the function do_irq() accesses the proper element of irq_desc and jumps to each handler in the chain of action structures. Here, we have finally made it to the actual handler function for the PIT: timer_interrupt(). See the following code segments from time.c. Maintaining the same order as in the source file, the handler starts at line 274:

```
------------------------------------------------------------------------
arch/i386/kernel/time.c
274 irqreturn_t timer_interrupt(int irq, void *dev_id, struct pt_regs *regs)
275 {
...
287   do_timer_interrupt(irq, NULL, regs);
...
290   return IRQ_HANDLED;
291 }
------------------------------------------------------------------------
```

Line 274

This is the entry point for the system timer interrupt handler.

Line 287

This is the call to do_timer_interrupt().

```
------------------------------------------------------------------------
arch/i386/kernel/time.c
208  static inline void do_timer_interrupt(int irq, void *dev_id,
209       struct pt_regs *regs)
210  {
   ...
227  do_timer_interrupt_hook(regs);
...
250  }
------------------------------------------------------------------------
```

Line 227

Call to do_timer_interrupt_hook(). This function is essentially a wrapper around the call to do_timer(). Let's look at it:

```
------------------------------------------------------------------------
include/asm-i386/mach-default/do_timer.h
016  static inline void do_timer_interrupt_hook(struct pt_regs   *regs)
017  {
018   do_timer(regs);
...
025   x86_do_profile(regs);
...
030  }
------------------------------------------------------------------------
```

Line 18

This is where the call to do_timer() gets made. This function performs the bulk of the work for updating the system time.

Line 25

The x86_do_profile() routine looks at the eip register for the code that was running before the interrupt. Over time, this data indicates how often processes are running.

At this point, the system timer interrupt returns from do_irq() to entry.S for system housekeeping and the interrupted thread resumes.

As previously discussed, the system timer is the heartbeat of the Linux operating system. Although we have used the timer as an example for interrupts in this chapter, its use is prevalent throughout the entire operating system.

Summary

Processes have to share the processor with other processes and define individual contexts of execution that hold all the information necessary to run the process. In the course of their execution processes, they go through various states that can be abstracted into blocked states, running states, and ready-to-be-run states.

The kernel stores information regarding tasks in a task_struct descriptor. The task_struct fields can be split up according to different functions that involve the process, including process attributes, process relationships, process memory access, process-related file management, credentials, resource limits, and scheduling. All these fields are necessary to keep track of the process context. A process can be composed of one or more threads that share the memory address space. Each thread has its own structure.

Process creation comes about with a call to one of fork(), vfork(), or clone() system calls. All three system calls end up calling the kernel routine do_fork(), which performs the bulk of the new process creation. During execution, a process goes from one state to another. A process goes from a ready state to a running state by way of scheduler selection, from a running state to a ready state if its timeslice ends or if it yields to another process, from a blocked state to a ready state if an awaited signal comes in, and from running state to a blocked state when awaiting a resource or when sleeping. Process death comes about with a call to the `exit()` system call.

We then delved into the basics of scheduler construction and the structures it uses, including the run queues and wait queues, and how it manages these structures to keep track of how processes are to be scheduled.

This chapter closed with a discussion of the asynchronous flows of process execution, which include exceptions and interrupts, by looking at how the x86 and the PPC hardware handle interrupts. We explored how the Linux kernel manages an interrupt after the hardware delivers it by using the system timer interrupt as an example.

Project: current System Variable

This chapter explored the `task_struct` and current, which is the system variable that points to the currently executing task's `task_struct`. This project's goal is to reinforce the idea that the kernel is an orderly yet ever-changing series of linked structures that are created and destroyed as programs run. As we have seen, the `task_struct` structure is one of the most important structures the kernel owns, in that it has all the information needed for any given task. This project module accesses that structure just as the kernel does and serves as a base for future explorations for the reader.

In this project, we access the current `task_struct` and print various elements from that structure. Starting with the file `include/linux/sched.h`, we find the `task_struct`. Using `sched.h`, we reference `current->pid` and `current->comm.`, the current process ID and name, and follow these structures to the parent's `pid` and `comm`. Next, we borrow a routine from `printk()` and send a message back to the current `tty` terminal we are using.

See the following code:

> NOTE From running the first program (`hellomod`), what do you think the name of the current process will be when the initialization routine prints out `current->comm`? What will be the name of the *parent* process? See the following code discussion.

Project Source Code[8]

```
----------------------------------------------------------------------
currentptr.c
001     #include <linux/module.h>
002     #include <linux//kernel.h>
003     #include <linux/init.h>
004     #include <linux/sched.h>
005     #include <linux/tty.h>
006
007             void tty_write_message1(struct tty_struct *, char *);
008
009             static int my_init( void )
010             {
011
012                     char *msg="Hello tty!";
013
014                     printk("Hello, from the kernel...\n");
015                     printk("parent pid =%d(%s)\n",current->parent-
>pid,current->parent->comm);
016                     printk("current pid =%d(%s)\n",current->pid,current->comm);
017
018                     tty_write_message1(current->signal->tty,msg);
019                     return 0;
020     }

022  static void my_cleanup( void )
{
  printk("Goodbye, from the kernel...\n");
}

027  module_init(my_init);
028  module_exit(my_cleanup);


// This routine was borrowed from <printk.c>
032  void tty_write_message1(struct tty_struct *tty, char *msg)
{
  if (tty && tty->driver->write)
   tty->driver->write(tty, 0, msg, strlen(msg));
  return;
037  }
----------------------------------------------------------------------
```

---

[8] You can use the project source as a starting point to explore the running kernel. Although the kernel has many useful routines to view, such as its internals (for example, strace()), building your own tools, such as this project, sheds light on the real-time aspects of the Linux kernel.

Line 4

`sched.h` contains `struct task_struct {}`, which is where we reference the process ID (`->pid`), and the name of the current task (`->comm.`), as well as the pointer to the parent PID (`->parent`), which references the parent task structure. We also find a pointer to the signal structure, which contains a reference to the `tty` structure (see lines 18–22).

Line 5

`tty.h` contains `struct tty_struct {}`, which is used by the routine we borrowed from `printk.c` (see lines 32–37).

Line 12

This is the simple message string we want to send back to our terminal.

Line 15

Here, we reference the parent PID and its name from our current task structure. The answer to the previous question is that the parent of our task is the current shell program; in this case, it was *Bash*.

Line 16

Here, we reference the current PID and its name from our current task structure. To answer the other half of the previous question, we entered *insmod* on the Bash command line and that is printed out as the current process.

Line 18

This is a function borrowed from `kernel/printk.c`. It is used to redirect messages to a specific `tty`. To illustrate our *current* point, we pass this routine the `tty_struct` of the `tty` (window or command line) from where we invoke our program. This is referenced by way of `current->signal->tty`. The `msg parm` is the string we declared on line 12.

Lines 32–38

The `tty write` function checks that the `tty` exists and then calls the appropriate device driver with the message.

Running the Code

Compile and `insmod()` the code as in the first project.

Exercises

1. When we described process states, we described the "waiting or blocking" state as the state a process finds itself in when it is not running nor ready to run. What are the differences between waiting and blocking? Under what conditions would a process find itself in the waiting state, and under what conditions would it be in the blocking state?

2. Find the kernel code where a process is set from a running state to the blocked state. To put it another way, find where the state of the current->state goes from TASK_RUNNING to TASK_STOPPED.

3. To get an idea of how long it would take a counter to "roll over," do the following calculations. If a 64-bit decrementer runs at 500MHz, how long would it take to terminate with the following values?

   a. 0x000000000000ffff
   b. 0x00000000ffffffff
   c. 0xffffffffffffffff

4. Older versions of Linux used `sti()` and `cli()` to disable interrupts when a section of code should not be interrupted. The newer versions of Linux use `spin_lock()` instead. What is the main advantage of the spinlock?

5. How does the x86 routine `do_IRQ()` and the PPC routine `ppc_irq_dispatch_handler()` allow for shared interrupts?

6. Why is it not recommended that a system call be accessed from kernel code?

7. How many run queues are there per CPU on a Linux system running the 2.6 kernel?

8. When a process forks a new process, does Linux require it to give up some of its timeslice? If so, why?

9. How can processes get reinserted into the active priority array of a run queue after their timeslice has expired? What is a normal process' priority range? What about real-time processes?

Chapter 4

Memory Management

In this chapter

Memory management is the method by which an application running on a computer accesses memory through a combination of hardware and software manipulation. The job of the memory management subsystem is to allocate available memory to requesting processes and to deallocate the memory from a process as it releases it, keeping track of memory as it is handled.

The operating system lifespan can be split up into two phases: normal execution and bootstrapping. The bootstrapping phase makes temporary use of memory. The normal execution phase splits the memory between a portion that is permanently assigned to the kernel code and data, and a second portion that is assigned for dynamic memory requests. Dynamic memory requests come about from process creation and growth. This chapter concentrates on normal execution.

We must understand a few high-level concepts regarding memory management before we delve into the specifics of implementation and how they tie together. This chapter first overviews what a memory management system is and what virtual memory is. Next, we discuss the various kernel structures and algorithms that aid in memory management. After we understand how the kernel manages memory, we consider how process memory is split up and managed and outline how it ties into the kernel structures in a top-down manner. After we cover process memory acquisition, management, and release, we look at page faults and how the two architectures—PowerPC and x86—handle them.

The simplest type of memory management system is one in which a running process has access to all the memory. For a process to work in this way, it must contain all the code necessary to manipulate any hardware it needs in the system, must keep track of its memory addresses, and must have all its data loaded into memory. This approach places a heavy responsibility on the program developer and assumes that processes can fit into the available memory. As these requirements have proven unrealistic given our increasingly complex program demands, available memory is usually divided between the operating system and user processes, relegating the task of memory management to the operating system.

The demands placed on operating systems today are such that multiple programs should be able to share system resources and that the limitations on memory be transparent to the program developer. **Virtual memory** is the result of a method that has been adopted to support programs with the need to access more memory than is physically available on the system and to facilitate the efficient sharing of memory among multiple programs. Physical, or core, memory is what is made available by the RAM chips in the system. Virtual memory allows programs to behave as though they have more memory available than that provided by the system's core memory by transparently making use of disk space. Disk space, which is less expensive and has more capacity for storage than physical memory, can be used as an extension of internal memory. We call this virtual memory because the disk storage effectively acts as though it were memory without being so. Figure 4.1 illustrates the relations between the various levels of data storage.

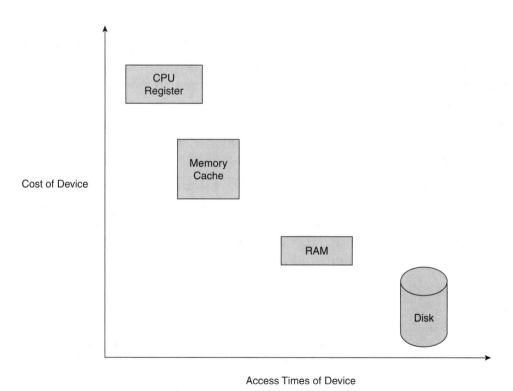

FIGURE 4.1
Data Access Hierarchy

To use virtual memory, the program data is split into basic units that can be moved from disk to memory and back. This way, the parts of the program that are being used can be placed into memory, taking advantage of the faster access times. The unused parts are temporarily placed on disk, which minimizes the impact of the disk's significantly higher access times while still having the data ready for access. These data units, or blocks of virtual memory, are called **pages**. In the same manner, physical memory needs to be split up into partitions that hold these pages. These partitions are called **page frames**. When a process requests an address, the page containing it is loaded into memory. All requests to data on that page yield access to the page. If no addresses in a page have been previously accessed, the page is not loaded into memory. The first access to an address in a page yields a miss or **page fault** because it is not available in memory and must be acquired from disk. A page fault is a trap. When this happens, the kernel must select a page frame and write its contents (the page) back to disk, replacing it with the contents of the page the program just requested.

When a program fetches data from memory, it uses addresses to indicate the portion of memory it needs to access. These addresses, called **virtual addresses**, make up the process **virtual address space**. Each process has its own range of virtual addresses that prevent it from reading or writing over another program's data. Virtual memory allows processes to "use" more memory than what's physically available. Hence, the operating system can afford to give each process its own virtual linear address space.[1]

The size of this address space is determined by the size of the architecture's word size. If a processor can hold a 32-bit value in its registers, the virtual address space of a program running on that processor consists of 2^{32} addresses.[2] Not only does virtual memory expand the amount of memory addressable, it makes certain limitations imposed by the nature of physical memory transparent to the user space

---

[1] Process addressing makes a few assumptions regarding process memory usage. The first is that a process will not make use of all the memory it requests at the same time. The second is that two or more processes instantiated from a common executable should need only to load the executable object once.

[2] Although the limit of memory available is technically the sum of memory and swap space, the addressable limit is imposed by the size of the architecture's word size. This means that even in a system with more than 4GB of memory, a process cannot malloc more than 3GB (after accounting for the top 1GB that is assigned to the kernel).

programmer. For example, the programmer does not need to manage any holes in memory. In our 32-bit example, we have a virtual address space that ranges from 0 to 4GB. If the system has 2GB of RAM, its physical address range spans from 0 to 2GB. Our programs might be 4GB programs, but they have to fit into the available memory. The entirety of the program is kept on disk and **pages** are moved in as they are used.

The act of moving a page from memory to disk and back is called **paging**. Paging includes the translation of the program virtual address onto the physical memory address.

The **memory manager** is a part of the operating system that keeps track of associations between virtual addresses and physical addresses and handles paging. To the memory manager, the page is the basic unit of memory. The **Memory Management Unit (MMU)**, which is a hardware agent, performs the actual translations.[3] The kernel provides **page tables**, indexed lists of the available pages, and their associated addresses that the MMU can access when performing address translations. These are updated whenever a page is loaded into memory.

Having seen the high-level concepts in memory management, let's start our view of how the kernel implements its memory manager with a view at the implementation of pages.

4.1   Pages

As the basic unit of memory managed by the memory manager, a page has a lot of state that it needs to be kept track of. For example, the kernel needs to know when pages become available for reallocation. To do this, the kernel uses page descriptors. Every physical page in memory is assigned a page descriptor.

This section describes various fields in the page descriptor and how the memory manager uses them. The page structure is defined in `include/linux/mm.h`.

---

[3] Some microprocessors, such as the Motorola 68000 (68K), lack an MMU altogether. uCLinux is a Linux distribution that has specifically ported Linux to run in MMU-less systems. Without an MMU, virtual addresses and physical addresses are one and the same.

```
--------------------------------------------------------------------------
include/linux/mm.h
170  struct page {
171    unsigned long flags;
172
173    atomic_t count;
174    struct list_head list;
175    struct address_space *mapping;
176    unsigned long index;
177    struct list_head lru;
178
179    union {
180      struct pte_chain *chain;
181
182      pte_addr_t direct;
183    } pte;
184    unsigned long private;
185
...
196  #if defined(WANT_PAGE_VIRTUAL)
197    void *virtual;
198
199  #endif
200  };
--------------------------------------------------------------------------
```

4.1.1 flags

Atomic flags describe the state of the page frame. Each flag is represented by one of the bits in the 32-bit value. Some helper functions allow us to manipulate and test particular flags. Also, some helper functions allow us to access the value of the bit corresponding to the particular flag. The flags themselves, as well as the helper functions, are defined in `include/linux/page-flags.h`. Table 4.1 identifies and explains some of the flags that can be set in the `flags` field of the page structure.

TABLE 4.1
Flag Values for page->flags

Flag Name	Description
PG_locked	This page is locked so it shouldn't be touched. This bit is used during disk I/O, being set before the I/O operation and reset upon completion.
PG_error	Indicates that an I/O error occurred on this page.

continues

TABLE 4.1
Continued

Flag Name	Description
PG_referenced	Indicates that this page was accessed for a disk I/O operation. This is used to determine which active or inactive page list the page is on.
PG_uptodate	Indicates that the page's contents are valid, being set when a read completes upon that page. This is mutually exclusive to having PG_error set.
PG_dirty	Indicates a modified page.
PG_lru	The page is in one of the Least Recently Used lists used for page swapping. See the description of lru page struct field in this section for more information regarding LRU lists.
PG_active	Indicates that the page is in the active page list.
PG_slab	This page belongs to a slab created by the slab allocator, which is described in the "Slab Allocator" section in this chapter.
PG_highmem	Indicates that this page is in the high memory zone (ZONE_HIGHMEM) and so it cannot be permanently mapped into the kernel virtual address space. The high memory zone pages are identified as such during kernel bootup in mem_init() (see Chapter 8, "Booting the Kernel," for more detail).
PG_checked	Used by the ext2 filesystem. Killed in 2.5.
PG_arch_1	Architecture-specific page state bit.
PG_reserved	Marks pages that cannot be swapped out, do not exist, or were allocated by the boot memory allocator.
PG_private	Indicates that the page is valid and is set if page->private contains a valid value.
PG_writeback	Indicates that the page is under writeback.
PG_mappedtodisk	This page has blocks currently allocated on a system disk.
PG_reclaim	Indicates that the page should be reclaimed.
PG_compound	Indicates that the page is part of a higher order compound page.

4.1.1.1   count

The `count` field serves as the usage or reference counter for a page. A value of 0 indicates that the page frame is available for reuse. A positive value indicates the number of processes that can access the page data.[4]

4.1.1.2   list

The `list` field is the structure that holds the next and prev pointers to the corresponding elements in a doubly linked list. The doubly linked list that this page is a member of is determined in part by the mapping it is associated with and the state of the page.

4.1.1.3   mapping

Each page can be associated with an `address_space` structure when it holds the data for a file memory mapping. The `mapping` field is a pointer to the `address_space` of which this page is a member. An `address_space` is a collection of pages that belongs to a memory object (for example, an inode). For more information on how `address_space` is used, go to Chapter 7, "Scheduling and Kernel Synchronization," Section 7.14.

4.1.1.4   lru

The `lru` field holds the next and prev pointers to the corresponding elements in the Least Recently Used (LRU) lists. These lists are involved with page reclamation and consist of two lists: `active_list`, which contains pages that are in use, and `incactive_list`, which contains pages that can be reused.

4.1.1.5   virtual

`virtual` is a pointer to the page's corresponding virtual address. In a system with highmem,[5] the memory mapping can occur dynamically, making it necessary to recalculate the virtual address when needed. In these cases, this value is set to NULL.

---

[4] A page is free when the data it was holding is no longer used or needed.

[5] Highmem is the physical memory that surpasses the virtually addressable range. See Section 4.2, "Memory Zones."

Compound Page

A compound page is a higher-order page. To enable compound page support in the kernel, "Huge TLB Page Support" must be enabled at compile time. A compound page is composed of more than one page, the first of which is called the "head" page and the remainder of which are called "tail" pages. All compound pages will have the `PG_compound` bit set in their respective `page->flags`, and the `page->lru.next` pointing to the head page.

4.2 Memory Zones

Not all pages are created equal. Some computer architectures have constraints on what certain physical address ranges of memory can be used for. For example, in x86, some ISA buses are only able to address the first 16MB of RAM. Although PPC does not have this constraint, the memory zone concepts are ported to simplify the architecture-independent portion of the code. In the architecture-dependent portion of the PPC code, these zones are set to overlap. Another such constraint is seen in a system that has more RAM than it can address with its linear address space.

A memory zone is composed of page frames or physical pages, which means that a page frame is allocated from a particular memory zone. Three memory zones exist in Linux: `ZONE_DMA` (used for DMA page frames), `ZONE_NORMAL` (non-DMA pages with virtual mapping), and `ZONE_HIGHMEM` (pages whose addresses are not contained in the virtual address space).

4.2.1 Memory Zone Descriptor

As with all objects that the kernel manages, a memory zone has a structure called **zone**, which stores all its information. The zone struct is defined in `include/linux/mmzone.h`. We now closely look at some of the most commonly used fields:

```
-------------------------------------------------------------------
include/linux/mmzone.h
66   struct zone {
...
70     spinlock_t    lock;
71     unsigned long   free_pages;
72     unsigned long   pages_min, pages_low, pages_high;
```

```
73
74    ZONE_PADDING(_pad1_)
75
76    spinlock_t    lru_lock;
77    struct list_head  active_list;
78    struct list_head  inactive_list;
79    atomic_t   refill_counter;
80    unsigned long    nr_active;
81    unsigned long    nr_inactive;
82    int    all_unreclaimable; /* All pages pinned */
83    unsigned long    pages_scanned;  /* since last reclaim */
84
85    ZONE_PADDING(_pad2_)
...
103   int temp_priority;
104   int prev_priority;
...
109   struct free_area   free_area[MAX_ORDER];
...
135   wait_queue_head_t  * wait_table;
136   unsigned long    wait_table_size;
137   unsigned long    wait_table_bits;
138
139   ZONE_PADDING(_pad3_)
140
...
157   } ____cacheline_maxaligned_in_smp;
```

4.2.1.1   lock

The zone descriptor must be locked when it is being manipulated to prevent
read/write errors. The `lock` field holds the spinlock that protects the descriptor
from this.

This is a lock for the descriptor itself and not for the memory range with which
it is associated.

4.2.1.2   free_pages

The `free_pages` field holds the number of free pages that are left in the zone.
This unsigned long is decremented every time a page is allocated from the particular zone and incremented every time a page is returned to the zone. The total

amount of free RAM returned by a call to `nr_free_pages()` is calculated by adding this value from all three zones.

4.2.1.3 pages_min, pages_low, and pages_high

The `pages_min`, `pages_low`, and `pages_high` fields hold the zone watermark values. When the number of available pages reaches each of these watermarks, the kernel responds to the memory shortage in ways suited for each decrementally serious situation.

4.2.1.4 lru_lock

The `lru_lock` field holds the spinlock for the free page list.

4.2.1.5 active_list and inactive_list

`active_list` and `inactive_list` are involved in the page reclamation functionality. The first is a list of the active pages and the second is a list of pages that can be reclaimed.

4.2.1.6 all_unreclaimable

The `all_unreclaimable` field is set to 1 if all pages in the zone are pinned. They will only be reclaimed by `kswapd`, which is the pageout daemon.

4.2.1.7 pages_scanned, temp_priority, and prev_priority

The `pages_scanned`, `temp_priority`, and `prev_priority` fields are all involved with page reclamation functionality, which is outside the scope of this book.

4.2.1.8 free_area

The buddy system uses the `free_area` bitmap.

4.2.1.9 wait_table, wait_table_size, and wait_table_bits

The `wait_table`, `wait_table_size`, and `wait_table_bits` fields are associated with process wait queues on the zone's pages.

Cache Aligning and Zone Padding

Cache aligning is done to improve performance on descriptor field accesses. Cache aligning improves performance by minimizing the number of instructions needed to copy a chunk of data. Take the case of having a 32-bit value not aligned on a word. The processor would need to make two "load word" instructions to get the data onto registers as opposed to just one. ZONE_PADDING shows how cache aligning is performed on a memory zone:

```
---------------------------------------------------------------------
include/linux/mmzone.h
#if defined(CONFIG_SMP)
struct zone_padding {
  int x;
} ____cacheline_maxaligned_in_smp;
#define ZONE_PADDING(name)  struct zone_padding name;
#else
#define ZONE_PADDING(name)
#endif
---------------------------------------------------------------------
```

If you want to know more about how cache aligning works in Linux, refer to include/linux/cache.h.

4.2.2 Memory Zone Helper Functions

When actions are commonly applied to an object, or information is often requested of an object, usually, helper functions make coding easier. Here, we present a couple of helper functions that facilitate memory zone manipulation.

4.2.2.1 for_each_zone()

The for_each_zone() macro iterates over all zones:

```
---------------------------------------------------------------------
include/linux/mmzone.h
268  #define for_each_zone(zone) \
269    for (zone = pgdat_list->node_zones; zone; zone = next_zone(zone))
---------------------------------------------------------------------
```

4.2.2.2 is_highmem() and is_normal()

The is_highmem() and is_normal() functions check if zone struct is in the highmem or normal zones, respectively:

```
--------------------------------------------------------------------------
include/linux/mmzone.h
315  static inline int is_highmem(struct zone *zone)
316  {
317    return (zone - zone->zone_pgdat->node_zones == ZONE_HIGHMEM);
318  }
319
320  static inline int is_normal(struct zone *zone)
321  {
322    return (zone - zone->zone_pgdat->node_zones == ZONE_NORMAL);
323  }
--------------------------------------------------------------------------
```

4.3 Page Frames

A **page frame** is the unit of memory that holds a page. When a process requests memory, the kernel can request a page frame. In the same manner, when a page frame is no longer being used, the kernel releases it to make it available for another process. The following functions are called to perform those operations.

4.3.1 Functions for Requesting Page Frames

A few routines can be called to request a page frame. We can split up the functions into two groups depending on the type of their return value. One group returns a pointer to the page struct (return type is void *) that corresponds to the page frame that is allocated to the request. This includes alloc_pages() and alloc_page(). The second group of functions returns the 32-bit virtual address (return type is a long) of the first allocated page. These include __get_free_page() and __get_dma_pages(). Many of these routines are simply wrappers around a lower-level interface. Figures 4.2 and 4.3 show the calling graphs of these routines.

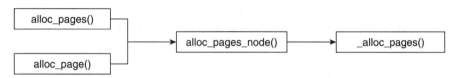

FIGURE 4.2
alloc_*() Calling Graph

The following macros and functions refer to the number of pages being handled (requested or released) in powers of 2. Pages are requested or released in contiguous page frames in powers of 2. We can request 1, 2, 4, 8, 16, and so on groups of pages.[6]

4.3.1.1   alloc_pages() and alloc_page()

alloc_page() requests a single page and thus has no order parameter. This function fills in a 0 value when calling alloc_pages_node(). Alternatively, alloc_pages() can request two order pages:

```
------------------------------------------------------------------------
include/linux/gfp.h
75  #define alloc_pages(gfp_mask, order) \
76     alloc_pages_node(numa_node_id(), gfp_mask, order)
77  #define alloc_page(gfp_mask) \
78     alloc_pages_node(numa_node_id(), gfp_mask, 0)
------------------------------------------------------------------------
```

As you can see from Figure 4.2, both macros then call __alloc_pages_node(), passing it the appropriate parameters. alloc_pages_node() is a wrapper function used for sanity checking of the order of requested page frames:

```
------------------------------------------------------------------------
include/linux/gfp.h
67  static inline struct page * alloc_pages_node(int nid, unsigned int gfp_mask,
unsigned int order)
68  {
69    if (unlikely(order >= MAX_ORDER))
70      return NULL;
71
72    return __alloc_pages(gfp_mask, order, NODE_DATA(nid)->node_zonelists +
(gfp_mask & GFP_ZONEMASK));
73  }
------------------------------------------------------------------------
```

As you can see, if the order of pages requested is greater than the allowed maximum order (MAX_ORDER), the request for page allocation does not go through. In alloc_page(), this value is always set to 0 and so the call always goes through. MAX_ORDER, which is defined in linux/mmzone.h, is set to 11. Thus, we can request up to 2,048 pages.

The __alloc_pages() function performs the meat of the page request. This function is defined in mm/page_alloc.c and requires knowledge of memory zones, which we discussed in the previous section.

---

[6]   Groups of pages requested or released are always continuous.

4.3.1.2   __get_free_page() and __get_dma_pages()

The __get_free_page() macro is a convenience for when only one page is requested. Like alloc_page(), it passes a 0 as the order of pages requested to __get_free_pages(), which then performs the bulk of the request. Figure 4.3 illustrates the calling hierarchy of these functions.

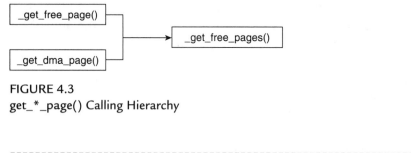

FIGURE 4.3
get_*_page() Calling Hierarchy

```
-----------------------------------------------------------------------------
include/linux/gfp.h
83   #define __get_free_page(gfp_mask) \
84       __get_free_pages((gfp_mask),0)
-----------------------------------------------------------------------------
```

The __get_dma_pages() macro specifies that the pages requested be from ZONE_DMA by adding that flag onto the page flag mask. ZONE_DMA refers to a portion of memory that is reserved for DMA accesses:

```
-----------------------------------------------------------------------------
include/linux/gfp.h
86   #define __get_dma_pages(gfp_mask, order) \
87       __get_free_pages((gfp_mask) | GFP_DMA,(order))
-----------------------------------------------------------------------------
```

4.3.2   Functions for Releasing Page Frames

There are multiple routines for releasing page frames: two macros and the two functions for which they each serve as a wrapper. Figure 4.4 shows the calling hierarchy of the page release routines. We can again split up the functions into two groups. This time, the split is based on the type of parameters they take. The first group, which includes __free_page() and __free_pages(), takes a pointer to the page descriptor that refers to the page that is to be released. The second group, free_page() and free_pages(), takes the address of the first page to be released.

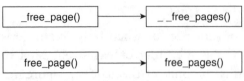

FIGURE 4.4
free_page() Calling Hierarchy

The __free_page() and free_page() macros release a single page. They pass a 0 as the order of pages to be released to the functions that perform the bulk of the work, __free_pages() and free_pages(), respectively:

```
---------------------------------------------------------------------------
include/linux/gfp.h
94  #define __free_page(page) __free_pages((page), 0)
95  #define free_page(addr) free_pages((addr),0)
---------------------------------------------------------------------------
```

free_pages() eventually calls __free_pages_bulk(), which is the freeing function for the Linux implementation of the buddy system. We explore the buddy system in more detail in the following section.

4.3.3   Buddy System

When page frames are allocated and deallocated, the system runs into a memory fragmentation problem called **external fragmentation**. This occurs when the available page frames are spread out throughout memory in such a way that large amounts of contiguous page frames are not available for allocation although the total number of available page frames is sufficient. That is, the available page frames are interrupted by one or more unavailable page frames, which breaks continuity. There are various approaches to reduce external fragmentation. Linux uses an implementation of a memory management algorithm called the **buddy system**.

Buddy systems maintain a list of available blocks of memory. Each list will point to blocks of memory of different sizes, but they are all sized in powers of two. The number of lists depends on the implementation. Page frames are allocated from the list of free blocks of the smallest possible size. This maintains larger contiguous block sizes available for the larger requests. When allocated blocks are returned, the buddy system searches the free lists for available blocks of memory that's the same size as the returned block. If any of these available blocks is contiguous to the returned block, they are merged into a block twice the size of each individual. These

blocks (the returned block and the available block that is contiguous to it) are called
buddies, hence the name "buddy system." This way, the kernel ensures that larger
block sizes become available as soon as page frames are freed.

Now, look at the functions that implement the buddy system in Linux. The page
frame allocation function is __alloc_pages() (mm/page_alloc.c). The page
frame deallocation functions is __free_pages_bulk():

```
-------------------------------------------------------------------------------
mm/page_alloc.c
585  struct page * fastcall
586  __alloc_pages(unsigned int gfp_mask, unsigned int order,
587      struct zonelist *zonelist)
588  {
589    const int wait = gfp_mask & __GFP_WAIT;
590    unsigned long min;
591    struct zone **zones;
592    struct page *page;
593    struct reclaim_state reclaim_state;
594    struct task_struct *p = current;
595    int i;
596    int alloc_type;
597    int do_retry;
598
599    might_sleep_if(wait);
600
601    zones = zonelist->zones;
602    if (zones[0] == NULL)  /* no zones in the zonelist */
603      return NULL;
604
605    alloc_type = zone_idx(zones[0]);
...
608    for (i = 0; zones[i] != NULL; i++) {
609      struct zone *z = zones[i];
610
611      min = (1<<order) + z->protection[alloc_type];
...
617      if (rt_task(p))
618        min -= z->pages_low >> 1;
619
620      if (z->free_pages >= min ||
621          (!wait && z->free_pages >= z->pages_high)) {
622        page = buffered_rmqueue(z, order, gfp_mask);
623        if (page) {
624          zone_statistics(zonelist, z);
625            goto got_pg;
626        }
627      }
628    }
629
```

```
630     /* we're somewhat low on memory, failed to find what we needed */
631     for (i = 0; zones[i] != NULL; i++)
632       wakeup_kswapd(zones[i]);
633
634     /* Go through the zonelist again, taking __GFP_HIGH into account */
635   for (i = 0; zones[i] != NULL; i++) {
636       struct zone *z = zones[i];
637
638       min = (1<<order) + z->protection[alloc_type];
639
640       if (gfp_mask & __GFP_HIGH)
641         min -= z->pages_low >> 2;
642       if (rt_task(p))
643         min -= z->pages_low >> 1;
644
645       if (z->free_pages >= min ||
646           (!wait && z->free_pages >= z->pages_high)) {
647         page = buffered_rmqueue(z, order, gfp_mask);
648         if (page) {
649           zone_statistics(zonelist, z);
650           goto got_pg;
651         }
652       }
653   }
...
720 nopage:
721   if (!(gfp_mask & __GFP_NOWARN) && printk_ratelimit()) {
722     printk(KERN_WARNING "%s: page allocation failure."
723       " order:%d, mode:0x%x\n",
724       p->comm, order, gfp_mask);
725     dump_stack();
726   }
727   return NULL;
728 got_pg:
729   kernel_map_pages(page, 1 << order, 1);
730   return page;
731 }
```

The Linux buddy system is zoned, which means that lists of available page frames are maintained separate by zone. Hence, every search for available page frames has three possible zones from which to get the page frames.

Line 586

The gfp_mask integer value allows the caller of __alloc_pages() to specify both the manner in which to look for page frames (action modifiers). The possible values are defined in include/linux/gfp.h, and Table 4.2 lists them.

TABLE 4.2
Action Modifiers for gfp_maks in Page Allocation

Flag	Description
__GFP_WAIT	Allows the kernel to block the process waiting for page frames. For an example of its use, see line 537 of `page_alloc.c`.
__GFP_COLD	Requesting cache cold pages.
__GFP_HIGH	Page frame can be found at the emergency memory pool.
__GFP_IO	Can perform I/O transfers.
__GFP_FS	Allowed to call down on low-level FS operations.
__GFP_NOWARN	Upon failure of page-frame allocation, the allocation function sends a failure warning. If this modifier is selected, this warning is suppressed. For an example of its use, see lines 665–666 of `page_alloc.c`.
__GFP_REPEAT	Retry the allocation.
__GFP_NORETRY	The request should not be retried because it might fail.
__GFP_DMA	The page frame is in `ZONE_DMA`.
__GFP_HIGHMEM	The page frame is in `ZONE_HIGHMEM`.

Table 4.3 provides a pointer to the zonelists that correspond to the modifiers from `gfp_mask`.

TABLE 4.3
Zonelist

Flag	Description
GFP_USER	Indicates that memory should be allocated not in kernel RAM
GFP_KERNEL	Indicates that memory should be allocated from kernel RAM
GFP_ATOMIC	Used in interrupt handlers making the call to `kmalloc` because it assures that the memory allocation will not sleep
GFP_DMA	Indicates that memory should be allocated from `ZONE_DMA`

Line 599

The function `might_sleep_if()` takes in the value of variable `wait`, which holds the logical `bit` AND of the `gfp_mask` and the value `__GFP_WAIT`. The value of `wait` is 0 if `__GFP_WAIT` was not set, and the value is 1 if it was. If Sleep-inside-spinlock checking is enabled (under the Kernel Hacking menu) during kernel configuration, this function allows the kernel to block the current process for a timeout value.

Lines 608–628

In this block, we proceed to go through the list of zone descriptors once searching for a zone with enough free pages to satisfy the request. If the number of free pages satisfies the request, or if the process is allowed to wait and the number of free pages is higher than or equal to the upper threshold value for the zone, the function `buffered_rmqueue()` is called.

The function `buffered_rmqueue()` takes three arguments: the zone descriptor of the zone with the available page frames, the order of the number of page frames requested, and the temperature of the page frames requested.

Lines 631–632

If we get to this block, we have not been able to allocate a page because we are low on available page frames. The intent here is to try and reclaim page frames to satisfy the request. The function `wakeup_kswapd()` performs this function and replenishes the zones with the appropriate page frames. It also appropriately updates the zone descriptors.

Lines 635–653

After we attempt to replenish the page frames in the previous block, we go through the zonelist again to search for enough free page frames.

Lines 720–727

This block is jumped to after the function determines that no page frames can be made available. If the modifier `GFP_NOWARN` is not selected, the function prints a warning of the page allocation failure, which indicates the name of the command that was called for the current process, the order of page frames requested, and the `gfp_mask` that was applied to this request. The function then returns `NULL`.

Lines 728–730

This block is jumped to after the requested pages are found. The function returns the address of a page descriptor. If more than one page frames were requested, it returns the address of the page descriptor of the first page frame allocated.

When a memory block is returned, the buddy system makes sure to coalesce it into a larger memory block if a buddy of the same order is available. The function __free_pages_bulk() performs this function. We now look at how it works:

```
--------------------------------------------------------------------------------
mm/page_alloc.c
178  static inline void __free_pages_bulk (struct page *page, struct page *base,
179      struct zone *zone, struct free_area *area, unsigned long mask,
180      unsigned int order)
181  {
182    unsigned long page_idx, index;
183
184    if (order)
185      destroy_compound_page(page, order);
186    page_idx = page - base;
187    if (page_idx & ~mask)
188      BUG();
189    index = page_idx >> (1 + order);
190
191   zone->free_pages -= mask;
192    while (mask + (1 << (MAX_ORDER-1))) {
193      struct page *buddy1, *buddy2;
194
195      BUG_ON(area >= zone->free_area + MAX_ORDER);
196      if (!__test_and_change_bit(index, area->map))
...
206      buddy1 = base + (page_idx ^ -mask);
207      buddy2 = base + page_idx;
208      BUG_ON(bad_range(zone, buddy1));
209      BUG_ON(bad_range(zone, buddy2));
210      list_del(&buddy1->lru);
211      mask <<= 1;
212     area++;
213      index >>= 1;
214     page_idx &= mask;
215     }
216    list_add(&(base + page_idx)->lru, &area->free_list);
217  }
--------------------------------------------------------------------------------
```

Lines 184–215

The __free_pages_bulk() function iterates over the size of the blocks corresponding to each of the free block lists. (MAX_ORDER is the order of the largest block size.) For each order and until it reaches the maximum order or finds the smallest possible buddy, it calls `__test_and_change_bit()`. This function tests to see whether the buddy page to our returned block is allocated. If so, we break out of the loop. If not, it sees if it can find a higher order buddy with which to merge our freed block of page frames.

Line 216

The free block is inserted into the proper list of free page frames.

4.4 Slab Allocator

We discussed that pages are the basic unit of memory for the memory manager. However, processes generally request memory on the order of bytes, not on the order of pages. To support the allocation of smaller memory requests made through calls to functions like `kmalloc()`, the kernel implements the **slab allocator**, which is a layer of the memory manager that acts on acquired pages.

The slab allocator seeks to reduce the cost incurred by allocating, initializing, destroying, and freeing memory areas by maintaining a ready cache of commonly used memory areas. This cache maintains the memory areas allocated, initialized, and ready to deploy. When the requesting process no longer needs the memory areas, they are simply returned to the cache.

In practice, the slab allocator is made up of many caches, each of which stores memory areas of different sizes. Caches can be **specialized** or **general purpose**. Specialized caches store memory areas that hold specific objects, such as descriptors. For example, process descriptors, the `task_structs`, are stored in a cache that the slab allocator maintains. The size of the memory areas held by this cache are `sizeof(task_struct)`. In the same manner, inode and dentry data structures are also maintained in caches. General caches are made of memory areas of predetermined sizes. These sizes include memory areas of 32, 64, 128, 256, 512, 1,024, 2,048, 4,096, 8,192, 16,384, 32,768, 65,536, and 131,072 bytes.[7]

If we run the command `cat /proc/slabinfo`, the existing slab allocator caches are listed. Looking at the first column of the output, we can see the names of data

---

[7] All general caches are L1 aligned for performance reasons.

structures and a group of entries following the `format size-*`. The first set corresponds to specialized object caches; the latter set corresponds to caches that hold general-purpose objects of the specified size.

You might also notice that the general-purpose caches have two entries per size, one of which ends with `(DMA)`. This exists because memory areas from either DMA or normal zones can be requested. The slab allocator maintains caches of both types of memory to facilitate these requests. Figure 4.5 shows the output of `/proc/slabinfo`, which shows the caches of both types of memory.

size-131072 (DMA)	0	0	131072	1	32	: tunables	8	4	0	: slabdata	0	0
size-131072	0	0	131072	1	32	: tunables	8	4	0	: slabdata	0	0
size-65536 (DMA)	0	0	65536	1	16	: tunables	8	4	0	: slabdata	0	0
size-65536	1	1	65536	1	16	: tunables	8	4	0	: slabdata	1	1
size-32768 (DMA)	0	0	32768	1	8	: tunables	8	4	0	: slabdata	0	0
size-32768	0	0	32768	1	8	: tunables	8	4	0	: slabdata	0	0
size-16384 (DMA)	0	0	16384	1	4	: tunables	8	4	0	: slabdata	0	0
size-16384	0	0	16384	1	4	: tunables	8	4	0	: slabdata	0	0
size-8192 (DMA)	0	0	8192	1	2	: tunables	8	4	0	: slabdata	0	0
size-8192	64	68	8192	1	2	: tunables	8	4	0	: slabdata	64	68
size-4096 (DMA)	0	0	4096	1	1	: tunables	24	12	0	: slabdata	0	0
size-4096	65	65	4096	1	1	: tunables	24	12	0	: slabdata	65	65
size-2048 (DMA)	0	0	2048	2	1	: tunables	24	12	0	: slabdata	0	0
size-2048	102	102	2048	2	1	: tunables	24	12	0	: slabdata	51	51
size-1024 (DMA)	0	0	1024	4	1	: tunables	54	27	0	: slabdata	0	0
size-1024	73	100	1024	4	1	: tunables	54	27	0	: slabdata	25	25
size-512(DMA)	0	0	512	8	1	: tunables	54	27	0	: slabdata	0	0
size-512	288	288	512	8	1	: tunables	54	27	0	: slabdata	36	36
size-256 (DMA)	0	0	256	15	1	: tunables	120	60	0	: slabdata	0	0
size-256	149	165	256	15	1	: tunables	120	60	0	: slabdata	11	11
size-128 (DMA)	0	0	128	30	1	: tunables	120	60	0	: slabdata	0	0
size-128	4906	10290	128	30	1	: tunables	120	60	0	: slabdata	343	343
size-64 (DMA)	0	0	64	58	1	: tunables	120	60	0	: slabdata	0	0
size-64	1565	2323	64	58	1	: tunables	120	60	0	: slabdata	40	40

FIGURE 4.5
cat /proc/slabinfo

A cache is further subdivided into containers called **slabs**. Each slab is made up of one or more contiguous page frames from which the smaller memory areas are allocated. That is why we say that the slabs contain the objects. The objects themselves are address intervals of a predetermined size within a page frame that belongs to a particular slab. Figure 4.6 shows the slab allocator anatomy.

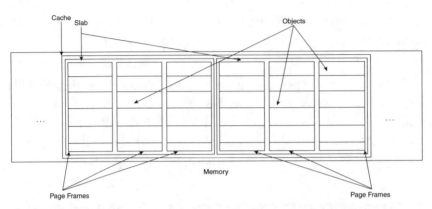

FIGURE 4.6
Slab Allocator Anatomy

The slab allocator uses three main structures to maintain object information: the cache descriptor called **kmem_cache**, the general caches descriptor called **cache_sizes**, and the slab descriptor called **slab**. Figure 4.7 summarizes the relationships between all the descriptors.

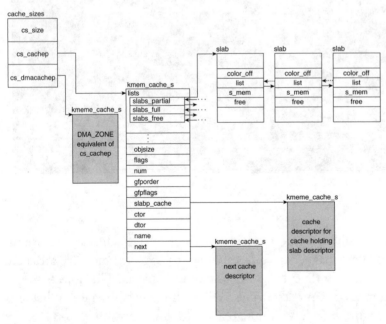

FIGURE 4.7
Slab Allocator Structures

4.4.1   Cache Descriptor

Every cache has a cache descriptor of type `kmem_cache_s`, which holds its information. Most of these values are set or calculated at cache-creation time in `kmem_cache_create()` (`mm/slab.c`). We discuss this function in a later section. First, let's look at some of the fields in the cache descriptor and understand the information they hold.

```
--------------------------------------------------------------------------------
mm/slab.c
246  struct kmem_cache_s {
...
252    struct kmem_list3  lists;
...
254    unsigned int    objsize;
255    unsigned int    flags;  /* constant flags */
256    unsigned int    num;  /* # of objs per slab */
...
263    unsigned int    gfporder;
264
265    /* force GFP flags, e.g. GFP_DMA */
266    unsigned int    gfpflags;
267
268    size_t    color; /* cache coloring range */
269    unsigned int    color_off;  /* color offset */
270    unsigned int    color_next;  /* cache coloring */
271    kmem_cache_t    *slabp_cache;
272    unsigned int    dflags;    /* dynamic flags */
273
273    /* constructor func */
274    void (*ctor)(void *, kmem_cache_t *, unsigned long);
275
276    /* de-constructor func */
277    void (*dtor)(void *, kmem_cache_t *, unsigned long);
278
279    /* 4) cache creation/removal */
280    const char    *name;
281    struct list_head  next;
282
...
301  };
--------------------------------------------------------------------------------
```

4.4.1.1   lists

The `lists` field is a structure that holds three lists heads, which each correspond to the three states that slabs can find themselves in: partial, full, and free. A cache can have one or more slabs in any of these states. It is by way of this data structure that the cache references the slabs. The lists themselves are doubly linked lists that are maintained by the slab descriptor field list. This is described in the "Slab Descriptor" section later in this chapter.

```
------------------------------------------------------------------------
mm/slab.c
217  struct kmem_list3 {
218    struct list_head   slabs_partial;
219    struct list_head   slabs_full;
220    struct list_head   slabs_free;
...
223    unsigned long  next_reap;
224    struct array_cache  *shared;
225  };
------------------------------------------------------------------------
```

lists.slabs_partial

lists.slabs_partial is the head of the list of slabs that are only partially allocated with objects. That is, a slab in the partial state has some of its objects allocated and some free to be used.

lists.slabs_full

lists.slabs_full is the head of the list of slabs whose objects have all been allocated. These slabs contain no available objects.

lists.slabs_free

lists.slabs_free is the head of the list of slabs whose objects are all free to be allocated. Not a single one of its objects has been allocated.

Maintaining these lists reduces the time it takes to find a free object. When an object from the cache is requested, the kernel searches the partial slabs. If the partial slabs list is empty, it then looks at the free slabs. If the free slabs list is empty, a new slab is created.

lists.next_reap

Slabs have page frames allocated to them. If these pages are not in use, it is better to return them to the main memory pool. Toward this end, the caches are reaped. This field holds the time of the next cache reap. It is set in kmem_cache_create() (mm/slab.c) at cache-creation time and is updated in cache_reap() (mm/slab.c) every time it is called.

4.4.1.2   objsize

The `objsize` field holds the size (in bytes) of the objects in the cache. This is determined at cache-creation time based on requested size and cache alignment concerns.

4.4.1.3   flags

The `flags` field holds the flag mask that describes constant characteristics of the cache. Possible flags are defined in `include/linux/slab.h` and Table 4.4 describes them.

TABLE 4.4
Slab Flags

Flag Name	Description
SLAB_POISON	Requests that a test pattern of a5a5a5a5 be written to the slab upon creation. This can then be used to verify memory that has been initialized.
SLAB_NO_REAP	When memory requests meet with insufficient memory conditions, the memory manager begins to reap memory areas that are not used. Setting this flag ensures that this cache won't be automatically reaped under these conditions.
SLAB_HWCACHE_ALIGN	Requests that objects be aligned to the processor's hardware cacheline to improve performance by cutting down memory cycles.
SLAB_CACHE_DMA	Indicates that DMA memory should used. When requesting new page frames, the GFP_DMA flag is passed to the buddy system.
SLAB_PANIC	Indicates that a panic should be called if kmem_cache_create() fails for any reason.

4.4.1.4   num

The `num` field holds the number of objects per slab in this cache. This is determined upon cache creation (also in `kmem_cache_create()`) based on `gfporder`'s value (see the next field), the size of the objects to be created, and the alignment they require.

4.4.1.5   gfporder

The `gfporder` is the order (base 2) of the number of contiguous page frames that are contained per slab in the cache. This value defaults to 0 and is set upon cache creation with the call to `kmem_cache_create()`.

4.4.1.6   gfpflags

The `gfpflags` flags specify the type of page frames to be requested for the slabs in this cache. They are determined based on the flags requested of the memory area. For example, if the memory area is intended for DMA use, the `gfpflags` field is set to `GFP_DMA`, and this is passed on upon page frame request.

4.4.1.7   slabp_cache

Slab descriptors can be stored within the cache itself or external to it. If the slab descriptors for the slabs in this cache are stored externally to the cache, the `slabp_cache` field holds a pointer to the cache descriptor of the cache that stores objects of the type slab descriptor. See the "Slab Descriptor" section for more information on slab descriptor storage.

4.4.1.8   ctor

The `ctor` field holds a pointer to the constructor[8] that is associated with the cache, if one exists.

4.4.1.9   dtor

Much like the `ctor` field, the `dtor` field holds a pointer to the destructor that is associated with the cache, if one exists.

Both the constructor and destructor are defined at cache-creation time and passed as parameters to `kmem_cache_create()`.

---

[8]   If you are familiar with object-oriented programming, the concept of constructors and destructors will not be new to you. The `ctor` field of the cache descriptor allows for the programming of a function that will get called every time a new cache descriptor is created. Likewise, the `dtor` field holds a pointer to a function that will be called every time a cache descriptor is destroyed.

4.4.1.10   name

The name field holds the human-readable string of the name that is displayed when /proc/slabinfo is opened. For example, the cache that holds file pointers has a value of filp in this field. This can be better understood by executing a call to cat /proc/slabinfo. The name field of a slab has to hold a unique value. Upon creation, the name requested for a slab is compared to the names of all other slabs in the list. No duplicates are allowed. The slab creation fails if another slab exists with the same name.

4.4.1.11   next

next is the pointer to the next cache descriptor in the singly linked list of cache descriptors.

4.4.2   General Purpose Cache Descriptor

As previously mentioned, the caches that hold the predetermined size objects for general use are always in pairs. One cache is for allocating the objects from DMA memory, and the other is for standard allocations from normal memory. If you recall the memory zones, you realize that the DMA cache is in ZONE_DMA and the standard cache is in ZONE_NORMAL. The struct cache_sizes is a useful way to store together all the information regarding general size caches.

```
---------------------------------------------------------------------------
include/linux/slab.h
69  struct cache_sizes {
70  size_t   cs_size;
71  kmem_cache_t  *cs_cachep;
72  kmem_cache_t  *cs_dmacachep;
73  };
---------------------------------------------------------------------------
```

4.4.2.1   cs_size

The cs_size field holds the size of the memory objects contained in this cache.

4.4.2.2   cs_cachep

The cs_cachep field holds the pointer to the normal memory cache descriptor for objects to be allocated from ZONE_NORMAL.

4.4.2.3   cs_dmacachep

The cs_dmacachep field holds the pointer to the DMA memory cache descriptor for objects to be allocated from ZONE_DMA.

One question comes to mind, "Where are the cache descriptors stored?" The slab allocator has a cache that is reserved just for that purpose. The cache_cache cache holds objects of the type cache descriptors. This slab cache is initialized statically during system bootstrapping to ensure that cache descriptor storage is available.

4.4.3   Slab Descriptor

Each slab in a cache has a descriptor that holds information particular to that slab. We just mentioned that cache descriptors are stored in the specialized cache called cache_cache. Slab descriptors in turn can be stored in two places: They are stored within the slab itself (specifically, the first-page frame) or externally within the first "general purpose" cache with objects large enough to hold the slab descriptor. This is determined upon cache creation based on space left over from object alignment. This space is determined upon cache creation.

Let's look at some of the slab descriptor fields:

```
----------------------------------------------------------------------
mm/slab.c
173  struct slab {
174    struct list_head  list;
175    unsigned long   coloroff;
176    void    *s_mem;  /* including color offset */
177    unsigned int   inuse;   /* num of objs active in slab */
178    kmem_bufctl_t   free;
179  };
----------------------------------------------------------------------
```

4.4.3.1   list

If you recall from the cache descriptor discussion, a slab can be in one of three states: free, partial, or full. The cache descriptor holds all slab descriptors in three lists—one for each state. All slabs in a particular state are kept in a doubly linked list by means of the list field.

4.4.3.2   s_mem

The s_mem field holds the pointer to the first object in the slab.

4.4.3.3 inuse

The value inuse keeps track of the number of objects that are occupied in that slab. For full and partial slabs, this is a positive number; for free slabs, this is 0.

4.4.3.4 free

The free field holds an index value to the array whose entries represent the objects in the slab. In particular, the free field contains the index value of the entry representing the first available object in the slab. The kmem_bufctl_t data type links all the objects within a slab. The data type is simply an unsigned integer and is defined in include/asm/types.h. These data types make up an array that is always stored right after the slab descriptor, regardless of whether the slab descriptor is stored internally or externally to the slab. This becomes clear when we look at the inline function slab_bufctl(), which returns the array:

```
--------------------------------------------------------------------------
mm/slab.c
1614   static inline kmem_bufctl_t *slab_bufctl(struct slab *slabp)
1615   {
1616     return (kmem_bufctl_t *)(slabp+1);
1617   }
--------------------------------------------------------------------------
```

The function slab_bufctl() takes in a pointer to the slab descriptor and returns a pointer to the memory area immediately following the slab descriptor.

When the cache is initialized, the slab->free field is set to 0 (because all objects will be free so it should return the first one), and each entry in the kmem_bufctl_t array is set to the index value of the next member of the array. This means that the 0th element holds the value 1, the 1st element holds the value 2, and so on. The last element in the array holds the value BUFCTL_END, which indicates that this is the last element in the array.

Figure 4.8 shows how the slab descriptor, the bufctl array, and the slab objects are laid out when the slab descriptors are stored internally to the slab. Table 4.5 shows the possible values of certain slab descriptor fields when the slab is in each of the three possible states.

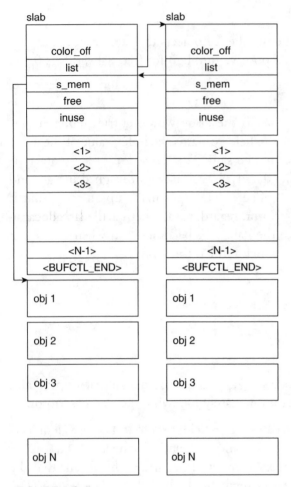

FIGURE 4.8
Slab Descriptor and bufctl

TABLE 4.5
Slab State and Descriptor Field Values

	Free	Partial	Full
slab->inuse	0	X	N
slab->free	0	X	N

N = Number of objects in slab
X = Some variable positive number

4.5   Slab Allocator's Lifecycle

Now, we explore the interaction of caches and the slab allocator throughout the lifecycle of the kernel. The kernel needs to make sure that certain structures are in place to support memory area requests on the part of processes and the creation of specialized caches on the part of dynamically loadable modules.

A few global structures play key roles for the slab allocator. Some of these were in passing previously in the chapter. Let's look at these global variables.

4.5.1   Global Variables of the Slab Allocator

There are a number of global variables that are associated with the slab allocator. These include

- **cache_cache.** The cache descriptor for the cache that is to contain all other cache descriptors. The human-readable name of this cache is kmem_cache. This cache descriptor is the only one that is statically allocated.

- **cache_chain.** The list element that serves as a pointer to the cache descriptor list.

- **cache_chain_sem.** The semaphore that controls access to cache_chain.[9] Every time an element (new cache descriptor) is added to the chain, this semaphore needs to be acquired with a down() and released with an up().

- **malloc_sizes**[]. The array that holds the cache descriptors for the DMA and non-DMA caches that correspond to a general cache.

Before the slab allocator is initialized, these structures are already in place. Let's look at their creation:

```
-------------------------------------------------------------------------
mm/slab.c
486   static kmem_cache_t cache_cache = {
487     .lists    = LIST3_INIT(cache_cache.lists),
488     .batchcount  = 1,
489     .limit    = BOOT_CPUCACHE_ENTRIES,
490     .objsize  = sizeof(kmem_cache_t),
491     .flags    = SLAB_NO_REAP,
492     .spinlock = SPIN_LOCK_UNLOCKED,
```

---

[9]   Semaphores are discussed in detail in Chapter 9, "Building the Linux Kernel."

```
493   .color_off  = L1_CACHE_BYTES,
494   .name       = "kmem_cache",
495   };
496
497   /* Guard access to the cache-chain. */
498   static struct semaphore  cache_chain_sem;
499
500   struct list_head cache_chain;
```

The cache_cache cache descriptor has the SLAB_NO_REAP flag. Even if memory is low, this cache is retained throughout the life of the kernel. Note that the cache_chain semaphore is only defined, not initialized. The initialization occurs during system initialization in the call to kmem_cache_init(). We explore this function in detail here:

----
mm/slab.c
```
462   struct cache_sizes malloc_sizes[] = {
463   #define CACHE(x) { .cs_size = (x) },
464   #include <linux/kmalloc_sizes.h>
465   { 0, }
466   #undef CACHE
467   };
```

This piece of code initializes the malloc_sizes[] array and sets the cs_size field according to the values defined in include/linux/kmalloc_sizes.h. As mentioned, the cache sizes can span from 32 bytes to 131,072 bytes depending on the specific kernel configurations.[10]

With these global variables in place, the kernel proceeds to initialize the slab allocator by calling kmem_cache_init() from init/main.c.[11] This function takes care of initializing the cache chain, its semaphore, the general caches, the kmem_cache cache—in essence, all the global variables that are used by the slab allocator for slab management. At this point, specialized caches can be created. The function used to create caches is kmem_cache_create().

------

[10] There are a few additional configuration options that result in more general caches of sizes larger than 131,072. For more information, see include/linux/kmalloc_sizes.h.

[11] Chapter 9 covers the initialization process linearly from power on. We see how kmem_cache_init() fits into the bootstrapping process.

4.5.2   Creating a Cache

The creation of a cache involves three steps:

1.   Allocation and initialization of the descriptor

2.   Calculation of the slab coloring and object size

3.   Addition of the cache to `cache_chain` list

General caches are set up during system initalization by `kmem_cache_init()` (`mm/slab.c`). Specialized caches are created by way of a call to `kmem_cache_create()`.

We now look at each of these functions.

4.5.2.1   kmem_cache_init()

This is where the `cache_chain` and general caches are created. This function is called during the initialization process. Notice that the function has `__init` preceding the function name. As discussed in Chapter 2, "Exploration Toolkit," this indicates that the function is loaded into memory that gets wiped after the bootstrap and initialization process is over.

```
---------------------------------------------------------------------
mm/slab.c
659  void __init kmem_cache_init(void)
660  {
661    size_t left_over;
662    struct cache_sizes *sizes;
663    struct cache_names *names;
...
669    if (num_physpages > (32 << 20) >> PAGE_SHIFT)
670      slab_break_gfp_order = BREAK_GFP_ORDER_HI;
671
672
---------------------------------------------------------------------
```

Lines 661–663

The variable sizes and names are the head arrays for the `kmalloc` allocated arrays (the general caches with geometrically distributes sizes). At this point, these arrays are located in the `__init` data area. Be aware that `kmalloc()` does not exist at this point. `kmalloc()` uses the `malloc_sizes` array and that is precisely what we are setting up now. At this point, all we have is the statically allocated `cache_cache` descriptor.

Lines 669–670

This code block determines how many pages a slab can use. The number of pages a slab can use is entirely determined by how much memory is available. In both x86 and PPC, the variable `PAGE_SHIFT` (`include/asm/page.h`) evaluates to 12. So, we are verifying if `num_physpages` holds a value greater than 8k. This would be the case if we have a machine with more than 32MB of memory. If this is the case, we fit `BREAK_GFP_ORDER_HI` pages per slab. Otherwise, one page is allocated per slab.

```
------------------------------------------------------------------------
mm/slab.c
690    init_MUTEX(&cache_chain_sem);
691    INIT_LIST_HEAD(&cache_chain);
692    list_add(&cache_cache.next, &cache_chain);
693    cache_cache.array[smp_processor_id()] = &initarray_cache.cache;
694
695    cache_estimate(0, cache_cache.objsize, 0,
696      &left_over, &cache_cache.num);
697    if (!cache_cache.num)
698      BUG();
699
...
------------------------------------------------------------------------
```

Line 690

This line initializes the `cache_chain` semaphore `cache_chain_sem`.

Line 691

Initialize the `cache_chain` list where all the cache descriptors are stored.

Line 692

Add the `cache_cache` descriptor to the `cache_chain` list.

Line 693

Create the per CPU caches. The details of this are beyond the scope of this book.

Lines 695–698

This block is a sanity check verifying that at least one cache descriptor can be allocated in `cache_cache`. Also, it sets the `cache_cache` descriptor's num field and calculates how much space will be left over. This is used for slab coloring.

Slab coloring is a method by which the kernel reduces cache alignment–related performance hits.

```
------------------------------------------------------------------------
mm/slab.c
705    sizes = malloc_sizes;
706    names = cache_names;
707
708    while (sizes->cs_size) {
...
714    sizes->cs_cachep = kmem_cache_create(
715     names->name, sizes->cs_size,
716     0, SLAB_HWCACHE_ALIGN, NULL, NULL);
717    if (!sizes->cs_cachep)
718      BUG();
719
...
725
726    sizes->cs_dmacachep = kmem_cache_create(
727     names->name_dma, sizes->cs_size,
728     0, SLAB_CACHE_DMA|SLAB_HWCACHE_ALIGN, NULL, NULL);
729    if (!sizes->cs_dmacachep)
730      BUG();
731
732    sizes++;
733    names++;
734    }
------------------------------------------------------------------------
```

Line 708

This line verifies if we have reached the end of the sizes array. The sizes array's last element is always set to 0. Hence, this case is true until we hit the last cell of the array.

Lines 714–718

Create the next `kmalloc` cache for normal allocation and verify that it is not empty. See the section, "`kmem_cache_create()`."

Lines 726–730

This block creates the caches for DMA allocation.

Lines 732–733

Go to the next element in the sizes and names arrays.

The remainder of the `kmem_cache_init()` function handles the replacement of the temporary bootstrapping data for `kmalloc` allocated data. We leave out the explanation of this because it is not directly pertinent to the actual initialization of the cache descriptors.

4.5.2.2   kmem_cache_create()

Times arise when the memory regions provided by the general caches are not sufficient. This function is called when a specialized cache needs to be created. The steps required to create a specialized cache are not unlike those required to create a general cache: create, allocate, and initialize the cache descriptor, align objects, align slab descriptors, and add the cache to the cache chain. This function does not have `__init` in front of the function name because persistent memory is available when it is called:

```
-----------------------------------------------------------------------
mm/slab.c
1027  kmem_cache_t *
1028  kmem_cache_create (const char *name, size_t size, size_t offset,
1029   unsigned long flags, void (*ctor)(void*, kmem_cache_t *, unsigned long),
1030   void (*dtor)(void*, kmem_cache_t *, unsigned long))
1031  {
1032   const char *func_nm = KERN_ERR "kmem_create: ";
1033   size_t left_over, align, slab_size;
1034   kmem_cache_t *cachep = NULL;
...
-----------------------------------------------------------------------
```

Let's look at the function parameters of `kmem_cache_create`.

name

This is the name used to identify the cache. This gets stored in the `name` field of the cache descriptor and displayed in `/proc/slabinfo`.

size

This parameter specifies the size (in bytes) of the objects that are contained in this cache. This value is stored in the `objsize` field of the cache descriptor.

offset

This value determines where the objects are placed within a page.

flags

The `flags` parameter is related to the slab. Refer to Table 4.4 for a description of the cache descriptor flags field and possible values.

ctor and dtor

`ctor` and `dtor` are respectively the constructor and destructor that are called upon creation or destruction of objects in this memory region.

This function performs sizable debugging and sanity checks that we do not cover here. See the code for more details:

```
------------------------------------------------------------------------
mm/slab.c
1079   /* Get cache's description obj. */
1080   cachep = (kmem_cache_t *) kmem_cache_alloc(&cache_cache, SLAB_KERNEL);
1081   if (!cachep)
1082    goto opps;
1083   memset(cachep, 0, sizeof(kmem_cache_t));
1084

...
1144   do {
1145    unsigned int break_flag = 0;
1146   cal_wastage:
1147    cache_estimate(cachep->gfporder, size, flags,
1148        &left_over, &cachep->num);
...
1174   } while (1);
1175
1176   if (!cachep->num) {
1177    printk("kmem_cache_create: couldn't create cache %s.\n", name);
1178    kmem_cache_free(&cache_cache, cachep);
1179    cachep = NULL;
1180    goto opps;
1181   }

------------------------------------------------------------------------
```

Lines 1079–1084

This is where the cache descriptor is allocated. Following this is the portion of the code that is involved with the alignment of objects in the slab. We leave this portion out of this discussion.

Lines 1144–1174

This is where the number of objects in cache is determined. The bulk of the work is done by `cache_estimate()`. Recall that the value is to be stored in the `num` field of the cache descriptor.

```
--------------------------------------------------------------------------
mm/slab.c
...
1201   cachep->flags = flags;
1202   cachep->gfpflags = 0;
1203   if (flags & SLAB_CACHE_DMA)
1204    cachep->gfpflags |= GFP_DMA;
1205   spin_lock_init(&cachep->spinlock);
1206   cachep->objsize = size;
1207   /* NUMA */
1208   INIT_LIST_HEAD(&cachep->lists.slabs_full);
1209   INIT_LIST_HEAD(&cachep->lists.slabs_partial);
1210   INIT_LIST_HEAD(&cachep->lists.slabs_free);
1211
1212   if (flags & CFLGS_OFF_SLAB)
1213    cachep->slabp_cache = kmem_find_general_cachep(slab_size,0);
1214   cachep->ctor = ctor;
1215   cachep->dtor = dtor;
1216   cachep->name = name;
1217
...
1242
1243   cachep->lists.next_reap = jiffies + REAPTIMEOUT_LIST3 +
1244     ((unsigned long)cachep)%REAPTIMEOUT_LIST3;
1245
1246   /* Need the semaphore to access the chain. */
1247   down(&cache_chain_sem);
1248   {
1249    struct list_head *p;
1250    mm_segment_t old_fs;
1251
1252    old_fs = get_fs();
1253    set_fs(KERNEL_DS);
1254    list_for_each(p, &cache_chain) {
1255     kmem_cache_t *pc = list_entry(p, kmem_cache_t, next);
1256     char tmp;
...
1265     if (!strcmp(pc->name,name)) {
1266       printk("kmem_cache_create: duplicate cache %s\n",name);
1267       up(&cache_chain_sem);
1268       BUG();
1269     }
1270    }
1271    set_fs(old_fs);
```

```
1272   }
1273
1274   /* cache setup completed, link it into the list */
1275   list_add(&cachep->next, &cache_chain);
1276   up(&cache_chain_sem);
1277  opps:
1278   return cachep;
1279  }
```

Just prior to this, the slab is aligned to the hardware cache and colored. The fields color and color_off of the slab descriptor are filled out.

Lines 1200–1217

This code block initializes the cache descriptor fields much like we saw in kmem_cache_init().

Lines 1243–1244

The time for the next cache reap is set.

Lines 1247–1276

The cache descriptor is initialized and all the information regarding the cache has been calculated and stored. Now, we can add the new cache descriptor to the cache_chain list.

4.5.3   Slab Creation and cache_grow()

When a cache is created, it starts empty of slabs. In fact, slabs are not allocated until a request for an object demonstrates a need for a new slab. This happens when the cache descriptor's lists.slabs_partial and lists.slabs_free fields are empty. At this point, we won't relate how the request for memory translates into the request for an object within a particular cache. For now, we take for granted that this translation has occurred and concentrate on the technical implementation within the slab allocator.

A slab is created within a cache by cache_grow(). When we create a slab, we not only allocate and initialize its descriptor; we also allocate the actual memory. To this end, we need to interface with the buddy system to request the pages. This is done by kmem_getpages() (mm/slab.c).

4.5.3.1   cache_grow()

The `cache_grow()` function grows the number of slabs within a cache by 1. It is called only when no free objects are available in the cache. This occurs when `lists.slabs_partial` and `lists.slabs_free` are empty:

```
mm/slab.c
1546   static int cache_grow (kmem_cache_t * cachep, int flags)
1547   {
...
```

The parameters passed to the function are

- **cachep**. This is the cache descriptor of the cache to be grown.

- **flags**. These flags will be involved in the creation of the slab.

```
mm/slab.c
1572   check_irq_off();
1573   spin_lock(&cachep->spinlock);
...
1581
1582     spin_unlock(&cachep->spinlock);
1583
1584     if (local_flags & __GFP_WAIT)
1585       local_irq_enable();
```

Lines 1572–1573

Prepare for manipulating the cache descriptor's fields by disabling interrupts and locking the descriptor.

Lines 1582–1585

Unlock the cache descriptor and reenable the interrupts.

```
mm/slab.c
...
1597   if (!(objp = kmem_getpages(cachep, flags)))
1598     goto failed;
1599
1600   /* Get slab management. */
1601   if (!(slabp = alloc_slabmgmt(cachep, objp, offset, local_flags)))
1602     goto opps1;
...
1605   i = 1 << cachep->gfporder;
```

```
1606    page = virt_to_page(objp);
1607    do {
1608     SET_PAGE_CACHE(page, cachep);
1609     SET_PAGE_SLAB(page, slabp);
1610     SetPageSlab(page);
1611     inc_page_state(nr_slab);
1612     page++;
1613    } while (--i) ;
1614
1615    cache_init_objs(cachep, slabp, ctor_flags);
```

Lines 1597–1598

Interface with the buddy system to acquire page(s) for the slab.

Lines 1601–1602

Place the slab descriptor where it needs to go. Recall that slab descriptors can be stored within the slab itself or within the first general purpose cache.

Lines 1605–1613

The pages need to be associated with the cache and slab descriptors.

Line 1615

Initialize all the objects in the slab.

```
mm/slab.c
1616    if (local_flags & __GFP_WAIT)
1617     local_irq_disable();
1618    check_irq_off();
1619    spin_lock(&cachep->spinlock);
1620
1621    /* Make slab active. */
1622    list_add_tail(&slabp->list, &(list3_data(cachep)->slabs_free));
1623    STATS_INC_GROWN(cachep);
1624    list3_data(cachep)->free_objects += cachep->num;
1625    spin_unlock(&cachep->spinlock);
1626    return 1;
1627  opps1:
1628    kmem_freepages(cachep, objp);
1629  failed:
1630    if (local_flags & __GFP_WAIT)
1631     local_irq_disable();
1632    return 0;
1633  }
```

Lines 1616–1619

Because we are about to access and change descriptor fields, we need to disable interrupts and lock the data.

Lines 1622–1624

Add the new slab descriptor to the `lists.slabs_free` field of the cache descriptor. Update the statistics that keep track of these sizes.

Lines 1625–1626

Unlock the spinlock and return because all succeeded.

Lines 1627–1628

This gets called if something goes wrong with the page request. Basically, we are freeing the pages.

Lines 1629–1632

Disable the interrupt disable, which now lets interrupts come through.

4.5.4   Slab Destruction: Returning Memory and kmem_cache_destroy()

Both caches and slabs can be destroyed. Caches can be shrunk or destroyed to return memory to the free memory pool. The kernel calls these functions when memory is low. In either case, slabs are being destroyed and the pages corresponding to them are being returned for the buddy system to recycle. `kmem_cache_destroy()` gets rid of a cache. We explore this function in depth. Caches can be reaped and shrunk by `kmem_cache_reap()` (`mm/slab.c`) and `kmem_cache_shrink()`, respectively (`mm/slab.c`). The function to interface with the buddy system is `kmem_freepages()` (`mm/slab.c`).

4.5.4.1   kmem_cache_destroy()

There are a few instances when a cache would need to be removed. Dynamically loadable modules (assuming no persistent memory across loading and unloading) that create caches must destroy them upon unloading to free up the memory and to ensure that the cache won't be duplicated the next time the module is loaded. Thus, the specialized caches are generally destroyed in this manner.

The steps to destroy a cache are the reverse of the steps to create one. Alignment issues are not a concern upon destruction of a cache, only the deletion of descriptors and freeing of memory. The steps to destroy a cache can be summarized as

1. Remove the cache from the cache chain.

2. Delete the slab descriptors.

3. Delete the cache descriptor.

```
-----------------------------------------------------------------------------
mm/slab.c
1421  int kmem_cache_destroy (kmem_cache_t * cachep)
1422  {
1423    int i;
1424
1425    if (!cachep || in_interrupt())
1426      BUG();
1427
1428    /* Find the cache in the chain of caches. */
1429    down(&cache_chain_sem);
1430    /*
1431    * the chain is never empty, cache_cache is never destroyed
1432    */
1433    list_del(&cachep->next);
1434    up(&cache_chain_sem);
1435
1436    if (__cache_shrink(cachep)) {
1437      slab_error(cachep, "Can't free all objects");
1438      down(&cache_chain_sem);
1439      list_add(&cachep->next,&cache_chain);
1440      up(&cache_chain_sem);
1441      return 1;
1442    }
1443
...
1450    kmem_cache_free(&cache_cache, cachep);
1451
1452    return 0;
1453  }
-----------------------------------------------------------------------------
```

The function parameter `cache` is a pointer to the cache descriptor of the cache that is to be destroyed.

Lines 1425–1426

This sanity check consists of ensuring that an interrupt is not in play and that the cache descriptor is not NULL.

Lines 1429–1434

Acquire the `cache_chain` semaphore, delete the cache from the cache chain, and release the cache chain semaphore.

Lines 1436–1442

This is where the bulk of the work related to freeing the unused slabs takes place. If the `__cache_shrink()` function returns true, that indicates that there are still slabs in the cache and, therefore, it cannot be destroyed. Thus, we reverse the previous step and reenter the cache descriptor into the `cache_chain`, again by first reacquiring the `cache_chain` semaphore, and releasing it once we finish.

Line 1450

We finish by releasing the cache descriptor.

4.6 Memory Request Path

Until now, we have approached the description of the slab allocator as though it were independent of any actual memory request. With the exception of the cache initialization functions, we have not tied together how all these functions come to be called. Now, we look at the flow of control associated with memory requests. When the kernel must obtain memory in byte-sized groupings, it uses the `kmalloc()` function, which eventually makes the call to `kmem_getpages` as follows:

```
kmalloc()->__cache_alloc()->kmem_cache_grow()->kmem_getpages()
```

4.6.1   kmalloc()

The `kmalloc()` function allocates memory objects in the kernel:

```
-------------------------------------------------------------------
mm/slab.c
2098  void * __kmalloc (size_t size, int flags)
2099  {
2100   struct cache_sizes *csizep = malloc_sizes;
2101
2102   for (; csizep->cs_size; csizep++) {
2103    if (size > csizep->cs_size)
2104      continue;
...
2112    return __cache_alloc(flags & GFP_DMA ?
2113      csizep->cs_dmacachep : csizep->cs_cachep, flags);
2114   }
2115   return NULL;
2116  }
-------------------------------------------------------------------
```

4.6.1.1   size

This is the number of bytes requested.

4.6.1.2   flags

Indicates the type of memory requested. These flags are passed on to the buddy system without affecting the behavior of kmalloc(). Table 4.6 shows the flags, and they are covered in detail in the "Buddy System" section.

Lines 2102–2104

Find the first cache with objects greater than the size requested.

Lines 2112–2113

Allocate an object from the memory zone specified by the flags parameter.

4.6.2   kmem_cache_alloc()

This is a wrapper function around __cache_alloc(). It does not perform any additional functionality because its parameters are passed as is:

```
------------------------------------------------------------------------
mm/slab.c
2070  void * kmem_cache_alloc (kmem_cache_t *cachep, int flags)
2071  {
2072   return __cache_alloc(cachep, flags);
2073  }
------------------------------------------------------------------------
```

4.6.2.1   cachep

The cachep parameter is the cache descriptor of the cache from which we want to allocate objects.

4.6.2.2   flags

The type of memory requested. This is passed directly as indicated to kmalloc().

To free byte-sized memory allocated with kmalloc(), the kernel provides the kfree() interface, which takes as a parameter the pointer to the memory returned by kmalloc(). Figure 4.9 illustrates the flow from kfree to kmem_freepages.

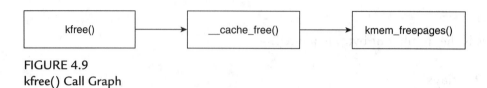

FIGURE 4.9
kfree( ) Call Graph

4.7 Linux Process Memory Structures

Until now, we covered how the kernel manages its own memory. We now turn our attention to user space programs and how the kernel manages program memory. The wonder of virtual memory allows a user space process to effectively operate as though it has access to all memory. In reality, the kernel manages what gets loaded, how it gets loaded, and when that happens. All that we have discussed until now in this chapter relates to how the kernel manages memory and is completely transparent to a user space program.

Upon creation, a user space process is assigned a virtual address space. As previously mentioned, a process' virtual address space is a range of unsegmented linear addresses that the process can use. The size of the range is defined by the size of the register in the system's architecture. Most systems have a 32-bit address space. A G5, for example, has processes with a 64-bit address space.

Upon creation, the address range the process is presented with can grow or shrink through the addition or removal of linear **address intervals**, respectively. The address interval (a range of addresses) represents yet another unit of memory called a **memory region** or a **memory area**. It is useful to split the process address range into areas of different types. These different types have different protection schemes or characteristics. The process-memory protection schemes are associated with process context. For example, certain parts of a program's code are marked read-only (text) while others are writable (variables) or executable (instructions). Also, a particular process might access only certain memory areas that belong to it.

Within the kernel, a process address space, as well as all the information related to it, is kept in an `mm_struct` descriptor. You might recall from Chapter 3, "Processes: The Principal Model of Execution," that this structure is referenced in the `task_struct` for the process. A memory area is represented by the `vm_area_struct` descriptor. Each memory area descriptor describes the contiguous address interval it represents. Throughout this section, we refer to the descriptor for an address interval as a memory area descriptor or as `vma_area_struct`. We now look at `mm_struct` and `vm_area_struct`. Figure 4.10 illustrates the relationship between these data structures.

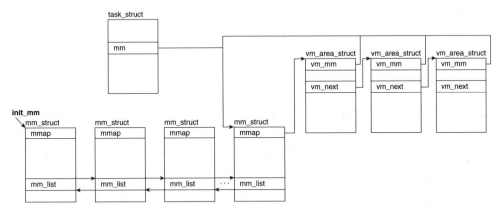

FIGURE 4.10
Process-Related Memory Structures

4.7.1 mm_struct

Every task has an `mm_struct` (`include/linux/sched.h`) structure that the kernel uses to represent its memory address range. All `mm_struct` descriptors are stored in a doubly linked list. The head of the list is the `mm_struct` that corresponds to process 0, which is the idle process. This descriptor is accessed by way of the global variable `init_mm`:

```
--------------------------------------------------------------------------
include/linux/sched.h
185   struct mm_struct {
186     struct vm_area_struct * mmap;
187     struct rb_root mm_rb;
188     struct vm_area_struct * mmap_cache;
189     unsigned long free_area_cache;
190     pgd_t * pgd;
191     atomic_t mm_users;
192     atomic_t mm_count;
193     int map_count;
194     struct rw_semaphore mmap_sem;
195     spinlock_t page_table_lock
196
197     struct list_head mmlist;
...
202     unsigned long start_code, end_code, start_data, end_data;
```

```
203    unsigned long start_brk, brk, start_stack;
204    unsigned long arg_start, arg_end, env_start, env_end;
205    unsigned long rss, total_vm, locked_vm;
206    unsigned long def_flags;
207    cpumask_t cpu_vm_mask;
208    unsigned long swap_address;
...
228  };
```

4.7.1.1   mmap

The memory area descriptors (which are defined in the next section) that have been assigned to a process are linked in a list. This list is accessed by means of the mmap field in the mm_struct. The list is traversed by way of the vm_next field of each vma_area_struct.

4.7.1.2   mm_rb

The simply linked list provides an easy way of traversing all the memory area descriptors that correspond to a particular process. However, if the kernel searches for a particular memory area descriptor, a simply linked list does not yield good search times. The memory area structures that correspond to a process address range are also stored in a red-black tree that is accessed through the mm_rb field. This yields faster search times when the kernel needs to access a particular memory area descriptor.

4.7.1.3   mmap_cache

mmap_cache is a pointer to the last memory area referenced by the process. The **principle of locality** states that when a memory address is referenced, memory areas that are close by tend to get referenced soon after. Hence, it is likely that the address being currently checked belongs to the same memory area as the last address checked. The hit rate of verifying whether the current address is in the last accessed memory area is approximately 35 percent.

4.7.1.4   pgd

The pgd field is a pointer to the page global directory that holds the entry for this memory area. In the mm_struct for the idle process (process 0), this field points to the `swapper_pg_dir`. See Section 4.9 for more information on what this field points to.

4.7.1.5   mm_users

The `mm_users` field holds the number of processes that access this memory area. Lightweight processes or threads share the same address intervals and memory areas. Thus, the `mm_struct` for threads generally have an `mm_users` field with a value greater than 1. This field is manipulated by way of the atomic functions: `atomic_set()`, `atomic_dec_and_lock()`, `atomic_read()`, and `atomic_inc()`.

4.7.1.6   mm_count

`mm_count` is the usage count for the `mm_struct`. When determining if the structure can be deallocated, a check is made against this field. If it holds the value of 0, no processes are using it; therefore, it can be deallocated.

4.7.1.7   map_count

The `map_count` field holds the number of memory areas, or `vma_area_struct` descriptors, in the process address space. Every time a new memory area is added to the process address space, this field is incremented alongside with the `vma_area_struct`'s insertion into the `mmap` list and `mm_rb` tree.

4.7.1.8   mm_list

The `mm_list` field of type `list_head` holds the address of adjacent `mm_structs` in the memory descriptor list. As previously mentioned, the head of the list is pointed to by the global variable `init_mm`, which is the memory descriptor for process 0. When this list is manipulated, `mmlist_lock` protects it from concurrent accesses.

The next 11 fields we describe deal with the various types of memory areas a process needs allocated to it. Rather than digress into an explanation that distracts from the description of the process memory–related structures, we now give a cursory description.

4.7.1.9   start_code and end_code

The `start_code` and `end_code` fields hold the starting and ending addresses for the code section of the processes' memory region (that is, the executable's text segment).

4.7.1.10   start_data and end_data

The `start_data` and `end_data` fields contain the starting and ending addresses for the initialized data (that found in the .data portion of the executable file).

4.7.1.11   start_brk and brk

The `start_brk` and `brk` fields hold the starting and ending addresses of the process heap.

4.7.1.12   start_stack

`start_stack` is the starting address of the process stack.

4.7.1.13   arg_start and arg_end

The `arg_start` and `arg_end` fields hold the starting and ending addresses of the arguments passed to the process.

4.7.1.14   env_start and env_end

The `env_start` and `env_end` fields hold the starting and ending addresses of the environment section.

This concludes the `mm_struct` fields that we focus on in this chapter. We now look at some of the fields for the memory area descriptor, `vm_area_struct`.

4.7.2   vm_area_struct

The `vm_area_struct` structure defines a virtual memory region. A process has various memory regions, but every memory region has exactly one `vm_area_struct` to represent it:

```
---------------------------------------------------------------------
include/linux/mm.h
51  struct vm_area_struct {
52    struct mm_struct * vm_mm;
```

```
53    unsigned long vm_start;
54    unsigned long vm_end;
...
57    struct vm_area_struct *vm_next;
...
60    unsigned long vm_flags;
61
62    struct rb_node vm_rb;
...
72    struct vm_operations_struct * vm_ops;
...
};
```

4.7.2.1   vm_mm

All memory regions belong to an address space that is associated with a process and represented by an `mm_struct`. The structure `vm_mm` points to a structure of type `mm_struct` that describes the address space to which this memory area belongs to.

4.7.2.2   vm_start and vm_end

A memory region is associated with an address interval. In the `vm_area_struct`, this interval is defined by keeping track of the starting and ending addresses. For performance reasons, the beginning address of the memory region must be a multiple of the page frame size. The kernel ensures that page frames are filled with data from a particular memory region by also demanding that the size of memory region be in multiples of the page frame size.

4.7.2.3   vm_next

The field `vm_next` points to the next `vm_area_struct` in the linked list that comprises all the regions within a process address space. The head of this list is referenced by way of the `mmap` field in the `mm_struct` for the address space.

4.7.2.4   vm_flags

Within this interval, a memory region also has associated characteristics that describe it. These are stored in the `vm_flags` field and apply to the pages within the memory region. Table 4.6 describes the possible flags.

TABLE 4.6
vm_area_struct->vm_flags Values

Flag	Description
VM_READ	Pages in this region can be read.
VM_WRITE	Pages in this region can be written.
VM_EXEC	Pages in this region can be executed.
VM_SHARED	Pages in this region are shared with another process.
VM_GROWSDOWN	The linear addresses are added onto the low side.
VM_GROWSUP	The linear addresses are added onto the high side.
VM_DENYWRITE	These pages cannot be written.
VM_EXECUTABLE	Pages in this region consist of executable code.
VM_LOCKED	Pages are locked.
VM_DONTCOPY	These pages cannot be cloned.
VM_DNTEXPAND	Do not expand this virtual memory area.

4.7.2.5   vm_rb

vm_rb holds the red-black tree node that corresponds to this memory area.

4.7.2.6   vm_ops

vm_ops consists of a structure of function pointers that handle the particular vm_area_struct. These functions include opening the memory area, closing, and unmapping it. Also, it holds a function pointer to the function called when a no-page exception occurs.

4.8   Process Image Layout and Linear Address Space

When a user space program is loaded into memory, it has its linear address space partitioned into various **memory areas** or segments. These segments are determined by functional differences in relation to the execution of the process. The functionally separated segments are mapped within the process address space. Six main segments are related to process execution:

- **Text**. This segment, also known as the code segment, holds the executable instructions of a program. As such, it has `execute` and `read` attributes. In the case that multiple processes can be loaded from a single program, it would be wasteful to load the same instructions twice. Linux allows for multiple processes to share this text segment in memory. The `start_code` and `end_code` fields of the `mm_struct` hold the addresses for the beginning and end of the text segment.

- **Data**. This section holds all initialized data. Initialized data includes statically allocated and global data that are initialized. The following code snippet shows an example of initialized data:

```
------------------------------------------------------------------
example1.c
int gvar = 10;

int main(){
...
}
------------------------------------------------------------------
```

- **gvar**. A global variable that is initialized and stored in the data segment. This section has read/write attributes but cannot be shared among processes running the same program. The `start_data` and `end_data` fields of the `mm_struct` hold the addresses for the beginning and end of the data segment.

- **BSS**. This section holds uninitialized data. This data consists of global variables that the system initializes with 0s upon program execution. Another name for this section is the zero-initialized data section. The following code snippet shows an example of non-initialized data:

```
------------------------------------------------------------------
example2.c
int gvar1[10];
long gvar2;

int main() {
...
}
------------------------------------------------------------------
```

Objects in this segment have only `name` and `size` attributes.

- **Heap**. This is used to grow the linear address space of a process. When a program uses `malloc()` to obtain dynamic memory, this memory is placed in the heap. The `start_brk` and `brk` fields of the `mm_struct` hold the addresses for the beginning and end of the heap. When `malloc()` is called to obtain dynamic memory, a call to the system call `sys_brk()` moves the `brk` pointer to its new location, thus growing the heap.

- **Stack**. This contains all the local variables that get allocated. When a function is called, the local variables for that function are pushed onto the stack. As soon as a function ends, the variables associated with the function are popped from the stack. Other information, including return addresses and parameters, is also stored in the stack. The field `start_stack` of the `mm_struct` marks the starting address of the process stack.

Although six main areas are related to process execution, they only map to three memory areas in the address space. These memory areas are called `text`, `data`, and `stack`. The `data` segment includes the executable's initialized `data` segment, the `bss`, and the heap. The `text` segment includes the executable's `text` segment. Figure 4.11 shows what the linear address space looks like and how the `mm_struct` keeps track of these segments.

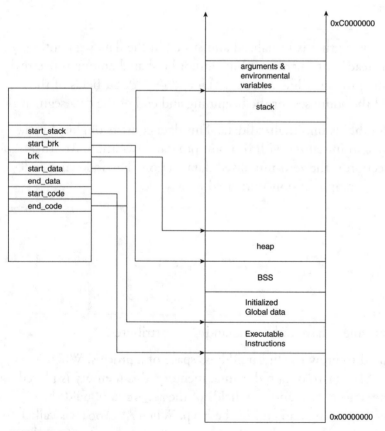

FIGURE 4.11
Process Address Space

The various memory areas are mapped in the /proc filesystem. The memory map of a process may be accessed through the output of /proc/<pid>/maps. We now look at an example program and see the list of memory areas in the process' address space. The code in example3.c shows the program being mapped.

```
----------------------------------------------------------------------
example3.c
#include <stdio.h>
int main(){
  while(1);
  return(0);
}
----------------------------------------------------------------------
```

The output of /proc/<pid>/maps for our example yields what's shown in Figure 4.12.

08048000-08049000	r-xp	00000000	03:05	1324039	/home/1kp/example3
08049000-0804a000	rw-p	00000000	03:05	1324039	/home/1kp/example3
40000000-40015000	r-xp	00000000	03:05	767058	/lib/ld-2.3.2.so
40015000-40016000	rw-p	00014000	03:05	767058	/lib/ld-2.3.2.so
40016000-40017000	rw-p	00000000	00:00	0	
42000000-4212e000	r-xp	00000000	03:05	1011853	/lib/tls/libc-2.3.2.so
4212e000-42131000	rw-p	0012e000	03:05	1011853	/lib/tls/libc-2.3.2.so
42131000-42133000	rw-p	00000000	00:00	0	
bfffe000-c0000000	rwxp	fffff000	00:00	0	

FIGURE 4.12
cat /proc/<pid>/maps

The left-most column shows the range of the memory segment. That is, the starting and ending addresses for a particular segment. The next column shows the access permissions for that segment. These flags are similar to the access permissions on files: r stands for readable, w stands for writeable, and x stands for executable. The last flag can be either a p, which indicates a private segment, or s, which indicates a shared segment. (A private segment is not necessarily unshareable.) The p indicates only that it is currently not being shared. The next column holds the offset for the segment. The fourth column from the left holds two numbers separated by a colon. These represent the major and minor numbers of the filesystem the file associated with that segment is found in. (Some segments do not have a file associated with them and, hence, just fill in this value with 00:00.) The fifth column holds the inode of the file and the sixth and right-most column holds the filename. For segments with no filename, this column is empty and the inode column holds a 0.

In our example, the first row holds a description of the text segment of our sample program. This can be seen on account of the permission flags set to executable. The next row describes our sample program's data segment. Notice that its permissions indicate that it is writeable.

Our program is dynamically linked, which means that functions it uses belonging to a library are loaded at runtime. These functions need to be mapped to the process' address space so that it can access them. The next six rows deal with dynamically linked libraries. The next three rows describe the `ld` library's `text`, `data`, and `bss`. These three rows are followed by descriptions of `libc`'s `test`, `data`, and `bss` segments in that order.

The final row, whose permissions indicated that it is readable, writeable, and executable, represents the process stack and extends up to 0xC0000000. 0xC000000 is the highest memory address accessible for user space processes.

4.9 Page Tables

Program memory is comfortably managed with virtual addresses. The problem with this is that when an instruction is issued to the processor, it cannot do anything with a virtual address. The processor operates on physical addresses. The association between the virtual address and the corresponding physical address is kept by the kernel (with help from the hardware) in page tables.

Page tables keep track of memory in page frame units. They are stored in RAM throughout the kernel's lifespan. Linux has what is called a three-level paging scheme. Three-level paging is sufficient to ensure that 64-bit architectures have enough space to maintain mappings of all their virtual-to-physical associations. As the name implies, three-level paging has three types of paging tables: The top level directory is called the Page Global Directory (PGD) and is represented by a `pgd_t` datatype; the second page is called the Page Middle Directory (PMD) and is represented by a `pmd_t` datatype; the final page is called a Page Table (PTE) and is represented by a `pte_t` datatype. Figure 4.13 illustrates the page tables.

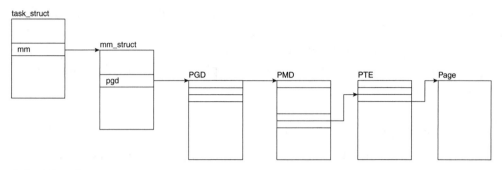

FIGURE 4.13
Page Tables in Linux

The PGD holds entries that refer to PMDs. The PMD holds entries that refer to PTEs, and the PTE holds entries that refer to specific pages. Each process has its own set of page tables. The `mm_struct->pgd` field points to the PGD for the process. The 32- or 64-bit virtual addresses are split up into variously sized (depending on the architecture) offset fields. Each field corresponds to an offset within the PGD, PMD, PTE, and the page itself.

4.10   Page Fault

Throughout the lifespan of a process, it is possible that it might attempt to access an address that belongs to its address space but is not loaded in RAM. It might alternatively access a page that is in RAM, but attempt action upon it that would violate the page's permission settings (for example, writing in a read-only area). When this happens, the system generates a **page fault**. The page fault is an exception handler that manages errors in a program's page access. Pages are fetched from storage when the hardware raises this page fault exception that the kernel traps. The kernel then allocates the missing page.

Each architecture has an architecture-dependent function that handles page faults. Both x86 and PPC call the function `do_page_fault()`. The x86 page fault handler `do_page_fault(*regs, error_code)` is located in `/arch/i386/mm/fault.c`. The PowerPC page fault handler `do_page_fault(*regs, address, error_code)` is located in `/arch/ppc/mm/fault.c`. The similarities are close enough that a discussion of `do_page_fault()` for the x86 covers the functionality of the PowerPC version.

The major difference in how the two architectures handle the page fault is in *how* the fault information is gathered and stored *before* do_page_fault() is called. We first explain the specifics of the x86 page fault handling and proceed to explain the do_page_fault() function. We follow this explanation by highlighting the differences seen in PowerPC.

4.10.1 x86 Page Fault Exception

The x86 page fault handler do_page_fault() is called as the result of a hardware interrupt 14. This interrupt occurs when the processor identifies the following conditions to be true:

1. Paging is enabled, and the present bit is clear in the page-directory or page-table entry needed for this address.

2. Paging is enabled, and the current privilege level is less than that needed to access the requested page.

Upon raising this interrupt, the processor saves two valuable pieces of information:

1. The nature of the error in the lower 4 bits of a word pushed on the stack. (Bit 3 is not used by do_page_fault().) See Table 4.7 to see what each bit value corresponds to.

2. The 32-bit linear address that caused the exception in cr2.

The regs parameter of do_page_fault() is a struct that contains the system registers, and the error_code parameter uses a 3-bit field to describe the source of the fault.

TABLE 4.7
Page Fault error_code

	Bit 2	Bit 1	Bit 0
Value = 0	Kernel	Read	Page not present
Value = 1	User	Write	Protection fault

4.10.2 Page Fault Handler

For both architectures, the do_page_fault() function uses the just-given information and takes one of several actions. These code segments follow a fairly complicated series of checks to end up with one of the following:

- The offending address being found by handle_mm_fault()

- The famous oops dump (no_context:) bad_page_fault() for PowerPC

- A segmentation fault (bad_area:) bad_page_fault() for PowerPC

- An error returned to the caller (fixup)

```
-----------------------------------------------------------------------------
arch/i386/mm/fault.c
212  asmlinkage void do_page_fault(struct pt_regs *regs, unsigned long
error_code)
213  {
214    struct task_struct *tsk;
215    struct mm_struct *mm;
216    struct vm_area_struct * vma;
217    unsigned long address;
218    unsigned long page;
219    int write;
220    siginfo_t info;
221
222    /* get the address */
223    __asm__("movl %%cr2,%0":"=r" (address));
...
232    tsk = current;
233
234    info.si_code = SEGV_MAPERR;
-----------------------------------------------------------------------------
```

Line 223

The address at which the page fault occurred is stored in the cr2 control register. The linear address is read and the local variable address is set to hold the value.

Line 232

The task_struct pointer tsk is set to point at the task_struct current.

Now, we are ready to find out more about where the address that generated the page fault comes from. Figure 4.14 illustrates the flow of the following lines of code:

```
-----------------------------------------------------------------------------
arch/i386/mm/fault.c
246  if (unlikely(address >= TASK_SIZE)) {
247    if (!(error_code & 5))
```

```
248   goto vmalloc_fault;
...
253   goto bad_area_nosemaphore;
254   }
...
257   mm = tsk->mm
...
```

Lines 246–248

This code checks if the address at which the page fault occurred was in kernel module space (that is, in a noncontiguous memory area). Noncontiguous memory area addresses have their linear address >= TASK_SIZE. If it was, it checks if bits 0 and 2 of the error_code are clear. Recall from Table 4.7 that this indicates that the error is caused by trying to access a kernel page that is not present. If so, this indicates that the page fault occurred in kernel mode and the code at label vmalloc_fault: is called.

Line 253

If we get here, it means that although the access occurred in a noncontiguous memory area, it occurred in user mode, hit a protection fault, or both. In this case, we jump to the label bad_area_semaphore:.

Line 257

This sets the local variable mm to point to the current task's memory descriptor. If the current task is a kernel thread, this value is NULL. This becomes significant in the next code lines.

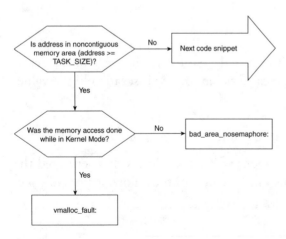

FIGURE 4.14
Page Fault I

At this point, we have determined that the page fault did not occur in a non-contiguous memory area. Again, Figure 4.15 illustrates the flow of the following lines of code:

```
--------------------------------------------------------------------------
arch/i386/mm/fault.c
...
262  if (in_atomic() || !mm)
263   goto bad_area_nosemaphore;
264
265  down_read(&mm->mmap_sem);
266
267  vma = find_vma(mm, address);
268  if (!vma)
269   goto bad_area;
270  if (vma->vm_start <= address)
271   goto good_area;
272  if (!(vma->vm_flags & VM_GROWSDOWN))
273   goto bad_area;
274  if (error_code & 4) {
...
281   if (address + 32 < regs->esp)
282     goto bad_area;
283  }
284  if (expand_stack(vma, address))
285   goto bad_area;
...
--------------------------------------------------------------------------
```

Lines 262–263

In this code block, we check to see if the fault occurred while executing within an interrupt handler or in kernel space. If it did, we jump to label bad_area_semaphore:.

Line 265

At this point, we are about to search through the memory areas of the current process, so we set a read lock on the memory descriptor's semaphore.

Lines 267–269

Given that, at this point, we know the address that generated the page fault is not in a kernel thread or in an interrupt handler, we search the address space of the process to see if the address is in one of its memory areas. If it is not there, jump to label bad_area:.

Lines 270–271

If we found a valid region within the process address space, we jump to label
`good_area:`.

Lines 272–273

If we found a region that is not valid, we check if the nearest region can grow to
fit the page. If not, we jump to the label `bad_area:`.

Lines 274–284

Otherwise, the offending address might be the result of a stack operation. If
expanding the stack does not help, jump to the label `bad_area:`.

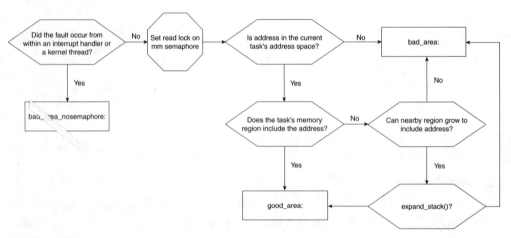

FIGURE 4.15
Page Fault II

Now, we proceed to explain what each of the label jump points do. We begin
with the label `vmalloc_fault`, which is illustrated in Figure 4.16:

```
--------------------------------------------------------------------------
arch/i386/mm/fault.c
473   vmalloc_fault:
   {

   int index = pgd_index(address);
   pgd_t *pgd, *pgd_k;
   pmd_t *pmd, *pmd_k;
   pte_t *pte_k;
```

```
      asm("movl %%cr3,%0":"=r" (pgd));
      pgd = index + (pgd_t *)__va(pgd);
      pgd_k = init_mm.pgd + index;

491   if (!pgd_present(*pgd_k))
      goto no_context;


      pmd = pmd_offset(pgd, address);
      pmd_k = pmd_offset(pgd_k, address);
      if (!pmd_present(*pmd_k))
       goto no_context;
      set_pmd(pmd, *pmd_k);

      pte_k = pte_offset_kernel(pmd_k, address);
506   if (!pte_present(*pte_k))
507     goto no_context;
508     return;
509   }
```

Lines 473–509

The current process Page Global Directory is referenced (by way of cr3) and saved in the variable pgd and the kernel Page Global Directory is referenced by pgd_k (likewise for the pmd and the pte variables). If the offending address is not valid in the kernel paging system, the code jumps to the no_context: label. Otherwise, the current process uses the kernel pgd.

vmalloc_fault:

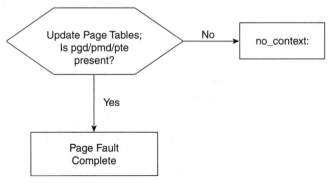

FIGURE 4.16
Label vmalloc_fault

Now, we look at the label `good_area:`. At this point, we know that the memory area holding the offending address exists within the address space of the process. Now, we need to ensure that the access permissions were correct. Figure 4.17 shows the flow diagram:

```
-------------------------------------------------------------------------
arch/i386/mm/fault.c
290  good_area:
291    info.si_code = SEGV_ACCERR;
292    write = 0;
293    switch (error_code & 3) {
294      default:  /* 3: write, present */
...
     /* fall through */
300      case 2:    /* write, not present */
301        if (!(vma->vm_flags & VM_WRITE))
302          goto bad_area;
303        write++;
304        break;
305      case 1:    /* read, present */
306        goto bad_area;
307      case 0:    /* read, not present */
308        if (!(vma->vm_flags & (VM_READ | VM_EXEC)))
309          goto bad_area;
310    }
-------------------------------------------------------------------------
```

Lines 294–304

If the page fault was caused by a memory access that was a write (recall that if this is the case, our left-most bit in the error code is set to 1), we check if our memory area is writeable. If it is not, we have a mismatch of permissions and we jump to the label `bad_area:`. If it was writeable, we fall through the case statement and eventually proceed to `handle_mm_fault()` with the local variable write set to 1.

Lines 305–309

If the page fault was caused by a read or execute access and the page is present, we jump to the label `bad_area:` because this constitutes a clear permissions violation. If the page is not present, we check to see if the memory area has read or execute permissions. If it does not, we jump to the label `bad_area:` because even if we were to fetch the page, the permissions would not allow the operation. If it does, we fall out of the case statement and eventually proceed to `handle_mm_fault()` with the local variable write set to 0.

good_area:

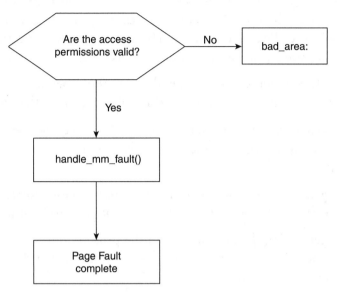

FIGURE 4.17
Label good_area

The following label marks the code we fall through to when the permissions checks comes out OK. It is appropriately labeled survive:.

```
-------------------------------------------------------------------------
arch/i386/mm/fault.c
survive:
318    switch (handle_mm_fault(mm, vma, address, write)) {
    case VM_FAULT_MINOR:
     tsk->min_flt++;
     break;
    case VM_FAULT_MAJOR:
     tsk->maj_flt++;
     break;
    case VM_FAULT_SIGBUS:
     goto do_sigbus;
    case VM_FAULT_OOM:
     goto out_of_memory;
329    default:
     BUG();
   }
-------------------------------------------------------------------------
```

Lines 318–329

The function `handle_mm_fault()` is called with the current memory descriptor (mm), the descriptor to the offending address' area, the offending address, and whether the access was a read/execute or write. The `switch` statement catches us if we fail at handling the fault, which ensures we exit gracefully.

The following code snippet describes the flow of the label `bad_area` and `bad_area_no_semaphore`. When we jump to this point, we know that either

1. The address generating the page fault is not in the process address space because we've searched its memory areas and did not find one that matched.

2. The address generating the page fault is not in the process address space and the region that would contain it cannot grow to hold it.

3. The address generating the page fault is in the process address space but the permissions of the memory area did not match the action we wanted to perform.

Now, we need to determine if the access is from within kernel mode. The following code and Figure 4.18 illustrates the flow of these labels:

```
----------------------------------------------------------------------
arch/i386/mm.fault.c
348  bad_area:
349    up_read(&mm->mmap_sem);
350
351  bad_area_nosemaphore:
352    /* User mode accesses just cause a SIGSEGV */
353    if (error_code & 4) {
354     if (is_prefetch(regs, address))
355       return;
356
357     tsk->thread.cr2 = address;
358     tsk->thread.error_code = error_code;
359     tsk->thread.trap_no = 14;
360     info.si_signo = SIGSEGV;
361     info.si_errno = 0;
362     /* info.si_code has been set above */
363     info.si_addr = (void *)address;
364     force_sig_info(SIGSEGV, &info, tsk);
365     return;
366    }
----------------------------------------------------------------------
```

Line 348

The function `up_read()` releases the read lock on the semaphore of the process' memory descriptor. Notice that we have only jumped to the label `bad_area` after we place read lock on the memory descriptor's semaphore to look through its memory areas to see if our address was within the process address space. Otherwise, we have jumped to the label `bad_area_nosemaphore`. The only difference between the two is the lifting of the read lock on the semaphore.

Lines 351–353

Because the address is not in the address space, we now check to see if the error was generated in user mode. If you recall from Table 4.7, an error code value of 4 indicates that the error occurred in user mode.

Lines 354–366

We have determined that the error occurred in user mode, so we send a `SIGSEGV` signal (trap 14).

bad_area:

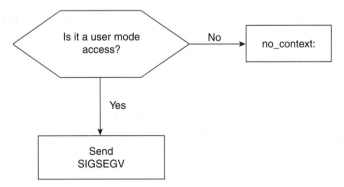

FIGURE 4.18
Label bad_area

The following code snippet describes the flow of the label `no_context`. When we jump to this point, we know that either

- One of the page tables is missing.

- The memory access was not done while in kernel mode.

Figure 4.19 illustrates the flow diagram of the label `no_context`:

```
------------------------------------------------------------------------
arch/i386/mm/fault.c
388  no_context:

390    if (fixup_exception(regs))
     return;

432    die("Oops", regs, error_code);
     bust_spinlocks(0);
     do_exit(SIGKILL);
------------------------------------------------------------------------
```

Line 390

The function `fixup_exception()` uses the `eip` passed in to search an exception table for the offending instruction. If the instruction is in the table, it must have already been compiled with "hidden" fault handling code built in. The page fault handler, `do_page__fault()`, uses the fault handling code as a return address and jumps to it. The code can then flag an error.

Line 432

If there is not an entry in the exception table for the offending instruction, the code that jumped to label `no_context` ends up with the `oops` screen dump.

no_context:

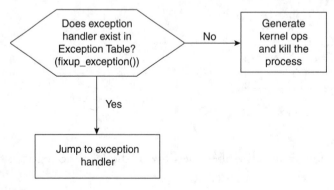

FIGURE 4.19
Label no_context

4.10.3   PowerPC Page Fault Exception

The PowerPC page fault handler `do_page_fault()` is called as a result of an instruction or data store exception. Because of the subtle differences between the various versions of the PowerPC processors, the error codes are in a slightly different format, but yield similar information. The bits of interest are whether the offending operation was a read or write, and if it was a protection fault. The PowerPC page fault handler `do_page_fault()` does not initiate the `oops` error.

In PowerPC, the label `no_context` code is combined with the label `bad_area` code and placed in a function called `bad_page_fault()`, which ends by producing a segmentation fault. This function also has the fixup function that traverses the `exception_table`.

Summary

This chapter began by overviewing all the concepts involved in memory management. We then explained the implementation of each concept. The first concept we looked at was pages, which is the basic unit of memory managed by the kernel and how pages are kept track of in the kernel. We then discussed memory zones as memory partitions that are subject to limitations from hardware. We followed this with a discussion about page frames and the memory allocation and deallocation algorithm that Linux uses, which is called the buddy system.

After we covered the basics of page and page frame management, we discussed the allocation of memory sizes smaller than a page, which is managed by the slab allocator. This introduced us to `kmalloc()` and the kernel memory allocation functions. We traced the execution of these functions down to how they interact with the slab allocator. This completed the discussion on the kernel memory management structures.

After the kernel management structures and algorithms were covered, we talked about user space process memory management. Process memory management is different from kernel memory management. We discussed memory layout for a process and how the various process parts are partitioned and mapped in memory. Following the discussion on process memory management flow, we introduced the concept of the page fault, the interrupt handler that is in charge of managing page misses from memory.

Project: Process Memory Map

We now look at what memory looks like for our own program. This project consists of an exploration of a user space program that illustrates where things are placed in memory. For this project, we create a simple shared library and a user space program that uses its function. From the program, we print the location of some of the variables and compare it against the process memory mappings to determine where the variables and functions are being stored.

The first step is to create the shared library. The shared library can have a single function, which we will call from our main program. We want to print the address of a local variable from within this function. Your shared library should look like this:

```
--------------------------------------------------------------------------
lkpsinglefoo.c
mylibfoo()
{
  int libvar;
  printf("variable libvar \t location: 0x%x\n", &libvar);
}
--------------------------------------------------------------------------
```

Compile and link `singlefoo.c` into a shared library:

```
#lkp>gcc -c lkpsinglefoo.c
#lkp>gcc lkpsinglefoo.o -o liblkpsinglefoo.so -shared -lc
```

The `-shared` and `-lc` flags are linker options. The `-shared` option requests that a shared object that can be linked with other objects be produced. The `-lc` flag indicates that the C library be searched when linking.

These commands generate a file called `liblkpsinglefoo.so`. To use it, you need to copy it to `/lib`.

The following is the main application we will call that links in your library:

```
--------------------------------------------------------------------------
lkpmem.c
#include <fcntl.h>

int globalvar1;
int globalvar2 = 3;

void mylocalfoo()
{
  int functionvar;
  printf("variable functionvar \t location: 0x%x\n", &functionvar);
}
```

```
int main()
{
  void *localvar1 = (void *)malloc(2048)
  printf("variable globalvar1 \t location: 0x%x\n", &globalvar1);
  printf("variable globalvar2 \t location: 0x%x\n", &globalvar2);
  printf("variable localvar1 \t location: 0x%x\n", &localvar1);

  mylibfoo();
  mylocalfoo();

  while(1);
  return(0);
}
```

Compile `lkpmem.c` as follows:

```
#lkp>gcc -o lkpmem lkpmem.c -llkplibsinglefoo
```

When you execute `lkpmem`, you get the print statements that indicate the memory locations of the various variables. The function blocks on the `while(1);` statement and does not return. This allows you to get the process PID and search the memory maps. To do so, use the following commands:

```
#lkp>./lkpmem
#lkp> ps aux | grep lkpmem
#lkp> cat /proc/<pid>/maps
```

Indicate the memory segment in which each variable is located.

Exercises

1. Why can't processes executed from a common executable or program not share the data segments of memory?

2. What would the stack of the following function look like after three iterations?

   ```
   foo(){
     int a;
     foo()
   }
   ```

   If it continues, what problem is this going to run into?

3. Fill in the values for the `vm_area_struct` descriptors that correspond to the memory map shown in Figure 4.11.

4. What is the relationship between pages and slabs?

5. A 32-bit system with Linux loaded does not use the Page Middle Directory. That is, it effectively has a two-level page table. The first 10 bits of the virtual address correspond to the offset within the Page Global Directory (PGD). The second 10 bits correspond to an offset into the Page Table (PTE). The remaining 12 bits correspond to the page offset.

   What is the page size in this Linux system? How many pages can a task access? How much memory?

6. What is the relationship between a memory zone and a page?

7. At the hardware level, how does "real" addressing differ from "virtual" addressing?

Chapter 5

Input/Output

In this chapter

The Linux kernel is a collection of code that runs on one or more processors. The processors' interface to the rest of the system is through the supporting hardware. At its lowest machine-dependent layer, the kernel communicates with these devices with simple assembly-language instructions. This chapter explores the relationship of the kernel to the surrounding hardware, focusing on file I/O and hardware devices. We illustrate how the Linux kernel ties together software and hardware by discussing how we go from the highest level of a virtual filesystem down to the lowest level of writing bits to physical media.

This chapter starts with an overview of just how the core of a computer, the processor, connects to the rest of the system. The concept of busses is also discussed, including how they connect the processor to other elements of the system (such as memory). We also introduce devices and controllers that make up the chipsets used in most x86 and PowerPC systems.

By having a basic understanding of the components of a system and their interconnection, we can begin to analyze the layers of software from an application to the operating system, to the specific block device used for storage—the hard drive and its controller. Although the concept of the filesystem is not covered until the next chapter, we discuss enough of the components to get us down to the generic block device layer and the most important method of communication for the block device; the request queue.

The important relationship between a mechanical device (the hard drive) and the system software is discussed when we introduce the concept of scheduling I/O. By understanding the physical geometry of a hard drive and how the operating system partitions the drive, we can begin to understand the timing between software and the underlying hardware.

Moving closer to the hardware, we see how the generic block driver interfaces to the specific block driver, which allows us to have common software control over various hardware devices. Finally, in our journey from the application level to the I/O level, we touch on the hardware I/O needed for a disc controller and point you to other examples of I/O and device drivers in this book.

We then discuss the other major device type—the character device—and how it differs from the block device and the network device. The importance of other devices—the DMA controller, the clock, and terminal devices—are also contrasted with these.

5.1   How Hardware Does It: Busses, Bridges, Ports, and Interfaces

The way a processor communicates with its surrounding devices is through a series of electrical connections, or **lines**. **Busses** are groups of these lines with similar function. The most common types of busses going to and from a processor are used for **addressing** the devices; for sending and receiving **data** from the devices; and for transmitting **control** information, such as device-specific initialization and characteristics. Thus, we can say the principal method for a device to communicate with the processor (and vice versa) is through its address bus, data bus, and control bus.

The most basic function of a processor in a system is to fetch and execute instructions. These instructions are collectively called a **computer program** or software. A program resides in a device (or group of devices) known as memory. The processor is attached to memory by way of the address, data, and control busses. When executing a program, the processor selects the location of an instruction in memory by way of the address bus and transfers (fetches) the instruction by way of the data bus. The control bus handles the direction (in or out of the processor) and type (in this case, memory) of transfer. Possibly adding to the confusion in this terminology is that, when we refer to a particular bus, such as the **front-side bus** or the **PCI bus**, we mean the address, data, and control busses all together.

The task of running software on a system requires a wide array of peripheral devices. Recent computer systems have two major peripheral devices (also called controllers), which are referred to as the **Northbridge** and the **Southbridge**. Traditionally, the term **bridge** describes a hardware device that connects two busses. Figure 5.1 illustrates how the Northbridge and the Southbridge interconnect other devices. Collectively, these controllers are the **chipset** of the system.

The Northbridge connects the high-speed, high-performance peripherals, such as the memory controller and the PCI controller. While there are chipset designs with graphics controllers integrated into the Northbridge, most recent designs include a high-performance bus, such as the Accelerated Graphics Port (AGP) or the PCI Express, to communicate with a dedicated graphics adaptor. To achieve speed and good performance, the Northbridge bridges the front-side bus[1] with, depending on the particular chipset design, the PCI bus and/or the memory bus.

---

[1]   In some PowerPC systems, the front-side bus equivalent is known as the processor-local bus.

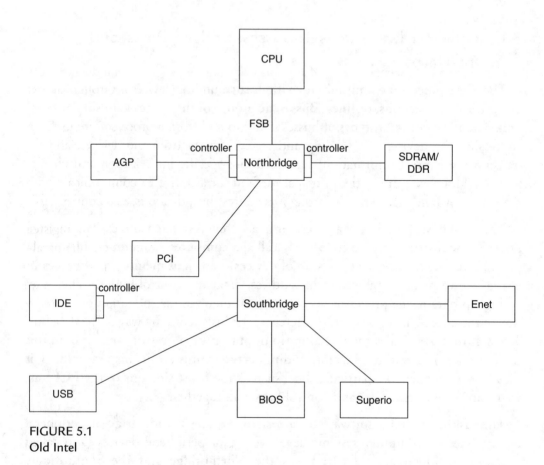

FIGURE 5.1
Old Intel

The Southbridge, which connects to the Northbridge, is also connected to a combination of low-performance devices. The Intel PIIX4, for example, has its Southbridge connected to the PCI-ISA bridge, the IDE controller, the USB, the real-time clock, the dual 82C59 interrupt controller (which is covered in Chapter 3, "Processes: The Principal Model of Execution"), the 82C54 timer, the dual 82C37 DMA controllers, and the I/O APIC support.

In the earliest x86-based personal computers, communication with basic peripherals, such as the keyboard, the serial port, and the parallel port, was done over an **I/O bus**. The I/O bus is a type of the control bus. The I/O bus is a relatively slow method of communication that controls peripherals. The x86 architecture has special I/O instructions, such as **inb** (read **in** a **b**yte) and **outb** (write **out** a **b**yte), which communicate over the I/O bus. The I/O bus is implemented by sharing the processor address and data lines. Control lines activated only when using the special I/O instructions prevented I/O devices from being confused with memory. The PowerPC architecture has a different method of controlling peripheral devices; it is known as **memory-mapped I/O**. With memory-mapped I/O, devices are assigned regions of address space for communication and control.

For example, in x86 architecture the first parallel port data register is located at **I/O port** 0x378, whereas in the PPC it could be, depending on the implementation, at memory location 0xf0000300. To read the first parallel port data register in x86, we execute the assembler instruction in al, 0x378. In this case, we activate a control line to the parallel port controller. This indicates to the bus that 0x378 is not a memory address but an I/O port. To read the first parallel port data register in PPC, we execute the assembly instruction lbz r3, 0(0xf0000300). The parallel port controller watches the address bus[2] and replies only to requests on a specific address range under which 0xf0000300 would fall.

As personal computers matured, more discrete I/O devices were consolidated into single integrated circuits called **Superio** chips. Superio function is often further consolidated into a Southbridge chip (as in the ALI M1543C). As an example of typical functionality found in a discrete Superio device, let's look at the SMSC FDC37C932. It includes a keyboard controller, a real-time clock, power management device, a floppy disk controller, serial port controllers, parallel ports, an IDE interface, and general purpose I/O. Other Southbridge chips contain integrated LAN controllers, PCI Express controllers, audio controllers, and the like.

The newer Intel system architecture has moved to the concept of **hubs**. The Northbridge is now known as the Graphics and Memory Controller Hub (GMCH). It supports a high-performance AGP and DDR memory controller. With PCI Express, Intel chipsets are moving to a Memory Controller Hub (MCH) for graphics and a DDR2 memory controller. The Southbridge is known as the I/O Controller Hub (ICH). These hubs are connected through a proprietary point-to-point bus called the Intel Hub Architecture (IHA). For more information, see the Intel chipset datasheets for the 865G[3] and the 925XE.[4] Figure 5.2 illustrates the ICH.

---

[2] Watching the address bus is also referred to as decoding the address bus.

[3] http://www.intel.com/design/chipsets/datashts/25251405.pdf.

[4] http://www.intel.com/design/chipsets/datashts/30146403.pdf.

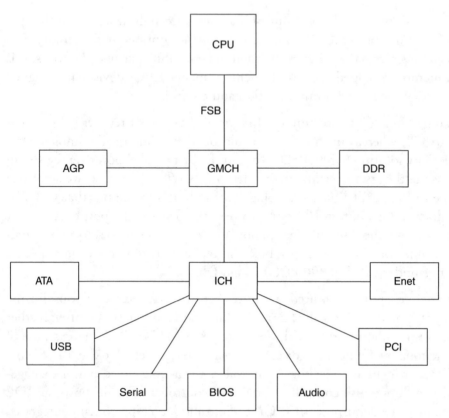

FIGURE 5.2
New Intel Hub

AMD has moved from the older Intel style of the Northbridge/Southbridge to the packetized **HyperTransport** technology between its major chipset components. To the operating system, HyperTransport is PCI compatible.[5] See AMD chipset datasheets for the 8000 Series chipsets. Figure 5.3 illustrates the HyperTransport technology.

Apple, using the PowerPC, has a proprietary design called the Universal Motherboard Architecture (UMA). UMA's goal is to use the same chipset across all Mac systems.

---

5 See AMD chipset datasheets for the 8000 series: http://www.amd.com/us-en/Processors/
ProductInformation/0,30_118_6291_4886,00.html.

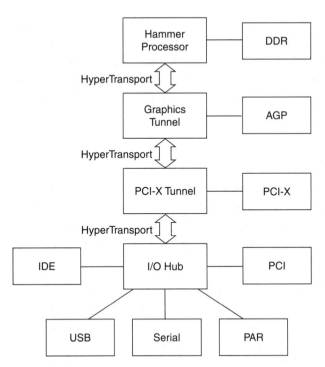

FIGURE 5.3
AMD HyperTransport

The G4 chipset includes the "UniNorth memory controller and PCI bus bridge" as a Northbridge and the "Key Largo I/O and disk-device controller" as a Southbridge. The UniNorth supports SDRAM, Ethernet, and AGP. The Key Largo Southbridge, connected to the UniNorth by a PCI-to-PCI bridge, supports the ATA busses, USB, wireless LAN (WLAN), and sound.

The G5 chipset includes a system controller Application Specific Integrated Circuit (ASIC), which supports AGP and DDR memory. Connected to the system controller via a HyperTransport bus is a PCI-X controller and a high-performance I/O device. For more information on this architecture, see the Apple developer pages.

By having this brief overview of the basic architecture of a system, we can now focus on the interface to these devices provided by the kernel. Chapter 1, "Overview," mentioned that devices are represented as files in the filesystem. File permissions, modes, and filesystem-related system calls, such as open() or read(), apply to these special files as they do to regular files. The significance of each call varies with respect to the device being handled and is customized to handle each type of device. In this way, the details of the device handling are made transparent to the application programmer and are hidden in the kernel. Suffice it to say that when a process applies one of the system calls on the device file, it translates to some kind of device-handling function. These handling functions are defined in the device driver. We now look at the types of devices.

5.2   Devices

Two kinds of device files exist: block device files and character device files. Block devices transfer data in chunks, and character devices (as the name implies) transfer data one character at a time. A third device type, the network device, is a special case that exhibits attributes of both block and character devices. However, network devices are not represented by files.

The old method of assigned numbers for devices where the major number usually referred to a device driver or controller, and the minor number was a particular device within that controller, is giving way to a new dynamic method called devfs. The history behind this change is that the major and minor numbers are both 8-bit values; this allows for little more than 200 **statically** allocated major devices for the entire planate. (Block and character devices each have their own list of 256 entries.) You can find the official listing of the allocated major and minor device numbers in /Documentation/devices.txt.

The Linux Device Filesystem (**devfs**) has been in the kernel since version 2.3.46. devfs is not included by default in the 2.6.7 kernel build, but it can be enabled by setting CONFIG_DEVFS_FS=Y in the configuration file. With devfs, a module can register a device by name rather than a major/minor number pair. For compatibility, devfs allows the use of old major/minor numbers or generates a unique 16-bit device number on any given **system**.

5.2.1   Block Device Overview

As previously mentioned, the Linux operating system sees all devices as files. Any given element in a block device can be randomly referenced. A good example of a block device is the disk drive. The filesystem name for the first IDE disk is /dev/hda. The associated major number of /dev/hda is 3, and the minor number is 0. The disk drive itself usually has a controller and is electro-mechanical by nature (that is, it has moving parts). The "General System File" section in Chapter 6, "Filesystems," discusses the basic construction of a hard disk.

5.2.1.1   Generic Block Device Layer

The device driver registers itself at driver initialization time. This adds the driver to the kernel's **driver table**, mapping the device number to the **block_device_ operations** structure. The `block_device_operations` structure contains the functions for starting and stopping a given block device in the system:

```
------------------------------------------------------------------------
include/linux/fs.h
760  struct block_device_operations {
761    int (*open) (struct inode *, struct file *);
762    int (*release) (struct inode *, struct file *);
763    int (*ioctl) (struct inode *, struct file *, unsigned, unsigned long);
764    int (*media_changed) (struct gendisk *);
765    int (*revalidate_disk) (struct gendisk *);
766    struct module *owner;
767  };
------------------------------------------------------------------------
```

The interfaces to the block device are similar to other devices. The functions `open()` (on line 761) and `release()` (on line 762) are **synchronous** (that is, they run to completion when called). The most important functions, `read()` and `write()`, are implemented differently with block devices because of their mechanical nature. Consider accessing a block of data from a disk drive. The amount of time it takes to position the head on the proper track and for the disk to rotate to the desired block can take a long time, from the processor's point of view. This **latency** is the driving force for the implementation of the **system request queue**. When the filesystem requests a block (or more) of data, and it is not in the local **page cache**, it places the request on a request queue and passes this queue on to the generic block device layer. The generic block device layer then determines the most efficient way to mechanically retrieve (or store) the information, and passes this on to the hard disk driver.

Most importantly, at initialization time, the block device driver registers a request queue handler with the kernel (specifically with the block device manager) to facilitate the read/write operations for the block device. The generic block device layer acts as an interface between the filesystem and the register level interface of the device and allows for per-queue tuning of the read and write queues to make better use of the new and smarter devices available. This is accomplished through the tagged command queuing helper utilities. For example, if a device on a given queue supports command queuing, read and write operations can be optimized to exploit the underlying hardware by reordering requests. An example of per-queue tuning in this case would be the ability to set how many requests are allowed to be pending. See Figure 5.4 for an illustration of how the application layer, the filesystem layer, the generic block device layer, and the device driver interrelate. The file `biodoc.txt` under `/Documentation/block>` has more helpful information on this layer and information regarding changes from earlier kernels.

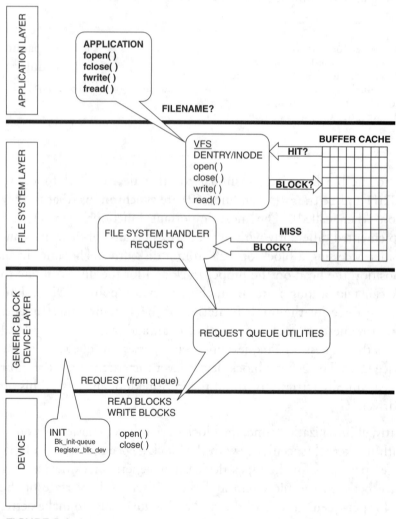

FIGURE 5.4
Block Read/Write

5.2.2   Request Queues and Scheduling I/O

When a read or write request traverses the layers from VFS, through the filesystem drivers and page cache,[6] it eventually ends up entering the block device driver to perform the actual I/O on the device that holds the data requested.

As previously mentioned, the block device driver creates and initializes a request queue upon initialization. This initialization also determines the I/O scheduling algorithm to use when a read or write is attempted on the block device. The I/O scheduling algorithm is also known as the **elevator algorithm**.

The default I/O scheduling algorithm is determined by the kernel at boot time with the default being the **anticipatory I/O scheduler**.[7] By setting the kernel parameter `elevator` to the following values, you can change the type of I/O scheduler:

- **`deadline`**. For the deadline I/O scheduler

- **`noop`**. For the no-operation I/O scheduler

- **`as`**. For the anticipatory I/O scheduler

As of this writing, a patch exists that makes the I/O schedulers fully modular. Using `modprobe`, the user can load the modules and switch between them on the fly.[8] With this patch, at least one scheduler must be compiled into the kernel to begin with.

Before we can describe how these I/O schedulers work, we need to touch on the basics of request queues.

Block devices use request queues to order the many block I/O requests the devices are given. Certain block devices, such as a RAM disk, might have little need for ordering requests because the I/O requests to the device have little overhead. Other block devices, like hard drives, need to order requests because there is a great overhead in reading and writing. As previously mentioned, the head of the hard drive has to move from track to track, and each movement is agonizingly slow from the CPU's perspective.

---

[6]   This traversal is described in Chapter 6.

[7]   Some block device drivers can change their I/O scheduler during runtime, if it's visible in sysfs.

[8]   For more information, do a Web search on "Jens Axboe" and "Modular IO Schedulers."

Request queues solve this problem by attempting to order block I/O read and write requests in a manner that optimizes throughput but does not indefinitely postpone requests. A common and useful analogy of I/O scheduling is to look at how elevators work.[9] If you were to order the stops an elevator took by the order of the requests, you would have the elevator moving inefficiently from floor to floor; it could go from the penthouse to the ground floor without ever stopping for anyone in between. By responding to requests that occur while the elevator travels in the same direction, it increases the elevator's efficiency and the riders' happiness. Similarly, I/O requests to a hard disk should be grouped together to avoid the high overhead of repeatedly moving the disk head back and forth. All the I/O schedulers mentioned (no-op, deadline, and anticipatory) implement this basic elevator functionality. The following sections look at these *elevators* in more detail.

5.2.2.1   No-Op I/O Scheduler

The no-op I/O scheduler[10] takes a request and scans through its queue to determine if it can be merged with an existing request. This occurs if the new request is close to an existing request. If the new request is for I/O blocks before an existing request, it is merged on the front of the existing request. If the new request is for I/O blocks after an existing request, it is merged on the back of the existing request. In normal I/O, we read the beginning of a file before the end, and thus, most requests are merged onto the back of existing requests.

If the no-op I/O scheduler finds that the new request cannot be merged into the existing request because it is not near enough, the scheduler looks for a place within the queue between existing requests. If the new request calls for I/O to sectors between existing requests it is inserted into the queue at the determined position. If there are no places the request can be inserted, it is placed on the tail of the request queue.

5.2.2.2   Deadline I/O Scheduler

The no-op I/O scheduler[11] suffers from a major problem; with enough close requests, new requests are never handled. Many new requests that are close to

---

[9]   This analogy is why I/O schedulers are also referred to as elevators.

[10]   The code for the no-op I/O scheduler is located in `drivers/block/noop-iosched.c`.

[11]   The code for the deadline I/O scheduler is located in `drivers/block/deadline-iosched.c`.

existing ones would be either merged or inserted between existing elements, and new requests would pile up at the tail of the request queue. The deadline scheduler attempts to solve this problem by assigning each request an expiration time and uses two additional queues to manage time efficiency as well as a queue similar to the no-op algorithm to model disk efficiency.

When an application makes a read request, it typically waits until that request is fulfilled before continuing. Write requests, on the other hand, will not normally cause an application to wait; the write can execute in the background while the application continues on to other tasks. The deadline I/O scheduler uses this information to favor read requests over write requests. A read queue and write queue are kept in addition to the queue sorted by a request's sector proximity. In the read and write queue, requests are ordered by time (FIFO).

When a new request comes in, it is placed on the sorted queue as in the no-op scheduler. The request is also placed on either the read queue or write queue depending on its I/O request. When the deadline I/O scheduler handles a request, it first checks the head of the read queue to see if that request has expired. If that requests expiration time has been reached, it is immediately handled. Similarly, if no read request has expired, the scheduler checks the write queue to see if the request at its head has expired; if so, it is immediately handled. The standard queue is checked only when no reads or writes have expired and requests are handled in nearly the same way as the no-op algorithm.

Read requests also expire faster than write requests: $\frac{1}{2}$ a second versus 5 seconds in the default case. This expiration difference and the preference of handling read requests over write requests can lead to write requests being starved by numerous read requests. As such, a parameter tells the deadline I/O scheduler the maximum number of times reads can starve a write; the default is 2, but because sequential requests can be treated as a single request, 32 sequential read requests could pass before a write request is considered starved.[12]

5.2.2.3   Anticipatory I/O Scheduling

One of the problems with the deadline I/O scheduling algorithm occurs during intensive write operations. Because of the emphasis on maximizing read efficiency,

---

[12] See lines 24–27 of `deadline-iosched.c` for parameter definitions.

a write request can be preempted by a read, have the disk head seek to new location, and then return to the write request and have the disk head seek back to its original location. Anticipatory I/O scheduling[13] attempts to anticipate what the next operation is and aims to improve I/O throughput in doing so.

Structurally, the anticipatory I/O scheduler is similar to the deadline I/O scheduler. There exist a read and write queue each ordered by time (FIFO) and a default queue that is ordered by sector proximity. The main difference is that after a read request, the scheduler does not immediately proceed to handling other requests. It does nothing for 6 milliseconds in anticipation of an additional read. If another read request does occur to an adjacent area, it is immediately handled. After the anticipation period, the scheduler returns to its normal operation as described under the deadline I/O scheduler.

This anticipation period helps minimize the I/O delay associated with moving the disk head from sector to sector across the block device.

Like the deadline I/O scheduler, a number of parameters control the anticipatory I/O scheduling algorithm. The default time for reads to expire is $\frac{1}{8}$ second and the default time for writes to expire is $\frac{1}{4}$ second. Two parameters control when to check to switch between streams of reads and writes.[14] A stream of reads checks for expired writes after $\frac{1}{4}$ second and a stream of writes checks for expired reads after $\frac{1}{16}$ second.

The default I/O scheduler is the anticipatory I/O scheduler because it optimizes throughput for most applications and block devices. The deadline I/O scheduler is sometimes better for database applications or those that require high disk performance requirements. The no-op I/O scheduler is usually used in systems where I/O seek time is near negligible, such as embedded systems running from RAM.

We now turn our attention from the various I/O schedulers in the Linux kernel to the request queue itself and the manner in which block devices initialize request queues.

---

[13] The code for anticipatory I/O scheduling is located in `drivers/block/as-iosched.c`.

[14] See lines 30–60 of `as-iosched.c` for parameter definitions.

5.2.2.4   Request Queue

In Linux 2.6, each block device has its own request queue that manages I/O requests to that device. A process can only update a device's request queue if it has obtained the lock of the request queue. Let's examine the `request_queue` structure:

```
-----------------------------------------------------------------------
include/linux/blkdev.h
270 struct request_queue
271 {
272    /*
273    * Together with queue_head for cacheline sharing
274    */
275    struct list_head  queue_head;
276    struct request   *last_merge;
277    elevator_t     elevator;
278
279    /*
280    * the queue request freelist, one for reads and one for writes
281    */
282    struct request_list  rq;
-----------------------------------------------------------------------
```

Line 275

This line is a pointer to the head of the request queue.

Line 276

This is the last request placed into the request queue.

Line 277

The scheduling function (elevator) used to manage the request queue. This can be one of the standard I/O schedulers (noop, deadline, or anticipatory) or a new type of scheduler specifically designed for the block device.

Line 282

The `request_list` is a structure composed of two `wait_queues`: one for queuing reads to the block device and one for queuing writes.

```
-----------------------------------------------------------------------
include/linux/blkdev.h
283
284    request_fn_proc  *request_fn;
```

```
285   merge_request_fn   *back_merge_fn;
286   merge_request_fn   *front_merge_fn;
287   merge_requests_fn   *merge_requests_fn;
288   make_request_fn    *make_request_fn;
289   prep_rq_fn      *prep_rq_fn;
290   unplug_fn      *unplug_fn;
291   merge_bvec_fn    *merge_bvec_fn;
292   activity_fn      *activity_fn;
293
--------------------------------------------------------------------------
```

Lines 283–293

These scheduler- (or elevator-) specific functions can be defined to control how requests are managed for the block device.

```
--------------------------------------------------------------------------
include/linux/blkdev.h
294   /*
295   * Auto-unplugging state
296   */
297   struct timer_list  unplug_timer;
298   int      unplug_thresh; /* After this many requests */
299   unsigned long  unplug_delay; /* After this many jiffies*/
300   struct work_struct  unplug_work;
301
302   struct backing_dev_info backing_dev_info;
303
--------------------------------------------------------------------------
```

Lines 294–303

These functions are used to unplug the I/O scheduling function used on the block device. **Plugging** refers to the practice of waiting for more requests to fill the request queue with the expectation that more requests allow the scheduling algorithm to order and sort I/O requests that enhance the time it takes to perform the I/O requests. For example, a hard drive "plugs" a certain number of read requests with the expectation that it moves the disk head less when more reads exist. It's more likely that the reads can be arranged sequentially or even clustered together into a single large read. **Unplugging** refers to the method in which a device decides that it can wait no longer and must service the requests it has, regardless of possible future optimizations. See `documentation/block/biodoc.txt` for more information.

```
------------------------------------------------------------------------
include/linux/blkdev.h
304    /*
305    * The queue owner gets to use this for whatever they like.
306    * ll_rw_blk doesn't touch it.
307    */
308    void     *queuedata;
309
310    void     *activity_data;
311
------------------------------------------------------------------------
```

Lines 304–311

As the inline comments suggest, these lines request queue management that is
specific to the device and/or device driver:

```
------------------------------------------------------------------------
include/linux/blkdev.h
312    /*
313    * queue needs bounce pages for pages above this limit
314    */
315    unsigned long   bounce_pfn;
316    int        bounce_gfp;
317
------------------------------------------------------------------------
```

Lines 312–317

Bouncing refers to the practice of the kernel copying high-memory buffer I/O
requests to low-memory buffers. In Linux 2.6, the kernel allows the device itself to
manage high-memory buffers if it wants. Bouncing now typically occurs only if the
device cannot handle high-memory buffers.

```
------------------------------------------------------------------------
include/linux/blkdev.h
318    /*
319    * various queue flags, see QUEUE_* below
320    */
321    unsigned long   queue_flags;
322
------------------------------------------------------------------------
```

Lines 318–321

The `queue_flags` variable stores one or more of the queue flags shown in
Table 5.1 (see `include/linux/blkdev.h`, lines 368–375).

TABLE 5.1
queue_flags

Flag Name	Flag Function
QUEUE_FLAG_CLUSTER	/* cluster several segments into 1 */
QUEUE_FLAG_QUEUED	/* uses generic tag queuing */
QUEUE_FLAG_STOPPED	/* queue is stopped */
QUEUE_FLAG_READFULL	/* read queue has been filled */
QUEUE_FLAG_WRITEFULL	/* write queue has been filled */
QUEUE_FLAG_DEAD	/* queue being torn down */
QUEUE_FLAG_REENTER	/* Re-entrancy avoidance */
QUEUE_FLAG_PLUGGED	/* queue is plugged */

```
----------------------------------------------------------------------
include/linux/blkdev.h
323    /*
324     * protects queue structures from reentrancy
325     */
326    spinlock_t    *queue_lock;
327
328    /*
329     * queue kobject
330     */
331    struct kobject kobj;
332
333    /*
334     * queue settings
335     */
336    unsigned long   nr_requests; /* Max # of requests */
337    unsigned int    nr_congestion_on;
338    unsigned int    nr_congestion_off;
339
340    unsigned short    max_sectors;
341    unsigned short    max_phys_segments;
342    unsigned short    max_hw_segments;
343    unsigned short    hardsect_size;
344    unsigned int    max_segment_size;
345
346    unsigned long    seg_boundary_mask;
347    unsigned int    dma_alignment;
348
349    struct blk_queue_tag *queue_tags;
350
```

```
351   atomic_t     refcnt;
352
353   unsigned int  in_flight;
354
355   /*
356    * sg stuff
357    */
358   unsigned int  sg_timeout;
359   unsigned int  sg_reserved_size;
360 };
```

Lines 323–360

These variables define manageable resources of the request queue, such as locks (line 326) and kernel objects (line 331). Specific request queue settings, such as the maximum number of requests (line 336) and the physical constraints of the block device (lines 340–347) are also provided. SCSI attributes (lines 355–359) can also be defined, if they're applicable to the block device. If you want to use tagged command queuing use the `queue_tags` structure (on line 349). The `refcnt` and `in_flight` fields (on lines 351 and 353) count the number of references to the queue (commonly used in locking) and the number of requests that are in process ("in flight").

Request queues used by block devices are initialized simply in the 2.6 Linux kernel by calling the following function in the devices' `__init` function. Within this function, we can see the anatomy of a request queue and its associated helper routines. In the 2.6 Linux kernel, each block device controls its own locking, which is contrary to some earlier versions of Linux, and passes a spinlock as the second argument. The first argument is a request function that the block device driver provides.

```
drivers/block/ll_rw_blk.c
1397 request_queue_t *blk_init_queue(request_fn_proc *rfn, spinlock_t *lock)
1398 {
1399   request_queue_t *q;
1400   static int printed;
1401
1402   q = blk_alloc_queue(GFP_KERNEL);
1403   if (!q)
1404   return NULL;
1405
1406   if (blk_init_free_list(q))
1407     goto out_init;
1408
```

```
1409   if (!printed) {
1410     printed = 1;
1411     printk("Using %s io scheduler\n", chosen_elevator->elevator_name);
1412   }
1413
1414   if (elevator_init(q, chosen_elevator))
1415     goto out_elv;
1416
1417   q->request_fn    = rfn;
1418   q->back_merge_fn    = ll_back_merge_fn;
1419   q->front_merge_fn   = ll_front_merge_fn;
1420   q->merge_requests_fn = ll_merge_requests_fn;
1421   q->prep_rq_fn    = NULL;
1422   q->unplug_fn    = generic_unplug_device;
1423   q->queue_flags    = (1 << QUEUE_FLAG_CLUSTER);
1424   q->queue_lock    = lock;
1425
1426   blk_queue_segment_boundary(q, 0xffffffff);
1427
1428   blk_queue_make_request(q, __make_request);
1429   blk_queue_max_segment_size(q, MAX_SEGMENT_SIZE);
1430
1431   blk_queue_max_hw_segments(q, MAX_HW_SEGMENTS);
1432   blk_queue_max_phys_segments(q, MAX_PHYS_SEGMENTS);
1433
1434   return q;
1435 out_elv:
1436   blk_cleanup_queue(q);
1437 out_init:
1438   kmem_cache_free(requestq_cachep, q);
1439   return NULL;
1440 }
```

Line 1402

Allocate the queue from kernel memory and zero its contents.

Line 1406

Initialize the request list that contains a read queue and a write queue.

Line 1414

Associate the chosen elevator with this queue and initialize.

Lines 1417–1424

Associate the elevator-specific functions with this queue.

Line 1426

This function sets the boundary for segment merging and checks that it is at least a minimum size.

Line 1428

This function sets the function used to get requests off the queue by the driver. It allows an alternate function to be used to bypass the queue.

Line 1429

Initialize the upper-size limit on a combined segment.

Line 1431

Initialize the maximum segments the physical device can handle.

Line 1432

Initialize the maximum number of physical segments per request.

The values for lines 1429–1432 are set in `include/linux/blkdev.h`.

Line 1434

Return the initialized queue.

Lines 1435–1439

Routines to clean up memory in the event of an error.

We now have the request queue in place and initialized.

Before we explore the generic device layer and the generic block driver, let's quickly trace the layers of software it takes to get to the manipulation of IO in the block device. (Refer to Figure 5.4.)

At the application level, an application has initiated a file operation such as `fread()`. This request is taken by the virtual filesystem (VFS) layer (covered in Chapter 4), where the file's `dentry` structure is found, and through the `inode` structure, where the file's `read()` function is called. The VFS layer tries to find the requested page in its buffer cache, but if it is a miss, the **filesystem handler** is called to acquire the appropriate physical blocks. The `inode` is linked to the filesystem handler, which is associated with the correct filesystem. The filesystem handler calls on the **request queue utilities**, which are part of the **generic block device layer** to create a request with the correct physical blocks and device. The request is put on the **request queue**, which is maintained by the **generic block device layer**.

5.2.3   Example: "Generic" Block Driver

We now look at the generic block device layer. Referring to Figure 5.4, it resides above the physical device layer and just below the filesystem layer. The most important job of the generic block layer is to maintain request queues and their related helper routines.

We first register our device with `register_blkdev(major, dev_name, fops)`. This function takes in the requested major number, the name of this block device (this appears in the `/dev` directory), and a pointer to the file operations structure. If successful, it returns the desired major number.

Next, we create the `gendisk` structure.

The function `alloc_disk(int minors)` in `include/linux/genhd.h` takes in the number of partitions and returns a pointer to the `gendisk` structure. We now look at the `gendisk` structure:

```
---------------------------------------------------------------------
include/linux/genhd.h
081  struct gendisk {
082    int major;     /* major number of driver */
083    int first_minor;
084    int minors;
085    char disk_name[16];   /* name of major driver */
086    struct hd_struct **part;   /* [indexed by minor] */
087    struct block_device_operations *fops;
088    struct request_queue *queue;
089    void *private_data;
090    sector_t capacity;
091
092    int flags;
093    char devfs_name[64];   /* devfs crap */
094    int number;     /* more of the same */
095    struct device *driverfs_dev;
096    struct kobject kobj;
097
098    struct timer_rand_state *random;
099    int policy;
100
```

```
101    unsigned sync_io;    /* RAID */
102    unsigned long stamp, stamp_idle;
103    int in_flight;
104  #ifdef  CONFIG_SMP
105    struct disk_stats *dkstats;
106  #else
107    struct disk_stats dkstats;
108  #endif
109  };
```

Line 82

The `major_num` field is filled in from the result of `register_blkdev()`.

Line 83

A block device for a hard drive could handle several physical drives. Although it is driver dependent, the minor number usually labels each physical drive. The `first_minor` field is the first of the physical drives.

Line 85

The `disk_name`, such as `hda` or `sdb`, is the text name for an entire disk. (Partitions within a disk are named `hda1`, `hda2`, and so on.) These are *logical* disks *within* a physical disk device.

Line 87

The `fops` field is the `block_device_operations` initialized to the file operations structure. The file operations structure contains pointers to the helper functions in the low-level device driver. These functions are driver dependent in that they are not all implemented in every driver. Commonly implemented file operations are `open`, `close`, `read`, and `write`. Chapter 4, "Memory Management," discusses the file operations structure.

Line 88

The `queue` field points to the list of requested operations that the driver must perform. Initialization of the request queue is discussed shortly.

Line 89

The `private_data` field is for driver-dependent data.

Line 90

The `capacity` field is to be set with the drive size (in 512KB sectors). A call to `set_capacity()` should furnish this value.

Line 92

The `flags` field indicates device attributes. In case of a disk drive, it is the type of media, such as CD, removable, and so on.

Now, we look at what is involved with initializing the request queue. With the queue already declared, we call `blk_init_queue(request_fn_proc, spinlock_t)`. This function takes, as its first parameter, the transfer function to be called on behalf of the filesystem. The function `blk_init_queue()` allocates the queue with `blk_alloc_queue()` and then initializes the queue structure. The second parameter to `blk_init_queue()` is a lock to be associated with the queue for all operations.

Finally, to make this block device visible to the kernel, the driver must call `add_disk()`:

```
-------------------------------------------------------------------------
Drivers/block/genhd.c
193   void add_disk(struct gendisk *disk)
194   {
195    disk->flags |= GENHD_FL_UP;
196    blk_register_region(MKDEV(disk->major, disk->first_minor),
197      disk->minors, NULL, exact_match, exact_lock, disk);
198    register_disk(disk);
199    blk_register_queue(disk);
200   }
-------------------------------------------------------------------------
```

Line 196

This device is mapped into the kernel based on size and number of partitions.

The call to `blk_register_region()` has the following six parameters:

1. The disk major number and *first* minor number are built into this parameter.

2. This is the range of minor numbers after the first (if this driver handles multiple minor numbers).

3. This is the loadable module containing the driver (if any).

4. `exact_match` is a routine to find the proper disk.

5. `exact_lock` is a locking function for this code once the
    `exact_match` routine finds the proper disk.

6. Disk is the handle used for the `exact_match` and `exact_lock`
    functions to identify a specific disk.

Line 198

`register_disk` checks for partitions and adds them to the filesystem.

Line 199

Register the request queue for this particular region.

5.2.4   Device Operations

The basic generic block device has `open`, `close` (release), `ioctl`, and most important, the `request` function. At the least, the `open` and `close` functions could be simple usage counters. The `ioctl()` interface can be used for debug and performance measurements by bypassing the various software layers. The `request` function, which is called when a request is put on the queue by the filesystem, extracts the request structure and acts upon its contents. Depending on whether the request is a read or write, the device takes the appropriate action.

The request queue is not accessed directly, but by a set of helper routines. (These can be found in `drivers/block/elevator.c` and `include/linux/blkdev.h`.) In keeping with our basic device model, we want to include the ability to act on the next request in our `request` function:

```
-------------------------------------------------------------------
drivers/block/elevator.c
186  struct request *elv_next_request(request_queue_t *q)
-------------------------------------------------------------------
```

This helper function returns a pointer to the next request structure. By examining the elements, the driver can glean all the information needed to determine the size, direction, and any other custom operations associated with this request.

When the driver finishes this request, it indicates this to the kernel by using the
`end_request()` helper function:

```
-----------------------------------------------------------------------
drivers/block/ll_rw_blk.c
2599  void end_request(struct request *req, int uptodate)
2600  {
2601  if (!end_that_request_first(req, uptodate, req->hard_cur_sectors)) {
2602  add_disk_randomness(req->rq_disk);
2603  blkdev_dequeue_request(req);
2604  end_that_request_last(req);
2605  }
2606  }
-----------------------------------------------------------------------
```

Line 2599

Pass in the request queue acquired from `elev_next_request()`,

Line 2601

`end_that_request_first()` transfers the proper number of sectors. (If sectors
are pending, `end_request()` simply returns.)

Line 2602

Add to the system entropy pool. The entropy pool is the system method for generating random numbers from a function fast enough to be called at interrupt time.
The basic idea is to collect bytes of data from various drivers in the system and generate a random number from them. Chapter10, "Adding Your Code to the Kernel,"
discusses this. Another explanation is at the head of the file `/drivers/char/
random.c`.

Line 2603

Remove request structure from the queue.

Line 2604

Collect statistics and make the structure available to be free.

From this point on, the generic driver services requests until it is released.

Referring to Figure 5.4, we now have the generic block device layer constructing
and maintaining the request queue. The final layer in the block I/O system is the
hardware (or specific) device driver. The hardware device driver uses the request

queue helper routines from the generic layer to service requests from its registered request queue and send notifications when the request is complete.

The hardware device driver has intimate knowledge of the underlying hardware with regard to register locations, I/O, timing, interrupts, and DMA (discussed in the "Direct Memory Access [DMA]" section of this chapter). The complexities of a complete driver for IDE or SCSI are beyond the scope of this chapter. We offer more on hardware device drivers in Chapter 10 and a series of projects to help you produce a skeleton driver to build on.

5.2.5   Character Device Overview

Unlike the block device, the character device sends a stream of data. All serial devices are character devices. When we use the classic examples of a keyboard controller or a serial terminal as a character stream device, it is intuitively clear we cannot (nor would we want to) access the data from these devices out of order. This introduces the gray area for packetized data transmission. The Ethernet medium at the physical transmission layer is a serial device, but at the bus level, it uses DMA to transfer large chunks of data to and from memory.

As device driver writers, we can make anything happen in the hardware, but real-time practicality is the governing force keeping us from randomly accessing an audio stream or streaming data to our IDE drive. Although both sound like attractive challenges, we still have two simple rules we must follow:

- All Linux device I/O is based on files.
- All Linux device I/O is either character or block.

The parallel port driver at the end of this chapter is a character device driver. Similarities between character and block drivers is the file I/O-based interface. Externally, both types use file operations such as open, close, read, and write. Internally, the most obvious difference between a character device driver and a block device driver is that the character device does not have the block device system of request queues for read and write operations (as previously discussed). It is often the case that for a non-buffered character device, an interrupt is asserted for each element (character) received. To contrast this to a block device, a chunk(s) of data is retrieved and an interrupt is then asserted.

5.2.6   A Note on Network Devices

Network devices have attributes of both block and character devices and are often thought of as a special set of devices. Like a character device, at the physical level, data is transmitted serially. Like a block device, data is packetized and moved to and from the network controller via direct memory access (discussed in the "Direct Memory Access [DMA]" section).

Network devices need to be mentioned as I/O in this chapter, but because of their complexity, they are beyond the scope of this book.

5.2.7   Clock Devices

Clocks are I/O devices that count the hardware *heartbeat* of the system. Without the concept of elapsed time, Linux would cease to function. Chapter 7, "Scheduling and Kernel Synchronization," covers the system and real-time clocks.

5.2.8   Terminal Devices

The earliest terminals were teletype machines (hence the name `tty` for the serial port driver). The teletypewriter had been in development since the turn of the century with the desire to send and read real text over telegraph lines. By the early 1960s, the teletype had matured with the early RS-232 standard, and it seemed to be a match for the growing number of the day's minicomputers. For communicating with computers, the teletype gave way to the terminal of the 1970s. True terminals are becoming a rare breed. Popular with mainframe and minicomputers in the 1970s to the mid 1980s, they have given way to PCs running terminal-emulator software packages. The terminal itself (often called a "dumb" terminal) was simply a monitor and keyboard device that communicated with a mainframe by using serial communications. Unlike the PC, it had only enough "smarts" to send and receive text data.

The main console (configurable at boot time) is the first terminal to come up on a Linux system. Often, a graphical interface is launched, and terminal emulator windows are used thereafter.

5.2.9   Direct Memory Access (DMA)

The DMA controller is a hardware device that is situated between an I/O device and (usually) the high-performance bus in the system. The purpose of the DMA controller is to move large amounts of data without processor intervention. The DMA controller can be thought of as a dedicated processor programmed to move blocks of data to and from main memory. At the register level, the DMA controller takes a source and destination address and length to complete its task. Then, while the main processor is idle, it can send a burst of data from a device to memory, or from memory to memory or from memory to a device.

Many controllers (disk, network, and graphics) have a DMA engine built-in and can therefore transfer large amounts of data without using precious processor cycles.

Summary

This chapter described how the Linux kernel handles input and output.

More specifically, we covered the following topics:

- We provided an overview of the hardware the Linux kernel uses to perform low-level input and output, such as bridges and busses.

- We covered how Linux represents and interfaces with block devices.

- We introduced the varieties of Linux schedulers and request queues: no-op, deadline, and anticipatory.

Project: Building a Parallel Port Driver

This project introduces a basic parallel port controller, which demonstrates how the I/O routines previously discussed coalesce. The parallel port, usually integrated into the Superio section of a chipset, is a good example for a character device-driver skeleton. This driver, or dynamically loaded **module**, is not extremely useful, but you can build upon and improve it. Because we address the device at the register level, this module can be used in a PowerPC system for accessing I/O as long as the register I/O mapping is documented.

Our parallel port device driver uses the standard `open()`, `close()`, and most importantly, the `ioctl()` interface to illustrate the architecture and inner workings of the device driver. We won't be using the `read()` or `write()` functions in this project because the `ioctl()` call returns register values. (Because our device driver is a dynamically loadable module, we simply refer to it as a module.)

We begin with a brief description on how to talk to the parallel port and then proceed to investigate our basic character device-driver module operations. We use the `ioctl()` interface to reference the individual registers in the device, and create an application to interface with our module.

Parallel Port Hardware

Any Web search of the parallel port yields a massive amount of information. Because our goal for this section is to describe a Linux module, we touch only on the basics of this device.

For this project, we use an x86 system for the experiment. This driver skeleton is easily ported to PowerPC; it just needs to talk to another device at the I/O level. Although the parallel port exists in many embedded PowerPC implementations, it is not widely used in desktops (such as the G4 and G5).

For the actual communication with the parallel port registers, we use `inb()` and `outb()`. We could have just as easily used `readb()` and `writeb()`, which are available in the file `io.h` for both x86 and PPC architectures. The `readb()` and `writeb()` macros are a good choice for architecture independence because they each resolve to the low-level I/O routines that are used for x86 and PPC.

The parallel port in x86 systems is usually included as a part of the Superio device or it could be a separate (PCI) card added to the system. If you go to your BIOS setup screen, you can see where the parallel port(s) is mapped in the system I/O space. For x86 systems, the parallel port will be at hex address 0x278, 0x378, or 0x3bc using IRQ 7. This is the **base** address of the device. The parallel port has three 8-bit registers, starting at the base address shown in Table 5.2. For this example, we use a base address of 0x378.

TABLE 5.2
Parallel Port Registers

Bit	7	6	5	4	3	2	1	0	I/O Port Address
Data register (output)	D7	D6	D5	D4	D3	D2	D1	D0	0x378 (base+0)
Status register (input)	Busy*	ACK	Paper end	Select	Error				0x379 (base+1)
Control register (output)					Select*	Init	Auto feed*	Strobe*	0x37A (base+2)

* Active low

The data register contains the 8 bits to write out to the pins on the connector.

The status register contains the input signals from the connector.

The control register sends specific control signals to the connector.

The connector for the parallel port is a 25-pin D-shell (DB-25). Table 5.3 shows how these signals map to the specific pins of the connector.

TABLE 5.3
Association of Signals to Pins of the Parallel Connector

Signal Name	Pin Number
Strobe	1
D0	2
D1	3
D2	4

continues

TABLE 5.3
Continued

Signal Name	Pin Number
D3	5
D4	6
D5	7
D6	8
D7	9
Acknowledge	10
Busy	11
Paper end	12
Select in	13
Auto feed	14
Error	15
Initialize	16
Select	17
Ground	18–25

CAUTION! The parallel port can be sensitive to static electricity and overcurrent. Do not use your integrated (built in to the motherboard) parallel port unless

· You are certain of your hardware skills.

· You have no problem destroying your port—or worse, your motherboard.

We **strongly suggest** that you use a parallel-port adapter card for these, and all, experiments.

For input operations, we will jumper **D7** (pin 9) to **Acknowledge** (pin 10) and **D6** (pin 8) to **Busy** (pin 11) with 470 ohm resistors. To monitor output, we drive LEDs with data pins **D0** through **D4** by using a 470 ohm **current limiting** resistor. We can do this by using an old printer cable or a 25-pin male D-Shell connector from a local electronics store.

NOTE A good register-level programmer should always know as much about the underlying hardware as possible. This includes finding the datasheet for your particular parallel port I/O device. In the datasheet, you can find the sink/source current limitations for your device. Many Web sites feature interface methods to the parallel port, including isolation, expanding the number of signals, and pull-up and pull-down resistors. They are a *must read* for any I/O controller work beyond the scope of this example.

This module addresses the parallel port by way of the `outb()` and `inb()` functions. Recall from Chapter 2, "Exploration Toolkit," that, depending on the platform compilation, these functions correctly implement the `in` and `out` instructions for x86 and the `lbz` and `stb` instructions for the memory-mapped I/O of the PowerPC. This inline code can be found in the `/io.h` file under the appropriate platform.

Parallel Port Software

The following discussion focuses on the pertinent driver functions for this project. The complete program listing for `parll.c`, along with `Make` and `parll.h` files, is included at the end of this book.

1) Setting Up the File Operations (fops)

As previously mentioned, this module uses `open()`, `close()`, and `ioctl()`, as well as the `init` and `cleanup` operations discussed in previous projects.

The first step is to set up our file operations structure. This structure defined in `/linux/fs.h` lists the possible functions we can choose to implement in our module. We do not have to itemize each operation—only the ones we want. A Web search of **C99** and **linux module** furnishes more information on this methodology. By using this structure, we inform the kernel of the location of our implementation (or entry points) of `open`, `release`, and `ioctl`.

```
-----------------------------------------------------------------------
parll.c
struct file_operations parlport_fops = {
    .open =    parlport_open,
    .ioctl =   parlport_ioctl,
    .release = parlport_close };

-----------------------------------------------------------------------
```

Next, we create the functions open() and close(). These are essentially dummy functions used to flag when we have opened and closed:

```
---------------------------------------------------------------------
parll.c

static int parlport_open(struct inode *ino, struct file *filp)
{
  printk("\n parlport open function");
  return 0;
}

static int parlport_close(struct inode *ino, struct file *filp)
{
  printk("\n parlport close function");
  return 0;
}

---------------------------------------------------------------------
```

Create the ioctl() function. Note the following declarations were made at the beginning of parll.c:

```
---------------------------------------------------------------------
#define MODULE_NAME  "parll"
static int base = 0x378;


parll.c
static int parlport_ioctl(struct inode *ino, struct file *filp,
     unsigned int ioctl_cmd, unsigned long parm)
{
  printk("\n parlport ioctl function");
  if(_IOC_TYPE(ioctl_cmd) != IOCTL_TYPE)
  {
   printk("\n%s wrong ioctl type",MODULE_NAME);
   return -1;
  }
  switch(ioctl_cmd)
  {
   case DATA_OUT:
    printk("\n%s ioctl data out=%x",MODULE_NAME,(unsigned int)parm);
    outb(parm & 0xff, base+0);
    return (parm & 0xff);

   case GET_STATUS:
    parm = inb(base+1);
    printk("\n%s ioctl get status=%x",MODULE_NAME,(unsigned int)parm);
    return parm;
```

```
  case CTRL_OUT:
   printk("\n%s ioctl ctrl out=%x",MODULE_NAME,(unsigned int)parm);
   outb(parm && 0xff, base+2);
   return 0;

 }  //end switch
 return 0;
} //end ioctl
```

The ioctl() function is made available to handle any user-defined command. In our module, we surface the three registers associated with the parallel port to the user. The DATA_OUT command sends a value to the **data** register, the GET_STATUS command reads from the **status** register, and finally, the CTRL_OUT command is available to set the control signals to the port. Although a better methodology would be to hide the device specifics behind the read() and write() routines, this module is mainly for experimentation with I/O, not data encapsulation.

The three commands just used are defined in the header file parll.h. They are created by using the IOCTL helper routines for type checking. Rather than using an integer to represent an IOCTL function, we use the IOCTL type checking macro IO(*type*, *number*), where the type is defined as *p* (for parallel port) and *number* is the actual IOCTL number used in the case statement. At the beginning of parlport_ioctl(), we check the type, which should be **p**. Because the **application** code uses the same header file as the driver, the interface will be consistent.

2) Setting Up the Module Initialization Routine

The initialization module is used to associate the module with the operating system. It can also be used for early initialization of any data structures if desired. Since the parallel port driver requires no complex data structures, we simply register the module.

```
parll.c
static int parll_init(void)
{
  int retval;

  retval= register_chrdev(Major, MODULE_NAME, &parlport_fops);
  if(retval < 0)
  {
   printk("\n%s: can't register",MODULE_NAME);
   return retval;
```

```
 }
 else
 {
  Major=retval;
  printk("\n%s:registered, Major=%d",MODULE_NAME,Major);

  if(request_region(base,3,MODULE_NAME))
   printk("\n%s:I/O region busy.",MODULE_NAME);

 }
 return 0;
}
```

The `init_module()` function is responsible for registering the module with the kernel. The `register_chrdev()` function takes in the requested major number (discussed in Section 5.2 and later in Chapter 10; if 0, the kernel assigns one to the module). Recall that the major number is kept in the `inode` structure, which is pointed to by the `dentry` structure, which is pointed to by a file struct. The second parameter is the name of the device as it will appear in `/proc/devices`. The third parameter is the file operations structure that was just shown.

Upon successfully registering, our `init` routine calls `request_region()` with the base address of the parallel port and the length (in bytes) of the range of registers we are interested in.

The `init_module()` function returns a negative number upon failure.

3) Setting Up the Module Cleanup Routine

The `cleanup_module()` function is responsible for unregistering the module and releasing the I/O range that we requested earlier:

----
parll.c

```
static void parll_cleanup( void )
{
    printk("\n%s:cleanup ",MODULE_NAME);
    release_region(base,3);
    unregister_chrdev(Major,MODULE_NAME);
}
```

Finally, we include the required `init` and cleanup entry points.

```
---------------------------------------------------------------------
parll.c
module_init(parll_init);
module_exit(parll_cleanup);
---------------------------------------------------------------------
```

4) Inserting the Module

We can now insert our module into the kernel, as in the previous projects, by using

```
Lkp:~# insmod parll.ko
```

Looking at `/var/log/messages` shows us our `init()` routine output as before, but make specific note of the **major** number returned.

In previous projects, we simply inserted and removed our module from the kernel. We now need to associate our module with the filesystem with the `mknod` command. From the command line, enter the following:

```
Lkp:~# mknod /dev/parll c <XXX> 0
```

The parameters:

- **c**. Create a character special file (as opposed to block)

- **/dev/parll**. The path to our device (for the open call)

- **XXX**. The **major** number returned at `init` time (from `/var/log/messages`)

- **0**. The minor number of our device (not used in this example)

For example, if you saw a major number of 254 in `/var/log/messages`, the command would look like this:

```
Lkp:~# mknod /dev/parll c 254 0
```

5) Application Code

Here, we created a simple application that opens our module and starts a binary count on the D0 through D7 output pins.

Compile this code with `gcc app.c`. The executable output defaults to `a.out`:

```
-------------------------------------------------------------------------
app.c
000  //application to use parallel port driver

#include <fcntl.h>
#include <linux/ioctl.h>
004  #include "parll.h"

main()
{
  int fptr;
  int i,retval,parm =0;

  printf("\nopening driver now");
012    if((fptr = open("/dev/parll",O_WRONLY))<0)
  {
   printf("\nopen failed, returned=%d",fptr);
   exit(1);
  }


018    for(i=0;i<0xff;i++)
  {
020      system("sleep .2");
021      retval=ioctl(fptr,DATA_OUT,parm);
022      retval=ioctl(fptr,GET_STATUS,parm);

024    if(!(retval & 0x80))
    printf("\nBusy signal count=%x",parm);
   if(retval & 0x40)
027      printf("\nAck signal count=%x",parm);
028  //   if(retval & 0x20)
//    printf("\nPaper end signal count=%x",parm);
//    if(retval & 0x10)
//    printf("\nSelect signal count=%x",parm);
//    if(retval & 0x08)
033  //     printf("\nError signal count=%x",parm);

   parm++;
  }

038    close(fptr);

}
-------------------------------------------------------------------------
```

Line 4

The header file common to both the application and the driver contains the new IOCTL helper macros for type checking.

Line 12

Open the driver to get a file handle for our module.

Line 18

Enter the loop.

Line 20

Slow down the loop so we can watch the lights/count.

Line 21

Using the file pointer, send a DATA_OUT command to the module, which in turn uses outb() to write the least significant 8 bits of the parameter to the data port.

Line 22

Read the status byte by way of the ioctl with a GET_STATUS command. This uses inb() and returns the value.

Lines 24–27

Watch for our particular bits of interest. Note that Busy* is an active low signal, so when the I/O is off, we read this as true.

Lines 28–33

Uncomment these as you improve on the design.

Line 38

Close our module.

If you have built the connector as outlined in Figure 5.5, the busy and ack signals come on when the two most significant bits of the count are on. The application code reads these bits and outputs accordingly.

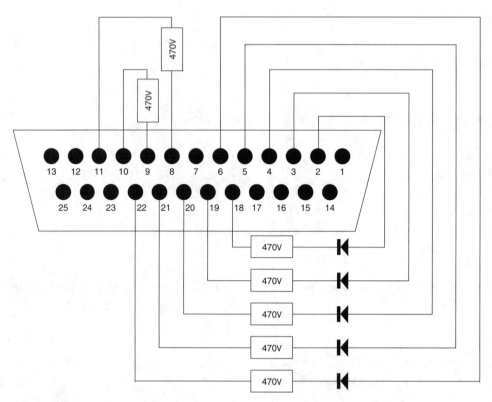

FIGURE 5.5
Built Connector

We just outlined the major elements for a character device driver. By knowing these functions, it is easier to trace through working code or create your own driver. Adding an interrupt handler to this module involves a call to request_irq() and passing in the desired IRQ and the name of the handler. This would be included in the init_module().

Here are some suggested additions to the driver:

- Make parallel port module service-timer interrupts to poll input.

  - How can we multiplex 8 bits of I/O into 16, 32, 64? What is sacrificed?

  - Send a character out the serial port from the write routine within the module.

  - Add an interrupt routine by using the ack signal.

Exercises

1. Load a module. What device file does the module become in the filesystem?

2. Find the major and minor number for the device file that was loaded.

3. When would it be advantageous to use the deadline I/O scheduler instead of an anticipatory I/O scheduler?

4. When would it be better to use the no-op I/O scheduler instead of the anticipatory I/O scheduler?

5. What are the characteristics of a Northbridge controller and a Southbridge controller?

6. What is the advantage of rolling up so much function into a Superio chip?

7. Why would we not see graphics or network communications rolled into a Superio chip at this time?

8. What is the main difference and advantage of a *journaled* filesystem, such as `ext3`, over a standard filesystem like `ext2`?

9. What is the basic theory behind anticipatory I/O scheduling? Is this methodology better suited for a hard disk drive or RAM disk?

10. What is the main difference between a *block* and a *character* device? Give examples of each.

11. What is DMA? Why is it an effective way of moving data?

12. What was the original use for the teletype machine?

Chapter 6

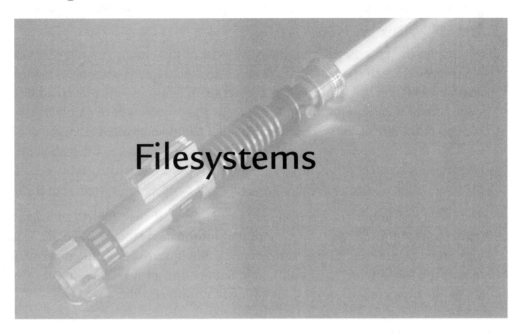

Filesystems

In this chapter

$\mathbf{C}$omputing revolves around the storage, retrieval, and manipulation of information.

In Chapter 3, "Processes: The Principal Model of Execution," we talked about how processes are the basic unit of execution and looked at how a process manipulates information by storing it in its address space. However, the process address space is limited in that it lasts only as long as the process is alive and it holds a fraction of the size of the system memory. The filesystem evolved from the need for large capacity, **non-volatile** storage of information in media other than system registers or memory. Non-volatile information is data that persists despite the termination of the process that manipulates it or operating-system shutdown.

The storage of information on external media presents the problem of how to represent the information. The basic unit of information storage is the **file**. The **filesystem**, or file-management subsystem, is the operating-system component that deals with the file structure, manipulation, and protection. This chapter covers the topics related to the Linux filesystem implementation.

6.1 General Filesystem Concepts

We begin with a description of the concepts behind the Linux filesystem. For many of you, these concepts are familiar because they are tied into Linux usage and the programming of user space applications. If you feel comfortable with general filesystem concepts, skip ahead to Section 6.2, "Linux Virtual Filesystem."

6.1.1 File and Filenames

The word file is terminology borrowed from the real world. Information was stored in files since before the advent of vacuum tubes. A real-world file is composed of one or more pieces of paper of a predetermined size. These files are generally stored in a cabinet.

In Linux, a file is a linear stream of bytes. The significance of these bytes is of no interest to the operating system, but they are of extreme importance to the user, much like the cabinet is indifferent to the contents of its files. The filesystem provides a user interface to data storage and transparently manipulates the physical data from the external drives.

A file in Linux has many attributes and characteristics. The attribute most familiar to a user is usually the file's name. The name of a file often indicates the file's
content. A filename can have a **filename extension**, which is an additional name
appended to the primary filename with a period. This extension provides an additional manner of distinguishing content to user space applications. For example, all
the example files we've looked at so far have a filename extension of .h or .c. User
space programs, such as compilers and linkers, use these as indicators that the files
are header files or source files, respectively.

Although the filename can be important to a user application such as a compiler,
the operating system is indifferent to filenames because it deals only with the file as
a container of bytes irrespective of its content or purpose.

6.1.2   File Types

Linux supports many file types, including regular files, directories, links, device
files, sockets, and pipes. **Regular files** include binary files and ASCII files. ASCII
files are simply lines of text that can be displayed and understood by a user without
any need for an interpreter program. Some ASCII files are executable and are called
scripts. These files are executed by programs called interpreters. The shell, at its
most basic, is an interpreter. Executable binary files are non-ASCII files that seem-
ingly display random data. These files have an internal format that is interpreted by
the kernel to run the program. The format is known as an **object file format**, and
each operating system interprets predetermined object file formats. Chapter 9,
"Building the Linux Kernel," covers object file formats in more detail.

In Linux, files are organized into a hierarchical directory system, such as the one shown
in Figure 6.1. A **directory** contains files and exists to maintain the filesystem structure.
The following sections look at directories and the Linux file structure in more detail.

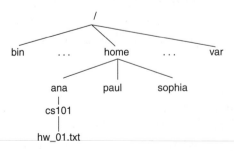

FIGURE 6.1
Filesystem Hierarchy

A **link** is a file that points to another file, a file pointer. These files simply contain the information necessary to access another file.

Device files are representations of I/O devices used to access these hardware devices. Programs that need to access an I/O device can use the same attributes that apply to files to affect the device on which it is acting. Two main types of devices exist: **block devices**, which transfer data in blocks, and **character devices**, which transfer data in characters. Chapter 5, "Input/Output," covers the details of I/O devices.

Sockets and **pipes** are forms of Interprocess Communication (IPC). These files support directional data flow between processes. We do not discuss these special files.

6.1.3   Additional File Attributes

A file has more attributes than its name, type, and data. The operating system associates additional information with each file, such as permissions for file access. File protection becomes increasingly important in multiuser systems, such as Linux. Users are classified into three categories:

- User or owner of the file

- Group or the users that belong to the group that owns the file

- Other, which is the catch-all for the rest of the users on the system who do not belong to the file's group

For each of these users, the file allows a particular set of permissions. Although many operations can be applied to a file, Linux summarizes permissions as they apply to three file operations: read, write, and execute. Because each of these three classes is applied to each of the three user categories, a file has nine sets of permissions associated with it.

Other attributes include file size, creation timestamp, and last-access timestamp, all of which are displayed by the core utility ls. When we look at the kernel's implementation of files, we see that many other attributes are not visible to the user.

6.1.4   Directories and Pathnames

A directory is a file that maintains the hierarchical structure of the filesystem. The directory keeps track of the files it contains, any directories beneath it, and information about itself. In Linux, each user gets his own "home directory," under which he stores his files and creates his own directory tree structure. In Figure 6.1, we see how the directory contributes to the tree structure of the filesystem.

With the arrangement of the filesystem into a tree structure, the filename alone is not sufficient to locate the file; we must know where it is located in the tree to find it. A file's **pathname** describes the location of the file. A file's location can be described with respect to the root of the tree, which is known as the **absolute pathname**. The absolute pathname starts with the root directory, which is referred to as `/`. A directory node's name is the directory name followed by a `/`, such as `bin/`. Thus, a file's absolute pathname is expressed as a collection of all the directory nodes one traverses in the tree until one reaches the file. In Figure 6.1, the absolute pathname of the file called `hw1.txt` is `/home/ana/cs101/hw1.txt`. Another way of representing a file is with a **relative pathname**. This depends on the **working directory** of the process associated with the file. The working directory, or current directory, is a directory associated with the execution of a process. Hence, if `/home/ana/` is the working directory for our process, we can refer to the file as `cs101/hw1.txt`.

In Linux, directories contain files that perform varying tasks during the operation of the operating system. For example, shareable files are stored under `/usr` and `/opt` whereas unshareable files are stored under `/etc/` and `/boot`. In the same manner, non-static files, those whose contents are changed by system programs, are stored under the `vcertain` directories under `/var`. Refer to `http://www.pathname.com/fhs` for more information on the filesystem hierarchy standard.

In Linux, each directory has two entries associated with it: `.` (pronounced "dot") and `..` (pronounced "dot dot"). The `.` entry denotes the current directory and `..` denotes the parent directory. For the root directory, `.` and `..` denote the current directory. (In other words, the root directory is its own parent.) This notation plays into relative pathnames in the following manner. In our previous example, the working directory was `/home/ana` and the relative pathname of our file was `csw101/hw1.txt`. The relative pathname of a `hw1.txt` file in `paul`'s directory from within our working directory is `../paul/cs101/hw1.txt` because we first have to go up a level.

6.1.5   File Operations

File operations include all operations that the system allows on the files. Generally, files can be created and destroyed, opened and closed, read and written.

Additionally, files can also be renamed and its attributes can be changed. The filesystem provides system calls as interfaces to these operations, and these are in turn placed in wrapper functions that are made accessible to user space applications by way of linkable libraries. We explore some of these operations as we traverse through the implementation of the Linux filesystem.

6.1.6   File Descriptors

A file descriptor is an `int` datatype that the system uses to identify an open file. The `open()` system call returns a file descriptor that can later be used on all future operations to be visited upon that file by that process. In a later section, we see what the file descriptor stands for in kernel terms.

Each process holds an array of file descriptors. When we discuss the kernel structures that support the filesystem, we see how this information is maintained in an array. It is by convention that the first element of the array (file descriptor 0) is associated with the process' standard input, the second (file descriptor 1) with standard output, and the third (file descriptor 2) with standard error. This allows applications to open a file on standard input, output, or error. Figure 6.2 illustrates the file descriptor array pertaining to a process.

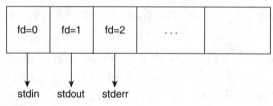

FIGURE 6.2
File Descriptor Array

File descriptors are assigned on a "lowest available index" basis. Thus, if a process is to open multiple files, the assigned file descriptors will be incrementally higher unless a previously opened file is closed before the new one. We see how the open and close system calls manipulate file descriptors to ensure this. Hence, within a process' lifetime, it might open two different files that will have the same file descriptor if one is closed before the other is opened. Conversely and separately, two different file descriptors can point to the same file.

6.1.7   Disk Blocks, Partitions, and Implementation

To understand the concerns of filesystem implementation, we need to understand some basic concepts about hard disks. Hard disks magnetically record data. A hard disk contains multiple rotating disks on which data is recorded. A **head**, which is mounted on a mechanical arm that moves over the surface of the disk, reads and writes the data by moving along the radius of the disks, much like the needle of a turntable. The disks themselves rotate much like LP's on a turntable. Each disk is broken up into concentric rings called **tracks**. Tracks are numbered starting from the outside to the inside of the disk. Groups of the same numbered tracks (across the disks) are called **cylinders**. Each track is in turn broken up into (usually) 512K byte sectors. Cylinders, tracks, and heads make up the **geometry** of a hard drive.

A blank disk must first be **formatted** before the filesystem is made. Formatting creates tracks, blocks, and **partitions** in a disk. A partition is a **logical disk** and is how the operating system allocates or uses the geometry of the hard drive. The partitions provide a way of dividing a single hard disk to look as though there were multiple disks. This allows different filesystems to reside in a common disk. Each partition is split up into tracks and blocks. The creation of **tracks** and **blocks** in a disk is done by way of programs such as `fdformat`[1] whereas the creation of logical partitions is done by programs such as `fdisk`. Both of these precede creation of the actual filesystem.

The Linux file tree can provide access to more than one filesystem. This means that if you have a disk with multiple partitions, each of which has a filesystem, it is possible to view all these filesystems from one logical namespace. This is done by attaching each filesystem to the main Linux filesystem tree by using the `mount` command. We say that a filesystem is mounted to refer to the fact that the device filesystem is attached and accessible from the main tree. Filesystems are mounted onto directories.[2] The directory onto which a filesystem is mounted is referred to as the **mount point**.

---

[1]   fdformat is used for low-level formatting (track and sector creation) of floppies. IDE and SCSI disks are generally preformatted at the factory.

[2]   In tree parlance, you would say that you are attaching a subtree to a node in the main tree.

One of the main difficulties in filesystem implementation is in determining how the operating system will keep track of the sequence of bytes that make up a file. As previously mentioned, the disk partition space is split into chunks of space called blocks. The size of a block varies by implementation. The management of blocks determines the speed of file access and the level of fragmentation[3] and therefore wasted space. For example, if we have a block size of 1,024 bytes and a file size of 1,567 bytes, the file spans two blocks. The operating system keeps track of the blocks that belong to a particular file by keeping the information in a structure called an **index node** (**inode**).

6.1.8   Performance

There are various ways in which the filesystem improves system performance. One way is by maintaining internal infrastructure in the kernel that quickly accesses an inode that corresponds to a given pathname. We see how the kernel does this when we explain filesystem implementation.

The page cache is another method in which the filesystem improves performance. The page cache is an in-memory collection of pages. It is designed to cache many different types of pages, originating from disk files, memory-mapped files, or any other page object the kernel can access. This caching mechanism greatly reduces disk accesses and thus improves system performance. This chapter shows how the page cache interacts with disk accesses in the course of file manipulation.

6.2   Linux Virtual Filesystem

The implementation of filesystems varies from system to system. For example, in Windows, the implementation of how a file relates to a disk block differs from how a file in a UNIX filesystem relates to a disk block. In fact, Microsoft has various implementations of filesystems that correspond to its various operating systems: MS-DOS for DOS and Win 3.x, VFAT for Windows 9x, and NTFS for Windows NT. UNIX operating systems also have various implementations, such as SYSV and MINIX. Linux specifically uses filesystems such as ext2, ext3, and ResierFS.

---

[3] We visited fragmentation in Chapter 4, "Memory Management," and saw how wasted holes in memory can be created. The same kind of fragmentation problems are seen with hard disk storage.

One of the best attributes of Linux is the many filesystems it supports. Not only can you view files from its own filesystems (ext2, ext3, and ReiserFS), but you can also view files from filesystems pertaining to other operating systems. On a single Linux system, you are capable of accessing files from numerous different formats. Table 6.1 lists the currently supported filesystems. To a user, there is no difference between one filesystem and another; he can indiscriminately mount any of the supported filesystems to his original tree namespace.

Linux supports more than on-disk filesystems. It also supports network-mounted filesystems and special filesystems that are used for things other than managing disk space. For example, `procfs` is a pseudo filesystem. This virtual filesystem provides information about different aspects of your system. A `procfs` filesystem does not take up hard disk space and files are created on the fly upon access. Another such filesystem is `devfs`,[4] which provides an interface to device drivers.

TABLE 6.1
Some of the Linux Supported Filesystems

Filesystem Name	Description
ext2	Second extended filesystem
ext3	ext3 journaling filesystem
Reiserfs	Journaling filesystem
JFS	IBM's journaled filesystem
XFS	SGI Irix's high-performance journaling filesystem
MINIX	Original Linux filesystem, minix OS filesystem
ISO9660	CD-ROM filesystem
JOLIET	Microsoft CRDOM filesystem extensions
UDF	Alternative CROM, DVD filesystem
MSDOS	Microsoft Disk Operating System
VFAT	Windows 95 Virtual File Allocation Table

continues

---

[4] In Linux 2.6, `devfs` is obsolete by `udev`, although minimal support is still available. For more information on udev, go to `http://www.kernel.org/pub/linux/utils/kernel/hotplug/udev-FAQ`.

TABLE 6.1
Continued

Filesystem Name	Description
NTFS	Windows NT, 2000, XP, 2003 filesystem
ADFS	Acorn Disk filesystem
HFS	Apple Macintosh filesystem
BEFS	BeOs filesystem
FreeVxfs	Veritas Vxfs support
HPFS	OS/2 support
SysVfs	System V filesystem support
NFS	Networking filesystem support
AFS	Andrew filesystem (also networking)
UFS	BSD filesystem support
NCP	NetWare filesystem
SMB	Samba

Linux achieves this "masquerading" of the physical filesystem specifics by introducing an intermediate layer of abstraction between user space and the physical filesystem. This layer is known as the **virtual filesystem (VFS)**. It separates the filesystem-specific structures and functions from the rest of the kernel. The VFS manages the filesystem-related system calls and translates them to the appropriate filesystem type functions. Figure 6.3 overviews the filesystem-management structure.

The user application accesses the generic VFS through system calls. Each supported filesystem must have an implementation of a set of functions that perform the VFS-supported operations (for example, open, read, write, and close). The VFS keeps track of the filesystems it supports and the functions that perform each of the operations. You know from Chapter 5 that a generic block device layer exists between the filesystem and the actual device driver. This provides a layer of abstraction that allows the implementation of the filesystem-specific code to be independent of the specific device it eventually accesses.

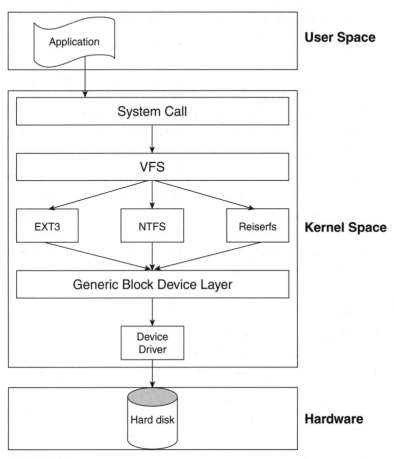

FIGURE 6.3
Linux VFS

6.2.1   VFS Data Structures

The VFS relies on data structures to hold its generic representation of a filesystem.
The data structures are as follows:

- **superblock structure.** Stores information relating to mounted filesystems
- **inode structure.** Stores information relating to files

- **file** structure. Stores information related to files opened by a process

- **dentry** structure. Stores information related to a pathname and the file pointed to

In addition to these structures, the VFS also uses additional structures such as vfsmount, and nameidata, which hold mounting information and pathname lookup information, respectively. We see how these two structures relate to the main ones just described, although we do not independently cover them.

The structures that compose the VFS are associated with actions that can be applied on the object represented by the structure. These actions are defined in a table of operations for each object. The tables of operations are lists of function pointers. We define the operations table for each object as we describe them. We now closely look at each of these structures. (Note that we do not focus on any locking mechanisms for the purposes of clarity and brevity.)

6.2.1.1   superblock Structure

When a filesystem is mounted, all information concerning it is stored is the super_block struct. One superblock structure exists for every mounted filesystem. We show the structure definition followed by explanations of some of the more important fields:

```
----------------------------------------------------------------------
include/linux/fs.h
666   struct super_block {
667     struct list_head    s_list;
668     dev_t       s_dev;
669     unsigned long       s_blocksize;
670     unsigned long       s_old_blocksize;
671     unsigned char       s_blocksize_bits;
672     unsigned char       s_dirt;
673     unsigned long long    s_maxbytes;
674     struct file_system_type   *s_type;
675     struct super_operations   *s_op;
676     struct dquot_operations   *dq_op;
677     struct quotactl_ops   *s_qcop;
678     struct export_operations   *s_export_op;
679     unsigned long       s_flags;
680     unsigned long       s_magic;
681     struct dentry       *s_root;
682     struct rw_semaphore   s_umount;
683     struct semaphore    s_lock;
```

```
684    int     s_count;
685    int     s_syncing;
686    int     s_need_sync_fs;
687    atomic_t    s_active;
688    void    *s_security;
689
690    struct list_head    s_dirty;
691    struct list_head    s_io;
692    struct hlist_head    s_anon;
693    struct list_head    s_files;
694
695    struct block_device    *s_bdev;
696    struct list_head    s_instances;
697    struct quota_info    s_dquot;
698
699    char    s_id[32];
700
701    struct kobject    kobj;
702    void    *s_fs_info;
...
708    struct semaphore    s_vfs_rename_sem;
709    };
```

Line 667

The s_list field is of type list_head,[5] which is a pointer to the next and previous elements in the circular doubly linked list in which this super_block is
embedded. Like many other structures in the Linux kernel, the super_block
structs are maintained in a circular doubly linked list. The list_head datatype
contains pointers to two other list_heads: the list_head of the next
superblock object and the list_head of the previous superblock objects. (The
global variable super_blocks (fs/super.c) points to the first element in the list.)

Line 672

On disk-based filesystems, the superblock structure is filled with information
originally maintained in a special disk sector that is loaded into the superblock
structure. Because the VFS allows editing of fields in the superblock structure, the
information in the superblock structure can find itself out of sync with the on-
disk data. This field identifies that the superblock structure has been edited and
needs to sync up with the disk.

---

[5] Chapter 2, "Exploration Toolkit," describes the list_head datatype in detail.

Line 673

This field of type unsigned long defines the maximum file size allowed in the filesystem.

Line 674

The `superblock` structure contains general filesystem information. However, it needs to be associated with the specific filesystem information (for example, MSDOS, ext2, MINIX, and NFS). The `file_system_type` structure holds filesystem-specific information, one for each type of filesystem configured into the kernel. This field points to the appropriate filesystem-specific struct and is how the VFS manages the interaction from general request to specific filesystem operation.

Figure 6.4 shows the relation between the `superblock` and the `file_system_type` structures. We show how the `superblock->s_type` field points to the appropriate `file_system_type` struct in the **file_systems** list. (In the "Global and Local List References" section later in this chapter, we show what the `file_systems` list is.)

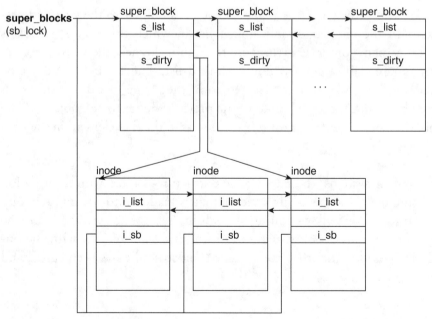

FIGURE 6.4
Relation Between superblock and file_system_type

Line 675

The field is a pointer of type `super_operations` struct. This datatype holds the table of `superblock` operations. The `super_operations` struct itself holds function pointers that are initialized with the particular filesystem's `superblock` operations. The next section explains `super_operations` in more detail.

Line 681

This field is a pointer to a `dentry` struct. The `dentry` struct holds the pathname of a file. This particular `dentry` object is the one associated with the mount directory whose `superblock` this belongs to.

Line 690

The `s_dirty` field (not to be confused with s_dirt) is a `list_head` struct that points to the first and last elements in the list of dirty inodes belonging to this filesystem.

Line 693

The `s_files` field is a `list_head` struct that points to the first element of a list of file structs that are both in use and assigned to the `superblock`. In the "file Structure" section, you see that this is one of the three lists in which a file structure can find itself.

Line 696

The field of `s_instances` is a `list_head` structure that points to the adjacent `superblock` elements in the list of `superblocks` with the same filesystem type. The head of this list is referenced by the `fs_supers` field of the `file_system_type` structure.

Line 702

This void * data type points to additional `superblock` information that is specific to a particular filesystem (for example, `ext3_sb_info`). This acts as a sort of catch-all for any `superblock` data on disk for that specific filesystem that was not abstracted out into the virtual filesystem `superblock` concept.

6.2.1.2   superblock Operations

The s_op field of the superblock points to a table of operations that the filesystem's superblock can perform. This list is specific to each filesystem because it
operates directly on the filesystem's implementation. The table of operations is
stored in a structure of type **super_operations**:

```
-------------------------------------------------------------------
include/linux/fs.h
struct super_operations {
  struct inode *(*alloc_inode)(struct super_block *sb);
  void (*destroy_inode)(struct inode *);

  void (*read_inode) (struct inode *);

  void (*dirty_inode) (struct inode *);
  void (*write_inode) (struct inode *, int);
  void (*put_inode) (struct inode *);
  void (*drop_inode) (struct inode *);
  void (*delete_inode) (struct inode *);
  void (*put_super) (struct super_block *);
  void (*write_super) (struct super_block *);
  int (*sync_fs)(struct super_block *sb, int wait);
  void (*write_super_lockfs) (struct super_block *);
  void (*unlockfs) (struct super_block *);
  int (*statfs) (struct super_block *, struct kstatfs *);
  int (*remount_fs) (struct super_block *, int *, char *);
  void (*clear_inode) (struct inode *);
  void (*umount_begin) (struct super_block *);

  int (*show_options)(struct seq_file *, struct vfsmount *);
};
-------------------------------------------------------------------
```

When the superblock of a filesystem is initialized, the s_op field is set to point
at the appropriate table of operations. In the "Moving from the Generic to the
Specific" section later in this chapter, we show how this table of operations is implemented in the ext2 filesystem. Table 6.2 shows the list of superblock operations.
Some of these functions are optional and are only filled in by a subset of the supported filesystems. Those that do not support a particular optional function set the
field to NULL in the operations struct.

TABLE 6.2
Superblock Operations

Superblock Operations Name	Description
alloc_inode	New in 2.6. It allocates and initializes a vfs inode under the superblock. The specifics of initialization are left up to the particular filesystem. The allocation is done with a call to kmem_cache_create() or kemem_cache_alloc() (see Chapter 4) on the inode's cache.
destroy_inode	New in 2.6. It deallocates the specified inode pertaining to the superblock. The deallocation is done with a call to kmem_cache_free().
read_inode	Reads the inode specified by the inode->i_ino field. The inode's fields are updated from the on-disk data. Particularly important is inode->i_op.
dirty_inode	Places an inode in the superblock's dirty inode list. The head and tail of the circular, doubly linked list is referenced by way of the superblock->s_dirty field. Figure 6.5 illustrates a superblock's dirty inode list.
write_inode	Writes the inode information to disk.
put_inode	Releases the inode from the inode cache. It's called by iput().
drop_inode	Called when the last access to an inode is dropped.
delete_inode	Deletes an inode from disk. Used on inodes that are no longer needed. It's called from generic_delete_inode().
put_super	Frees the superblock (for example, when unmounting a filesystem).

continues

TABLE 6.2
Continued

Superblock Operations Name	Description
write_super	Writes the superblock information to disk.
sync_fs	Currently used only by ext3, Resiserfs, XFS, and JFS, this function writes out dirty `superblock` struct data to the disk.
write_super_lockfs	In use by ext3, JFS, Resierfs, and XFS, this function blocks changes to the filesystem. It then updates the disk superblock.
unlockfs	Reverses the block set by the `write_super_lockfs()` function.
stat_fs	Called to get filesystem statistics.
remount_fs	Called when the filesystem is remounted to update any mount options.
clear_inode	Releases the inode and all pages associated with it.
umount_begin	Called when a mount operation must be interrupted.
show_options	Used to get filesystem information from a mounted filesystem.

This completes our introduction of the `superblock` structure and its operations. Now, we explore the `inode` structure in detail.

6.2.1.3   inode Structure

We mentioned that inodes are structures that keep track of file information, such as pointers, to the blocks that contain all the file data. Recall that directories, devices, and pipes (for example) are also represented as files in the kernel, so an inode can represent one of them as well. Inode objects exist for the full lifetime of the file and contain data that is maintained on disk.

Inodes are kept in lists to facilitate referencing. One list is a hash table that reduces the time it takes to find a particular inode. An inode also finds itself in one of three types of doubly linked list. Table 6.3 shows the three list types. Figure 6.5 shows the relationship between a `superblock` structure and its list of dirty inodes.

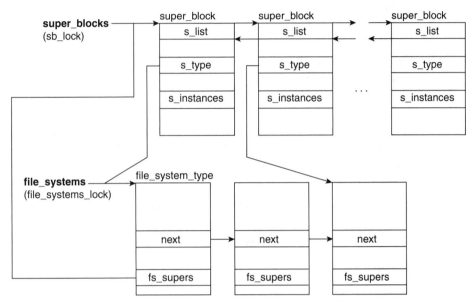

FIGURE 6.5
Relation Between Superblock and Inode

The `inode` struct is large and has many fields. The following is a description of a small subset of the `inode` struct fields:

```
----------------------------------------------------------------
include/linux/fs.h
368  struct inode {
369    struct hlist_node    i_hash;
370    struct list_head     i_list;
371    struct list_head     i_dentry;
372    unsigned long        i_ino;
373    atomic_t     i_count;
...
390    struct inode_operations   *i_op;
...
392    struct super_block    *i_sb;
...
407    unsigned long     i_state;
...
421  };
----------------------------------------------------------------
```

Line 369

The `i_hash` field is of type `hlist_node`.[6] This contains a pointer to the hash list, which is used for speedy inode lookup. The inode hash list is referenced by the global variable `inode_hashtable`.

Line 370

This field links to the adjacent structures in the inode lists. Inodes can find themselves in one of the three linked lists.

TABLE 6.3
Inode Lists

List	i_count	Dirty	Reference Pointer
Valid, unused	i_count = 0	Not dirty	`inode_unused` (global)
Valid, in use	i_count > 0	Not dirty	`inode_in_use` (global)
Dirty inodes	i_count > 0	Dirty	`superblock's s_dirty` field

Line 371

This field points to a list of `dentry` structs that corresponds to the file. The `dentry` struct contains the pathname pertaining to the file being represented by the inode. A file can have multiple `dentry` structs if it has multiple aliases.

Line 372

This field holds the unique inode number. When an inode gets allocated within a particular superblock, this number is an automatically incremented value from a previously assigned inode ID. When the superblock operation `read_inode()` is called, the inode indicated in this field is read from disk.

Line 373

The `i_count` field is a counter that gets incremented with every inode use. A value of 0 indicates that the inode is unused and a positive value indicates that it is in use.

---

[6] `hlist_node` is a type of list pointer for double-linked lists, much like `list_head`. The difference is that the list head (type `hlist_head`) contains a single pointer that points at the first element rather than two (where the second one points at the tail of the list). This reduces overhead for hash tables.

Line 392

This field holds the pointer to the superblock of the filesystem in which the file resides. Figure 6.5 shows how all the inodes in a superblocks' dirty inode list will have their `i_sb` field pointing to a common superblock.

Line 407

This field corresponds to inode state flags. Table 6.4 lists the possible values.

TABLE 6.4
Inode States

Inode State Flags	Description
I_DIRTY_SYNC	See `I_DIRTY` description.
I_DIRTY_DATASYNC	See `I_DIRTY` description.
I_DIRTY_PAGES	See `I_DIRTY` description.
I_DIRTY	This macro correlates to any of the three `I_DIRTY_*` flags. It enables a quick check for any of those flags. The `I_DIRTY*` flags indicate that the contents of the inode have been written to and need to be synchronized.
I_LOCK	Set when the inode is locked and cleared when the inode is unlocked. An inode is locked when it is first created and when it is involved in I/O transfers.
I_FREEING	Gets set when an inode is being removed. This flag serves the purpose of tagging the inode as unusable as it is being deleted so no one takes a new reference to it.
I_CLEAR	Indicates that the inode is no longer useful.
I_NEW	Gets set upon inode creation. The flag gets removed the first time the new inode is unlocked.

An inode with the `I_LOCK` or `I_DIRTY` flags set finds itself in the `inode_in_use` list. Without either of these flags, it is added to the `inode_unused` list.

6.2.1.4   dentry Structure

The `dentry` structure represents a directory entry and the VFS uses it to keep track of relations based on directory naming, organization, and logical layout of files. Each `dentry` object corresponds to a component in a pathname and associates other structures and information that relates to it. For example, in the path `/home/lkp/Chapter06.txt`, there is a `dentry` created for `/`, `home`, `lkp`, and `Chapter06.txt`. Each `dentry` has a reference to that component's inode, superblock, and related information. Figure 6.6 illustrates the relationship between the `superblock`, the `inode`, and the `dentry` structs.

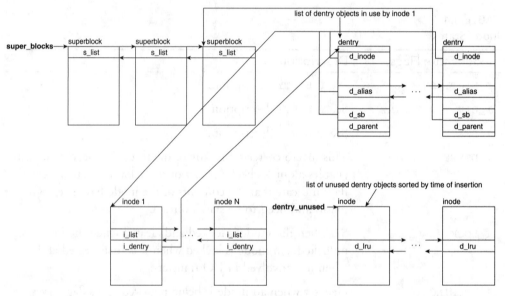

FIGURE 6.6
Relations Between superblock, dentry, and inode

We now look at some of the fields of the `dentry` struct:

```
-----------------------------------------------------------------
include/linux/dcache.h
81   struct dentry {
...
85       struct inode   * d_inode;
86       struct list_head  d_lru;
87       struct list_head  d_child;   /* child of parent list */
88       struct list_head  d_subdirs;   /* our children */
89       struct list_head  d_alias;
90       unsigned long  d_time;   /* used by d_revalidate */
91       struct dentry_operations *d_op;
92       struct super_block  * d_sb;
...
```

```
100    struct dentry   * d_parent;
...
105    } ____cacheline_aligned;
```

Line 85

The `d_inode` field points to the inode corresponding with the file associated with the `dentry`. In the case that the pathname component corresponding with the `dentry` does not have an associated inode, the value is `NULL`.

Lines 85–88

These are the pointers to the adjacent elements in the `dentry` lists. A `dentry` object can find itself in one of the kinds of lists shown in Table 6.5.

TABLE 6.5
Dentry Lists

Listname	List Pointer	Description
Used dentrys	`d_alias`	The inode with which these dentrys are associated points to the head of the list via the `i_dentry` field.
Unused dentrys	`d_lru`	These dentrys are no longer in use but are kept around in case the same components are accessed in a pathname.

Line 91

The `d_op` field points to the table of `dentry` operations.

Line 92

This is a pointer to the superblock associated with the component represented by the `dentry`. Refer to Figure 6.6 to see how a dentry is associated with a `superblock` struct.

Line 100

This field holds a pointer to the parent `dentry`, or the `dentry` corresponding to the parent component in the pathname. For example, in the pathname `/home/paul`, the `d_parent` field of the `dentry` for `paul` points to the `dentry` for `home`, and the `d_parent` field of this `dentry` in turn points to the `dentry` for `/`.

6.2.1.5 file Structure

Another structure that the VFS uses is the file structure. When a process manipulates a file, the file structure is the datatype the VFS uses to hold information regarding the process/file association. Unlike other structures, no original on-disk data is held by a file structure; file structures are created on-the-fly upon the issue of the `open()` syscall and are destroyed upon issue of the `close()` syscall. Recall from Chapter 3 that throughout the lifetime of a process, the file structures representing files opened by the process are referenced through the process descriptor (the `task_struct`). Figure 6.7 illustrates how the file structure associates with the other VFS structures. The `task_struct` points to the file descriptor table, which holds a list of pointers to all the file descriptors that process has opened. Recall that the first three entries in the descriptor table correspond to the file descriptors for `stdin`, `stdout`, and `stderr`, respectively.

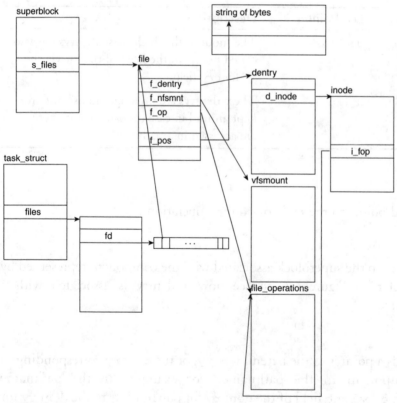

FIGURE 6.7
File Objects

The kernel keeps file structures in circular doubly linked lists. There are three lists in which a file structure can find itself embedded depending on its usage and assignment. Table 6.6 describes the three lists.

The kernel creates the file structure by way of get_empty_filp(). This routine returns a pointer to the file structure or returns NULL if there are no more free structures or if the system has run out of memory.

We now look at some of the more important fields in the file structure:

```
-------------------------------------------------------------------------
include/linux/fs.h
506  struct file {
507    struct list_head    f_list;
508    struct dentry      *f_dentry;
509    struct vfsmount    *f_vfsmnt;
510    struct file_operations  *f_op;
511    atomic_t      f_count;
512    unsigned int      f_flags;
513    mode_t      f_mode;
514    loff_t      f_pos;
515    struct fown_struct    f_owner;
516    unsigned int      f_uid, f_gid;
517    struct file_ra_state    f_ra;
...
527    struct address_space  *f_mapping;
...
529  };
-------------------------------------------------------------------------
```

Line 507

The f_list field of type list_head holds the pointers to the adjacent file structures in the list.

TABLE 6.6
File Lists

Name	Reference Pointer to Head of List	Description
The free file object list	Global variable free_list	A doubly linked list composed of all file objects that are available. The size of this list is always at least NR_RESERVED_FILES large.
The in-use but unassigned file object list	Global variable anon_list	A doubly linked list composed of all file objects that are being used but have not been assigned to a superblock.

continues

TABLE 6.6
Continued

Name	Reference Pointer to Head of List	Description
Superblock file object list	Superblock field `s_files`	A doubly linked list composed of all file objects that have a file associated with a superblock.

Line 508

This is a pointer to the `dentry` structure associated with the file.

Line 509

This is a pointer to the `vfsmount` structure that is associated with the mounted filesystem that the file is in. All filesystems that are mounted have a `vfsmount` structure that holds the related information. Figure 6.8 illustrates the data structures associated with vfsmount structures.

Line 510

This is a pointer to the `file_operations` structure, which holds the table of file operations that can be applied to a file. (The `inodes` field `i_fop` points to the same structure.) Figure 6.7 illustrates this relationship.

Line 511

Numerous processes can concurrently access a file. The `f_count` field is set to 0 when the file structure is unused (and, therefore, available for use). The `f_count` field is set to 1 when it's associated with a file and incremented by one thereafter with each process that handles the file. Thus, if a file object that is in use represents a file accessed by four different processes, the `f_count` field holds a value of 5.

Line 512

The `f_flags` field contains the flags that are passed in via the `open()` syscall. We cover this in more detail in the "open()" section.

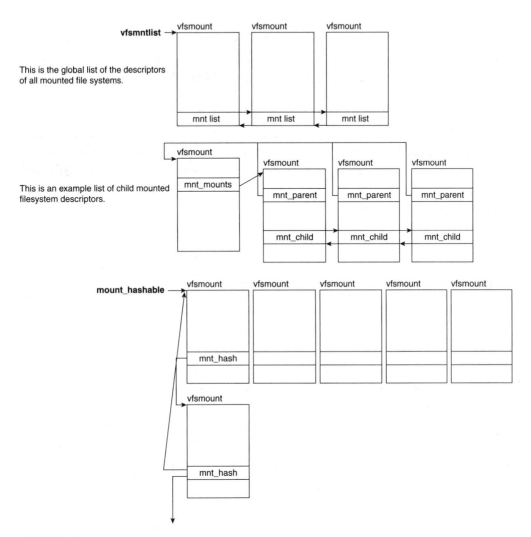

FIGURE 6.8
vfsmount Objects

Line 514

The f_pos field holds the file offset. This is essentially the read/write pointer that some of the methods in the file operations table use to refer to the current position in the file.

Line 516

We need to know who the owner of the process is to determine file access permissions when the file is manipulated. These fields correspond to the uid and the gid of the user who started the process and opened the file structure.

Line 517

A file can read pages from the page cache, which is the in-memory collection of pages, in advance. The read-ahead optimization involves reading adjacent pages of a file prior to any of them being requested to reduce the number of costly disk accesses. The f_ra field holds a structure of type file_ra_state, which contains all the information related to the file's read-ahead state.

Line 527

This field points to the address_space struct, which corresponds to the page-caching mechanism for this file. This is discussed in detail in the "Page Cache" section.

6.2.2   Global and Local List References

The Linux kernel uses global variables that hold pointers to linked lists of the structures previously mentioned. All structures are kept in a doubly linked list. The kernel keeps a pointer to the head of the list using this as an access point to the list. The structures all have fields of type list_head,[7] which they use to point to the previous and next elements in the list. Table 6.7 summarizes the global variables that the kernel holds and the type of list it keeps a reference to.

The super_block, file_system_type, dentry, and vfsmount structures are all kept in their own list. Inodes can find themselves in either global inode_in_use or inode_unused, or in the local list of the superblock under which they correspond. Figure 6.9 shows how some of these structures interrelate.

---

[7]   The inode struct has a variation of this called hlist_node, as we saw in Section 6.2.1.3, "inode Structure."

TABLE 6.7
VFS-Related Global Variables

Global Variable	Structure Type
super_blocks	super_block
file_systems	file_system_type
dentry_unused	dentry
vfsmntlist	vfsmount
inode_in_use	inode
inode_unused	inode

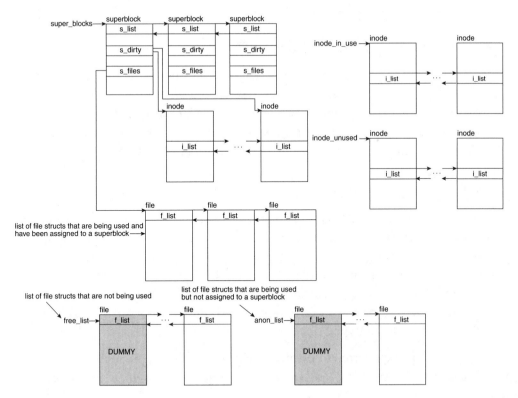

FIGURE 6.9
VFS-Related Global Variables

The `super_blocks` variable points to the head of the superblock list with the elements pointing to the previous and next elements in the list by means of the `s_list` field. The `s_dirty` field of the superblock structure in turn points to the inodes it owns, which need to be synchronized with the disk. Inodes not in a local superblock list are in the `inode_in_use` or `inode_unused` lists. All inodes point to the next and previous elements in the list by way of the `i_list` field.

The superblock also points to the head of the list containing the file structs that have been assigned to that superblock by way of the `s_files` list. The file structs that have not been assigned are placed in one of the `free_list` lists of the `anon_list` list. Both lists have a dummy file struct as the head of the list. All file structs point to the next and previous elements in their list by using the `f_list` field.

Refer to Figure 6.6 to see how the inode points to the list of `dentry` structures by using the `i_dentry` field.

6.3   Structures Associated with VFS

Other than the four main VFS structures, a few other structures interact with VFS: `fs_struct`, `files_struct`, `namespace`, and `fd_set`. The structures `fs_struct`, `files_stuct`, and `namespace` are all process-related objects that contain file-related data. Figure 6.10 relates how a process descriptor associates with file-related structures. We now look at these additional structures.

6.3.1   fs_struct Structure

In Linux, multiple processes could refer to a single file. As a result, the Linux VFS must store information about how processes and files interact. For example, a process started by one user might differ from a process started by another user with respect to permissions related to file operations. The `fs_struct` structure holds all the information associating a particular process to a file. We need to examine the `fs_struct` structure prior to examining the `files_struct` structure because it uses the `fs_struct` datatype.

`fs_struct` can be referred to by multiple process descriptors, so it is not uncommon that an `fs_struct` representing a file is referenced by many `task_struct` descriptors:

```
include/linux/fs_struct.h
 7   struct fs_struct {
 8     atomic_t count;
```

```
 9    rwlock_t lock;
10    int umask;
11    struct dentry * root, * pwd, * altroot;
12    struct vfsmount * rootmnt, * pwdmnt, * altrootmnt;
13    };
```

6.3.1.1   count

The count field holds the number of process descriptors that reference the particular fs_struct.

6.3.1.2   umask

The umask field holds the mask representing the permissions to be set on files opened.

6.3.1.3   root, pwd, and altroot

The root and pwd fields are pointers to the dentry object associated with the process' root directory and current working directory, respectively. altroot is a pointer to the dentry structure of an alternative root directory. This field is used for emulation environments.

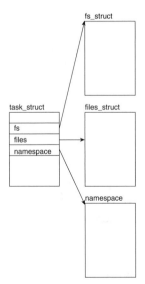

FIGURE 6.10
Process-Related Objects

6.3.1.4   rootmnt, pwdmnt, and altrootmnt

The fields `rootmnt`, `pwdmnt`, and `altrootmnt` are pointers to the mounted
filesystem object of the process' root, current working, and alternative root directories, respectively.

6.3.2   files_struct Structure

`files_struct` contains information related to open files and their descriptors.
In the introduction, we mentioned that file descriptors are unique `int` datatypes
associated with an open file. In kernel terms, the file descriptor is the index into the
`fd` array of the files object of the current task's `task_struct` or `current->files-`
`>fd`. Figure 6.7 shows the `fd` array of a `task_struct` and how it points to the file's
file structure.

Linux can associate sets of file descriptors according to shared qualities, such as
read-only or read-write. The `fd_struct` structure represents the file descriptor sets.
The `files_struct` uses these sets to group its file descriptors:

```
------------------------------------------------------------------
include/linux/file.h
22   struct files_struct {
23     atomic_t count;
24    spinlock_t file_lock
25     int max_fds;
26     int max_fdset;
27     int next_fd;
28     struct file ** fd;
29     fd_set *close_on_exec;
30     fd_set *open_fds;
31     fd_set close_on_exec_init;
32     fd_set open_fds_init;
33     struct file * fd_array[NR_OPEN_DEFAULT];
34   };
------------------------------------------------------------------
```

Line 23

The `count` field exists because the `files_struct` can be referred to by multiple process descriptors, much like the `fs_struct`. This field is incremented in the
kernel routine `fget()` and decremented in the kernel routine `fput()`. These functions are called during the file-closing process.

Line 25

The max_fds field keeps track of the maximum number of files that the process can have open. The default of max_fds is 32 as associated with NR_OPEN_DEFAULT size of the fd_array. When a file wants to open more than 32 files, this value is grown.

Line 26

The max_fdset field keeps track of the maximum number of file descriptors. Similar to max_fds, this field can be expanded if the total number of files the process has open exceeds its value.

Line 27

The next_fd field holds the value of the next file descriptor to be assigned. We see how it is manipulated through the opening and closing of files, but one thing should be understood: File descriptors are assigned in an incremental manner unless a previously assigned file descriptor's associated file is closed. In this case, the next_fd field is set to that value. Thus, file descriptors are assigned in a lowest available value manner.

Line 28

The fd array points to the open file object array. It defaults to fd_array, which holds 32 file descriptors. When a request for more than 32 file descriptors comes in, it points to a newly generated array.

Lines 30–32

close_on_exec, open_fds, close_on_exec_init, and open_fds_init are all fields of type fd_set. We mentioned that the fd_set structure holds sets of file descriptors. Before explaining each field individually, we look at the fd_set structure.

The fd_set datatype can be traced back to a struct that holds an array of unsigned longs, each of which holds a file descriptor:

```
-----------------------------------------------------------------
include/linux/types.h
22  typedef __kernel_fd_set    fd_set;
-----------------------------------------------------------------
```

The `fd_set` datatype is a type definition of `__kernel_fd_set`. This datatype structure holds an array of unsigned longs:

```
include/linux/posix_types.h
36  typedef struct {
37    unsigned long fds_bits [__FDSET_LONGS];
38  } __kernel_fd_set;
```

`__FDSET_LONGS` has a value of 32 on a 32-bit system and 16 on a 64-bit system, which ensures that `fd_sets` always has a bitmap of size 1,024. This is where `__FDSET_LONGS` is defined:

```
include/linux/posix_types.h
 6  #undef __NFDBITS
 7  #define __NFDBITS  (8 * sizeof(unsigned long))
 8
 9  #undef __FD_SETSIZE
10  #define __FD_SETSIZE  1024
11
12  #undef __FDSET_LONGS
13  #define __FDSET_LONGS  (__FD_SETSIZE/__NFDBITS)
```

Four macros are available for the manipulation of these file descriptor sets (see Table 6.8).

TABLE 6.8
File Descriptor Set Macros

Macro	Description
FD_SET	Sets the file descriptor in the set.
FD_CLR	Clears the file descriptor from the set.
FD_ZERO	Clears the file descriptor set.
FD_ISSET	Returns if the file descriptor is set.

Now, we look at the various fields.

6.3.2.1 close_on_exec

The `close_on_exec` field is a pointer to the set of file descriptors that are marked to be closed on `exec()`. It initially (and usually) points to the `close_on_exec_init`

field. This changes if the number of file descriptors marked to be open on exec()
grows beyond the size of the close_on_exec_init bit field.

6.3.2.2   open_fds

The open_fds field is a pointer to the set of file descriptors that are marked as
open. Like close_on_exec, it initially points to the open_fds_init field and
changes if the number of file descriptors marked as open grows beyond the size of
open_fds_init bit field.

6.3.2.3   close_on_exec

The close_on_exec_init field holds the bit field that keeps track of the file
descriptors of files that are to be closed on exec().

6.3.2.4   open_fds_init

The open_fds_init field holds the bit field that keeps track of the file descriptors of files that are open.

6.3.2.5   fd_array

The fd_array array pointer points to the first 32 open file descriptors.

The fs_struct structures are initialized by the INIT_FILES macro:

```
---------------------------------------------------------------------
include/linux/init_task.h
 6  #define INIT_FILES \
 7  {
 8    .count     = ATOMIC_INIT(1),
 9    .file_lock  = SPIN_LOCK_UNLOCKED,
10    .max_fds   = NR_OPEN_DEFAULT,
11    .max_fdset  = __FD_SETSIZE,
12    .next_fd   = 0,
13    .fd      = &init_files.fd_array[0],
14    .close_on_exec  = &init_files.close_on_exec_init,
15    .open_fds  = &init_files.open_fds_init,
16    .close_on_exec_init = { { 0, } },
17    .open_fds_init  = { { 0, } },
18    .fd_array   = { NULL, }
19  }
---------------------------------------------------------------------
```

Figure 6.11 illustrates what the fs_struct looks like after it is initialized.

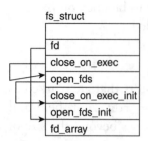

FIGURE 6.11
init fs_struct

```
------------------------------------------------------------------
include/linux/file.h
6  #define NR_OPEN_DEFAULT BITS_PER_LONG
------------------------------------------------------------------
```

The NR_OPEN_DEFAULT global definition is set to BITS_PER_LONG, which is 32 on 32-bit systems and 64 on 64-bit systems.

6.4   Page Cache

In the introductory sections, we mentioned that the page cache is an in-memory collection of pages. When data is frequently accessed, it is important to be able to quickly access the data. When data is duplicated and synchronized across two devices, one of which typically is smaller in storage size but allows much faster access than the other, we call it a cache. A page cache is how an operating system stores parts of the hard drive in memory for faster access. We now look at how it works and is implemented.

When you perform a write to a file on your hard drive, that file is broken into chunks called pages, that are swapped into memory (RAM). The operating system updates the page in memory and, at a later date, the page is written to disk.

If a page is copied from the hard drive to RAM (which is called swapping into memory), it can become either clean or dirty. A dirty page has been modified in memory but the modifications have not yet been written to disk. A clean page exists in memory in the same state that it exists on disk.

In Linux, the memory is divided into zones.[8] Each zone has a list of active and inactive pages. When a page is inactive for a certain amount of time, it gets

---

[8]   See Chapter 4 for more on memory zones.

swapped out (written back to disk) to free memory. Each page in the zones list has a pointer to an `address_space`. Each `address_space` has a pointer to an `address_space_operations` structure. Pages are marked dirty by calling the `set_dirty_page()` function of the `address_space_operation` structure. Figure 6.12 illustrates this dependency.

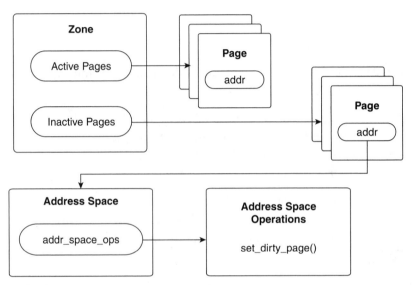

FIGURE 6.12
Page Cache and Zones

6.4.1   address_space Structure

The core of the page cache is the `address_space` object. Let's take a close look at it.

```
-------------------------------------------------------------------
include/linux/fs.h
326 struct address_space {
327    struct inode    *host;  /* owner: inode, block_device */
328    struct radix_tree_root page_tree; /* radix tree of all pages */
329    spinlock_t    tree_lock; /* and spinlock protecting it */
330    unsigned long   nrpages;  /* number of total pages */
331    pgoff_t     writeback_index;/* writeback starts here */
332    struct address_space_operations *a_ops; /* methods */
```

```
333   struct prio_tree_root i_mmap;  /* tree of private mappings */
334   unsigned int    i_mmap_writable;/* count VM_SHARED mappings */
335   struct list_head  i_mmap_nonlinear;/*list VM_NONLINEAR mappings */
336   spinlock_t      i_mmap_lock; /* protect tree, count, list */
337   atomic_t      truncate_count; /* Cover race condition with truncate */
338   unsigned long   flags;    /* error bits/gfp mask */
339   struct backing_dev_info *backing_dev_info; /* device readahead, etc */
340   spinlock_t      private_lock; /* for use by the address_space */
341   struct list_head  private_list; /* ditto */
342   struct address_space *assoc_mapping; /* ditto */
343 };
```

The inline comments of the structure are fairly descriptive. Some additional explanation might help in understanding how the page cache operates.

Usually, an `address_space` is associated with an inode and the host field points to this inode. However, the generic intent of the page cache and address space structure need not require this field. It could be `NULL` if the `address_space` is associated with a kernel object that is not an inode.

The `address_space` structure has a field that should be intuitively familiar to you by now: `address_space_operations`. Like the file structure `file_operations`, `address_space_operations` contains information about what operations are valid for this `address_space`.

```
-----------------------------------------------------------------
include/linux/fs.h
297 struct address_space_operations {
298   int (*writepage)(struct page *page, struct writeback_control *wbc);
299   int (*readpage)(struct file *, struct page *);
300   int (*sync_page)(struct page *);
301
302   /* Write back some dirty pages from this mapping. */
303   int (*writepages)(struct address_space *, struct writeback_control *);
304
305   /* Set a page dirty */
306   int (*set_page_dirty)(struct page *page);
307
308   int (*readpages)(struct file *filp, struct address_space *mapping,
309       struct list_head *pages, unsigned nr_pages);
310
311   /*
312   * ext3 requires that a successful prepare_write() call be followed
313   * by a commit_write() call - they must be balanced
314   */
315   int (*prepare_write)(struct file *, struct page *, unsigned, unsigned);
316   int (*commit_write)(struct file *, struct page *, unsigned, unsigned);
317   /* Unfortunately this kludge is needed for FIBMAP. Don't use it */
318   sector_t (*bmap)(struct address_space *, sector_t);
```

```
319    int (*invalidatepage) (struct page *, unsigned long);
320    int (*releasepage) (struct page *, int);
321    ssize_t (*direct_IO)(int, struct kiocb *, const struct iovec *iov,
322        loff_t offset, unsigned long nr_segs);
323 };
```

These functions are reasonably straightforward. readpage() and writepage() read and write pages associated with an address space, respectively. Multiple pages can be written and read via readpages() and writepages(). Journaling filesystems, such as ext3, can provide functions for prepare_write() and commit_write().

When the kernel checks the page cache for a page, it must be blazingly fast. As such, each address space has a radix_tree, which performs a quick search to determine if the page is in the page cache or not.

Figure 6.13 illustrates how files, inodes, address spaces, and pages relate to each other; this figure is useful for the upcoming analysis of the page cache code.

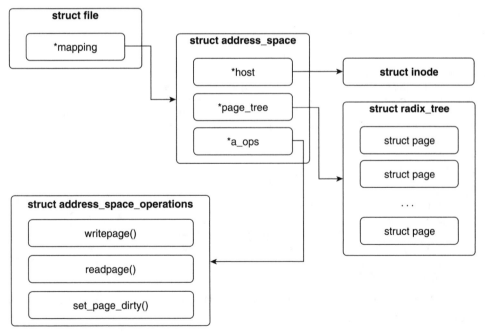

FIGURE 6.13
Files, Inodes, Address Spaces, and Pages

6.4.2 buffer_head Structure

Each sector on a block device is represented by the Linux kernel as a
`buffer_head` structure. A `buffer_head` contains all the information necessary to
map a physical sector to a buffer in physical memory. The `buffer_head` structure
is illustrated in Figure 6.14.

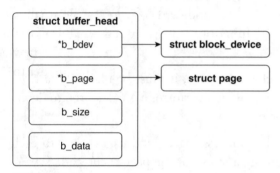

FIGURE 6.14
buffer_head Structure

```
--------------------------------------------------------------------
include/linux/buffer_head.h
47 struct buffer_head {
48   /* First cache line: */
49   unsigned long b_state;   /* buffer state bitmap (see above) */
50   atomic_t b_count;     /* users using this block */
51   struct buffer_head *b_this_page;/* circular list of page's buffers */
52   struct page *b_page;    /* the page this bh is mapped to */
53
54   sector_t b_blocknr;     /* block number */
55   u32 b_size;       /* block size */
56   char *b_data;       /* pointer to data block */
57
58   struct block_device *b_bdev;
59   bh_end_io_t *b_end_io;   /* I/O completion */
60   void *b_private;     /* reserved for b_end_io */
61   struct list_head b_assoc_buffers; /* associated with another mapping */
62 };
--------------------------------------------------------------------
```

The physical sector that a `buffer_head` structure refers to is logical block
`b_blocknr` on device `b_dev`.

The physical memory that a `buffer_head` structure refers to is a block of memory starting at `b_data` of `b_size` bytes. This memory block is within the physical
page of `b_page`.

The other definitions within the `buffer_head` structure are used for managing housekeeping tasks for how the physical sector is mapped to the physical memory. (Because this is a digression on bio structures and not `buffer_head` structures, refer to `mpage.c` for more detailed information on struct `buffer_head`.)

As mentioned in Chapter 4, each physical memory page in the Linux kernel is represented by a struct page. A page is composed of a number of I/O blocks. As each I/O block can be no larger than a page (although it can be smaller), a page is composed of one or more I/O blocks.

In older versions of Linux, block I/O was only done via buffers, but in 2.6, a new way was developed, using bio structures. The new way allows the Linux kernel to group block I/O together in a more manageable way.

Suppose we write a portion of the top of a text file and the bottom of a text file. This update would likely need two `buffer_head` structures for the data transfer: one that points to the top and one that points to the bottom. A bio structure allows file operations to bundle discrete chunks together in a single structure. This alternate way of looking at buffers and pages occurs by looking at the contiguous memory segments of a buffer. The `bio_vec` structure represents a contiguous memory segment in a buffer. The `bio_vec` structure is illustrated in Figure 6.15.

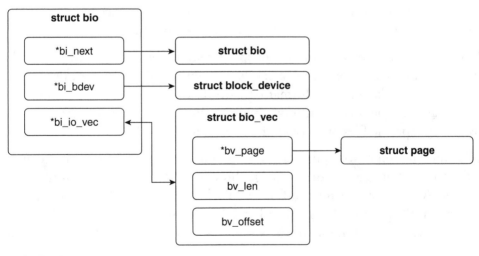

FIGURE 6.15
Bio Structure

```
-------------------------------------------------------------------
include/linux/bio.h
47 struct bio_vec {
48    struct page  *bv_page;
49    unsigned int bv_len;
50    unsigned int bv_offset;
51 };
-------------------------------------------------------------------
```

The `bio_vec` structure holds a pointer to a page, the length of the segment, and the offset of the segment within the page.

A bio structure is composed of an array of `bio_vec` structures (along with other housekeeping fields). Thus, a bio structure represents a number of contiguous memory segments of one or more buffers on one or more pages.[9]

6.5   VFS System Calls and the Filesystem Layer

Until this point, we covered all the structures that are associated with the VFS and the page cache. Now, we focus on two of the system calls used in file manipulation and trace their execution down to the kernel level. We see how the `open()`, `close()`, `read()`, and `write()` system calls make use of the structures previously described.

We mentioned that in the VFS, files are treated as complete abstractions. You can open, read, write, or close a file, but the specifics of what physically happens are unimportant to the VFS layer. Chapter 5 covers these specifics.

Hooked into the VFS is the filesystem-specific layer that translates the VFS' file I/O to pages and blocks. Because you can have many specific filesystem types on a computer system, like an `ext2` formatted hard disk and an `iso9660 cdrom`, the filesystem layer can be divided into two main sections: the generic filesystem operations and the specific filesystem operations (refer to Figure 6.3).

Following our top-down approach, this section traces a read and write request from the VFS call of `read()`, or `write()`, through the filesystem layer until a specific block I/O request is handed off to the block device driver. In our travels, we move between the generic filesystem and specific filesystem layer. We use the `ext2` filesystem driver as the example of the specific filesystem layer, but keep in mind

---

[9]   See include/linux/bio.h for detailed information on struct bio.

that different filesystem drivers could be accessed depending on what file is being acted upon. As we progress, we will also encounter the page cache, which is a construct within Linux that is positioned in the generic filesystem layer. In older versions of Linux, a buffer cache and page cache exist, but in the 2.6 kernel, the page cache has consumed any buffer cache functionality.

6.5.1 open ()

When a process wants to manipulate the contents of a file, it issues the open() system call:

```
-------------------------------------------------------------------
synopsis
#include <sys/types.h>
#include <sys/stat.h>
#include <fcntl.h>
int open(const char *pathname, int flags);
int open(const char *pathname, int flags, mode_t mode);
int creat(const char *pathname, mode_t mode);
-------------------------------------------------------------------
```

The open syscall takes as its arguments the pathname of the file, the flags to identify access mode of the file being opened, and the permission bit mask (if the file is being created). open() returns the file descriptor of the opened file (if successful) or an error code (if it fails).

The flags parameter is formed by bitwise ORing one or more of the constants defined in include/linux/fcntl.h. Table 6.9 lists the flags for open() and the corresponding value of the constant. Only one of O_RDONLY, O_WRONLY, or O_RDWR flags has to be specified. The additional flags are optional.

TABLE 6.9
open() Flags

Flag Name	Value	Description
O_RDONLY	0	Opens file for reading.
O_WRONLY	1	Opens file for writing.
O_RDWR	2	Opens file for reading and writing.
O_CREAT	100	Indicates that, if the file does not exist, it should be created. The creat() function is equivalent to the open() function with this flag set.

continues

TABLE 6.9
Continued

Flag Name	Value	Description
O_EXCL	200	Used in conjunction with O_CREAT, this indicates the open() should fail if the file does exist.
O_NOCTTY	400	In the case that pathname refers to a terminal device, the process should not consider it a controlling terminal.
O_TRUNC	0×1000	If the file exists, truncate it to 0 bytes.
O_APPEND	0×2000	Writes at the end of the file.
O_NONBLOCK	0×4000	Opens the file in non-blocking mode.
O_NDELAY	0×4000	Same value as O_NONBLOCK.
O_SYNC	0×10000	Writes to the file have to wait for the completion of physical I/O. Applied to files on block devices.
O_DIRECT	0×20000	Minimizes cache buffering on I/O to the file.
O_LARGEFILE	0×100000	The large filesystem allows files of sizes greater than can be represented in 31 bits. This ensures they can be opened.
O_DIRECTORY	0×200000	If the pathname does not indicate a directory, the open is to fail.
O_NOFOLLOW	0×400000	If the pathname is a symbolic link, the open is to fail.

Let's look at the system call:

```
------------------------------------------------------------------
fs/open.c
927  asmlinkage long sys_open (const char __user * filename, int flags, int
mode)
928  {
929    char * tmp;
930    int fd, error;
931
932 #if BITS_PER_LONG != 32
933    flags |= O_LARGEFILE;
934  #endif
935    tmp = getname(filename);
936    fd = PTR_ERR(tmp);
937    if (!IS_ERR(tmp)) {
```

```
938    fd = get_unused_fd();
939    if (fd >= 0) {
940      struct file *f = filp_open(tmp, flags, mode);
941      error = PTR_ERR(f);
942      if (IS_ERR(f))
943        goto out_error;
944      fd_install(fd, f);
945    }
946  out:
947    putname(tmp);
948    }
949    return fd;
950
951  out_error:
952    put_unused_fd(fd);
953    fd = error;
954    goto out;
955    }
```

Lines 932–934

Verify if our system is non-32-bit. If so, enable the large filesystem support flag
O_LARGEFILE. This allows the function to open files with sizes greater than those
represented by 31 bits.

Line 935

The getname() routine copies the filename from user space to kernel space by
invoking strncpy_from_user().

Line 938

The get_unused_fd() routine returns the first available file descriptor (or
index into fd array: current->files->fd) and marks it busy. The local variable
fd is set to this value.

Line 940

The filp_open() function performs the bulk of the open syscall work and
returns the file structure that will associate the process with the file. Let's take a
closer look at the filp_open() routine:

```
fs/open.c
740  struct file *filp_open(const char * filename, int flags, int mode)
741  {
742    int namei_flags, error;
```

```
743    struct nameidata nd;
744
745    namei_flags = flags;
746    if ((namei_flags+1) & O_ACCMODE)
747      namei_flags++;
748    if (namei_flags & O_TRUNC)
749      namei_flags |= 2;
750
751    error = open_namei(filename, namei_flags, mode, &nd);
752    if (!error)
753      return dentry_open(nd.dentry, nd.mnt, flags);
754
755    return ERR_PTR(error);
```

Lines 745–749

The pathname lookup functions, such as open_namei(), expect the access mode flags encoded in a specific format that is different from the format used by the open system call. These lines copy the access mode flags into the namei_flags variable and format the access mode flags for interpretation by open_namei().

The main difference is that, for pathname lookup, it can be the case that the access mode might not require read or write permission. This "no permission" access mode does not make sense when trying to open a file and is thus not included under the open system call flags. "No permission" is indicated by the value of 00. Read permission is then indicated by setting the value of the low-order bit to 1 whereas write permission is indicated by setting the value of the high-order bit to 1. The open system call flags for O_RDONLY, O_WRONLY, and O_RDWR evaluate to 00, 01, and 02, respectively as seen in include/asm/fcntl.h.

The namei_flags variable can extract the access mode by logically bit ANDing it with the O_ACCMODE variable. This variable holds the value of 3 and evaluates to true if the variable to be ANDed with it holds a value of 1, 2, or 3. If the open system call flag was set to O_RDONLY, O_WRONLY, and O_RDWR, adding a 1 to this value translates it into the pathname lookup format and evaluates to true when ANDed with O_ACCMODE. The second check just assures that if the open system call flag is set to allow for file truncation, the high-order bit is set in the access mode specifying write access.

Line 751

The `open_namei()` routine performs the pathname lookup, generates the associated `nameidata` structure, and derives the corresponding inode.

Line 753

The `dentry_open()` is a wrapper routine around `dentry_open_it()`, which creates and initializes the file structure. It creates the file structure via a call to the kernel routine `get_empty_filp()`. This routine returns ENFILE if the `files_stat.nr_files` is greater than or equal to `files_stat.max_files`. This case indicates that the system's limit on the total number of open files has been reached.

Let's look at the `dentry_open_it()` routine:

```
------------------------------------------------------------------------
fs/open.c
844  struct file *dentry_open_it(struct dentry *dentry, struct 845     vfsmount
*mnt, int flags, struct lookup_intent *it)
846  {
847    struct file * f;
848    struct inode *inode;
849    int error;
850
851    error = -ENFILE;
852    f = get_empty_filp();
...
855    f->f_flags = flags;
856    f->f_mode = (flags+1) & O_ACCMODE;
857    f->f_it = it;
858    inode = dentry->d_inode;
859    if (f->f_mode & FMODE_WRITE) {
860      error = get_write_access(inode);
861      if (error)
862        goto cleanup_file;
863    }
...
866    f->f_dentry = dentry;
867    f->f_vfsmnt = mnt;
868    f->f_pos = 0;
869    f->f_op = fops_get(inode->i_fop);
870    file_move(f, &inode->i_sb->s_files);
871
872    if (f->f_op && f->f_op->open) {
```

```
873     error = f->f_op->open(inode,f);
874     if (error)
875      goto cleanup_all;
876     intent_release(it);
877   }
...
891  return f;
...
907  }
```

Line 852

The file struct is assigned by way of the call to `get_empty_filp()`.

Lines 855–856

The `f_flags` field of the file struct is set to the flags passed in to the open system call. The `f_mode` field is set to the access modes passed to the open system call, but in the format expected by the pathname lookup functions.

Lines 866–869

The files struct's `f_dentry` field is set to point to the `dentry` struct that is associated with the file's pathname. The `f_vfsmnt` field is set to point to the `vmfsmount` struct for the filesystem. `f_pos` is set to 0, which indicates that the starting position of the `file_offset` is at the beginning of the file. The `f_op` field is set to point to the table of operations pointed to by the file's inode.

Line 870

The `file_move()` routine is called to insert the file structure into the filesystem's superblock list of file structures representing open files.

Lines 872–877

This is where the next level of the open function occurs. It is called here if the file has more file-specific functionality to perform to open the file. It is also called if the file operations table for the file contains an open routing.

This concludes the `dentry_open_it()` routine.

By the end of `filp_open()`, we will have a file structure allocated, inserted at the head of the superblock's `s_files` field, with `f_dentry` pointing to the `dentry` object, `f_vfsmount` pointing to the `vfsmount` object, `f_op` pointing to the inode's `i_fop` file operations table, `f_flags` set to the access flags, and `f_mode` set to the permission mode passed to the `open()` call.

Line 944

The `fd_install()` routine sets the `fd` array pointer to the address of the file object returned by `filp_open()`. That is, it sets `current->files->fd[fd]`.

Line 947

The `putname()` routine frees the kernel space allocated to store the filename.

Line 949

The file descriptor `fd` is returned.

Line 952

The `put_unused_fd()` routine clears the file descriptor that has been allocated. This is called when a file object failed to be created.

To summarize, the hierarchical call of the `open()` syscall process looks like this:

sys_open:

- **getname()**. Moves filename to kernel space
- **get_unused_fd()**. Gets next available file descriptor
- **filp_open()**. Creates the `nameidata` struct
- **open_namei()**. Initializes the `nameidata` struct
- **dentry_open()**. Creates and initializes the file object
- **fd_install()**. Sets `current->files->fd[fd]` to the file object
- **putname()**. Deallocates kernel space for filename

Figure 6.16 illustrates the structures that are initialized and set and identifies the routines where this was done.

Table 6.10 shows some of the `sys_open()` return errors and the kernel routines that find them.

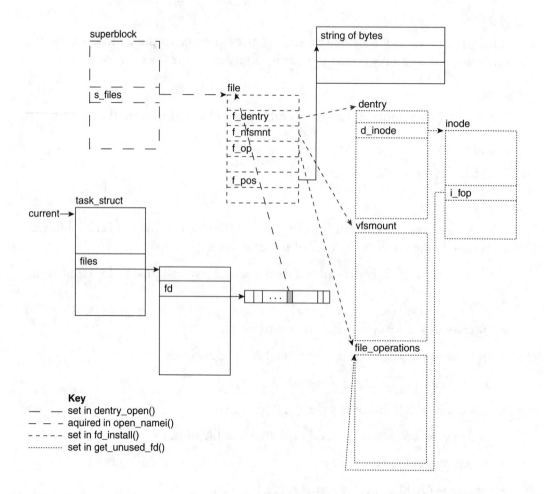

FIGURE 6.16
Filesystem Structures

TABLE 6.10
sys_open() Errors

Error Code	Description	Function Returning Error
ENAMETOOLONG	Pathname too long.	getname()
ENOENT	File does not exist (and flag O_CREAT not set).	getname()
EMFILE	Process has maximum number of files open.	get_unused_fd()
ENFILE	System has maximum number of files open.	get_unused_filp()

6.5.2   close ()

After a process finishes with a file, it issues the close() system call:

```
synopsis
#include <unistd.h>

int close(int fd);
```

The close system call takes as parameter the file descriptor of the file to be closed. In standard C programs, this call is made implicitly upon program termination. Let's delve into the code for sys_close():

```
fs/open.c
1020  asmlinkage long sys_close(unsigned int fd)
1021  {
1022    struct file * filp;
1023    struct files_struct *files = current->files;
1024
1025    spin_lock(&files->file_lock);
1026    if (fd >= files->max_fds)
1027      goto out_unlock;
1028    filp = files->fd[fd];
1029    if (!filp)
1030      goto out_unlock;
1031    files->fd[fd] = NULL;
1032    FD_CLR(fd, files->close_on_exec);
1033    __put_unused_fd(files, fd);
```

346 Chapter 6 • Filesystems

```
1034    spin_unlock(&files->file_lock);
1035    return filp_close(filp, files);
1036
1037  out_unlock:
1038    spin_unlock(&files->file_lock);
1039    return -EBADF;
1040  }
```

Line 1023

The current `task_struct`'s files field point at the `files_struct` that corresponds to our file.

Lines 1025–1030

These lines begin by locking the file so as to not run into synchronization problems. We then check that the file descriptor is valid. If the file descriptor number is greater than the highest allowable file number for that file, we remove the lock and return the error `-EBADF`. Otherwise, we acquire the file structure address. If the file descriptor index does not yield a file structure, we also remove the lock and return the error as there would be nothing to close.

Lines 1031–1032

Here, we set the `current->files->fd[fd]` to `NULL`, removing the pointer to the file object. We also clear the file descriptor's bit in the file descriptor set referred to by `files->close_on_exec`. Because the file descriptor is closed, the process need not worry about keeping track of it in the case of a call to `exec()`.

Line 1033

The kernel routine `__put_unused_fd()` clears the file descriptor's bit in the file descriptor set `files->open_fds` because it is no longer open. It also does something that assures us of the "lowest available index" assignment of file descriptors:

```
fs/open.c
897  static inline void __put_unused_fd(struct files_struct *files,  unsigned
int fd)
898  {
899    __FD_CLR(fd, files->open_fds);
890    if (fd < files->next_fd)
891      files->next_fd = fd;
892  }
```

Lines 890–891

The next_fd field holds the value of the next file descriptor to be assigned. If the current file descriptor's value is less than that held by files->next_fd, this field will be set to the value of the current file descriptor instead. This assures that file descriptors are assigned on the basis of the lowest available value.

Lines 1034–1035

The lock on the file is now released and the control is passed to the filp_close() function that will be in charge of returning the appropriate value to the close system call. The filp_close() function performs the bulk of the close syscall work. Let's take a closer look at the filp_close() routine:

```
-----------------------------------------------------------------------
fs/open.c
987  int filp_close(struct file *filp, fl_owner_t id)
988  {
989  int retval;
990  /* Report and clear outstanding errors */
991  retval = filp->f_error;
992  if (retval)
993    filp->f_error = 0;
994
995  if (!file_count(filp)) {
996    printk(KERN_ERR "VFS: Close: file count is 0\n");
997    return retval;
998  }
999
1000  if (filp->f_op && filp->f_op->flush) {
1001    int err = filp->f_op->flush(filp);
1002    if (!retval)
1003      retval = err;
1004  }
1005
1006  dnotify_flush(filp, id);
1007  locks_remove_posix(filp, id);
1008  fput(filp);
1009  return retval;
1010  }
-----------------------------------------------------------------------
```

Lines 991–993

These lines clear any outstanding errors.

Lines 995–997

This is a sanity check on the conditions necessary to close a file. A file with a `file_count` of 0 should already be closed. Hence, in this case, `filp_close` returns an error.

Lines 1000–1001

Invokes the file operation `flush()` (if it is defined). What this does is determined by the particular filesystem.

Line 1008

`fput()` is called to release the file structure. The actions performed by this routine include calling file operation `release()`, removing the pointer to the `dentry` and `vfsmount` objects, and finally, releasing the file object.

The hierarchical call of the `close()` syscall process looks like this:

sys_close():

- **__put_unused_fd()**. Returns file descriptor to the available pool
- **filp_close()**. Prepares file object for clearing
- **fput()**. Clears file object

Table 6.11 shows some of the `sys_close()` return errors and the kernel routines that find them.

TABLE 6.11
sys_close() Errors

Error	Function	Description
EBADF	sys_close()	Invalid file descriptor

6.5.3   read()

When a user level program calls `read()`, Linux translates this to a system call, `sys_read()`:

```
-------------------------------------------------------------------
fs/read_write.c
272 asmlinkage ssize_t sys_read(unsigned int fd, char __user * buf, size_t count)
273 {
```

```
274   struct file *file;
275   ssize_t ret = -EBADF;
276   int fput_needed;
277
278   file = fget_light(fd, &fput_needed);
279   if (file) {
280     ret = vfs_read(file, buf, count, &file->f_pos);
281     fput_light(file, fput_needed);
282   }
283
284   return ret;
285 }
```

Line 272

`sys_read()` takes a file descriptor, a user-space buffer pointer, and a number of bytes to read from the file into the buffer.

Lines 273–282

A file lookup is done to translate the file descriptor to a file pointer with `fget_light()`. We then call `vfs_read()`, which does all the main work. Each `fget_light()` needs to be paired with `fput_light(,)` so we do that after our `vfs_read()` finishes.

The system call, `sys_read()`, has passed control to `vfs_read()`, so let's continue our trace:

```
--------------------------------------------------------------------
fs/read_write.c
200 ssize_t vfs_read(struct file *file, char __user *buf, size_t count,
loff_t *pos)
201 {
202   struct inode *inode = file->f_dentry->d_inode;
203   ssize_t ret;
204
205   if (!(file->f_mode & FMODE_READ))
206     return -EBADF;
207   if (!file->f_op || (!file->f_op->read && \            !file->f_op->aio_read))
208     return -EINVAL;
209
210   ret = locks_verify_area(FLOCK_VERIFY_READ, inode,
file, *pos, count);
211   if (!ret) {
212     ret = security_file_permission (file, MAY_READ);
213     if (!ret) {
214       if (file->f_op->read)
215         ret = file->f_op->read(file,
buf, count, pos);
```

```
216         else
217             ret = do_sync_read(file, buf,
count, pos);
218         if (ret > 0)
219            dnotify_parent(file->f_dentry,
DN_ACCESS);
220       }
221     }
222
223   return ret;
224 }
```

Line 200

The first three parameters are all passed via, or are translations from, the original `sys_read()` parameters. The fourth parameter is the offset within **file**, where the read should start. This could be non-zero if `vfs_read()` is called explicitly because it could be called from within the kernel.

Line 202

We store a pointer to the file's inode.

Lines 205–208

Basic checking is done on the file operations structure to ensure that read or asynchronous read operations have been defined. If no read operation is defined, or if the operations table is missing, the function returns the `EINVAL` error at this point. This error indicates that the file descriptor is attached to a structure that cannot be used for reading.

Lines 210–214

We verify that the area to be read is not locked and that the file is authorized to be read. If it is not, we notify the parent of the file (on lines 218–219).

Lines 215–217

These are the guts of `vfs_read()`. If the read file operation has been defined, we call it; otherwise, we call `do_sync_read()`.

In our tracing, we follow the standard file operation read and not the `do_sync_read()` function. Later, it becomes clear that both calls eventually reach the same underlying point.

6.5.3.1   Moving from the Generic to the Specific

This is our first encounter with one of the many abstractions where we move between the generic filesystem layer and the specific filesystem layer. Figure 6.17 illustrates how the file structure points to the specific filesystem table or operations. Recall that when `read_inode()` is called, the inode information is filled in, including having the `fop` field point to the appropriate table of operations defined by the specific filesystem implementation (for example, `ext2`).

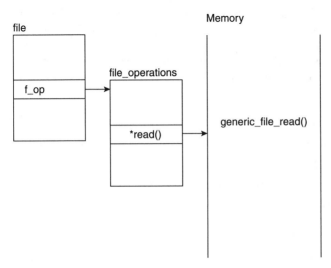

FIGURE 6.17
File Operations

When a file is created, or mounted, the specific filesystem layer initializes its file operations structure. Because we are operating on a file on an `ext2` filesystem, the file operations structure is as follows:

```
-----------------------------------------------------------------
fs/ext2/file.c
42 struct file_operations ext2_file_operations = {
43    .llseek   = generic_file_llseek,
44    .read    = generic_file_read,
45    .write   = generic_file_write,
46    .aio_read  = generic_file_aio_read,
47    .aio_write = generic_file_aio_write,
48    .ioctl   = ext2_ioctl,
49    .mmap    = generic_file_mmap,
50    .open    = generic_file_open,
51    .release  = ext2_release_file,
```

```
52   .fsync   = ext2_sync_file,
53   .readv   = generic_file_readv,
54   .writev  = generic_file_writev,
55   .sendfile = generic_file_sendfile,
56 };
```

You can see that for nearly every file operation, the ext2 filesystem has decided that the Linux defaults are acceptable. This leads us to ask when a filesystem would want to implement its own file operations. When a filesystem is sufficiently unlike a UNIX filesystem, extra steps might be necessary to allow Linux to interface with it. For example, MSDOS- or FAT-based filesystems need to implement their own write but can use the generic read.[10]

Discovering that the specific filesystem layer for ext2 passes control to the generic filesystem layer, we now examine generic_file_read():

```
mm/filemap.c
924 ssize_t
925 generic_file_read(struct file *filp, char __user *buf, size_t count, loff_t
*ppos)
926 {
927   struct iovec local_iov = { .iov_base = buf, .iov_len = count };
928   struct kiocb kiocb;
929   ssize_t ret;
930
931   init_sync_kiocb(&kiocb, filp);
932   ret = __generic_file_aio_read(&kiocb, &local_iov, 1, ppos);
933   if (-EIOCBQUEUED == ret)
934     ret = wait_on_sync_kiocb(&kiocb);
935   return ret;
936 }
937
938 EXPORT_SYMBOL(generic_file_read);
```

Lines 924–925

Notice that the same parameters are simply being passed along from the upper-level reads. We have filp, the file pointer; buf, the pointer to the memory buffer where the file will be read into; count, the number of characters to read; and ppos, the position within the file to begin reading from.

---

[10] See fs/fat/file.c for more information.

Line 927

An `iovec` structure is created that contains the address and length of the user space buffer that the results of the read are to be stored in.

Lines 928 and 931

A `kiocb` structure is initialized using the file pointer. (`kiocb` stands for **kernel I/O** control block.)

Line 932

The bulk of the read is done in the generic asynchronous file read function.

Asynchronous I/O Operations

`kiocb` and `iovec` are two datatypes that facilitate asynchronous I/O operations within the Linux kernel.

Asynchronous I/O is desirable when a process wishes to perform an input or output operation without immediately waiting for the result of the operation. It is extremely desirable for high I/O environments, as you can allow the device the opportunity to order and schedule the I/O requests instead of the process.

In Linux, an I/O vector (iovec) represents an address range of memory and is defined as

```
-------------------------------------------------------------------
include/linux/uio.h

20 struct iovec
21 {
22   void __user *iov_base; /* BSD uses caddr_t (1003.1g requires void *)
*/
23   __kernel_size_t iov_len; /* Must be size_t (1003.1g) */
24 };
-------------------------------------------------------------------
```

This is simply a pointer to a section of memory and the length of the memory.

The kernel I/O control block (`kiocb`) is a structure that is required to help manage how and when the I/O vector gets operated upon asynchronously.

`__generic_file_aio_read()` function uses the `kiocb` and `iovec` structures to read the `page_cache` directly.

Lines 933–935

After we send off the read, we wait until the read finishes and then return the result of the read operation.

Recall the `do_sync_read()` path in `vfs_read()`; it would have eventually called this same function via another path. Let's continue the trace of file I/O by examining `__generic_file_aio_read()`:

```
-----------------------------------------------------------------------
mm/filemap.c
835 ssize_t
836 __generic_file_aio_read(struct kiocb *iocb,
const struct iovec *iov,
837     unsigned long nr_segs, loff_t *ppos)
838 {
839   struct file *filp = iocb->ki_filp;
840   ssize_t retval;
841   unsigned long seg;
842   size_t count;
843
844   count = 0;
845   for (seg = 0; seg < nr_segs; seg++) {
846     const struct iovec *iv = &iov[seg];
...
852     count += iv->iov_len;
853     if (unlikely((ssize_t)(count|iv->iov_len) <
 0))
854       return -EINVAL;
855     if (access_ok(VERIFY_WRITE, iv->iov_base,
iv->iov_len))
856       continue;
857     if (seg == 0)
858       return -EFAULT;
859     nr_segs = seg;
860     count -= iv->iov_len
861     break;
862   }
...
-----------------------------------------------------------------------
```

Lines 835–842

Recall that `nr_segs` was set to 1 by our caller and that `iocb` and `iov` contain the file pointer and buffer information. We immediately extract the file pointer from `iocb`.

Lines 845–862

This `for` loop verifies that the `iovec` struct passed is composed of valid segments. Recall that it contains the user space buffer information.

```
------------------------------------------------------------------------
mm/filemap.c
...
863
864    /* coalesce the iovecs and go direct-to-BIO for O_DIRECT */
865    if (filp->f_flags & O_DIRECT) {
866      loff_t pos = *ppos, size;
867      struct address_space *mapping;
868      struct inode *inode;
869
870      mapping = filp->f_mapping;
871      inode = mapping->host;
872      retval = 0;
873      if (!count)
874        goto out; /* skip atime */
875      size = i_size_read(inode);
876      if (pos < size) {
877        retval = generic_file_direct_IO(READ, iocb,
878              iov, pos, nr_segs);
879        if (retval >= 0 && !is_sync_kiocb(iocb))
880          retval = -EIOCBQUEUED;
881        if (retval > 0)
882          *ppos = pos + retval;
883      }
884      file_accessed(filp);
885      goto out;
886    }
...
------------------------------------------------------------------------
```

Lines 863–886

This section of code is only entered if the read is direct I/O. Direct I/O bypasses the page cache and is a useful property of certain block devices. For our purposes, however, we do not enter this section of code at all. Most file I/O takes our path as the page cache, which we describe soon, which is much faster than the underlying block device.

```
------------------------------------------------------------------------
mm/filemap.c
...
887
888    retval = 0;
889    if (count) {
890      for (seg = 0; seg < nr_segs; seg++) {
```

```
891        read_descriptor_t desc;
892
893        desc.written = 0;
894        desc.buf = iov[seg].iov_base;
895        desc.count = iov[seg].iov_len;
896        if (desc.count == 0)
897          continue;
898        desc.error = 0;
899        do_generic_file_read(filp,ppos,&desc,file_read_actor);
900        retval += desc.written;
901        if (!retval) {
902          retval = desc.error;
903          break;
904        }
905      }
906    }
907 out:
08   return retval;
909 }
```

Lines 889–890

Because our `iovec` is valid and we have only one segment, we execute this `for` loop once only.

Lines 891–898

We translate the `iovec` structure into a `read_descriptor_t` structure. The `read_descriptor_t` structure keeps track of the status of the read. Here is the description of the `read_descriptor_t` structure:

```
include/linux/fs.h
837  typedef struct {
838    size_t written;
839    size_t count;
840    char __user * buf;
841    int error;
842  } read_descriptor_t;
```

Line 838

The field written keeps a running count of the number of bytes transferred.

Line 839

The field count keeps a running count of the number of bytes left to be transferred.

Line 840

The field buf holds the current position into the buffer.

Line 841

The field error holds any error code encountered during the read operation.

Lines 899

We pass our new read_descriptor_t structure **desc** to do_generic_file_read(), along with our file pointer filp and our position ppos. file_read_actor() is a function that copies a page to the user space buffer located in desc.[11]

Lines 900–909

The amount read is calculated and returned to the caller.

At this point in the read() internals, we are about to access the page cache[12] and determine if the sections of the file we want to read already exist in RAM, so we don't have to directly access the block device.

6.5.3.2   Tracing the Page Cache

Recall that the last function we encountered passed a file pointer filp, an offset ppos, a read_descriptor_t desc, and a function file_read_actor into do_generic_file_read().

```
-----------------------------------------------------------------
include/linux/fs.h
1420 static inline void do_generic_file_read(struct file * filp, loff_t *ppos,
1421          read_descriptor_t * desc,
1422          read_actor_t actor)
1423 {
1424   do_generic_mapping_read(filp->f_mapping,
1425          &filp->f_ra,
1426          filp,
1427          ppos,
1428          desc,
1429          actor);
1430 }
-----------------------------------------------------------------
```

---

[11] file_read_actor() can be found on line 794 of mm/filemap.c.

[12] The page cache is described in Section 6.4, "Page Cache."

Lines 1420–1430

do_generic_file_read() is simply a wrapper to do_generic_mapping_read(). filp->f_mapping is a pointer to an address_space object and filp->f_ra is a structure that holds the address of the file's read-ahead state.[13]

So, we've transformed our read of a file into a read of the page cache via the address_space object in our file pointer. Because do_generic_mapping_read() is an extremely long function with a number of separate cases, we try to make the analysis of the code as painless as possible.

```
------------------------------------------------------------------
mm/filemap.c
645 void do_generic_mapping_read(struct address_space *mapping,
646          struct file_ra_state *_ra,
647          struct file * filp,
648          loff_t *ppos,
649          read_descriptor_t * desc,
650          read_actor_t actor)
651 {
652   struct inode *inode = mapping->host;
653   unsigned long index, offset;
654   struct page *cached_page;
655   int error;
656   struct file_ra_state ra = *_ra;
657
658   cached_page = NULL;
659   index = *ppos >> PAGE_CACHE_SHIFT;
660   offset = *ppos & ~PAGE_CACHE_MASK;
------------------------------------------------------------------
```

Line 652

We extract the inode of the file we're reading from address_space.

Lines 658–660

We initialize cached_page to NULL until we can determine if it exists within the page cache. We also calculate index and offset based on page cache constraints. The index corresponds to the page number within the page cache, and the offset corresponds to the displacement within that page. When the page size is 4,096 bytes, a right bit shift of 12 on the file pointer yields the index of the page.

---

[13] See the "file Structure" section for more information about this field and read-ahead optimization.

"The page cache can [be] done in larger chunks than one page, because it allows for more efficient throughput" (`linux/pagemap.h`). `PAGE_CACHE_SHIFT` and `PAGE_CACHE_MASK` are settings that control the structure and size of the page cache:

```
mm/filemap.c
661
662  for (;;) {
663     struct page *page;
664     unsigned long end_index, nr, ret;
665     loff_t isize = i_size_read(inode);
666
667     end_index = isize >> PAGE_CACHE_SHIFT;
668
669     if (index > end_index)
670       break;
671     nr = PAGE_CACHE_SIZE;
672     if (index == end_index) {
673       nr = isize & ~PAGE_CACHE_MASK;
674       if (nr <= offset)
675         break;
676     }
677
678     cond_resched();
679     page_cache_readahead(mapping, &ra, filp, index);
680
681     nr = nr - offset;
```

Lines 662–681

This section of code iterates through the page cache and retrieves enough pages to fulfill the bytes requested by the `read` command.

```
mm/filemap.c
682 find_page:
683     page = find_get_page(mapping, index);
684     if (unlikely(page == NULL)) {
685       handle_ra_miss(mapping, &ra, index);
686       goto no_cached_page;
687     }
688     if (!PageUptodate(page))
689       goto page_not_up_to_date;
```

Lines 682–689

We attempt to find the first page required. If the page is not in the page cache, we jump to the `no_cached_page` label. If the page is not up to date, we jump to the `page_not_up_to_date` label. `find_get_page()` uses the address space's radix tree to find the page at `index`, which is the specified offset.

```
------------------------------------------------------------------------
mm/filemap.c
690 page_ok:
691      /* If users can be writing to this page using arbitrary
692       * virtual addresses, take care about potential aliasing
693       * before reading the page on the kernel side.
694       */
695      if (mapping_writably_mapped(mapping))
696        flush_dcache_page(page);
697
698      /*
699       * Mark the page accessed if we read the beginning.
700       */
701      if (!offset)
702        mark_page_accessed(page);
...
714      ret = actor(desc, page, offset, nr);
715      offset += ret;
716      index += offset >> PAGE_CACHE_SHIFT;
717      offset &= ~PAGE_CACHE_MASK;
718
719      page_cache_release(page);
720      if (ret == nr && desc->count)
721        continue;
722      break;
723
------------------------------------------------------------------------
```

Lines 690–723

The inline comments are descriptive so there's no point repeating them. Notice that on lines 656–658, if more pages are to be retrieved, we immediately return to the top of the loop where the index and offset manipulations in lines 714–716 help choose the next page to retrieve. If no more pages are to be read, we break out of the `for` loop.

```
------------------------------------------------------------------------
mm/filemap.c
724 page_not_up_to_date:
725      /* Get exclusive access to the page ... */
726      lock_page(page);
727
728      /* Did it get unhashed before we got the lock? */
729      if (!page->mapping) {
730        unlock_page(page);
731        page_cache_release(page);
```

```
732        continue;
734
735        /* Did somebody else fill it already? */
736        if (PageUptodate(page)) {
737          unlock_page(page);
738          goto page_ok;
739        }
740
```

Lines 724–740

If the page is not up to date, we check it again and return to the `page_ok` label
if it is, now, up to date. Otherwise, we try to get exclusive access; this causes us to
sleep until we get it. Once we have exclusive access, we see if the page attempts to
remove itself from the page cache; if it is, we hasten it along before returning to the
top of the `for` loop. If it is still present and is now up to date, we unlock the page
and jump to the `page_ok` label.

```
mm/filemap.c
741 readpage:
742   /* ... and start the actual read. The read will unlock the page. */
743     error = mapping->a_ops->readpage(filp, page);
744
745     if (!error) {
746       if (PageUptodate(page))
747         goto page_ok;
748       wait_on_page_locked(page);
749       if (PageUptodate(page))
750         goto page_ok;
751       error = -EIO;
752     }
753
754     /* UHHUH! A synchronous read error occurred. Report it */
755     desc->error = error;
756     page_cache_release(page);
757     break;
758
```

Lines 741–743

If the page was not up to date, we can fall through the previous label with the
page lock held. The actual read, `mapping->a_ops->readpage(filp, page)`,
unlocks the page. (We trace `readpage()` further in a bit, but let's first finish the
current explanation.)

Lines 746–750

If we read a page successfully, we check that it's up to date and jump to `page_ok` when it is.

Lines 751–758

If a synchronous read error occurred, we log the error in `desc`, release the page from the page cache, and break out of the `for` loop.

```
--------------------------------------------------------------------
mm/filemap.c
759 no_cached_page:
760     /*
761      * Ok, it wasn't cached, so we need to create a new
762      * page..
763      */
764     if (!cached_page) {
765         cached_page = page_cache_alloc_cold(mapping);
766         if (!cached_page) {
767             desc->error = -ENOMEM;
768             break;
769         }
770     }
771     error = add_to_page_cache_lru(cached_page, mapping,
772             index, GFP_KERNEL);
773     if (error) {
774         if (error == -EEXIST)
775             goto find_page;
776         desc->error = error;
777         break;
778     }
779     page = cached_page;
780     cached_page = NULL;
781     goto readpage;
782 }
--------------------------------------------------------------------
```

Lines 698–772

If the page to be read wasn't cached, we allocate a new page in the address space and add it to both the least recently used (LRU) cache and the page cache.

Lines 773–775

If we have an error adding the page to the cache because it already exists, we jump to the `find_page` label and try again. This could occur if multiple processes attempt to read the same uncached page; one would attempt allocation and succeed, the other would attempt allocation and find it already existing.

Lines 776–777

If there is an error in adding the page to the cache other than it already existing, we log the error and break out of the `for` loop.

Lines 779–781

When we successfully allocate and add the page to the page cache and LRU cache, we set our page pointer to the new page and attempt to read it by jumping to the `readpage` label.

```
-------------------------------------------------------------------
mm/filemap.c
784    *_ra = ra;
785
786    *ppos = ((loff_t) index << PAGE_CACHE_SHIFT) + offset;
787    if (cached_page)
788      page_cache_release(cached_page);
789    file_accessed(filp);
790 }
-------------------------------------------------------------------
```

Line 786

We calculate the actual offset based on our page cache index and offset.

Lines 787–788

If we allocated a new page and could add it correctly to the page cache, we remove it.

Line 789

We update the file's last accessed time via the inode.

The logic described in this function is the core of the page cache. Notice how the page cache does not touch any specific filesystem data. This allows the Linux kernel to have a page cache that can cache pages regardless of the underlying filesystem structure. Thus, the page cache can hold pages from MINIX, ext2, and MSDOS all at the same time.

The way the page cache maintains its specific filesystem layer agnosticism is by using the `readpage()` function of the address space. Each specific filesystem implements its own `readpage()`. So, when the generic filesystem layer calls `mapping->a_ops->readpage()`, it calls the specific `readpage()` function from the filesystem driver's `address_space_operations` structure. For the ext2 filesystem, `readpage()` is defined as follows:

```
fs/ext2/inode.c
676 struct address_space_operations ext2_aops = {
677   .readpage      = ext2_readpage,
678   .readpages     = ext2_readpages,
679   .writepage     = ext2_writepage,
680   .sync_page     = block_sync_page,
681   .prepare_write = ext2_prepare_write,
682   .commit_write  = generic_commit_write,
683   .bmap          = ext2_bmap,
684   .direct_IO     = ext2_direct_IO,
685   .writepages    = ext2_writepages,
686 };
```

Thus, `readpage()` actually calls `ext2_readpage()`:

```
fs/ext2/inode.c
616 static int ext2_readpage(struct file *file, struct page *page)
617 {
618   return mpage_readpage(page, ext2_get_block);
619 }
```

`ext2_readpage()` calls `mpage_readpage()`, which is a generic filesystem layer call, but passes it the specific filesystem layer function `ext2_get_block()`.

The generic filesystem function `mpage_readpage()` expects a `get_block()` function as its second argument. Each filesystem implements certain I/O functions that are specific to the format of the filesystem; `get_block()` is one of these. Filesystem `get_block()` functions map logical blocks in the `address_space` pages to actual device blocks in the specific filesystem layout. Let's look at the specifics of `mpage_readpage()`:

```
fs/mpage.c
358 int mpage_readpage(struct page *page, get_block_t get_block)
359 {
360   struct bio *bio = NULL;
361   sector_t last_block_in_bio = 0;
362
363   bio = do_mpage_readpage(bio, page, 1,
364       &last_block_in_bio, get_block);
365   if (bio)
366     mpage_bio_submit(READ, bio);
367   return 0;
368 }
```

Lines 360–361

We allocate space for managing the bio structure the address space uses to manage the page we are trying to read from the device.

Lines 363–364

`do_mpage_readpage()` is called, which translates the logical page to a bio structure composed of actual pages and blocks. The bio structure keeps track of information associated with block I/O.

Lines 365–367

We send the newly created bio structure to `mpage_bio_submit()` and return.

Let's take a moment and recap (at a high level) the flow of the read function so far:

1. Using the file descriptor from a call to `read()`, we locate the file pointer from which we obtain an inode.

2. The filesystem layer checks the in-memory page cache for a page, or pages, that correspond to the given inode.

3. If no page is found, the filesystem layer uses the specific filesystem driver to translate the requested sections of the file to I/O blocks on a given device.

4. We allocate space for pages in the page cache `address_space` and create a bio structure that ties the new pages with the sectors on the block device.

`mpage_readpage()` is the function that creates the bio structure and ties together the newly allocated pages from the page cache to the bio structure. However, no data exists in the pages yet. For that, the filesystem layer needs the block device driver to do the actual interfacing to the device. This is done by the `submit_bio()` function in `mpage_bio_submit()`:

```
-------------------------------------------------------------------
fs/mpage.c
90 struct bio *mpage_bio_submit(int rw, struct bio *bio)
91 {
92   bio->bi_end_io = mpage_end_io_read;
93   if (rw == WRITE)
94     bio->bi_end_io = mpage_end_io_write;
```

```
95    submit_bio(rw, bio);
96    return NULL;
97 }
```

Line 90

The first thing to notice is that `mpage_bio_submit()` works for both read and write calls via the `rw` parameter. It submits a bio structure that, in the read case, is empty and needs to be filled in. In the write case, the bio structure is filled and the block device driver copies the contents to its device.

Lines 92–94

If we are reading or writing, we set the appropriate function that will be called when I/O ends.

Lines 95–96

We call `submit_bio()` and return `NULL`. Recall that `mpage_readpage()` doesn't do anything with the return value of `mpage_bio_submit()`.

`submit_bio()` is part of the generic block device driver layer of the Linux kernel.

```
drivers/block/ll_rw_blk.c
2433 void submit_bio(int rw, struct bio *bio)
2434 {
2435    int count = bio_sectors(bio);
2436
2437    BIO_BUG_ON(!bio->bi_size);
2438    BIO_BUG_ON(!bio->bi_io_vec);
2439    bio->bi_rw = rw;
2440    if (rw & WRITE)
2441       mod_page_state(pgpgout, count);
2442    else
2443       mod_page_state(pgpgin, count);
2444
2445    if (unlikely(block_dump)) {
2446       char b[BDEVNAME_SIZE];
2447       printk(KERN_DEBUG "%s(%d): %s block %Lu on %s\n",
2448          current->comm, current->pid,
2449          (rw & WRITE) ? "WRITE" : "READ",
2450          (unsigned long long)bio->bi_sector,
2451          bdevname(bio->bi_bdev,b));
```

```
2452    }
2453
2454    generic_make_request(bio);
2455 }
```

Lines 2433–2443

These calls enable some debugging: Set the read/write attribute of the bio structure, and perform some page state housekeeping.

Lines 2445–2452

These lines handle the rare case that a block dump occurs. A debug message is thrown.

Line 2454

`generic_make_request()` contains the main functionality and uses the specific block device driver's request queue to handle the block I/O operation.

Part of the inline comments for `generic_make_request()` are enlightening:

```
drivers/block/ll_rw_blk.c
2336 * The caller of generic_make_request must make sure that bi_io_vec
2337 * are set to describe the memory buffer, and that bi_dev and bi_sector
are
2338 * set to describe the device address, and the
2339 * bi_end_io and optionally bi_private are set to describe how
2340 * completion notification should be signaled.
```

In these stages, we constructed the bio structure, and thus, the `bio_vec` structures are mapped to the memory buffer mentioned on line 2337, and the bio struct is initialized with the device address parameters as well. If you want to follow the read even further into the block device driver, refer to the "Block Device Overview" section in Chapter 5, which describes how the block device driver handles request queues and the specific hardware constraints of its device. Figure 6.18 illustrates how the `read()` system call traverses through the layers of kernel functionality.

After the block device driver reads the actual data and places it in the bio structure, the code we have traced unwinds. The newly allocated pages in the page cache are filled, and their references are passed back to the VFS layer and copied to the section of user space specified so long ago by the original `read()` call.

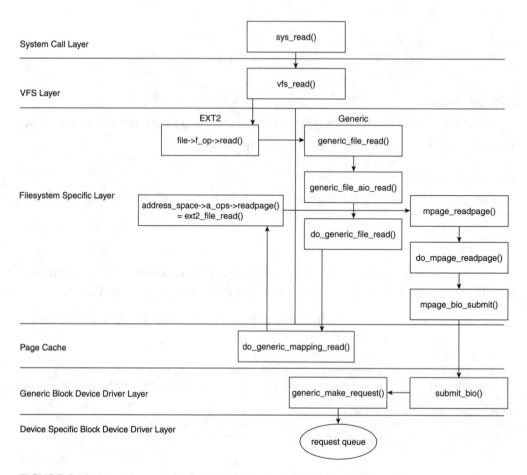

FIGURE 6.18
read() Top-Down Traversal

However, we hear you ask, "Isn't this only half of the story? What if we wanted to write instead of read?"

We hope that these descriptions made it somewhat clear that the path a read() call takes through the Linux kernel is similar to the path a write() call takes. However, we now outline some differences.

6.5.4   write()

A `write()` call gets mapped to `sys_write()` and then to `vfs_write()` in the same manner as a `read()` call:

```
------------------------------------------------------------------
fs/read_write.c
244 ssize_t vfs_write(struct file *file, const char __user *buf, size_t count,
loff_t *pos)
245 {
...
259         ret = file->f_op->write(file, buf, count, pos);
...
268 }
------------------------------------------------------------------
```

`vfs_write()` uses the generic `file_operations` write function to determine what specific filesystem layer write to use. This is translated, in our example ext2 case, via the `ext2_file_operations` structure:

```
------------------------------------------------------------------
fs/ext2/file.c
42 struct file_operations ext2_file_operations = {
43   .llseek   = generic_file_llseek,
44   .read     = generic_file_read,
45   .write    = generic_file_write,
...
56 };
------------------------------------------------------------------
```

Lines 44–45

Instead of calling `generic_file_read()`, we call `generic_file_write()`.

`generic_file_write()` obtains a lock on the file to prevent two writers from simultaneously writing to the same file, and calls `generic_file_write_nolock()`. `generic_file_write_nolock()` converts the file pointers and buffers to the `kiocb` and `iovec` parameters and calls the page cache write function `generic_file_aio_write_nolock()`.

Here is where a write diverges from a read. If the page to be written isn't in the page cache, the write does not fall through to the device itself. Instead, it reads the page into the page cache and then performs the write. Pages in the page cache are not immediately written to disk; instead, they are marked as "dirty" and, periodically, all dirty pages are written to disk.

There are analogous functions to the `read()` functions' `readpage()`. Within `generic_file_aio_write_nolock()`, the `address_space_operations` pointer accesses `prepare_write()` and `commit_write()`, which are both specific to the filesystem type the file resides upon. Recall `ext2_aops`, and we see that the `ext2` driver uses its own function, `ext2_prepare_write()`, and a generic function `generic_commit_write()`.

```
-------------------------------------------------------------------
fs/ext2/inode.c
628 static int
629 ext2_prepare_write(struct file *file, struct page *page,
630      unsigned from, unsigned to)
631 {
632   return block_prepare_write(page,from,to,ext2_get_block);
633 }
-------------------------------------------------------------------
```

Line 632

`ext2_prepare_write` is simply a wrapper for the generic filesystem function `block_prepare_write()`, which passes in the `ext2` filesystem-specific `get_block()` function.

`block_prepare_write()` allocates any new buffers that are required for the write. For example, if data is being appended to a file enough buffers are created, and linked with pages, to store the new data.

`generic_commit_write()` takes the given page and iterates over the buffers within it, marking each dirty. The `prepare` and the `commit` sections of a write are separated to prevent a partial write being flushed from the page cache to the block device.

6.5.4.1 Flushing Dirty Pages

The `write()` call returns after it has inserted—and marked dirty—all the pages it has written to. Linux has a daemon, `pdflush`, which writes the dirty pages from the page cache to the block device in two cases:

- **The system's free memory falls below a threshold.** Pages from the page cache are flushed to free up memory.

- **Dirty pages reach a certain age.** Pages that haven't been written to disk after a certain amount of time are written to their block device.

The `pdflush` daemon calls the filesystem-specific function `writepages()` when it is ready to write pages to disk. So, for our example, recall the `ext2_file_operation` structure, which equates `writepages()` with `ext2_writepages()`.[14]

```
670 static int
671 ext2_writepages(struct address_space *mapping, struct writeback_control
*wbc)
672 {
673    return mpage_writepages(mapping, wbc, ext2_get_block);
674 }
```

Like other specific implementations of generic filesystem functions, `ext2_writepages()` simply calls the generic filesystem function `mpage_writepages()` with the filesystem-specific `ext2_get_block()` function.

`mpage_writepages()` loops over the dirty pages and calls `mpage_writepage()` on each dirty page. Similar to `mpage_readpage()`, `mpage_writepage()` returns a bio structure that maps the physical device layout of the page to its physical memory layout. `mpage_writepages()` then calls `submit_bio()` to send the new bio structure to the block device driver to transfer the data to the device itself.

Summary

This chapter began by looking at the structures and global variables that make up the common file model. The structures include the `superblock`, the `inode`, the `dentry`, and the file structures. We then looked at the structures associated with VFS. We saw how VFS works to support various filesystems.

We then looked at VFS-associated system calls, open and close, to illustrate how it all works together. We then traced the `read()` and `write()` user space call through VFS and throughout the twists and turns of the generic filesystem layer and the specific filesystem layer. Using the `ext2` filesystem driver as an example of the specific filesystem layer, we showed how the kernel intertwines calls to specific filesystem driver functions and generic filesystem functions. This lead us to discuss the page cache, which is a section of memory that stores recently accessed pages from the block devices attached to the system.

---

[14] The `pdflush` daemon is fairly involved, and for our purposes of tracing a write, we can ignore the complexity. However, if you are interested in the details, `mm/pdflush.c`, `mm/fs-writeback.c`, and `mm/page-writeback.c` contain the relevant code.

Exercises

1. Under what circumstances would you use the inode `i_hash` field as opposed to the `i_list` field? Why have both a hash list and a linear list for the same structures?

2. Of all the file structures we've seen, name the ones that have corresponding data structures in the hard disk.

3. For what types of operations are `dentry` objects used? Why not just use inodes?

4. What is the association between a file descriptor and a file structure? Is it one-to-one? Many-to-one? One-to-many?

5. What is the use of the `fd_set` structure?

6. What type of data structure ensures that the page cache operates at maximum speed?

7. Suppose that you are writing a new filesystem driver. You're replacing the `ext2` filesystem driver with a new driver (`media_fs`) that optimizes file I/O for multimedia. Where would you make changes to the Linux kernel to ensure that your new driver is used instead of the `ext2` driver?

8. How does a page get dirty? How does a dirty page get written to disk?

Chapter 7

Scheduling and Kernel Synchronization

In this chapter

The Linux kernel is a multitasking kernel, which means that many processes can run as if they were the only process on the system. The way in which an operating system chooses which process at a given time has access to a system's CPU(s) is controlled by a scheduler.

The scheduler is responsible for swapping CPU access between different processes and for choosing the order in which processes obtain CPU access. Linux, like most operating systems, triggers the scheduler by using a timer interrupt. When this timer goes off, the kernel needs to decide whether to yield the CPU to a process different than the current process and, if a yield occurs, which process gets the CPU next. The amount of time between the timer interrupt is called a **timeslice**.

System processes tend to fall into two types: interactive and non-interactive. Interactive processes are heavily dependent upon I/O and, as a result, do not usually use their entire timeslice and, instead, yield the CPU to another process. Non-interactive processes are heavily dependent on the CPU and typically use most, if not all, of their timeslice. The scheduler has to balance the requirements of these two types of processes and attempt to ensure every process gets enough time to accomplish its task without detrimentally affecting the execution of other processes.

Linux, like some schedulers, distinguishes between one more type of process: a real-time process. Real-time processes must execute in real time. Linux has support for real-time processes, but those exist outside of the scheduler logic. Put simply, the Linux scheduler treats any process marked as real-time as a higher priority than any other process. It is up to the developer of the real-time processes to ensure that these processes do not hog the CPU and eventually yield.

Schedulers typically use some type of process queue to manage the execution of processes on the system. In Linux, this process queue is called the run queue. The run queue is described fully in Chapter 3, "Processes: The Principal Model of Execution,"[1] but let's recap some of the fundamentals here because of the close tie between the scheduler and the run queue.

---

[1] Section 3.6 discusses the run queue.

In Linux, the run queue is composed of two priority arrays:

- **Active.** Stores processes that have not yet used up their timeslice
- **Expired.** Stores processes that have used up their timeslice

From a high level, the scheduler's job in Linux is to take the highest priority active processes, let them use the CPU to execute, and place them in the expired array when they use up their timeslice. With this high-level framework in mind, let's closely look at how the Linux scheduler operates.

7.1 Linux Scheduler

The 2.6 Linux kernel introduces a completely new scheduler that's commonly referred to as the O(1) scheduler. The scheduler can perform the scheduling of a task in constant time.[2] Chapter 3 addressed the basic structure of the scheduler and how a newly created process is initialized for it. This section describes how a task is executed on a single CPU system. There are some mentions of code for scheduling across multiple CPU (SMP) systems but, in general, the same scheduling process applies across CPUs. We then describe how the scheduler switches out the currently running process, performing what is called a context switch, and then we touch on the other significant change in the 2.6 kernel: preemption.

From a high level, the scheduler is simply a grouping of functions that operate on given data structures. Nearly all the code implementing the scheduler can be found in `kernel/sched.c` and `include/linux/sched.h`. One important point to mention early on is how the scheduler code uses the terms "task" and "process" interchangeably. Occasionally, code comments also use "thread" to refer to a task or process. A task, or process, in the scheduler is a collection of data structures and flow of control. The scheduler code also refers to a `task_struct`, which is a data structure the Linux kernel uses to keep track of processes.[3]

---

[2] O(1) is big-oh notation, which means constant time.

[3] Chapter 3 explains the `task_struct` structure in depth.

7.1.1   Choosing the Next Task

After a process has been initialized and placed on a run queue, at some time, it should have access to the CPU to execute. The two functions that are responsible for passing CPU control to different processes are `schedule()` and `scheduler_tick()`. `scheduler_tick()` is a system timer that the kernel periodically calls and marks processes as needing rescheduling. When a timer event occurs, the current process is put on hold and the Linux kernel itself takes control of the CPU. When the timer event finishes, the Linux kernel normally passes control back to the process that was put on hold. However, when the held process has been marked as needing rescheduling, the kernel calls `schedule()` to choose which process to activate instead of the process that was executing before the kernel took control. The process that was executing before the kernel took control is called the current process. To make things slightly more complicated, in certain situations, the kernel can take control from the kernel; this is called kernel preemption. In the following sections, we assume that the scheduler decides which of two user space processes gains CPU control.

Figure 7.1 illustrates how the CPU is passed among different processes as time progresses. We see that *Process A* has control of the CPU and is executing. The system timer `scheduler_tick()` goes off, takes control of the CPU from *A*, and marks *A* as needing rescheduling. The Linux kernel calls `schedule()`, which chooses *Process B* and the control of the CPU is given to *B*.

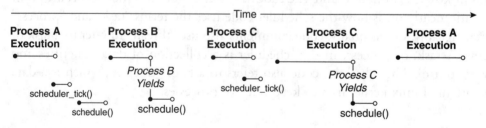

FIGURE 7.1
Scheduling Processes

Process B executes for a while and then voluntarily yields the CPU. This commonly occurs when a process waits on some resource. *B* calls `schedule()`, which chooses *Process C* to execute next.

Process C executes until `scheduler_tick()` occurs, which does not mark *C* as needing rescheduling. This results in `schedule()` not being called and *C* regains control of the CPU.

Process C yields by calling `schedule()`, which determines that *Process A* should gain control of the CPU and *A* starts to execute again.

We first examine `schedule()`, which is how the Linux kernel decides which process to execute next, and then we examine `scheduler_tick()`, which is how the kernel determines which processes need to yield the CPU. The combined effects of these functions demonstrate the flow of control within the scheduler:

```
------------------------------------------------------------------
kernel/sched.c
2184 asmlinkage void schedule(void)
2185 {
2186   long *switch_count;
2187   task_t *prev, *next;
2188   runqueue_t *rq;
2189   prio_array_t *array;
2190   struct list_head *queue;
2191   unsigned long long now;
2192   unsigned long run_time;
2193   int idx;
2194
2195   /*
2196   * Test if we are atomic. Since do_exit() needs to call into
2197   * schedule() atomically, we ignore that path for now.
2198   * Otherwise, whine if we are scheduling when we should not be.
2199   */
2200   if (likely(!(current->state & (TASK_DEAD | TASK_ZOMBIE)))) {
2201     if (unlikely(in_atomic())) {
2202       printk(KERN_ERR "bad: scheduling while atomic!\n  ");
2203       dump_stack();
2204     }
2205   }
2206
2207 need_resched:
2208   preempt_disable();
2209   prev = current;
2210   rq = this_rq();
2211
2212   release_kernel_lock(prev);
2213   now = sched_clock();
2214   if (likely(now - prev->timestamp < NS_MAX_SLEEP_AVG))
2215     run_time = now - prev->timestamp;
2216   else
2217     run_time = NS_MAX_SLEEP_AVG;
2218
2219   /*
```

```
2220    * Tasks with interactive credits get charged less run_time
2221    * at high sleep_avg to delay them losing their interactive
2222    * status
2223    */
2224    if (HIGH_CREDIT(prev))
2225    run_time /= (CURRENT_BONUS(prev) ? : 1);
```

Lines 2213–2218

We calculate the length of time for which the process on the scheduler has been active. If the process has been active for longer than the average maximum sleep time (NS_MAX_SLEEP_AVG), we set its runtime to the average maximum sleep time.

This is what the Linux kernel code calls a timeslice in other sections of the code. A **timeslice** refers to both the amount of time between scheduler interrupts and the length of time a process has spent using the CPU. If a process exhausts its timeslice, the process expires and is no longer active. The **timestamp** is an absolute value that determines for how long a process has used the CPU. The scheduler uses time-stamps to decrement the timeslice of processes that have been using the CPU.

For example, suppose Process A has a timeslice of 50 clock cycles. It uses the CPU for 5 clock cycles and then yields the CPU to another process. The kernel uses the timestamp to determine that Process A has 45 cycles left on its timeslice.

Lines 2224–2225

Interactive processes are processes that spend much of their time waiting for input. A good example of an interactive process is the keyboard controller—most of the time the controller is waiting for input, but when it has a task to do, the user expects it to occur at a high priority.

Interactive processes, those that have an interactive credit of more than 100 (default value), get their effective run_time divided by (sleep_avg/ max_sleep_avg * MAX_BONUS(10)):[4]

```
kernel/sched.c
2226
2227    spin_lock_irq(&rq->lock);
2228
2229    /*
2230    * if entering off of a kernel preemption go straight
2231    * to picking the next task.
2232    */
```

---

[4] Bonuses are scheduling modifiers for high priority.

```
2233    switch_count = &prev->nivcsw;
2234    if (prev->state && !(preempt_count() & PREEMPT_ACTIVE)) {
2235      switch_count = &prev->nvcsw;
2236      if (unlikely((prev->state & TASK_INTERRUPTIBLE) &&
2237          unlikely(signal_pending(prev))))
2238        prev->state = TASK_RUNNING;
2239      else
2240        deactivate_task(prev, rq);
2241    }
```

Line 2227

The function obtains the run queue lock because we're going to modify it.

Lines 2233–2241

If we have entered `schedule()` with the previous process being a kernel pre-emption, we leave the previous process running if a signal is pending. This means that the kernel has preempted normal processing in quick succession; thus, the code is contained in two `unlikely()` statements.[5] If there is no further preemption, we remove the preempted process from the run queue and continue to choose the next process to run.

```
kernel/sched.c
2243    cpu = smp_processor_id();
2244    if (unlikely(!rq->nr_running)) {
2245      idle_balance(cpu, rq);
2246      if (!rq->nr_running) {
2247        next = rq->idle;
2248        rq->expired_timestamp = 0;
2249        wake_sleeping_dependent(cpu, rq);
2250        goto switch_tasks;
2251      }
2252    }
2253
2254    array = rq->active;
2255    if (unlikely(!array->nr_active)) {
2256      /*
2257      * Switch the active and expired arrays.
2258      */
2259      rq->active = rq->expired;
2260      rq->expired = array;
2261      array = rq->active;
2262      rq->expired_timestamp = 0;
2263      rq->best_expired_prio = MAX_PRIO;
2264    }
```

---

[5]   For more information on the unlikely routine, see Chapter 2, "Exploration Toolkit."

Line 2243

We grab the current CPU identifier via `smp_processor_id()`.

Lines 2244–2252

If the run queue has no processes on it, we set the next process to the idle process and reset the run queue's expired timestamp to 0. On a multiprocessor system, we first check if any processes are running on other CPUs that this CPU can take. In effect, we load balance idle processes across all CPUs in the system. Only if no processes can be moved from the other CPUs do we set the run queue's next process to idle and reset the expired timestamp.

Lines 2255–2264

If the run queue's active array is empty, we switch the active and expired array pointers before choosing a new process to run.

```
-------------------------------------------------------------------
kernel/sched.c
2266    idx = sched_find_first_bit(array->bitmap);
2267    queue = array->queue + idx;
2268    next = list_entry(queue->next, task_t, run_list);
2269
2270    if (dependent_sleeper(cpu, rq, next)) {
2271      next = rq->idle;
2272      goto switch_tasks;
2273    }
2274
2275    if (!rt_task(next) && next->activated > 0) {
2276      unsigned long long delta = now - next->timestamp;
2277
2278      if (next->activated == 1)
2279        delta = delta * (ON_RUNQUEUE_WEIGHT * 128 / 100) / 128;
2280
2281      array = next->array;
2282      dequeue_task(next, array);
2283      recalc_task_prio(next, next->timestamp + delta);
2284      enqueue_task(next, array);
2285    }
next->activated = 0;
-------------------------------------------------------------------
```

Lines 2266–2268

The scheduler finds the highest priority process to run via `sched_find_first_bit()` and then sets up `queue` to point to the list held in the priority array at the specified location. `next` is initialized to the first process in `queue`.

Lines 2270–2273

If the process to be activated is dependent on a sibling that is sleeping, we choose a new process to be activated and jump to `switch_tasks` to continue the scheduling function.

Suppose that we have Process A that spawned Process B to read from a device and that Process A was waiting for Process B to finish before continuing. If the scheduler chooses Process A for activation, this section of code, `dependent_sleeper()`, determines that Process A is waiting on Process B and chooses an entirely new process to activate.

Lines 2275–2285

If the process' activated attribute is greater than 0, and the next process is not a real-time task, we remove it from `queue`, recalculate its priority, and enqueue it again.

Line 2286

We set the process' activated attribute to 0, and then run with it.

```
kernel/sched.c
2287 switch_tasks:
2288   prefetch(next);
2289   clear_tsk_need_resched(prev);
2290   RCU_qsctr(task_cpu(prev))++;
2291
2292   prev->sleep_avg -= run_time;
2293   if ((long)prev->sleep_avg <= 0) {
2294     prev->sleep_avg = 0;
2295     if (!(HIGH_CREDIT(prev) || LOW_CREDIT(prev)))
2296       prev->interactive_credit--;
2297   }
2298   prev->timestamp = now;
2299
2300   if (likely(prev != next)) {
2301     next->timestamp = now;
2302     rq->nr_switches++;
2303     rq->curr = next;
2304     ++*switch_count;
2305
```

```
2306        prepare_arch_switch(rq, next);
2307        prev = context_switch(rq, prev, next);
2308        barrier();
2309
2310        finish_task_switch(prev);
2311    } else
2312        spin_unlock_irq(&rq->lock);
2313
2314    reacquire_kernel_lock(current);
2315    preempt_enable_no_resched();
2316    if (test_thread_flag(TIF_NEED_RESCHED))
2317        goto need_resched;
2318 }
```

Line 2288

We attempt to get the memory of the new process' task structure into the CPU's L1 cache. (See include/linux/prefetch.h for more information.)

Line 2290

Because we're going through a context switch, we need to inform the current CPU that we're doing so. This allows a multi-CPU device to ensure data that is shared across CPUs is accessed exclusively. This process is called read-copy updating. For more information, see http://lse.sourceforge.net/locking/rcupdate.html.

Lines 2292–2298

We decrement the previous process' sleep_avg attribute by the amount of time it ran, adjusting for negative values. If the process is neither interactive nor non-interactive, its interactive credit is between high and low, so we decrement its interactive credit because it had a low sleep average. We update its timestamp to the current time. This operation helps the scheduler keep track of how much time a given process has spent using the CPU and estimate how much time it will use the CPU in the future.

Lines 2300–2304

If we haven't chosen the same process, we set the new process' timestamp, increment the run queue counters, and set the current process to the new process.

Lines 2306–2308

These lines describe the assembly language `context_switch()`. Hold on for a few paragraphs as we delve into the explanation of context switching in the next section.

Lines 2314–2318

We reacquire the kernel lock, enable preemption, and see if we need to reschedule immediately; if so, we go back to the top of `schedule()`.

It's possible that after we perform the `context_switch()`, we need to reschedule. Perhaps `scheduler_tick()` has marked the new process as needing rescheduling or, when we enable preemption, it gets marked. We keep rescheduling processes (and context switching them) until one is found that doesn't need rescheduling. The process that leaves `schedule()` becomes the new process executing on this CPU.

7.1.2 Context Switch

Called from `schedule()` in `/kernel/sched.c`, `context_switch()` does the machine-specific work of switching the memory environment and the processor state. In the abstract, `context_switch` swaps the current task with the next task. The function `context_switch()` begins executing the next task and returns a pointer to the task structure of the task that was running before the call:

```
-------------------------------------------------------------------
kernel/sched.c
1048 /*
1049 * context_switch - switch to the new MM and the new
1050 * thread's register state.
1051 */
1052 static inline
1053 task_t * context_switch(runqueue_t *rq, task_t *prev, task_t *next)
1054 {
1055    struct mm_struct *mm = next->mm;
1056    struct mm_struct *oldmm = prev->active_mm;
...
1063      switch_mm(oldmm, mm, next);
...
1072    switch_to(prev, next, prev);
1073
1074    return prev;
1075 }
-------------------------------------------------------------------
```

Here, we describe the two jobs of `context_switch`: one to switch the virtual memory mapping and one to switch the task/thread structure. The first job, which the function `switch_mm()` carries out, uses many of the hardware-dependent memory management structures and registers:

```
-------------------------------------------------------------------
/include/asm-i386/mmu_context.h
026  static inline void switch_mm(struct mm_struct *prev,
027      struct mm_struct *next,
028      struct task_struct *tsk)
029  {
030   int cpu = smp_processor_id();
031
032   if (likely(prev != next)) {
033    /* stop flush ipis for the previous mm */
034    cpu_clear(cpu, prev->cpu_vm_mask);
035  #ifdef CONFIG_SMP
036    cpu_tlbstate[cpu].state = TLBSTATE_OK;
037    cpu_tlbstate[cpu].active_mm = next;
038  #endif
039    cpu_set(cpu, next->cpu_vm_mask);
040
041    /* Re-load page tables */
042    load_cr3(next->pgd);
043
044    /*
045     * load the LDT, if the LDT is different:
046     */
047    if (unlikely(prev->context.ldt != next->context.ldt))
048      load_LDT_nolock(&next->context, cpu);
049   }
050  #ifdef CONFIG_SMP
051   else {
-------------------------------------------------------------------
```

Line 39

Bind the new task to the current processor.

Line 42

The code for switching the memory context utilizes the x86 hardware register `cr3`, which holds the base address of all paging operations for a given process. The new page global descriptor is loaded here from `next->pgd`.

Line 47

Most processes share the same LDT. If another LDT is required by this process, it is loaded here from the new `next->context` structure.

The other half of function `context_switch()` in `/kernel/sched.c` then calls the macro `switch_to()`, which calls the C function `__switch_to()`. The delineation of architecture *in*dependence to architecture dependence for both x86 and PPC is the `switch_to()` macro.

7.1.2.1 Following the x86 Trail of switch_to()

The x86 code is more compact than PPC. The following is the architecture-dependent code for `__switch_to()`. `task_struct` (not `thread_struct`) is passed to `__switch_to()`. The code discussed next is inline assembler code for calling the C function `__switch_to()` (line 23) with the proper `task_struct` structures as parameters.

The `context_switch` takes three task pointers: `prev`, `next`, and `last`. In addition, there is the current pointer.

Let us now explain, at a high level, what occurs when `switch_to()` is called and how the task pointers change after a call to `switch_to()`.

Figure 7.2 shows three `switch_to()` calls using three processes: A, B, and C.

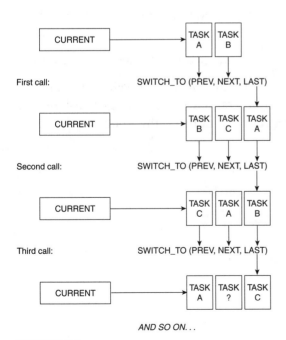

FIGURE 7.2
switch_to Calls

We want to switch A and B. Before, the **first call** we have

- Current → A
- Prev → A, next → B

After the **first call**:

- Current → B
- Last → A

Now, we want to switch B and C. Before the **second call**, we have

- Current → B
- Prev → B, next → C

After the **second call**:

- Current → C
- Last → B

Returning from the **second call**, current now points to task (C) and last points to (B).

The method continues with task (A) being swapped in once again, and so on.

The inline assembly of the switch_to() function is an excellent example of assembly magic in the kernel. It is also a good example of the gcc C extensions. See Chapter 2, "Exploration Toolkit," for a tutorial featuring this function. Now, we carefully walk through this code block.

```
--------------------------------------------------------------------
/include/asm-i386/system.h
012   extern struct task_struct * FASTCALL(__switch_to(struct task_struct *prev,
struct task_struct *next));

015   #define switch_to(prev,next,last) do {        \
016     unsigned long esi,edi;          \
017     asm volatile("pushfl\n\t"        \
018     "pushl %%ebp\n\t"         \
019     "movl %%esp,%0\n\t"   /* save ESP */     \
020     "movl %5,%%esp\n\t"   /* restore ESP */    \
021     "movl $1f,%1\n\t"    /* save EIP */    \
022     "pushl %6\n\t"    /* restore EIP */    \
023     "jmp __switch_to\n"          \
```

```
023    "1:\t"                \
024    "popl %%ebp\n\t"          \
025    "popfl"          \
026    :"=m" (prev->thread.esp),"=m" (prev->thread.eip),  \
027    "=a" (last),"=S" (esi),"=D" (edi)        \
028    :"m" (next->thread.esp),"m" (next->thread.eip),   \
029    "2" (prev), "d" (next));        \
030    } while (0)
```

Line 12

The FASTCALL macro resolves to __attribute__ regparm(3), which forces
the parameters to be passed in registers rather than stack.

Lines 15–16

The do {} while (0) construct allows (among other things) the macro to have
local the variables esi and edi. Remember, these are just local variables with familiar names.

Current and the Task Structure

As we explore the kernel, whenever we need to retrieve or store information on the
task (or process) which is *currently* running on a given processor, we use the global
variable current to reference its task structure. For example, current->pid holds
the process ID. Linux allows for a quick (and clever) method of referencing the current task structure.

Every process is assigned 8K of contiguous memory when it is created. (With Linux
2.6, there is a compile-time option to use 4K instead of 8K.) This 8K segment is
occupied by the task structure and the kernel stack for the given process. Upon
process creation, Linux puts the task structure at the low end of the 8K memory and
the kernel stack pointer starts at the high end. The kernel stack pointer (especially for
x86 and r1 for PPC) decrements as data is pushed onto the stack. Because this 8K
memory region is page-aligned, its starting address (in hex notation) always ends in
0x000 (multiples of 4k bytes).

As you might have guessed, the clever method by which Linux references the current
task structure is to AND the contents of the stack pointer with 0xffff_f000. Recent versions of the PPC Linux kernel have taken this one step further by dedicating General
Purpose Register 2 to holding the current pointer.

Lines 17 and 30

The construct `asm volatile ()`[6] encloses the inline assembly block and the volatile keyword assures that the compiler will not change (optimize) the routine in any way.

Lines 17–18

Push the `flags` and `ebp` registers onto the stack. (Note: We are still using the stack associated with the `prev` task.)

Line 19

This line saves the current stack pointer `esp` to the `prev` task structure.

Line 20

Move the stack pointer from the next task structure to the current processor `esp`.

> NOTE By definition, we have just made a context switch.

We are now with a new kernel stack and thus, any reference to current is to the new (`next`) task structure.

Line 21

Save the return address for `prev` into its task structure. This is where the `prev` task resumes when it is restarted.

Line 22

Push the return address (from when we return from `__switch_to()`) onto the stack. This is the `eip` from `next`. The `eip` was saved into its task structure (on line 21) when it was stopped, or preempted the last time.

Line 23

Jump to the C function `__switch_to()` to update the following:

- The next thread structure with the kernel stack pointer

- Thread local storage descriptor for this processor

- `fs` and `gs` for `prev` and `next`, if needed

---

[6] See Chapter 2 for more information on `volatile`.

- Debug registers, if needed
- I/O bitmaps, if needed

`__switch_to()` then returns the updated `prev` task structure.

Lines 24–25
Pop the base pointer and flags registers from the new (next task) kernel stack.

Lines 26–29
These are the output and input parameters to the inline assembly routine. See the "Inline Assembly" section in Chapter 2 for more information on the *constraints* put on these parameters.

Line 29
By way of assembler magic, `prev` is returned in `eax`, which is the third positional parameter. In other words, the input parameter `prev` is passed out of the `switch_to()` macro as the output parameter last.

Because `switch_to()` is a macro, it was executed inline with the code that called it in `context_switch()`. It does not return as functions normally do.

For the sake of clarity, remember that `switch_to()` passes back `prev` in the `eax` register, execution then continues in `context_switch()`, where the next instruction is `return prev` (line 1074 of `kernel/sched.c`). This allows `context_switch()` to pass back a pointer to the last task running.

7.1.2.2   Following the PPC context_switch()

The PPC code for `context_switch()` has slightly more work to do for the same results. Unlike the `cr3` register in x86 architecture, the PPC uses hash functions to point to context environments. The following code for `switch_mm()` touches on these functions, but Chapter 4, "Memory Management," offers a deeper discussion.

Here is the routine for `switch_mm()` which, in turn, calls the routine `set_context()`.

```
-----------------------------------------------------------------
/include/asm-ppc/mmu_context.h
155  static inline void switch_mm(struct mm_struct *prev, struct
mm_struct *next,struct task_struct *tsk)
156  {
157    tsk->thread.pgdir = next->pgd;
```

```
158    get_mmu_context(next);
159    set_context(next->context, next->pgd);
160  }
```

Line 157

The page global directory (segment register) for the new thread is made to point to the next->pgd pointer.

Line 158

The context field of the mm_struct (next->context) passed into switch_mm() is updated to the value of the appropriate context. This information comes from a global reference to the variable context_map[], which contains a series of bitmap fields.

Line 159

This is the call to the assembly routine set_context. Below is the code and discussion of this routine. Upon execution of the blr instruction on line 1468, the code returns to the switch_mm routine.

```
---------------------------------------------------------------------
/arch/ppc/kernel/head.S
1437  _GLOBAL(set_context)
1438  mulli  r3,r3,897  /* multiply context by skew factor */
1439  rlwinm r3,r3,4,8,27  /* VSID = (context & 0xfffff) << 4 */
1440  addis  r3,r3,0x6000  /* Set Ks, Ku bits */
1441  li   r0,NUM_USER_SEGMENTS
1442  mtctr  r0
...
1457  3:  isync
...
1461  mtsrin  r3,r4
1462  addi  r3,r3,0x111  /* next VSID */
1463  rlwinm r3,r3,0,8,3  /* clear out any overflow from VSID field */
1464  addis  r4,r4,0x1000  /* address of next segment */
1465  bdnz  3b
1466  sync
1467  isync
1468  blr
---------------------------------------------------------------------
```

Lines 1437–1440

The context field of the mm_struct (next->context) passed into set_context() by way of r3, sets up the hash function for PPC segmentation.

Lines 1461–1465

The `pgd` field of the `mm_struct` (`next->pgd`) passed into `set_context()` by way of `r4`, points to the segment registers.

Segmentation is the basis of PPC memory management (refer to Chapter 4). Upon returning from `set_context()`, the `mm_struct` next is initialized to the proper memory regions and is returned to `switch_mm()`.

7.1.2.3   Following the PPC Trail of switch_to()

The result of the PPC implementation of `switch_to()` is necessarily identical to the x86 call; it takes in the `current` and `next` task pointers and returns a pointer to the previously running task:

```
------------------------------------------------------------------------
include/asm-ppc/system.h
88 extern struct task_struct *__switch_to(struct task_struct *,
89   struct task_struct *);
90 #define switch_to(prev, next, last)
((last) = __switch_to((prev), (next)))
91
92 struct thread_struct;
93 extern struct task_struct *_switch(struct thread_struct *prev,
94        struct thread_struct *next);
------------------------------------------------------------------------
```

On line 88, `__switch_to()` takes its parameters as `task_struct` type and, at line 93, `_switch()` takes its parameters as *thread*_struct. This is because the thread entry within `task_struct` contains the architecture-dependent processor register information of interest for the given thread. Now, let us examine the implementation of `__switch_to()`:

```
------------------------------------------------------------------------
/arch/ppc/kernel/process.c
200  struct task_struct *__switch_to(struct task_struct *prev,
   struct task_struct *new)
201  {
202    struct thread_struct *new_thread, *old_thread;
203    unsigned long s;
204    struct task_struct *last;
205    local_irq_save(s);
...
247    new_thread = &new->thread;
248    old_thread = &current->thread;
249    last = _switch(old_thread, new_thread);
250    local_irq_restore(s);
251    return last;
252  }
------------------------------------------------------------------------
```

Line 205

Disable interrupts before the context switch.

Lines 247–248

Still running under the context of the *old* thread, pass the pointers to the thread structure to the _switch() function.

Line 249

_switch() is the assembly routine called to do the work of switching the two thread structures (see the following section).

Line 250

Enable interrupts after the context switch.

To better understand what needs to be swapped within a PPC thread, we need to examine the thread_struct passed in on line 249.

Recall from the exploration of the x86 context switch that the switch does not officially occur until we are pointing to a new kernel stack. This happens in _switch().

Tracing the PPC Code for _switch()

By convention, the parameters of a PPC C function (from left to right) are held in r3, r4, r5, ...r12. Upon entry into switch(), r3 points to the thread_struct for the current task and r4 points to the thread_struct for the new task:

```
-------------------------------------------------------------------
/arch/ppc/kernel/entry.S
437  _GLOBAL(_switch)
438   stwu  r1,-INT_FRAME_SIZE(r1)
439   mflr  r0
440   stw   r0,INT_FRAME_SIZE+4(r1)
441   /* r3-r12 are caller saved -- Cort */
442   SAVE_NVGPRS(r1)
443   stw   r0,_NIP(r1)  /* Return to switch caller */
444   mfmsr  r11
...
458  1:  stw r11,_MSR(r1)
459   mfcr  r10
460   stw   r10,_CCR(r1)
461   stw   r1,KSP(r3)  /* Set old stack pointer */
462
463   tophys(r0,r4)
```

```
464    CLR_TOP32(r0)
465    mtspr  SPRG3,r0/* Update current THREAD phys addr */
466    lwz  r1,KSP(r4)  /* Load new stack pointer */
467    /* save the old current 'last' for return value */
468    mr  r3,r2
469    addi  r2,r4,-THREAD  /* Update current */
...
478    lwz  r0,_CCR(r1)
479    mtcrf  0xFF,r0
480    REST_NVGPRS(r1)
481
482    lwz  r4,_NIP(r1)  /* Return to _switch caller in new task */
483    mtlr  r4
484    addi  r1,r1,INT_FRAME_SIZE
485    blr
```

The byte-for-byte mechanics of swapping out the previous thread_struct for
the new is left as an exercise for you. It is worth noting, however, the use of r1, r2,
r3, SPRG3, and r4 in _switch() to see the basics of this operation.

Lines 438–460

The environment is saved to the current stack with respect to the current stack
pointer, r1.

Line 461

The entire environment is then saved into the current thread_struct pointer
passed in by way of r3.

Lines 463–465

SPRG3 is updated to point to the thread structure of the new task.

Line 466

KSP is the offset into the task structure (r4) of the new task's kernel stack pointer.
The stack pointer r1 is now updated with this value. (**This is the point of the PPC
context switch.**)

Line 468

The current pointer to the previous task is returned from _switch() in r3. This
represents the last task.

Line 469

The current pointer (r2) is updated with the pointer to the new task structure (r4).

Lines 478–486

Restore the rest of the environment from the new stack and return to the caller with the previous task structure in r3.

This concludes the explanation of context_switch(). At this point, the processor has swapped the two processes prev and next as called by context_switch in schedule().

```
------------------------------------------------------------------
kernel/sched.c
1709   prev = context_switch(rq, prev, next);
------------------------------------------------------------------
```

prev now points to the process that we have just switched away from and next points to the current process.

Now that we've discussed how tasks are scheduled in the Linux kernel, we can examine how tasks are told to be scheduled. Namely, what causes schedule() to be called and one process to yield the CPU to another process?

7.1.3   Yielding the CPU

Processes can voluntarily yield the CPU by simply calling schedule(). This is most commonly used in kernel code and device drivers that want to sleep or wait for a signal to occur.[7] Other tasks want to continually use the CPU and the system timer must tell them to yield. The Linux kernel periodically seizes the CPU, in so doing stopping the active process, and then does a number of timer-based tasks. One of these tasks, scheduler_tick(), is how the kernel forces a process to yield. If a process has been running for too long, the kernel does not return control to that process and instead chooses another one. We now examine how scheduler_tick() determines if the current process must yield the CPU:

```
------------------------------------------------------------------
kernel/sched.c
1981 void scheduler_tick(int user_ticks, int sys_ticks)
1982 {
1983   int cpu = smp_processor_id();
1984   struct cpu_usage_stat *cpustat = &kstat_this_cpu.cpustat;
1985   runqueue_t *rq = this_rq();
1986   task_t *p = current;
1987
```

---

[7]   Linux convention specifies that you should *never* call schedule while holding a spinlock because this introduces the possibility of system deadlock. This is good advice!

```
1988    rq->timestamp_last_tick = sched_clock();
1989
1990    if (rcu_pending(cpu))
1991      rcu_check_callbacks(cpu, user_ticks);
```

Lines 1981–1986

This code block initializes the data structures that the scheduler_tick() function needs. cpu, cpu_usage_stat, and rq are set to the processor ID, CPU stats and run queue of the current processor. p is a pointer to the current process executing on cpu.

Line 1988

The run queue's last tick is set to the current time in nanoseconds.

Lines 1990–1991

On an SMP system, we need to check if there are any outstanding read-copy updates to perform (RCU). If so, we perform them via rcu_check_callback().

```
kernel/sched.c
1993    /* note: this timer irq context must be accounted for as well */
1994    if (hardirq_count() - HARDIRQ_OFFSET) {
1995        cpustat->irq += sys_ticks;
1996        sys_ticks = 0;
1997    } else if (softirq_count()) {
1998        cpustat->softirq += sys_ticks;
1999        sys_ticks = 0;
2000    }
2001
2002    if (p == rq->idle) {
2003        if (atomic_read(&rq->nr_iowait) > 0)
2004          cpustat->iowait += sys_ticks;
2005        else
2006          cpustat->idle += sys_ticks;
2007        if (wake_priority_sleeper(rq))
2008          goto out;
2009        rebalance_tick(cpu, rq, IDLE);
2010        return;
2011    }
2012    if (TASK_NICE(p) > 0)
2013        cpustat->nice += user_ticks;
2014    else
2015        cpustat->user += user_ticks;
2016    cpustat->system += sys_ticks;
```

Lines 1994–2000

cpustat keeps track of kernel statistics, and we update the hardware and software interrupt statistics by the number of system ticks that have occurred.

Lines 2002–2011

If there is no currently running process, we atomically check if any processes are waiting on I/O. If so, the CPU I/O wait statistic is incremented; otherwise, the CPU idle statistic is incremented. In a uniprocessor system, rebalance_tick() does nothing, but on a multiple processor system, rebalance_tick() attempts to load balance the current CPU because the CPU has nothing to do.

Lines 2012–2016

More CPU statistics are gathered in this code block. If the current process was niced, we increment the CPU nice counter; otherwise, the user tick counter is incremented. Finally, we increment the CPU's system tick counter.

```
------------------------------------------------------------------
kernel/sched.c
2019   if (p->array != rq->active) {
2020     set_tsk_need_resched(p);
2021     goto out;
2022   }
2023   spin_lock(&rq->lock);
------------------------------------------------------------------
```

Lines 2019–2022

Here, we see why we store a pointer to a priority array within the task_struct of the process. The scheduler checks the current process to see if it is no longer active. If the process has expired, the scheduler sets the process' rescheduling flag and jumps to the end of the scheduler_tick() function. At that point (lines 2092–2093), the scheduler attempts to load balance the CPU because there is no active task yet. This case occurs when the scheduler grabbed CPU control before the current process was able to schedule itself or clean up from a successful run.

Line 2023

At this point, we know that the current process was running and not expired or nonexistent. The scheduler now wants to yield CPU control to another process; the first thing it must do is take the run queue lock.

```
kernel/sched.c
2024   /*
2025   * The task was running during this tick - update the
2026   * time slice counter. Note: we do not update a thread's
2027   * priority until it either goes to sleep or uses up its
2028   * timeslice. This makes it possible for interactive tasks
2029   * to use up their timeslices at their highest priority levels.
2030   */
2031   if (unlikely(rt_task(p))) {
2032      /*
2033       * RR tasks need a special form of timeslice management.
2034       * FIFO tasks have no timeslices.
2035       */
2036      if ((p->policy == SCHED_RR) && !--p->time_slice) {
2037         p->time_slice = task_timeslice(p);
2038         p->first_time_slice = 0;
2039         set_tsk_need_resched(p);
2040
2041         /* put it at the end of the queue: */
2042         dequeue_task(p, rq->active);
2043         enqueue_task(p, rq->active);
2044      }
2045      goto out_unlock;
2046   }
```

Lines 2031–2046

The easiest case for the scheduler occurs when the current process is a real-time task. Real-time tasks always have a higher priority than any other tasks. If the task is a FIFO task and was running, it should continue its operation so we jump to the end of the function and release the run queue lock. If the current process is a round-robin real-time task, we decrement its timeslice. If the task has no more timeslice, it's time to schedule another round-robin real-time task. The current task has its new timeslice calculated by task_timeslice(). Then the task has its first time-slice reset. The task is then marked as needing rescheduling and, finally, the task is put at the end of the round-robin real-time tasklist by removing it from the run queue's active array and adding it back in. The scheduler then jumps to the end of the function and releases the run queue lock.

```
kernel/sched.c
2047   if (!--p->time_slice) {
2048      dequeue_task(p, rq->active);
2049      set_tsk_need_resched(p);
2050      p->prio = effective_prio(p);
```

```
2051        p->time_slice = task_timeslice(p);
2052        p->first_time_slice = 0;
2053
2054        if (!rq->expired_timestamp)
2055          rq->expired_timestamp = jiffies;
2056        if (!TASK_INTERACTIVE(p) || EXPIRED_STARVING(rq)) {
2057          enqueue_task(p, rq->expired);
2058          if (p->static_prio < rq->best_expired_prio)
2059            rq->best_expired_prio = p->static_prio;
2060        } else
2061          enqueue_task(p, rq->active);
2062      } else {
```

Lines 2047–2061

At this point, the scheduler knows that the current process is not a real-time process. It decrements the process' timeslice and, in this section, the process' timeslice has been exhausted and reached 0. The scheduler removes the task from the active array and sets the process' rescheduling flag. The priority of the task is recalculated and its timeslice is reset. Both of these operations take into account prior process activity.[8] If the run queue's expired timestamp is 0, which usually occurs when there are no more processes on the run queue's active array, we set it to jiffies.

Jiffies

Jiffies is a 32-bit variable counting the number of ticks since the system has been booted. This is approximately 497 days before the number wraps around to 0 on a 100HZ system. The macro on line 20 is the suggested method of accessing this value as a u64. There are also macros to help detect wrapping in `include/jiffies.h`.

```
include/linux/jiffies.h
017  extern unsigned long volatile jiffies;
020  u64 get_jiffies_64(void);
```

We normally favor interactive tasks by replacing them on the active priority array of the run queue; this is the `else` clause on line 2060. However, we don't want to starve expired tasks. To determine if expired tasks have been waiting too long for CPU time, we use `EXPIRED_STARVING()` (see `EXPIRED_STARVING` on line 1968).

---

[8] See `effective_prio()` and `task_timeslice()`.

The function returns true if the first expired task has been waiting an "unreasonable" amount of time or if the expired array contains a task that has a greater priority than the current process. The unreasonableness of waiting is load-dependent and the swapping of the active and expired arrays decrease with an increasing number of running tasks.

If the task is not interactive or expired tasks are starving, the scheduler takes the current process and enqueues it onto the run queue's expired priority array. If the current process' static priority is higher than the expired run queue's highest priority task, we update the run queue to reflect the fact that the expired array now has a higher priority than before. (Remember that high-priority tasks have low numbers in Linux, thus, the (<) in the code.)

```
-------------------------------------------------------------------
kernel/sched.c
2062   } else {
2063       /*
2064        * Prevent a too long timeslice allowing a task to monopolize
2065        * the CPU. We do this by splitting up the timeslice into
2066        * smaller pieces.
2067        *
2068        * Note: this does not mean the task's timeslices expire or
2069        * get lost in any way, they just might be preempted by
2070        * another task of equal priority. (one with higher
2071        * priority would have preempted this task already.) We
2072        * requeue this task to the end of the list on this priority
2073        * level, which is in essence a round-robin of tasks with
2074        * equal priority.
2075        *
2076        * This only applies to tasks in the interactive
2077        * delta range with at least TIMESLICE_GRANULARITY to requeue.
2078        */
2079       if (TASK_INTERACTIVE(p) && !((task_timeslice(p) -
2080           p->time_slice) % TIMESLICE_GRANULARITY(p)) &&
2081           (p->time_slice >= TIMESLICE_GRANULARITY(p)) &&
2082           (p->array == rq->active)) {
2083
2084           dequeue_task(p, rq->active);
2085           set_tsk_need_resched(p);
2086           p->prio = effective_prio(p);
2087           enqueue_task(p, rq->active);
2088       }
2089   }
2090 out_unlock:
2091   spin_unlock(&rq->lock);
2092 out:
2093   rebalance_tick(cpu, rq, NOT_IDLE);
2094 }
-------------------------------------------------------------------
```

Lines 2079–2089

The final case before the scheduler is that the current process was running and still has timeslices left to run. The scheduler needs to ensure that a process with a large timeslice doesn't hog the CPU. If the task is interactive, has more timeslices than TIMESLICE_GRANULARITY, and was active, the scheduler removes it from the active queue. The task then has its reschedule flag set, its priority recalculated, and is placed back on the run queue's active array. This ensures that a process at a certain priority with a large timeslice doesn't starve another process of an equal priority.

Lines 2090–2094

The scheduler has finished rearranging the run queue and unlocks it; if executing on an SMP system, it attempts to load balance.

Combining how processes are marked to be rescheduled, via scheduler_tick() and how processes are scheduled, via schedule() illustrates how the scheduler operates in the 2.6 Linux kernel. We now delve into the details of what the scheduler means by "priority."

7.1.3.1   Dynamic Priority Calculation

In previous sections, we glossed over the specifics of how a task's dynamic priority is calculated. The priority of a task is based on its prior behavior, as well as its user-specified nice value. The function that determines a task's new dynamic priority is recalc_task_prio():

```
-------------------------------------------------------------------
kernel/sched.c
381 static void recalc_task_prio(task_t *p, unsigned long long now)
382 {
383   unsigned long long __sleep_time = now - p->timestamp;
384   unsigned long sleep_time;
385
386   if (__sleep_time > NS_MAX_SLEEP_AVG)
387     sleep_time = NS_MAX_SLEEP_AVG;
388   else
389     sleep_time = (unsigned long)__sleep_time;
390
391   if (likely(sleep_time > 0)) {
392     /*
393      * User tasks that sleep a long time are categorised as
394      * idle and will get just interactive status to stay active &
395      * prevent them suddenly becoming cpu hogs and starving
396      * other processes.
397      */
```

```
398     if (p->mm && p->activated != -1 &&
399       sleep_time > INTERACTIVE_SLEEP(p)) {
400         p->sleep_avg = JIFFIES_TO_NS(MAX_SLEEP_AVG -
401            AVG_TIMESLICE);
402         if (!HIGH_CREDIT(p))
403            p->interactive_credit++;
404     } else {
405        /*
406         * The lower the sleep avg a task has the more
407         * rapidly it will rise with sleep time.
408         */
409        sleep_time *= (MAX_BONUS - CURRENT_BONUS(p)) ? : 1;
410
411        /*
412         * Tasks with low interactive_credit are limited to
413         * one timeslice worth of sleep avg bonus.
414         */
415        if (LOW_CREDIT(p) &&
416         sleep_time > JIFFIES_TO_NS(task_timeslice(p)))
417           sleep_time = JIFFIES_TO_NS(task_timeslice(p));
418
419        /*
420         * Non high_credit tasks waking from uninterruptible
421         * sleep are limited in their sleep_avg rise as they
422         * are likely to be cpu hogs waiting on I/O
423         */
424        if (p->activated == -1 && !HIGH_CREDIT(p) && p->mm) {
425           if (p->sleep_avg >= INTERACTIVE_SLEEP(p))
426              sleep_time = 0;
427           else if (p->sleep_avg + sleep_time >=
428                INTERACTIVE_SLEEP(p)) {
429              p->sleep_avg = INTERACTIVE_SLEEP(p);
430              sleep_time = 0;
431           }
432        }
433
434        /*
435         * This code gives a bonus to interactive tasks.
436         *
437         * The boost works by updating the 'average sleep time'
438         * value here, based on ->timestamp. The more time a
439         * task spends sleeping, the higher the average gets -
440         * and the higher the priority boost gets as well.
441         */
442        p->sleep_avg += sleep_time;
443
444        if (p->sleep_avg > NS_MAX_SLEEP_AVG) {
445           p->sleep_avg = NS_MAX_SLEEP_AVG;
446           if (!HIGH_CREDIT(p))
447              p->interactive_credit++;
448        }
```

```
449     }
450    }
452
452    p->prio = effective_prio(p);
453 }
```

Lines 386–389

Based on the time `now`, we calculate the length of time the process `p` has slept for and assign it to `sleep_time` with a maximum value of `NS_MAX_SLEEP_AVG`. (`NS_MAX_SLEEP_AVG` defaults to 10 milliseconds.)

Lines 391–404

If process `p` has slept, we first check to see if it has slept enough to be classified as an interactive task. If it has, when `sleep_time > INTERACTIVE_SLEEP(p)`, we adjust the process' sleep average to a set value and, if `p` isn't classified as interactive yet, we increment `p`'s `interactive_credit`.

Lines 405–410

A task with a low sleep average gets a higher sleep time.

Lines 411–418

If the task is CPU intensive, and thus classified as non-interactive, we restrict the process to having, at most, one more timeslice worth of a sleep average bonus.

Lines 419–432

Tasks that are not yet classified as interactive (not `HIGH_CREDIT`) that awake from uninterruptible sleep are restricted to having a sleep average of `INTERACTIVE()`.

Lines 434–450

We add our newly calculated `sleep_time` to the process' sleep average, ensuring it doesn't go over `NS_MAX_SLEEP_AVG`. If the processes are not considered interactive but have slept for the maximum time or longer, we increment its interactive credit.

Line 452

Finally, the priority is set using `effective_prio()`, which takes into account the newly calculated `sleep_avg` field of `p`. It does this by scaling the sleep average of 0..MAX_SLEEP_AVG into the range of -5 to +5. Thus, a process that has a static priority of 70 can have a dynamic priority between 65 and 85, depending on its prior behavior.

One final thing: A process that is not a real-time process has a range between 101 and 140. Processes that are operating at a very high priority, 105 or less, cannot cross the real-time boundary. Thus, a high priority, highly interactive process could never have a dynamic priority of lower than 101. (Real-time processes cover 0..100 in the default configuration.)

7.1.3.2 Deactivation

We already discussed how a task gets inserted into the scheduler by forking and how tasks move from the active to expired priority arrays within the CPU's run queue. But, how does a task ever get removed from a run queue?

A task can be removed from the run queue in two major ways:

- The task is preempted by the kernel and its state is not running, and there is no signal pending for the task (see line 2240 in kernel/sched.c).

- On SMP machines, the task can be removed from a run queue and placed on another run queue (see line 3384 in kernel/sched.c).

The first case normally occurs when schedule() gets called after a process puts itself to sleep on a wait queue. The task marks itself as non-running (TASK_INTERRUPTIBLE, TASK_UNINTERRUPTIBLE, TASK_STOPPED, and so on) and the kernel no longer considers it for CPU access by removing it from the run queue.

The case in which the process is moved to another run queue is dealt with in the SMP section of the Linux kernel, which we do not explore here.

We now trace how a process is removed from the run queue via deactivate_task():

```
-----------------------------------------------------------------
kernel/sched.c
507 static void deactivate_task(struct task_struct *p, runqueue_t *rq)
508 {
509   rq->nr_running--;
510   if (p->state == TASK_UNINTERRUPTIBLE)
511     rq->nr_uninterruptible++;
512   dequeue_task(p, p->array);
513   p->array = NULL;
514 }
-----------------------------------------------------------------
```

Line 509

The scheduler first decrements its count of running processes because p is no longer running.

Lines 510–511

If the task is uninterruptible, we increment the count of uninterruptible tasks on the run queue. The corresponding decrement operation occurs when an uninterruptible process wakes up (see `kernel/sched.c` line 824 in the function `try_to_wake_up()`).

Line 512–513

Our run queue statistics are now updated so we actually remove the process from the run queue. The kernel uses the `p->array` field to test if a process is running and on a run queue. Because it no longer is either, we set it to NULL.

There is still some run queue management to be done; let's examine the specifics of `dequeue_task()`:

```
-----------------------------------------------------------------
kernel/sched.c
303 static void dequeue_task(struct task_struct *p, prio_array_t *array)
304 {
305     array->nr_active--;
306     list_del(&p->run_list);
307     if (list_empty(array->queue + p->prio))
308         __clear_bit(p->prio, array->bitmap);
309 }
-----------------------------------------------------------------
```

Line 305

We adjust the number of active tasks on the priority array that process p is on—either the expired or the active array.

Lines 306–308

We remove the process from the list of processes in the priority array at p's priority. If the resulting list is empty, we need to clear the bit in the priority array's bitmap to show there are no longer any processes at priority `p->prio()`.

`list_del()` does all the removal in one step because `p->run_list` is a `list_head` structure and thus has pointers to the previous and next entries in the list.

We have reached the point where the process is removed from the run queue and has thus been completely deactivated. If this process had a state of `TASK_INTERRUPTIBLE` or `TASK_UNINTERRUPTIBLE`, it could be awoken and placed back on a run queue. If the process had a state of `TASK_STOPPED`, `TASK_ZOMBIE`, or `TASK_DEAD`, it has all of its structures removed and discarded.

7.2 Preemption

Preemption is the switching of one task to another. We mentioned how `schedule()` and `scheduler_tick()` decide which task to switch to next, but we haven't described how the Linux kernel decides when to switch. The 2.6 kernel introduces kernel preemption, which means that both user space programs and kernel space programs can be switched at various times. Because kernel preemption is the standard in Linux 2.6, we describe how full kernel and user preemption operates in Linux.

7.2.1 Explicit Kernel Preemption

The easiest preemption to understand is explicit kernel preemption. This occurs in kernel space when kernel code calls `schedule()`. Kernel code can call `schedule()` in two ways, either by directly calling `schedule()` or by blocking.

When the kernel is explicitly preempted, as in a device driver waiting with a `wait_queue`, the control is simply passed to the scheduler and a new task is chosen to run.

7.2.2 Implicit User Preemption

When the kernel has finished processing a kernel space task and is ready to pass control to a user space task, it first checks to see which user space task it should pass control to. This might not be the user space task that passed its control to the kernel. For example, if Task A invokes a system call, after the system call completes, the kernel could pass control of the system to Task B.

Each task on the system has a "rescheduling necessary" flag that is set whenever a task should be rescheduled:

```
------------------------------------------------------------------
include/linux/sched.h
988 static inline void set_tsk_need_resched(struct task_struct *tsk)
989 {
990   set_tsk_thread_flag(tsk,TIF_NEED_RESCHED);
991 }
992
993 static inline void clear_tsk_need_resched(struct task_struct *tsk)
994 {
995   clear_tsk_thread_flag(tsk,TIF_NEED_RESCHED);
996 }
...
1003 static inline int need_resched(void)
1004 {
1005   return unlikely(test_thread_flag(TIF_NEED_RESCHED));
1006 }
------------------------------------------------------------------
```

Lines 988–996

`set_tsk_need_resched` and `clear_tsk_need_resched` are the interfaces provided to set the architecture-specific flag `TIF_NEED_RESCHED`.

Lines 1003–1006

`need_resched` tests the current thread's flag to see if `TIF_NEED_RESCHED` is set.

When the kernel is returning to user space, it chooses a process to pass control to, as described in `schedule()` and `scheduler_tick()`. Although `scheduler_tick()` can mark a task as needing rescheduling, only `schedule()` operates on that knowledge. `schedule()` repeatedly chooses a new task to execute until the newly chosen task does not need to be rescheduled. After `schedule()` completes, the new task has control of the processor.

Thus, while a process is running, the system timer causes an interrupt that triggers `scheduler_tick()`. `scheduler_tick()` can mark that task as needing rescheduling and move it to the expired array. Upon completion of kernel operations, `scheduler_tick()` could be followed by other interrupts and the kernel would continue to have control of the processor—`schedule()` is invoked to choose the next task to run. So, the `scheduler_tick()` marks processes and rearranges queues, but `schedule()` chooses the next task and passes CPU control.

7.2.3 Implicit Kernel Preemption

New in Linux 2.6 is the implementation of implicit kernel preemption. When a kernel task has control of the CPU, it can only be preempted by another kernel task if it does not currently hold any locks. Each task has a field, `preempt_count`, which marks whether the task is preemptible. The count is incremented every time the task obtains a lock and decremented whenever the task releases a lock. The `schedule()` function disables preemption while it determines which task to run next.

There are two possibilities for implicit kernel preemption: Either the kernel code is emerging from a code block that had preemption disabled or processing is returning to kernel code from an interrupt. If control is returning to kernel space from an interrupt, the interrupt calls `schedule()` and a new task is chosen in the same way as just described.

If the kernel code is emerging from a code block that disabled preemption, the act of enabling preemption can cause the current task to be preempted:

```
------------------------------------------------------------------
include/linux/preempt.h
46 #define preempt_enable() \
47 do { \
48   preempt_enable_no_resched(); \
49   preempt_check_resched(); \
50 } while (0)
------------------------------------------------------------------
```

Lines 46–50

`preempt_enable()` calls `preempt_enable_no_resched()`, which decrements the `preempt_count` on the current task by one and then calls `preempt_check_resched()`:

```
------------------------------------------------------------------
include/linux/preempt.h
40 #define preempt_check_resched() \
41 do { \
42   if (unlikely(test_thread_flag(TIF_NEED_RESCHED))) \
43     preempt_schedule(); \
44 } while (0)
------------------------------------------------------------------
```

Lines 40–44

`preempt_check_resched()` sees if the current task has been marked for rescheduling; if so, it calls `preempt_schedule()`.

```
-------------------------------------------------------------------
kernel/sched.c
2328 asmlinkage void __sched preempt_schedule(void)
2329 {
2330   struct thread_info *ti = current_thread_info();
2331
2332   /*
2333    * If there is a non-zero preempt_count or interrupts are disabled,
2334    * we do not want to preempt the current task. Just return..
2335    */
2336   if (unlikely(ti->preempt_count || irqs_disabled()))
2337      return;
2338
2339 need_resched:
2340   ti->preempt_count = PREEMPT_ACTIVE;
2341   schedule();
2342   ti->preempt_count = 0;
2343
2344  /* we could miss a preemption opportunity between schedule and now */
2345   barrier();
2346   if (unlikely(test_thread_flag(TIF_NEED_RESCHED)))
2347      goto need_resched;
2348 }
-------------------------------------------------------------------
```

Line 2336–2337

If the current task still has a positive preempt_count, likely from nesting preempt_disable() commands, or the current task has interrupts disabled, we return control of the processor to the current task.

Line 2340–2347

The current task has no locks because preempt_count is 0 and IRQs are enabled. Thus, we set the current tasks preempt_count to note it's undergoing preemption, and call schedule(), which chooses another task.

If the task emerging from the code block needs rescheduling, the kernel needs to ensure it's safe to yield the processor from the current task. The kernel checks the task's value of preempt_count. If preempt_count is 0, and thus the current task holds no locks, schedule() is called and a new task is chosen for execution. If preempt_count is non-zero, it is unsafe to pass control to another task, and control is returned to the current task until it releases all of its locks. When the current task releases locks, a test is made to see if the current task needs rescheduling.

When the current task releases its final lock and `preempt_count` goes to 0, scheduling immediately occurs.

7.3   Spinlocks and Semaphores

When two or more processes require dedicated access to a shared resource, they
might need to enforce the condition that they are the sole process to operate in a
given section of code. The basic form of locking in the Linux kernel is the spinlock.

Spinlocks take their name from the fact that they continuously loop, or *spin*,
waiting to acquire a lock. Because spinlocks operate in this manner, it is imperative
not to have any section of code inside a spinlock attempt to acquire a lock twice.
This results in deadlock.

Before operating on a spinlock, the `spin_lock_t` structure must be initialized.
This is done by calling `spin_lock_init()`:

```
-----------------------------------------------------------------
include/linux/spinlock.h
63 #define spin_lock_init(x) \
64   do { \
65     (x)->magic = SPINLOCK_MAGIC; \
66     (x)->lock = 0; \
67     (x)->babble = 5; \
68     (x)->module = __FILE__; \
69     (x)->owner = NULL; \
70     (x)->oline = 0; \
71   } while (0)
-----------------------------------------------------------------
```

This section of code sets the `spin_lock` to "unlocked," or 0, on line 66 and initializes the other variables in the structure. The `(x)->lock` variable is the one we're
concerned about here.

After a `spin_lock` is initialized, it can be acquired by calling `spin_lock()` or
`spin_lock_irqsave()`. The `spin_lock_irqsave()` function disables interrupts
before locking, whereas `spin_lock()` does not. If you use `spin_lock()`, the
process could be interrupted in the locked section of code.

To release a `spin_lock` after executing the critical section of code, you need to call
`spin_unlock()` or `spin_unlock_irqrestore()`. The `spin_unlock_irqrestore()`
restores the state of the interrupt registers to the state they were in when
`spin_lock_irq()` was called.

Let's examine the `spin_lock_irqsave()` and `spin_unlock_irqrestore()` calls:

```
-------------------------------------------------------------------
include/linux/spinlock.h
258 #define spin_lock_irqsave(lock, flags) \
259 do { \
260   local_irq_save(flags); \
261   preempt_disable(); \
262   _raw_spin_lock_flags(lock, flags); \
263 } while (0)
...
321 #define spin_unlock_irqrestore(lock, flags) \
322 do { \
323   _raw_spin_unlock(lock); \
324   local_irq_restore(flags); \
325   preempt_enable(); \
326 } while (0)
-------------------------------------------------------------------
```

Notice how preemption is disabled during the lock. This ensures that any operation in the critical section is not interrupted. The IRQ flags saved on line 260 are restored on line 324.

The drawback of spinlocks is that they busily loop, waiting for the lock to be freed. They are best used for critical sections of code that are fast to complete. For code sections that take time, it is better to use another Linux kernel locking utility: the semaphore.

Semaphores differ from spinlocks because the task sleeps, rather than busy waits, when it attempts to obtain a contested resource. One of the main advantages is that a process holding a semaphore is safe to block; they are SMP and interrupt safe:

```
-------------------------------------------------------------------
include/asm-i386/semaphore.h
44 struct semaphore {
45   atomic_t count;
46   int sleepers;
47   wait_queue_head_t wait;
48 #ifdef WAITQUEUE_DEBUG
49   long __magic;
50 #endif
51 };
-------------------------------------------------------------------

-------------------------------------------------------------------
include/asm-ppc/semaphore.h
24 struct semaphore {
25   /*
```

```
26    * Note that any negative value of count is equivalent to 0,
27    * but additionally indicates that some process(es) might be
28    * sleeping on 'wait'.
29    */
30    atomic_t count;
31    wait_queue_head_t wait;
32 #ifdef WAITQUEUE_DEBUG
33    long __magic;
34 #endif
35 };
```

Both architecture implementations provide a pointer to a `wait_queue` and a count. The count is the number of processes that can hold the semaphore at the same time. With semaphores, we could have more than one process entering a critical section of code at the same time. If the count is initialized to 1, only one process can enter the critical section of code; a semaphore with a count of 1 is called a mutex.

Semaphores are initialized using `sema_init()` and are locked and unlocked by calling `down()` and `up()`, respectively. If a process calls `down()` on a locked semaphore, it blocks and ignores all signals sent to it. There also exists `down_interruptible()`, which returns 0 if the semaphore is obtained and `-EINTR` if the process was interrupted while blocking.

When a process calls `down()`, or `down_interruptible()`, the count field in the semaphore is decremented. If that field is less than 0, the process calling `down()` is blocked and added to the semaphore's `wait_queue`. If the field is greater than or equal to 0, the process continues.

After executing the critical section of code, the process should call `up()` to inform the semaphore that it has finished the critical section. By calling `up()`, the process increments the `count` field in the semaphore and, if the count is greater than or equal to 0, wakes a process waiting on the semaphore's `wait_queue`.

7.4 System Clock: Of Time and Timers

For scheduling, the kernel uses the system clock to know how long a task has been running. We already covered the system clock in Chapter 5 by using it as an example for the discussion on interrupts. Here, we explore the Real-Time Clock and its uses and implementation; but first, let's recap clocks in general.

The clock is a periodic signal applied to a processor, which allows it to function in the time domain. The processor depends on the clock signal to know when it can perform its next function, such as adding two integers or fetching data from memory. The speed of this clock signal (1.4GHz, 2GHz, and so on) has historically been used to compare the processing speed of systems at the local electronics store.

At any given moment, your system has several clocks and/or timers running. Simple examples include the time of day displayed in the bottom corner of your screen (otherwise known as wall time), the cursor patiently pulsing on a cluttered desktop, or your laptop screensaver taking over because of inactivity. More complicated examples of timekeeping include audio and video playback, key repeat (holding a key down), how fast communications ports run, and, as previously discussed, how long a task can run.

7.4.1   Real-Time Clock: What Time Is It?

The Linux interface to *wall clock time* is accomplished through the /dev/rtc device driver ioctl() function. The device for this driver is called a Real-Time Clock (RTC). The RTC[9] provides timekeeping functions with a small 114-byte user NVRAM. The input to this device is a 32.768KHz oscillator and a connection for battery backup. Some discrete models of the RTC have the oscillator and battery built in, while other RTCs are now built in to the peripheral bus controller (for example, the Southbridge) of a processor chipset. The RTC not only reports the time of day, but it is also a programmable timer that is capable of interrupting the system. The frequency of interrupts varies from 2Hz to 8,192Hz. The RTC can also interrupt daily, like an alarm clock. Here, we explore the RTC code:

```
-----------------------------------------------------------------
/include/linux/rtc.h

/*
 * ioctl calls that are permitted to the /dev/rtc interface, if
 * any of the RTC drivers are enabled.
 */

70   #define RTC_AIE_ON    _IO('p', 0x01)  /* Alarm int. enable on */
71   #define RTC_AIE_OFF   _IO('p', 0x02)  /* ... off    */
72   #define RTC_UIE_ON    _IO('p', 0x03)  /* Update int. enable on  */
73   #define RTC_UIE_OFF   _ IO('p', 0x04)  /* ... off     */
74   #define RTC_PIE_ON    _IO('p', 0x05)  /* Periodic int. enable on  */
```

[9] Manufactured by several vendors, most notably Motorola, with the mc146818. (This RTC is no longer in production. The Dallas DS12885 or equivalent is used instead.)

```
75  #define RTC_PIE_OFF    _IO('p', 0x06)  /* ... off    */
76  #define RTC_WIE_ON   _IO('p', 0x0f) /* Watchdog int. enable on  */
77  #define RTC_WIE_OFF   _IO('p', 0x10) /* ... off    */

78  #define RTC_ALM_SET    _IOW('p', 0x07, struct rtc_time) /* Set alarm time */
79  #define RTC_ALM_READ   _IOR('p', 0x08, struct rtc_time) /* Read alarm time*/
80  #define RTC_RD_TIME    _IOR('p', 0x09, struct rtc_time) /* Read RTC time */
81  #define RTC_SET_TIME   _IOW('p', 0x0a, struct rtc_time) /* Set RTC time */
82  #define RTC_IRQP_READ _IOR('p', 0x0b, unsigned long)   /* Read IRQ rate*/
83  #define RTC_IRQP_SET   _IOW('p', 0x0c, unsigned long)  /* Set IRQ rate */
84  #define RTC_EPOCH_READ _IOR('p', 0x0d, unsigned long)  /* Read epoch */
85  #define RTC_EPOCH_SET   _IOW('p', 0x0e, unsigned long)  /* Set epoch */
86
87  #define RTC_WKALM_SET   _IOW('p', 0x0f, struct rtc_wkalrm)/*Set wakeupalarm*/
88  #define RTC_WKALM_RD  _IOR('p', 0x10, struct rtc_wkalrm)/*Get wakeupalarm*/
89
90  #define RTC_PLL_GET    _IOR('p', 0x11, struct rtc_pll_info) /* Get PLL
correction */
91  #define RTC_PLL_SET    _IOW('p', 0x12, struct rtc_pll_info) /* Set PLL
correction */
```

The ioctl() control functions are listed in include/linux/rtc.h. At this writing, not all the ioctl() calls for the RTC are implemented for the PPC architecture. These control functions each call lower-level hardware-specific functions (if implemented). The example in this section uses the RTC_RD_TIME function.

The following is a sample ioctl() call to get the time of day. This program simply opens the driver and queries the RTC hardware for the current date and time, and prints the information to stderr. Note that only one user can access the RTC driver at a time. The code to enforce this is shown in the driver discussion.

```
Documentation/rtc.txt
/*
 *  Trimmed down version of code in /Documentation/rtc.txt
 *
 */


int main(void) {

int fd, retval = 0;
//unsigned long tmp, data;
struct rtc_time rtc_tm;

fd = open ("/dev/rtc", O_RDONLY);


/* Read the RTC time/date */
```

```
retval = ioctl(fd, RTC_RD_TIME, &rtc_tm);

/* print out the time from the rtc_tm variable */

close(fd);
return 0;

} /* end main */
```

This code is a segment of a more complete example in /Documentation/
rtc.txt. The two main lines of code in this program are the open() command
and the ioctl() call. open() tells us which driver we will use (/dev/rtc) and
ioctl() indicates a specific path through the code down to the physical RTC
interface by way of the RTC_RD_TIME command. The driver code for the open()
command resides in the driver source, but its only significance to this discussion is
which device driver was opened.

7.4.2 Reading the PPC Real-Time Clock

At kernel compile time, the appropriate code tree (x86, PPC, MIPS, and so on)
is inserted. The source branch for PPC is discussed here in the source code file for
the generic RTC driver for non-x86 systems:

```
/drivers/char/genrtc.c
276  static int gen_rtc_ioctl(struct inode *inode, struct file *file,
277     unsigned int cmd, unsigned long arg)
278  {
279     struct rtc_time wtime;
280     struct rtc_pll_info pll;
281
282     switch (cmd) {
283
284     case RTC_PLL_GET:
...
290     case RTC_PLL_SET:
...
298     case RTC_UIE_OFF:   /* disable ints from RTC updates.  */
...
302     case RTC_UIE_ON:   /* enable ints for RTC updates.  */
...
305     case RTC_RD_TIME:   /* Read the time/date from RTC   */
306
307       memset(&wtime, 0, sizeof(wtime));
308       get_rtc_time(&wtime);
309
310       return copy_to_user((void *)arg,&wtime,sizeof(wtime)) ? -EFAULT:0;
311
```

```
312   case RTC_SET_TIME:   /* Set the RTC */
313    return -EINVAL;
314    }
...
353   static int gen_rtc_open(struct inode *inode, struct file *file)
354   {
355    if (gen_rtc_status & RTC_IS_OPEN)
356     return -EBUSY;
357    gen_rtc_status |= RTC_IS_OPEN;
```

This code is the case statement for the `ioctl` command set. Because we made the `ioctl` call from the user space test program with the `RTC_RD_TIME` flag, control is transferred to line 305. The next call is at line 308, `get_rtc_time(&wtime)` in `rtc.h` (see the following code). Before leaving this code segment, note line 353. This allows only one user to access, via `open()`, the driver at a time by setting the status to `RTC_IS_OPEN`:

```
include/asm-ppc/rtc.h
045   static inline unsigned int get_rtc_time(struct rtc_time *time)
046   {
047     if (ppc_md.get_rtc_time) {
048      unsigned long nowtime;
049
050      nowtime = (ppc_md.get_rtc_time)();
051
052      to_tm(nowtime, time);
053
054      time->tm_year -= 1900;
055    time->tm_mon -= 1; /* Make sure userland has a 0-based month */
056     }
057    return RTC_24H;
058   }
```

The inline function `get_rtc_time()` calls the function that the structure variable pointed at by `ppc_md.get_rtc_time` on line 50. Early in the kernel initialization, this variable is set in `chrp_setup.c`:

```
arch/ppc/platforms/chrp_setup.c
447   chrp_init(unsigned long r3, unsigned long r4, unsigned long r5,
448   unsigned long r6, unsigned long r7)
449   {
...
477    ppc_md.time_init  = chrp_time_init;
478    ppc_md.set_rtc_time = chrp_set_rtc_time;
479    ppc_md.get_rtc_time = chrp_get_rtc_time;
480    ppc_md.calibrate_decr = chrp_calibrate_decr;
```

The function `chrp_get_rtc_time()` (on line 479) is defined in `chrp_time.c` in the following code segment. Because the time information in CMOS memory is updated on a periodic basis, the block of read code is enclosed in a `for` loop, which rereads the block if the update is in progress:

```
--------------------------------------------------------------------
arch/ppc/platforms/chrp_time.c
122  unsigned long __chrp chrp_get_rtc_time(void)
123  {
124   unsigned int year, mon, day, hour, min, sec;
125   int uip, i;
...
141   for ( i = 0; i<1000000; i++) {
142    uip = chrp_cmos_clock_read(RTC_FREQ_SELECT);
143    sec = chrp_cmos_clock_read(RTC_SECONDS);
144    min = chrp_cmos_clock_read(RTC_MINUTES);
145    hour = chrp_cmos_clock_read(RTC_HOURS);
146    day = chrp_cmos_clock_read(RTC_DAY_OF_MONTH);
147    mon = chrp_cmos_clock_read(RTC_MONTH);
148    year = chrp_cmos_clock_read(RTC_YEAR);
149    uip |= chrp_cmos_clock_read(RTC_FREQ_SELECT);
150    if ((uip & RTC_UIP)==0) break;
151   }
152   if (!(chrp_cmos_clock_read(RTC_CONTROL)
153   & RTC_DM_BINARY) || RTC_ALWAYS_BCD)
154   {
155    BCD_TO_BIN(sec);
156    BCD_TO_BIN(min);
157    BCD_TO_BIN(hour);
158    BCD_TO_BIN(day);
159    BCD_TO_BIN(mon);
160    BCD_TO_BIN(year);
161   }
...
054  int __chrp chrp_cmos_clock_read(int addr)
055  {   if (nvram_as1 != 0)
056   outb(addr>>8, nvram_as1);
057   outb(addr, nvram_as0);
058   return (inb(nvram_data));
059  }
--------------------------------------------------------------------
```

Finally, in `chrp_get_rtc_time()`, the values of the individual components of the time structure are read from the RTC device by using the function `chrp_cmos_clock_read`. These values are formatted and returned in the `rtc_tm` structure that was passed into the `ioctl` call back in the userland test program.

7.4.3 Reading the x86 Real-Time Clock

The methodology for reading the RTC on the x86 system is similar to, but somewhat more compact and robust than, the PPC method. Once again, we follow the open driver /dev/rtc, but this time, the build has compiled the file rtc.c for the x86 architecture. The source branch for x86 is discussed here:

```
--------------------------------------------------------------------
drivers/char/rtc.c
...
352  static int rtc_do_ioctl(unsigned int cmd, unsigned long arg, int kernel)
353  {
...
switch (cmd) {
...
482  case RTC_RD_TIME:   /* Read the time/date from RTC   */
483  {
484   rtc_get_rtc_time(&wtime);
485   break;
486  }
...
1208  void rtc_get_rtc_time(struct rtc_time *rtc_tm)
1209  {
...
1238    spin_lock_irq(&rtc_lock);
1239    rtc_tm->tm_sec = CMOS_READ(RTC_SECONDS);
1240    rtc_tm->tm_min = CMOS_READ(RTC_MINUTES);
1241    rtc_tm->tm_hour = CMOS_READ(RTC_HOURS);
1242    rtc_tm->tm_mday = CMOS_READ(RTC_DAY_OF_MONTH);
1243    rtc_tm->tm_mon = CMOS_READ(RTC_MONTH);
1244    rtc_tm->tm_year = CMOS_READ(RTC_YEAR);
1245    ctrl = CMOS_READ(RTC_CONTROL);
...
1249    spin_unlock_irq(&rtc_lock);
1250
1251    if (!(ctrl & RTC_DM_BINARY) || RTC_ALWAYS_BCD)
1252    {
1253     BCD_TO_BIN(rtc_tm->tm_sec);
1254     BCD_TO_BIN(rtc_tm->tm_min);
1255     BCD_TO_BIN(rtc_tm->tm_hour);
1256     BCD_TO_BIN(rtc_tm->tm_mday);
1257     BCD_TO_BIN(rtc_tm->tm_mon);
1258     BCD_TO_BIN(rtc_tm->tm_year);
1259    }
--------------------------------------------------------------------
```

The test program uses the ioctl() flag RTC_RD_TIME in its call to the driver rtc.c. The ioctl switch statement then fills the time structure from the CMOS

memory of the RTC. Here is the x86 implementation of how the RTC hardware
is read:

```
-------------------------------------------------------------------
include/asm-i386/mc146818rtc.h
...
018  #define CMOS_READ(addr) ({ \
019    outb_p((addr),RTC_PORT(0)); \
020    inb_p(RTC_PORT(1)); \
021  })
-------------------------------------------------------------------
```

Summary

This chapter covered the Linux scheduler, preemption in Linux, and the Linux
system clock and timers.

More specifically, we covered the following topics:

- We introduced the new Linux 2.6 scheduler and outlined its new features.

- We described how the scheduler chooses the next task from among all tasks
  it can choose and the algorithms the scheduler uses to do so.

- We discussed the context switch that the scheduler uses to actually swap a
  process and traced the function into the low-level architecture-specific code.

- We covered how processes in Linux can yield the CPU to other processes by
  calling `schedule()` and how the kernel then marks that process as "to be
  scheduled."

- We delved into how the Linux kernel calculates dynamic priority based on
  the previous behavior of an individual process and how a process eventually
  gets removed from the scheduling queue.

- We then moved on and covered implicit and explicit user- and kernel-level
  preemption and how each is dealt with in the 2.6 Linux kernel.

- Finally, we explored timers and the system clock and how the system clock is
  implemented in both x86 and PPC architectures.

Exercises

1. How does Linux notify the scheduler to run periodically?

2. Describe the difference between interactive and non-interactive processes.

3. With respect to the scheduler, what's special about real-time processes?

4. What happens when a process runs out of scheduler ticks?

5. What's the advantage of an O(1) scheduler?

6. What kind of data structure does the scheduler use to manage the priority of the processes running on a system?

7. What happens if you were to call `schedule()` while holding a spinlock?

8. How does the kernel decide whether a kernel task can be implicitly preempted?

Booting the Kernel

In this chapter

So far, we presented the subsystems of the Linux kernel and the structures central to their operation. Every chapter has assumed that the subsystem was up and running, and we focused on the typical kernel subsystem management and handling operations. However, each subsystem must be initialized before it can be used. This initialization occurs during the kernel bootup, which is a process that begins after the bootloader finishes loading the kernel image into memory and passes processing control to it.

We chose to follow the kernel initialization process in the linear order in which it occurs. We begin with a discussion of what happens on power-on through to the call to the first architecture-independent function, start_kernel(), and follow the process up to the invocation of /sbin/init. Figure 8.1 illustrates the order of events from system power on to power off.

FIGURE 8.1
Kernel Inception and Boot Process

We begin with a discussion of BIOS and Open Firmware, which is the first code that runs in the x86 and PPC systems upon power on, respectively. This is followed by a discussion of bootloaders commonly used with Linux and how they load the kernel and pass execution control to it. We then discuss in detail the step known as **kernel initialization**, where all the subsystems are initialized. The end of the kernel initialization is marked by the call to /sbin/init by process 1. The init program continues on with what is known as **system initialization** by enabling processes that need to be running before users can log in.

It soon becomes obvious that part of the nature of kernel initialization consists of interleaved subsystem bring-up. This makes it difficult to follow the initialization of a given subsystem from start to end without being interrupted. However, following the linear order of the Linux kernel bootup allows us to trace the setup of kernel subsystems as they occur and illustrates the complexity of the bootstrapping process.

We refer to many of the structures introduced in previous chapters because this is where these structures are first brought up and initialized. We begin by looking at the first step: BIOS and Open Firmware.

8.1   BIOS and Open Firmware

Upon power-on the processor first accesses an address that usually resides in read-only memory. This read-only memory is often referred to as **Flash ROM** (or just **Flash**). This is where the first code that runs on the system resides. This code is responsible for enabling enough of the system to handle the loading of the kernel.

For x86 systems, this is where the system BIOS resides. The **Basic Input Output System (BIOS)** is a block of hardware-specific system initialization code that boots the system. In x86 systems, the boot loader and, in turn Linux, depend on BIOS to bring the system to a known state. The interface to BIOS is a uniform set of functions known as **interrupts**. At load time, Linux uses these interrupts to query available system resources. After BIOS completes its initialization, it copies the first 512 bytes from the boot device (which is discussed in the next section) to address 0x7c00 and jumps to it. Although in some installations, BIOS loads the operating system over a network connection, this discussion is confined to the process when loading Linux from the hard drive. When Linux is loaded, BIOS is still in memory and its functions are accessible and called by way of interrupts.

For PowerPC, the type of initialization code depends on the age of the specific PowerPC architecture. Older IBM systems use **PowerPC Reference Platform (PreP)** whereas more recent IBM systems use **Common Hardware Reference Platform (CHRP)**. G4 systems and later have been called "True New World" and use **Open Firmware (OF)** bound to a particular architecture implementation. (For more information on this processor and system-independent boot firmware and how it is bound to one of these formats, see the Open Firmware home page at www.openfirmware.org.)

8.2   Boot Loaders

Boot loaders are programs that reside on the boot device of a computer. The first boot device is usually the first hard disk in the system. A boot loader is called by BIOS (x86) or firmware (PPC) after enough system initialization has occurred to support the memory, interrupts, and I/O required to load the kernel. Once loaded, the kernel initializes and configures the operating system.

For x86 systems, the BIOS allows the user to set the order of boot devices for their system. These boot devices are typically the floppy, CD-ROM, and the hard drive. Formatting a disk (with `fdisk`, for example) creates the **Master Boot Record** (**MBR**), which resides in the first sector (sector 0, cylinder 0, head 0) of the boot device. The MBR contains a small program and a four-entry partition table. The end of the boot sector has a hex marker 0xAA55 at location 510. Table 8.1 shows the components of the MBR.

TABLE 8.1
MBR Components

Offset	Length	Purpose
0x00	0x1bd	MBR program code
0x1be	0x40	Partition table
0x1fe	0x2	Hex marker or signature

The MBR's partition table holds information pertinent to each of the hard disk primary partitions. Table 8.2 shows what each 16-byte entry of the MBR's partition table looks like:

TABLE 8.2
MBR 16-byte Entries

Offset	Length	Purpose
0x00	1	Active Boot Partition Flag
0x01	3	Starting Cylinder/Head/Sector of boot partition
0x04	1	Partition Type (Linux uses 0x83,PPC PReP uses 0x41)
0x05	3	Ending Cylinder/Head/Sector of boot partition

TABLE 8.2
Continued

Offset	Length	Purpose
0x08	4	Partition starting sector number
0x0c	4	Partition length (in sectors)

   At the end of self-test and hardware identification, the system initialization code (Firmware or BIOS) accesses the hard drive controller to read the MBR. After the type of boot drive is identified, one can follow a documented interface (for example, on an IDE drive) to access head 0, cylinder 0, and sector 0.

   After the boot device is located, the MBR is copied to memory address 0x7c00 and executed. The small program at the head of the MBR moves itself out of the way and searches its partition table for the location of the active boot partition. The MBR then copies the code from the active boot partition to address 0x7c00 and begins executing it. From this point, DOS is usually booted on an x86 system. However, the active boot partition can have a bootloader that, in turn, loads the operating system. We now discuss some of the most common bootloaders that Linux uses. Figure 8.2 shows what memory looks like at bootup time.

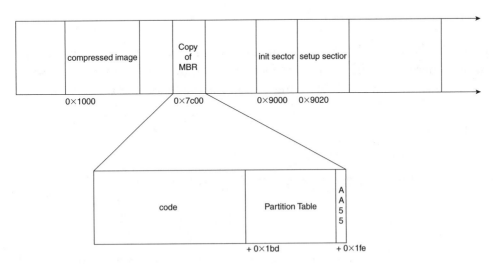

FIGURE 8.2
View of Memory at Bootup Time

8.2.1   GRUB

The **Grand Unified Bootloader (GRUB)** is an x86-based bootloader that's used to load Linux. GRUB 2 is in the process of being ported to PPC at the time of writing. Ample documentation exists on `www.gnu.org/software/grub`, including its history and future designs. GRUB recognizes filesystems on the boot drives, and the kernel can be loaded by specifying the filename, drive, and partition where the kernel resides. GRUB is a **two-stage bootloader.**[1] Stage 1 is installed in the MBR and is called by BIOS. Stage 2 is partially loaded by Stage 1 and then finishes loading itself from the filesystem. The breakdown of events ocurring in each of the stages is the following:

Stage 1

  1.   Initialization.

  2.   Detect the loading drive.

  3.   Load the first sector of Stage 2.

  4.   Jump to Stage 2.

Stage 2

  1.   Load the rest of Stage 2.

  2.   Jump to loaded code.

GRUB can be accessed through an interactive command line or a menu-driven interface. When using the menu interface, a configuration file must be created. Here is a stanza from the GRUB configuration file that loads the Linux kernel:

```
------------------------------------------------------------------------
/boot/menu.lst
...
title     Kernel 2.6.7, test kernel
root      (hd0,0)
kernel        /boot/bzImage-2.6.7-mytestkernel root=/dev/hda1 ro [2]
...
------------------------------------------------------------------------
```

---

[1]   Sometimes, GRUB is used with a Stage 1.5, but we discuss only the usual two stages.

[2]   The kernel accepts specifications at boot time by way of the kernel command line. This is a string describing a list of parameters that specify information such as hardware specifications, default values, etc. Go to `www.tldp.org/HOWTO/BootPrompt-HOWTO.html` for more information on the Linux boot prompt.

The options are `title`, which holds a label for the setup; `root`, which sets the current *root device* to `hd0`, partition `0`; and `kernel`, which loads the primary boot image of the kernel from the specified file. The rest of the information in the kernel entry is passed as boot time parameters to the kernel.

Certain aspects of booting, such as the location of where the kernel image is loaded and uncompressed, are configured in the architecture-specific sections of the Linux kernel code. Let's look at `arch/i386/boot/setup.s` where this is done for x86:

```
-------------------------------------------------------------------
arch/i836/boot/setup.S
61 INITSEG = DEF_INITSEG   # 0x9000, we move boot here, out of the way
62 SYSSEG = DEF_SYSSEG    # 0x1000, system loaded at 0x10000 (65536).
63 SETUPSEG = DEF_SETUPSEG   # 0x9020, this is the current segment
-------------------------------------------------------------------
```

This configuration specifies that Linux boots and loads the executable image to linear address 0x9000 and jumps to 0x9020. At this point, the uncompressed part of the Linux kernel decompresses the compressed portion to address 0x10000 and kernel initialization begins.

GRUB is based on the *Multiboot Specification*. At the time of this writing, Linux does not have all the structures in place to be multiboot-compliant, but it is worth discussing multiboot requirements.

8.2.1.1   Multiboot Specification

The **Multiboot Specification** describes an interface between any potential bootloader and any potential operating system. The Multiboot Specification does not say how a bootloader should work, but how it must interface with the operating system being loaded. Currently targeted at x86 architectures and free 32-bit operating systems, it provides a standard means for a bootloader to pass configuration information to an operating system. The OS image can be of any type (ELF or special), but must contain a *multiboot header* in the first 8K of the image, as well as the magic number 0x1BADB002. The multiboot-compliant loader should also provide a method for auxiliary boot modules or drivers to be used by the OS at boot time as certain OSes do not load all the programs necessary for operation into the bootable kernel image. This is often done to modularize boot kernels and keep the boot kernel to a manageable size.

The Multiboot Specification dictates that, when the bootloader invokes the OS, the system must be in a specific 32-bit real mode state such that the OS can successfully make calls back into BIOS if desired. Finally, the bootloader must present the OS with a data structure filled with essential machine data. We now look at the multiboot information data structure.

```
-------------------------------------------------------------------
typedef struct multiboot_info
{
ulong flags;    // indicate following fields
ulong mem_lower;   // if flags[0],amnt of mem < 1M
ulong mem_upper;   // if flags[0],amnt of mem > 1M
ulong boot_device;   // if flags[1],drive,part1,2,3
ulong cmdline;    // if flags[2],addr of cmd line
ulong mods_count;   // if flags[3],#of boot modules
ulong mods_addr;   // if flags[3],addr of first
        boot module.
union
{
aout_symbol_table_t aout_sym; // if flags[4], symbol table
    from a.out kernel image
elf_section_header_table_t elf_sec;// if flags[5], header
      from ELF kernel.
} u;
ulong mmap_length;   // if flags[6],BIOS mem map len
ulong mmap_addr;   // if flags[6],BIOS map addr
ulong drives_length;   // if flags[7],BIOS drive info structs
ulong drives_length;   // if flags[7],first BIOS drive info
        struct.
ulong config_table   // if flags[8],ROM config table
ulong boot_loader_name   // if flags[9],addr of string
ulong apm_table   // if flags[10],addr of APM info table
ulong vbe_control_info   // if flags[11],video mode settings
ulong vbe_mode_info
ulong vbe_mode
ulong vbe_interface_seg
ulong vbe_interface_off
ulong vbe_interface_len
};
-------------------------------------------------------------------
```

A pointer to this structure is passed in EBX when control is passed to the OS. The first field, **flags**, indicates which of the following fields are valid. Unused fields must be 0. You can learn more about the Multiboot Specification at www.gnu.org/software/grub/manual/multiboot/multiboot.html.

8.2.2   LILO

The **LInux LOader (LILO)** has been used for years as an x86 loader for Linux. It was one of the earliest boot-loading programs available to assist in the configuration and loading of the Linux kernel. LILO is similar to GRUB in the sense that it is a two-stage bootloader. LILO uses a configuration file and does not have a command-line interface.

Again, we start with BIOS initializing the system and loading the MBR (Stage 1) into memory and transferring control to it. The breakdown of the events occurring in each of LILO's stages is as follows:

Stage 1

1.   Begins execution and displays "L."

2.   Detects disk geometry and displays "I."

3.   Loads Stage 2 code.

Stage 2

1.   Begins execution and displays "L."

2.   Locates boot data and OS and displays "O."

3.   Determines which OS to start and jumps to it.

A stanza from the LILO configuration file looks like this:

```
-------------------------------------------------------------------
/etc/lilo.conf
image=/boot/bzImage-2.6.7-mytestkernel
label=Kernel 2.6.7, my test kernel
root=/dev/hda6
read-only
-------------------------------------------------------------------
```

The parameters are `image`, which indicates the pathname of the kernel; `label`, which is a string describing the configuration; `root`, which indicates the partition where the root filesystem resides; and `read-only`, which indicates that the root partition cannot be altered during boot.

Here is a list of the differences between GRUB and LILO:

- LILO stores configuration information in the MBR. If any changes are made, `/sbin/lilo` must be run to update the MBR.

- LILO cannot read various filesystems.

- LILO has no interactive command-line interface.

Let's review what happens when LILO is the bootloader. First, the MBR (which contains LILO) is copied to 0x7c00 and begins execution. LILO begins by copying the kernel image referenced in `/etc/lilo.conf` from the hard drive. This image, created by `build.c`, is made up of the `init` sector (loaded at 0x90000), the setup sector (loaded at 0x90200), and the compressed image (loaded at 0x10000). LILO then jumps to label `start_of_setup` at address 0x90200.

8.2.3   PowerPC and Yaboot

Yaboot is a bootloader based on the **Open Firmware** (**OF**) of New World PowerPC machines. Similar to LILO and GRUB, Yaboot uses a configuration file and a utility such as `ybin` or `ybootconfig` to set up a bootstrap partition containing Yaboot. Similar to the x86 BIOS, OF allows configuration of the boot device. However, in the OF case, it varies by system. OF settings can be usually found by pressing "Command+Option/Alt+o+f.?"

Yaboot uses the following steps to boot:

1. Yaboot gets called by OF.

2. Finds boot device, boot path, and opens boot partition.

3. Opens `/etc/yaboot.conf` or command shell.

4. Loads image or kernel and `initrd`.

5. Executes image.

As you can see, the kernel-loading stanza for Yaboot is similar to LILO and GRUB:

```
------------------------------------------------------------------
yaboot.conf
label=Linux
root=/dev/hda11
sysmap=/boot/System.map
read-only
------------------------------------------------------------------
```

As in LILO, `ybin` installs Yaboot to the boot partition. Any updates/changes to the Yaboot configuration require rerunning `ybin`.

Documentation on Yaboot can be found at `www.penguinppc.org`.

8.3   Architecture-Dependent Memory Initialization

We now take a moment to discuss hardware management features in PPC and x86. Both x86 and PowerPC architectures have hardware memory-management features to support real and virtual addressing environments. As in all operating systems, Linux Memory Management depends on the underlying hardware architecture. This section describes the hardware initialization of both architectures. Because the initialization of memory management is extremely hardware dependent, the hardware specifications need to be understood in order to follow the initialization process. Memory management is one of the first subsystems to be initialized and begins prior to the execution of `start_kernel()` because of its highly architecture-dependent nature.

8.3.1   PowerPC Hardware Memory Management

Also known as "storage control" in the PowerPC world, this section describes the hardware-supported features of address translation specific to the PowerPC architecture. We follow up with a discussion on how Linux uses (or disregards, for the sake of portability) these features from system power-on through kernel initialization.

8.3.1.1   Real Addressing Mode

From embedded up to high performance, all PowerPC processors come out of hardware reset in **real mode**.[3] PowerPC real-addressing mode is defined as having the processor in a state of disabled address translation. Address translation is controlled by the **instruction relocate (IR)** and **data relocate (DR)** bits in the **Machine State Register (MSR)**. For fetch instructions, if the IR bit is 0, the **effective address (EA)** is the same as the real address. For load and store instructions, the DR bit in the MSR plays a similar role.

---

[3]   Even the 440 series of processors, which technically have no real mode, start with a "shadow" TLB that maps linear addresses to physical addresses.

The MSR, which is illustrated in Figure 8.3, is a 64- or 32-bit register that describes the current state of the processor. On a 32-bit implementation, the IR and DR are bits 26 and 27.

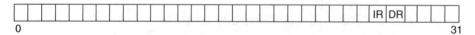

0   31

FIGURE 8.3
PowerPC Machine State Register (MSR)

Because address translation in Linux is a combination of hardware and software structures, real mode is fundamental to the boot process of initializing the memory subsystem and the memory-management structures of Linux. The need to enable address translation is exemplified by the inherent limitations of real mode. Real mode is only capable of addressing the implemented address width; this is 64- or 32-bit in most applications. The two major limitations are as follows:

- There is no hardware protection for load/store operations.

- Any access (instruction or data) to or from an address that does not have a device physically attached to the bus might cause a Machine Check (also known as a Checkstop), which in most cases, is unrecoverable.

8.3.1.2   Address Translation

The lack of address translation is real addressing. Address translation opens the door to virtual addressing where every possible address is not physically available at any given instance, but through the clever use of hardware and software, every possible address can be made virtually available when accessed.

With address translation enabled, the PowerPC architecture translates an EA by one of two methods: **Segmented Address Translation** or **Block Address Translation** (see Figure 8.4). If the EA can be translated by *both* methods, Block Address Translation takes precedence. Address translation is said to be enabled when $MSR_{IR}=1$, or $MSR_{DR}=1$, or both. Segmented Address Translation breaks virtual memory into segments, which are divided into 4KB pages, each representing physical memory. Block Address Translation breaks memory into regions ranging from 128MB to 256MB.

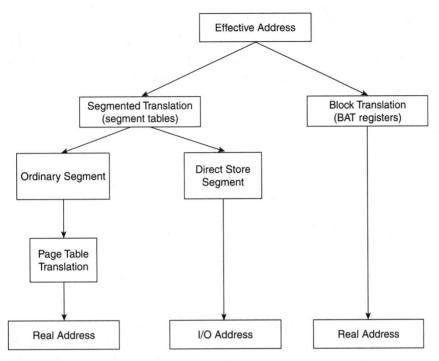

FIGURE 8.4
32-Bit Address Translation

Memory Addressing Terminology

When we reference memory, we really only have two distinct methodologies or modes: real addressing, where each increment of the address specifies a specific base unit (usually a byte) in physical memory; and virtual addressing, where the address is a computation in hardware and/or software. Here are some example terms used for each:

- **Real addressing**. Physical, bus
- **Virtual addressing**. Effective, protected, and translated

In PowerPC, effective address space is considered a subset of virtual address space.

Terms such as linear, flat, and logical can apply to both modes.

Segmented Address Translation Direct Store Segment T

The next level of translation is determined by the T bit, which is located in the **Segment Register.** Bits 0:3 of the EA select one of 16 segment registers (SRs) in the PowerPC 7*xx* series. Figure 8.5 illustrates the segment register.

T	Ks	Kp	reserved	VSID

0   1   2   8   31

Bit 0	T=1, Segment Translation. T=0, Block Translation
Bit 1	Ks, Supervisor state storage
Bit 2	Kp, Problem state storage
Bit 8:31	Virtual Segment ID

FIGURE 8.5
Segment Register

With the T bit set, the segment is deemed a **direct store segment** to an I/O device, and there is no reference to hardware page tables. The I/O address is made up of a permission bit, the BUID, the controller-specific field, and bits 4:31 of the EA. Linux does not use direct store segmentation.

When the Segmented Address Translation Ordinary Segment T is not set, the **virtual segment ID (VSID)** field is used.

Referring to Figure 8.6, a 52-bit **virtual address (VA)** is formed by concatenating bits 20:31 of the EA (the offset within a given page), bits 4:19 of the EA, and bits 8:31 of the selected segment register VSID field. The most significant 40 bits of the VA make up the **virtual page number (VPN)**. The PowerPC architecture uses a Hashed Page Table to map VPNs to real page numbers (the real address of a desired page in memory). The hash function uses the VPN and the value in **Storage Description Register 1 (SDR1)** to store and retrieve a **Page Table Entry (PTE)**. The PTE, which is illustrated in Figure 8.7, is an 8-byte structure that contains all the necessary attributes of a page in memory.

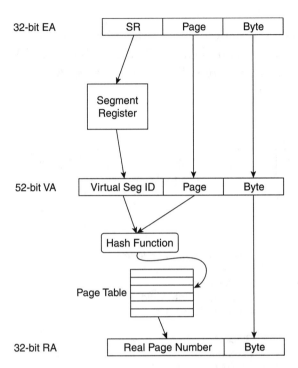

FIGURE 8.6
Segment Translation

0 1		24 25 26		31
V	VSID	H	API	
RPN		R C	WIMG	PP
0	19 23	24 25	28	30 31

Word 0	Bit 0	V=1, Entry Valid. V=0. Entry Invalid
	Bits 1:24	Virtual Segment ID
	Bit 25	Hash function identifier
	Bits 26:31	Abbreviated Page Index
Word 1	Bits 0:19	Real Page Number
	Bits: 20:22	reserved
	Bit 23	Reference bit
	Bit 24	Change bit
	Bit 25:28	WIMG
	Bits 30:31	Page Protection

FIGURE 8.7
Page Table Entry

Block Address Translation

As its name implies, **Block Address Translation (BAT)** is an addressing mechanism that allows for mapping blocks of contiguous memory from 125KB to 256MB. BAT registers are privileged **special purpose registers (SPRs)** in the PowerPC architecture. Figure 8.8 illustrates the BAT register.

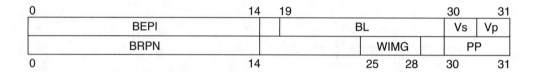

	Upper register	Bits 0:14	Block Effective Page Index
		Bits 15:18Bit 25	reserved
		Bits 19:29	Block Length
		Bit 30	Supervisor State Valid
		Bit 31	Problem State Valid
	Lower register	Bits 0:14	Block Real Page Number
		Bits 15:24	reserved
		Bits 25:28	WIMG (see sidebar)
		Bit 29	reserved
		Bits 30:31	Protection bits for BAT area

FIGURE 8.8
BAT Register

The formation of a real address from a BAT register can be seen in Figure 8.9. Four **Instruction BAT (IBAT)** registers and four **Data BAT (DBAT)** registers can be read or written using `mtspr` and `mfspr` PPC instructions.[4]

---

[4] Block Address Translation is not implemented on all PowerPC processors. Notably, it was not implemented on G4 or G5. It is implemented in the 4xx-embedded processors.

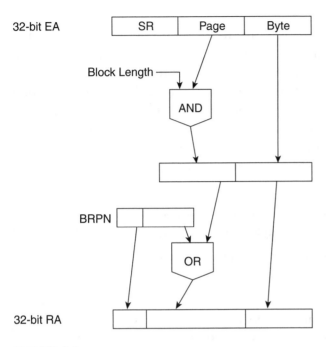

FIGURE 8.9
BAT Real

Translation Lookaside Buffers

The **Translation Lookaside Buffers** (**TLBs**) can be thought of as a hardware cache with hardware protection for the paging system. The TLB varies in length with PowerPC architectures and contains an index of the most recently used PTEs. The paging software must be sure to keep the TLBs in sync with the page table. When the processor cannot find a page in the hash table,[5] the Linux page tables are then searched. If the page is still not found, a normal page fault is generated. Information on optimization of the synchronization between the Linux page tables and PPC hash tables can be found in the document, "Low Level Optimizations in the PowerPC/Linux Kernels," by Paul Mackerras.

---

[5] Hash tables are not implemented on all PowerPC processors. They are absent in the 4xx- and 8xx-embedded systems where a TLB miss generates an exception in the hardware and the paging software, and then brings the page in.

Storage Access Mode Control

When address translation is enabled (MSR_{IR}=1, or MSR_{DR}=1, or both) and accomplished by way of Segmented Address Translation or Block Address Translation, the storage mode is determined by four control bits: W, I, M, and G. For Segmented Address Translation, they are bits 25:28 of the second word of a PTE, and the same bits for the second SPR of the DBAT. (The G-bit is reserved in the IBAT.) Two more bits—Reference and Control, which are located in the PTE—are available for Segmented Address Translation. The R and C bits are set by hardware or software. (See the following sidebar for a discussion of the W, I, M, G, R, and C bits.)

Control Bits

The W, I, M, G, R, and C bits control how the processor accesses the cache and main memory:

- **W (Write Through)**. If data is in the cache and a store operation is performed on it, if W=1, the copy in main memory must also be updated.
- **I (Cache Inhibit)**. Updates bypass cache and goes straight through to main memory.
- **M (Memory Coherence)**. When M=1, hardware memory coherency is enforced.
- **G (Guarded)**. When G=1, speculative execution is suppressed.
- **R (Referenced)**. When R=1, the Page Table entry has been referenced.
- **C (Changed)**. When C=1, the Page Table entry has been changed.

8.3.1.3   How Linux Uses PPC Address Translation

We now look at the code that influences memory management in PPC.

The following code is the first in the kernel distribution to get control. This routine calls back into the Firmware for allocation of temporary regions by using the `claim()` function. The kernel is then decompressed into its proper location:

```
------------------------------------------------------------------
arch/ppc/boot/openfirmware/newworldmain.c
40  void boot(int a1, int a2, void *prom)
...
54  claim(initrd_start, RAM_END - initrd_start, 0);
55  printf("initial ramdisk moving 0x%x <- 0x%p (%x bytes)\n\r",
56   initrd_start, (char *)(&__ramdisk_begin), initrd_size);
```

```
57   memcpy((char *)initrd_start, (char *)(&__ramdisk_begin), initrd_size);
...
63   /* claim 3MB starting at PROG_START */
64    claim(PROG_START, PROG_SIZE, 0);
65    dst = (void *) PROG_START;
66    if (im[0] == 0x1f && im[1] == 0x8b) {
67   /* claim some memory for scratch space */
68   avail_ram = (char *) claim(0, SCRATCH_SIZE, 0x10);
69   begin_avail = avail_high = avail_ram;
70   end_avail = avail_ram + SCRATCH_SIZE;
71   printf("heap at 0x%p\n", avail_ram);
72   printf("gunzipping (0x%p <- 0x%p:0x%p)...", dst, im, im+len);
73   gunzip(dst, PROG_SIZE, im, &len);
74   printf("done %u bytes\n", len);
75   printf("%u bytes of heap consumed, max in use %u\n",
76    avail_high - begin_avail, heap_max);
...
86    sa = (unsigned long)PROG_START;
87    printf("start address = 0x%x\n", sa);
88
89    (*(kernel_start_t)sa)(a1, a2, prom);
```

Line 40

Entry point to this file is the function boot(a1, a2, *prom).

Line 54

Function claim() is called to allocate memory just below 1M and ramdisk is copied into that memory.

Line 64

Function claim() is called to allocate 3M of memory, starting at 0x1_0000 for the image.

Line 68

Function claim() is called to allocate 8K of memory starting at 0x00 for scratch/heap.

Line 73

The image is gunzipped to address 0x1_0000 (PROG_START).

Line 89

Jump to 0x1_0000 ((*kernel_start_t)sa) with parameters (a1, a2, and prom) where a1 holds the value in r3 (equal to the boot ramdisk start), a2 holds the value in `r4` (equal to the boot ramdisk size or 0xdeadbeef in the case of `no ramdisk`) and `prom` holds the value in `r5` (code stored in system ROM).

The next code block readies the hardware memory-management features of the various PowerPC processors. The first 16M of RAM is mapped to 0xc0000000:

```
------------------------------------------------------------------
arch/ppc/kernel/head.S
131  __start:
...
150  bl   early_init   in <arch/ppc/kernel/setup.c> (283)
...
170  bl   mmu_off
...
171    RFI: SRR0=>IP, SRR1=>MSR
172  #ifndef CONFIG_POWER4
173    bl   clear_bats
174    bl   flush_tlbs
175
176    bl   initial_bats
177  #if !defined(CONFIG_APUS) && defined(CONFIG_BOOTX_TEXT)
178    bl   setup_disp_bat
179  #endif
180  #else /* CONFIG_POWER4 */
181    bl   reloc_offset
182    bl   initial_mm_power4
183  #endif /* CONFIG_POWER4 */
185    /*
186    * Call setup_cpu for CPU 0 and initialize 6xx Idle
187    */
188    bl   reloc_offset
189    li   r24,0      /* cpu# */
190    bl   call_setup_cpu   /* Call setup_cpu for this CPU */
195  #ifdef CONFIG_POWER4
196    bl   reloc_offset
197  bl   init_idle_power4
198  #endif /* CONFIG_POWER4 */
199
210  bl   reloc_offset
211  mr   r26,r3
212  addis  r4,r3,KERNELBASE@h  /* current address of _start */
213  cmpwi  0,r4,0    /* are we already running at 0? */
214  bne   relocate_kernel
215
...
224  turn_on_mmu:
225  mfmsr  r0
226  ori   r0,r0,MSR_DR|MSR_IR
227  mtspr  SRR1,r0
228  lis   r0,start_here@h
229  ori   r0,r0,start_here@l
230  mtspr  SRR0,r0
```

```
231  SYNC
232  RFI      /* enables MMU */
```

Line 131

This is the entry point to this code. Get minimal mmu environment set up. (Note that APUS stands for Amiga Power Up System.)

Line 150

There might be a difference between where the kernel is loaded and where it is linked. The function early_init returns the physical address of the current code.

Line 170

Shut off memory-management unit of PPC. If both IR and DR are enabled, leave them on; otherwise, shut off relocation.

Lines 173–176

If not power4 or G5, clear the BAT registers, flush TLBs, and set up BATs to map the first 16M of RAM to 0xc0000000.

Note the various labels for kernel memory used throughout the kernel:

```
arch/ppc/defconfig
CONFIG_KERNEL_START=0xc0000000
```
---

and

```
include/asm-ppc/page.h
#define PAGE_OFFSET  CONFIG_KERNEL_START
#define KERNELBASE  PAGE_OFFSET
```

Lines 181–182

By using segmentation, set up kernel memory for power4 and G5.

Lines 188–198

setup_cpu() initializes the kernel and user features, such as cache configuration, or whether an FPU or MMU exists. (Note that at this writing, init_idle_power4 is a noop.)

Line 210

Relocate kernel to KERNELBASE or 0x00, depending on the platform.

Lines 224–232

Turn on the MMU (if it is not already) by enabling IR and DR in MSR. Then, execute an RFI instruction causing a jump to the label `start_here:`. (Note: The RFI instruction loads the MSR with the contents of SRR1 and branches to the address in SRR0.)

The following code is where the kernel starts. It sets up all memory in the system based on the command line:

```
-------------------------------------------------------------------
arch/ppc/kernel/head.S
1337   start_here:
...
1364   bl   machine_init
1365   bl   MMU_init
...
1385   lis  r4,2f@h
1386   ori  r4,r4,2f@l
1387   tophys(r4,r4)
1388   li   r3,MSR_KERNEL & ~(MSR_IR|MSR_DR)
1389   FIX_SRR1(r3,r5)
1390   mtspr  SRR0,r4
1391   mtspr  SRR1,r3
1392   SYNC
1393   RFI
1394   /* Load up the kernel context */
1395   2:  bl   load_up_mmu
...
1411   /* Now turn on the MMU for real! */
1412   li   r4,MSR_KERNEL
1413   FIX_SRR1(r4,r5)
1414   lis  r3,start_kernel@h
1415   ori  r3,r3,start_kernel@l
1416   mtspr  SRR0,r3
1417   mtspr  SRR1,r4
1418   SYNC
1419   RFI

-------------------------------------------------------------------
```

Line 1337

This line is the entry point to this section.

Line 1364

`machine_init()` (see the file `arch/ppc/kernel/setup.c`, line 532) sets up machine-specific information, such as NVRAM, L2, CPU cache line size, debugging, and so on.

Line 1365

`MMU_init()` (see file `arch/ppc/mm/init.c`, line 234) discovers the total memory size for `highmem` and `lowmem`. It then initializes the MMU hardware (`MMU_init_hw()`, line 267), sets up Hash Page Table (`arch/ppc/mm/hashtable.s`), maps all RAM starting at `KERNELBASE` (`mapin_ram()`, line 272), maps all I/O (`setup_io_mappings()`, line 285), and initializes context management (`mmu_context_init()`, line 288).

Line 1385

Shut off IR and DR to set up SDR1. This holds the real address of the Page Table and how many bits from the hash are used in the Page Table Index.

Line 1395

Clear TLBs, load SDR1 (hash table base and size), set up segmentation, and, depending on the particular PPC platform, initialize the BAT registers.

Lines 1412–1419

Turn on IR, DR, and RFI to `start_kernel` in `/init/main.c`. Note that at interrupt time in the PowerPC architecture, the contents of the **Instruction Address Registser (ISR)** holds the address the processor must return to after servicing the interrupt. This value is saved in the **Save Restore Register 0 (SRR0)**. The Machine Status Register is in turn saved in the **Save Restore Register 1 (SRR1)**. In shorthand, at interrupt time:

- **IAR->SRR0**
- **MSR->SRR1**

The `RFI` instruction, which is normally executed at the end of an interrupt routine, is the inverse of this procedure, where `SRR0` is restored to the `IAR` and `SRR1` is restored to the `MSR`. In shorthand:

- **SRR0->IAR**
- **SRR1->MSR**

The code in lines 1385–1419 uses this methodology to turn memory management on and off by this three-step process:

1. Sets the desired bits for the MSR (refer to Figure 8.1) in SRR1.

2. Sets the desired address we want to jump to in SRR0.

3. Executes the RFI instruction.

8.3.2   x86 Intel-Based Hardware Memory Management

At power-on, all Intel processors are in real address mode. Real addressing is a compatibility mode to the early Intel processors. As processors grew more complex, legacy code was always in use that newer processors still needed to be able to run. In real address mode, the processor can execute a program written for the 8086 and 8088 processors using the same instructions and, more importantly, the same method of addressing or **address translation**. The end result of address translation is how the processor accesses the system memory. The early Intel processors had a 20-bit address bus, which accessed approximately 64K bytes of memory. This is the limitation put on the early code in the system. In real address mode, the *linear address* is the same as the *physical address*. As we move through the code that initializes memory management, we see more of the features of the later processors being used in the hardware and more complex structures added to the software.

The code in `setup.s` performs several important functions with respect to memory initialization:

```
-------------------------------------------------------------------
arch/i386/boot/setup.S
307   #define SMAP 0x534d4150
308
309   meme820:
310     xorl  %ebx, %ebx    # continuation counter
311     movw  $E820MAP, %di    # point into the whitelist
312           # so we can have the bios
313           # directly write into it.
314
315   jmpe820:
316     movl  $0x0000e820, %eax    # e820, upper word zeroed
317     movl  $SMAP, %edx    # ascii 'SMAP'
318     movl  $20, %ecx    # size of the e820rec
319     pushw %ds    # data record.
320     popw  %es
321     int   $0x15    # make the call
322     jc    bail820    # fall to e801 if it fails
```

```
323
324   cmpl  $SMAP, %eax     # check the return is 'SMAP'
325   jne  bail820       # fall to e801 if it fails
326
...
333  good820:
334   movb  (E820NR), %al     # up to 32 entries
335   cmpb  $E820MAX, %al
336   jnl  bail820
337
338   incb  (E820NR)
339   movw  %di, %ax
340   addw  $20, %ax
341   movw  %ax, %di
342  again820:
343   cmpl  $0, %ebx     # check to see if
344   jne  jmpe820     # %ebx is set to EOF
345  bail820:
```

Lines 307–345

Looking at the code segment, we first see (on line 321) a call to the BIOS
int15h function with ax= 0xe820. This returns the addresses and lengths of the
many different types of memory of which BIOS is aware. This simple memory map
represents the basic pool from which all the pages of memory in Linux are obtained.
As seen from further studying of the code, the memory map can be obtained by
three methods: 0xe820, 0xe801, and 0x88. All three methods have to do with
compatibility with existing BIOS distributions and their platforms.

```
arch/i386/boot/setup.S
595 # Now we move the system to its rightful place ... but we check if we have
a # big-kernel. In that case we *must* not move it ...
597   testb $LOADED_HIGH, %cs:loadflags
598   jz  do_move0    # .. then we have a normal low
599        # loaded zImage
600        # .. or else we have a high
601        # loaded bzImage
602   jmp  end_move    # ... and we skip moving
603
604  do_move0:
605   movw  $0x100, %ax    # start of destination segment
606   movw  %cs, %bp    # aka SETUPSEG
607   subw  $DELTA_INITSEG, %bp    # aka INITSEG
608   movw  %cs:start_sys_seg, %bx    # start of source segment
609   cld
610  do_move:
```

```
611   movw  %ax, %es    # destination segment
612   incb  %ah       # instead of add ax,#0x100
613   movw  %bx, %ds    # source segment
614   addw  $0x100, %bx
615   subw  %di, %di
616   subw  %si, %si
617   movw  $0x800, %cx
618   rep
619   movsw
620   cmpw  %bp, %bx    # assume start_sys_seg > 0x200,
621         # so we will perhaps read one
622         # page more than needed, but
623         # never overwrite INITSEG
624         # because destination is a
625         # minimum one page below source
626   jb  do_move
627
628   end_move:
```

Lines 595–628

This code is the kernel image created by build.c and loaded by LILO. It is made up of the init sector (at address 0x9000), the setup sector (at address 0x9200), and the compressed image. The image is originally loaded at address 0x10000. If it is LARGE (>0X7FF), it is left in place; otherwise, it is moved down to 0x1000.

```
arch/i386/boot/setup.S
723   # Try enabling A20 through the keyboard controller
724   #endif /* CONFIG_X86_VOYAGER */
725   a20_kbc:
726     call  empty_8042
727
728   #ifndef CONFIG_X86_VOYAGER
729     call  a20_test    # Just in case the BIOS worked
730     jnz   a20_done    # but had a delayed reaction.
731   #endif
732
733     movb  $0xD1, %al    # command write
734     outb  %al, $0x64
735     call  empty_8042
736
737     movb  $0xDF, %al    # A20 on
738     outb  %al, $0x60
739     call  empty_8042
```

Forming the 20-bit Physical Address in Intel Real Address Mode

The Intel 8088 processor in the original IBM PC had only 20 address lines [0...19]. This allowed the system to access up to 1 megabyte plus approximately 64K bytes of memory (0 to 0x10_FFEF) internally, but *physically* (on the bus) the last 64K of addressable memory was actually the *first* 64K of real memory!

Internal to the processor, a 20-bit address is formed from a 16-bit segment selector and a 16-bit segment offset. The selector is shifted left 4 bits and added to the offset, which is extended by 4 bits. The sum of these registers is the physical address seen on the bus.

For example:

To obtain the highest address, we load a segment selector (CS, DS, ES, and so on) with a value of **0xFFFF** and an index register (SI, DI, and so on) with a value of **0xFFFF**. *Internal* to the processor, the segment selector is shifted left 4 bits and added to the offset.

0xFFFF shifted left 4 bits	=	0x0F_FFF0
Add the offset	+	0x00_FFFF
Internal sum	=	0x10_FFEF
External Physical Address	=	0x00_FFEF

This resulting Physical Address is the same as a segment selector with the value of **0x0000** and an offset value of **0xFFEF** (**0000:FFEF**).

Accessing the highest address and above would wrap back into low memory at 0xFFEF. Certain programs written for this processor would depend on this 20-bit wrap-around behavior. The introduction of the Intel 286 and later processors with wider address busses incorporated Real Addressing to maintain backward compatibility with 8088 and 8086. Real Addressing mode did not take into account legacy software that depended on the 20-bit wrap-around. The A20M# signal pin was added to mimic this "feature" of the earlier processors. Asserting this signal would mask off the A20 signal allowing the low memory to be accessed once again.

A logic gate was used to enable or disable the memory bus A20 signal. The original design to assert this gate was to use an extra I/O signal from the keyboard controller that was controlled by I/O ports 0x60 and 0x64. A "Fast Gate A20" method was later developed which used I/O port 0x92 designed into the system board. Since all x86 processors come out of reset in Real Address mode, it is wise for boot code to make certain address line A20 is enabled by one or both of these methods.

Lines 723–739

This code is a fascinating throwback to the early Intel processors. This is a mere nuisance in the setup of Memory Management.

```
arch/i386/boot/setup.S
790  # set up gdt and idt
791  lidt  idt_48       # load idt with 0,0
792  xorl  %eax, %eax    # Compute gdt_base
793  movw  %ds, %ax      # (Convert %ds:gdt to a linear ptr)
794  shll  $4, %eax
795  addl  $gdt, %eax
796  movl  %eax, (gdt_48+2)
797  lgdt  gdt_48       # load gdt with whatever is
798        # appropriate
...
981  gdt:
982  .fill GDT_ENTRY_BOOT_CS,8,0
983
984  .word  0xFFFF       # 4Gb - (0x100000*0x1000 = 4Gb)
985  .word  0        # base address = 0
986  .word  0x9A00       # code read/exec
987  .word  0x00CF       # granularity = 4096, 386
988         # (+5th nibble of limit)
989
990  .word  0xFFFF       # 4Gb - (0x100000*0x1000 = 4Gb)
991  .word  0        # base address = 0
992  .word  0x9200       # data read/write
993  .word  0x00CF       # granularity = 4096, 386
994         # (+5th nibble of limit)
995  gdt_end:
996  .align  4
997
998  .word  0       # alignment byte
999  idt_48:
1000  .word  0        # idt limit = 0
1001  .word  0, 0      # idt base = 0L
1002
1003  .word  0       # alignment byte
1004  gdt_48:
1005  .word  gdt_end - gdt - 1   # gdt limit
1006  .word  0, 0      # gdt base (filled in later)
```

Lines 790–797

The structures and data for the provisional GDT and IDT are compiled into the end of setup.S. These tables are implemented in their simplest form.

Lines 981–1006

These lines are the compiled-in values for the provisional GDT. The GDT has a code and data descriptor, each representing 4GB of memory starting at 0x00. The IDT is left initialized to 0x00 and is filled in later.

As far as memory management on an Intel platform is concerned, entering protected mode is one of the most important phases. At this point, the hardware begins to build a virtual address space for the operating system.

Protected Mode

The Intel method of memory management is called protected mode. The protection refers to multiple independent segmented address spaces that are protected from each other. The other half of Intel memory management is paging or page translation. System programmers can make use of various combinations of segmentation and paging, but Linux uses a flat model where segmentation is all but eliminated. In the flat model, each process has access to its entire 32-bit address space (4GB).

```
arch/i386/boot/setupS
830  movw  $1, %ax      # protected mode (PE) bit
831  lmsw  %ax       # This is it!
832  jmp   flush_instr
833
834  flush_instr:
835    xorw  %bx, %bx    # Flag to indicate a boot
836    xorl  %esi, %esi     # Pointer to real-mode code
837    movw  %cs, %si
838    subw  $DELTA_INITSEG, %si
839    shll  $4, %esi
```

Lines 830–831

Set the PE bit in the Machine Status Word to enter protected mode. The `jmp` instruction begins executing in protected mode.

Lines 834–839

Save a 32-bit pointer to real-mode for decompressing and loading the kernel later on in `startup_32()`.

Recall that in real addressing mode, code is executed by using 16-bit instructions. The current file is compiled using the `.code16` assembler directive, which enforces this mode; this is also known as a 16-bit module in the *Intel Programmer's Reference*. To jump from a 16-bit module to a 32-bit module, the Intel architecture (and assembler magic) allows us to build a 32-bit instruction in a 16-bit module.

Build and execute the 32-bit jump:

```
arch/i386/boot/setup.S
841  # jump to startup_32 in arch/i386/kernel/head.S
842  #
843  # NOTE: For high loaded big kernels we need a
844  #   jmpi 0x100000,__BOOT_CS
845  #
846  #  but we haven't yet reloaded the CS register, so the default size
847  #  of the target offset still is 16 bit.
848  #  However, using an operand prefix (0x66), the CPU will properly
849  #  take our 48 bit far pointer. (INTeL 80386 Programmer's Reference
850  #  Manual, Mixing 16-bit and 32-bit code, page 16-6)
851
852   .byte 0x66, 0xea    # prefix + jmpi-opcode
853  code32:  .long  0x1000     # will be set to 0x100000
854         # for big kernels
855   .word __BOOT_CS
```

Line 852

This line builds the 32-bit jump instruction.

After this jump is executed, the system uses the provisional GDT and the code is executing in 32-bit protected mode, starting at the label `startup_32` in `arch/i386/kernel/head.S` line 57.

8.3.2.1   Protected Mode

Until this point, the discussion has been how to get the Intel system ready to set up paging. As we trace through the code in `head.S`, we see what initialization needs to take place and how Linux uses the x86-based protected mode paging system. This is the final code before the kernel is started in `main.c`. For complete information on the many possible modes and settings that relate to memory initialization and Intel processors, look at the *Intel Architecture Software Developers Manual*, Volume 3.

```
arch/i386/kernel/head.S
057  ENTRY(startup_32)
058
059  /*
```

```
060    * Set segments to known values.
061    */
062    cld
063    lgdt boot_gdt_descr - __PAGE_OFFSET
064    movl $(__BOOT_DS),%eax
065    movl %eax,%ds
066    movl %eax,%es
067    movl %eax,%fs
068    movl %eax,%gs
068
081    /*
082    * Initialize page tables. This creates a PDE and a set of page
083    * tables, which are located immediately beyond _end. The variable
084    * init_pg_tables_end is set up to point to the first "safe" location.
085    * Mappings are created both at virtual address 0 (identity mapping)
086    * and PAGE_OFFSET for up to _end+sizeof(page tables)+INIT_MAP_BEYOND_END.
087    *
088    * Warning: don't use %esi or the stack in this code. However, %esp
089    * can be used as a GPR if you really need it...
090    */
091    page_pde_offset = (__PAGE_OFFSET >> 20);
092
093    movl $(pg0 - __PAGE_OFFSET), %edi
094    movl $(swapper_pg_dir - __PAGE_OFFSET), %edx
095    movl $0x007, %eax       /* 0x007 = PRESENT+RW+USER */
096    10:
097      leal 0x007(%edi),%ecx    /* Create PDE entry */
098    movl %ecx,(%edx)      /* Store identity PDE entry */
099    movl %ecx,page_pde_offset(%edx)   /* Store kernel PDE entry */
100    addl $4,%edx
101    movl $1024, %ecx
102    11:
103    stosl
104    addl $0x1000,%eax
105    loop 11b
106    /* End condition: we must map up to and including INIT_MAP_BEYOND_END */
107    /* bytes beyond the end of our own page tables; the +0x007 is the
attribute bits */
108    leal (INIT_MAP_BEYOND_END+0x007)(%edi),%ebp
109    cmpl %ebp,%eax
110    jb 10b
111    movl %edi,(init_pg_tables_end - __PAGE_OFFSET)
112
113    #ifdef CONFIG_SMP
...
156    3:
157    #endif /* CONFIG_SMP */
158
159    /*
160    * Enable paging
161    */
162    movl $swapper_pg_dir-__PAGE_OFFSET,%eax
163    movl %eax,%cr3   /* set the page table pointer.. */
164    movl %cr0,%eax
165    orl $0x80000000,%eax
166    movl %eax,%cr0   /* ..and set paging (PG) bit */
```

```
167    ljmp $__BOOT_CS,$1f  /* Clear prefetch and normalize %eip */
168    1:
169    /* Set up the stack pointer */
170    lss stack_start,%esp
...
177    pushl $0
178    popfl
179
180    #ifdef CONFIG_SMP
181    andl %ebx,%ebx
182    jz 1f      /* Initial CPU cleans BSS */
183    jmp checkCPUtype
184    1:
185    #endif /* CONFIG_SMP */
186
187    /*
188    * start system 32-bit setup. We need to re-do some of the things done
189    * in 16-bit mode for the "real" operations.
190    */
191    call setup_idt
192
193    *
194    * Copy bootup parameters out of the way.
195    * Note: %esi still has the pointer to the real-mode data.
196    */
197    movl $boot_params,%edi
198    movl $(PARAM_SIZE/4),%ecx
199    cld
200    rep
201    movsl
202    movl boot_params+NEW_CL_POINTER,%esi
203    andl %esi,%esi
204    jnz 2f     # New command line protocol
205    cmpw $(OLD_CL_MAGIC),OLD_CL_MAGIC_ADDR
206    jne 1f
207    movzwl OLD_CL_OFFSET,%esi
208    addl $(OLD_CL_BASE_ADDR),%esi
209    2:
210    movl $saved_command_line,%edi
211    movl $(COMMAND_LINE_SIZE/4),%ecx
212    rep
213    movsl
214    1:
215    checkCPUtype:
...
279    lgdt cpu_gdt_descr
280    lidt idt_descr
...
303    call start_kernel
```

Line 57

This line is the 32-bit protected mode entry point for the kernel code. Currently, the code uses the provisional GDT.

Line 63

This code initializes the GDTR with the base address of the *boot* GDT. This boot GDT is the same as the provisional GDT used in `setup.s` (4GB code and data starting at address 0x00000000) and is used only by this boot code.

Lines 64–68

Initialize the remaining segment registers with `__BOOT_DS`, which resolves to 24 (see `/include/asm-i386/segment.h`). This value points to the 24th selector (starting at 0) in the final GDT, which is set later in this code.

Lines 91–111

Create a page directory entry (PDE) in `swapper_pg_dir` that references a page table (`pg0`) with 0 based (identity) entries and duplicate `PAGE_OFFSET` (kernel memory) entries.

Lines 113–157

This code block initializes secondary (non-boot) processors to the page tables. For this discussion, we focus on the boot processor.

Lines 162–164

The `cr3` register is the entry point for x86 hardware paging. This register is initialized to point to the base of the **Page Directory**, which in this case, is `swapper_pg_dir`.

Lines 165–168

Set the `PG` (paging) bit in `cr0` of the boot processor. The `PG` bit enables the paging mechanism in the x86 architecture. The jump instruction (on line 167) is recommended when changing the `PG` bit to ensure that all instructions *within* the processor are serialized at the moment of entering or exiting paging mode.

Line 170

Initialize the stack to the start of the data segment (see also lines 401–403).

Lines 177–178

The `eflags` register is a read/write system register that contains the status of interrupts, modes, and permissions. This register is cleared by pushing a 0 onto the stack and directly popping it into the register with the `popfl` instruction.

Lines 180–185

The general-purpose register ebx is used as a flag to indicate whether it is the boot processor to the processor that runs this code. Because we are tracing this code as the boot processor, ebx has been cleared (0), and we jump to the call to setup_idt.

Line 191

The routine setup_idt initializes an Interrupt Descriptor Table (IDT) where each entry points to a *dummy* handler. The IDT, discussed in Chapter 7, "Scheduling and Kernel Synchronization," is a table of functions (or *handlers*) that are called when the processor needs to immediately execute time-critical code.

Lines 197–214

The user can pass certain parameters to Linux at boot time. They are stored here for later use.

Lines 215–303

The code listed on these lines does a large amount of necessary (but tedious) x86 processor-version checking and some minor initialization. By way of the cupid instruction (or lack thereof), certain bits are set in the eflags register and cr0. One notable setting in cr0 is bit 4, the extension type (ET). This bit indicates the support of math-coprocessor instructions in older x86 processors. The most important lines of code in this block are lines 279–280. This is where the IDT and the GDT are loaded (by way of the lidt and lgdt instructions) into the idtr and gdtr registers. Finally, on line 303, we jump to the routine start_kernel().

With the code in head.s, the system can now map a **logical** address to a **linear** address to finally a **physical** address (see Figure 8.10). Starting with a **logical address**, the **selector** (in the CS, DS, ES, etc., registers) references one of the **descriptors** in the GDT. The **offset** is the flat address that we seek. The information from the **descriptor** and the **offset** are combined to form the **logical** address.

In the code walkthrough, we saw how the Page Directory (swapper_pg_dir) and Page Table (pg0) were created and that cr3 was initialized to point to the Page Directory. As previously discussed, the processor becomes aware of where to look for the paging components by cr3's setting, and setting cr0 (PG bit) is how the processor is informed to start using them. On the **logical** address, bits 22:31 indicate the **Page Directory Entry (PDE)**, bits 12:21 indicate the **Page Table Entry (PTE)**, and bits 0:11 indicate the **offset** (in this example, 4KB) into the physical page.

The system now has 8MB of memory mapped out using a provisional paging system. The next step is to call the function start_kernel() in init/main.c.

8.3.3   PowerPC and x86 Code Convergence

Notice that both the PowerPC code and the x86 code have now converged on `start_kernel()` in `init/main.c`. This routine, which is located in the architecture-independent section of the code, calls architecture-specific routines to finish memory initialization.

The first function called in this file is `setup_arch()` in `arch/i386/kernel/setup.c`, which then calls `paging_init()` in `arch/i386/mm/init.c`, which then calls `pagetable_init()` in the same file. The remainder of system memory is allocated here to produce the final page tables.

In the PowerPC world, much has already been done. The `setup_arch()` file in `arch/ppc/kernel/setup.c` then calls `paging_init()` in `arch/ppc/mm/init.c`. The one notable function performed in `paging_init()` for PPC is to set all pages to be in the DMA zone.

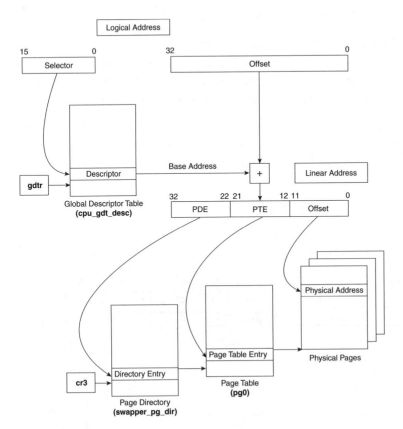

FIGURE 8.10
Boot-Time Paging

8.4   Initial RAM Disk

LILO, GRUB, and Yaboot support the loading of the initial RAM disk (`initrd`). `initrd` acts as a root filesystem before the final root filesystem is loaded and initialized. We refer to the loading of the final root filesystem as **pivoting** the root.

This initial step allows Linux to initially come up with certain modules precompiled and then dynamically load other modules and drivers from `initrd`. The major difference to the bootloader is that it loads a minimal kernel and the RAM disk during Stage 2. The kernel initializes using the RAM disk, mounts the final root filesystem, and then removes the `initrd`.

`initrd` allows for

- Configuring a kernel at boot time
- Keeping a small general-purpose kernel
- Having one kernel for several hardware configurations

The previously referenced stanzas are the most common for loading Linux with Yaboot, GRUB, and LILO. Each bootloader has a rich set of commands for their configuration files. For a customized or special function boot process, a quick Web search on GRUB and LILO configuration files yields good information on the subject.

Now that we have seen how the kernel is loaded and how memory initialization starts, let's look at the process of kernel initialization.

8.5   The Beginning: start_kernel()

This discussion begins with the jump to the `start_kernel()` (init/main.c) function, the first architecture-independent part of the code to be called.

With the jump to `start_kernel()`, we execute **Process 0**, which is otherwise known as the **root thread**. Process 0 spawns off **Process 1**, known as the **init process**. Process 0 then becomes the idle thread for the CPU. When `/sbin/init` is called, we have only those two processes running:

```
------------------------------------------------------------------
init/main.c
396  asmlinkage void __init start_kernel(void)
397  {
398    char * command_line;
```

```
399    extern char saved_command_line[];
400    extern struct kernel_param __start___param[], __stop___param[];
...
405    lock_kernel();
406    page_address_init();
407    printk(linux_banner);
408    setup_arch(&command_line);
409    setup_per_cpu_areas();
...
415    smp_prepare_boot_cpu();
...
422    sched_init();
423
424    build_all_zonelists();
425    page_alloc_init();
426    printk("Kernel command line: %s\n", saved_command_line);
427    parse_args("Booting kernel", command_line, __start___param,
428      __stop___param - __start___param,
429      &unknown_bootoption);
430    sort_main_extable();
431    trap_init();
432    rcu_init();
433    init_IRQ();
434    pidhash_init();
435    init_timers();
436    softirq_init();
437    time_init();
...
444    console_init();
445    if (panic_later)
446     panic(panic_later, panic_param) ;
447    profile_init();
448    local_irq_enable();
449    #ifdef CONFIG_BLK_DEV_INITRD
450    if (initrd_start && !initrd_below_start_ok &&
451      initrd_start < min_low_pfn << PAGE_SHIFT) {
452    printk(KERN_CRIT "initrd overwritten (0x%08lx < 0x%08lx) - "
453      "disabling it.\n",initrd_start,min_low_pfn << PAGE_SHIFT);
454    initrd_start = 0;
455    }
456    #endif
457    mem_init();
458    kmem_cache_init();
459    if (late_time_init)
460     late_time_init();
461    calibrate_delay();
462    pidmap_init();
463    pgtable_cache_init();
464    prio_tree_init();
465    anon_vma_init();
466    #ifdef CONFIG_X86
```

```
467   if (efi_enabled)
468     efi_enter_virtual_mode();
469  #endif
470   fork_init(num_physpages);
471   proc_caches_init();
472   buffer_init();
473   unnamed_dev_init();
474   security_scaffolding_startup();
475   vfs_caches_init(num_physpages);
476   radix_tree_init();
477   signals_init();
478   /* rootfs populating might need page-writeback */
479   page_writeback_init();
480  #ifdef CONFIG_PROC_FS
481   proc_root_init();
482  #endif
483   check_bugs();
...
490   init_idle(current, smp_processor_id());
...
493   rest_init();
494  }
```

8.5.1   The Call to lock_kernel()

Line 405

In the 2.6 Linux kernel, the default configuration is to have a preemptible kernel. A preemptible kernel means that the kernel itself can be interrupted by a higher priority task, such as a hardware interrupt, and control is passed to the higher priority task. The kernel must save enough state so that it can return to executing when the higher priority task finishes.

Early versions of Linux implemented kernel preemption and SMP locking by using the **Big Kernel Lock (BKL)**. Later versions of Linux correctly abstracted preemption into various calls, such as `preempt_disable()`. The BKL is still with us in the initialization process. It is a recursive spinlock that can be taken several times by a given CPU. A side effect of using the BKL is that it disables preemption, which is an important side effect during initialization.

Locking the kernel prevents it from being interrupted or preempted by any other task. Linux uses the BKL to do this. When the kernel is locked, no other process can execute. This is the antithesis of a preemptible kernel that can be interrupted at any point. In the 2.6 Linux kernel, we use the BKL to lock the kernel upon startup and initialize the various kernel objects without fear of being interrupted. The kernel is unlocked on line 493 within the `rest_init()` function. Thus, all of `start_kernel()` occurs with the kernels locked. Let's look at what happens in `lock_kernel()`:

```
-----------------------------------------------------------------
include/linux/smp_lock.h
42 static inline void lock_kernel(void)
43 {
44   int depth = current->lock_depth+1;
45   if (likely(!depth))
46     get_kernel_lock();
47   current->lock_depth = depth;
48 }
-----------------------------------------------------------------
```

Lines 44–48

The `init` task has a special `lock_depth` of -1. This ensures that in multi-processor systems, different CPUs do not attempt to simultaneously grab the kernel lock. Because only one CPU runs the `init` task, only it can grab the big kernel lock because `depth` is 0 only for `init` (otherwise, `depth` is greater than 0). A similar trick is used in `unlock_kernel()` where we test (`--current->lock_depth < 0`). Let's see what happens in `get_kernel_lock()`:

```
-----------------------------------------------------------------
include/linux/smp_lock.h
10 extern spinlock_t kernel_flag;
11
12 #define kernel_locked()     (current->lock_depth >= 0)
13
14 #define get_kernel_lock()   spin_lock(&kernel_flag)
15 #define put_kernel_lock()   spin_unlock(&kernel_flag)
...
59 #define lock_kernel()         do { } while(0)
60 #define unlock_kernel()       do { } while(0)
61 #define release_kernel_lock(task)    do { } while(0)
62 #define reacquire_kernel_lock(task)    do { } while(0)
63 #define kernel_locked()       1
-----------------------------------------------------------------
```

Lines 10–15

These macros describe the big kernel locks that use standard spinlock routines. In multiprocessor systems, it is possible that two CPUs might try to access the same data structure. Spinlocks, which are explained in Chapter 7, prevent this kind of contention.

Lines 59–63

In the case where the kernel is not preemptible and not operating over multiple CPUs, we simply do nothing for `lock_kernel()` because nothing can interrupt us anyway.

The kernel has now seized the BKL and will not let go of it until the end of `start_kernel()`; as a result, all the following commands cannot be preempted.

8.5.2   The Call to page_address_init()

Line 406

The call to `page_address_init()` is the first function that is involved with the initialization of the memory subsystem in this architecture-dependent portion of the code. The definition of `page_address_init()` varies according to three different compile-time parameter definitions. The first two result in `page_address_init()` being stubbed out to do nothing by defining the body of the function to be `do { } while (0)`, as shown in the following code. The third is the operation we explore here in more detail. Let's look at the different definitions and discuss when they are enabled:

```
------------------------------------------------------------------
include/linux/mm.h
376 #if defined(WANT_PAGE_VIRTUAL)
382 #define page_address_init() do { } while(0)

385 #if defined(HASHED_PAGE_VIRTUAL)
388 void page_address_init(void);

391 #if !defined(HASHED_PAGE_VIRTUAL) && !defined(WANT_PAGE_VIRTUAL)
394 #define page_address_init() do { } while(0)
------------------------------------------------------------------
```

The `#define` for `WANT_PAGE_VIRTUAL` is set when the system has direct memory mapping, in which case simply calculating the virtual address of the memory location is sufficient to access the memory location. In cases where all of RAM is not mapped into the kernel address space (as is often the case when `himem` is configured), we need a more involved way to acquire the memory address. This is why the initialization of page addressing is defined only in the case where `HASHED_PAGE_VIRTUAL` is set.

We now look at the case where the kernel has been told to use
HASHED_PAGE_VIRTUAL and where we need to initialize the virtual memory that
the kernel is using. Keep in mind that this happens only if himem has been configured; that is, the amount of RAM the kernel can access is larger than that mapped
by the kernel address space (generally 4GB).

In the process of following the function definition, various kernel objects are
introduced and revisited. Table 8.2 shows the kernel objects introduced during the
process of exploring page_address_init().

TABLE 8.2
Objects Introduced During the Call to page_address_init()

Object Name	Description
page_address_map	Struct
page_address_slot	Struct
page_address_pool	Global variable
page_address_maps	Global variable
page_address_htable	Global variable

```
----------------------------------------------------------------
mm/highmem.c
510 static struct page_address_slot {
511   struct list_head lh;
512 spinlock_t lock;
513 } ____cacheline_aligned_in_smp page_address_htable[1<<PA_HASH_ORDER];
...
591 static struct page_address_map page_address_maps[LAST_PKMAP];
592
593 void __init page_address_init(void)
594 {
595   int i;
596
597   INIT_LIST_HEAD(&page_address_pool);
598   for (i = 0; i < ARRAY_SIZE(page_address_maps); i++)
599     list_add(&page_address_maps[i].list, &page_address_pool)  ;
600   for (i = 0; i < ARRAY_SIZE(page_address_htable); i++) {
601     INIT_LIST_HEAD(&page_address_htable[i].lh);
602     spin_lock_init(&page_address_htable[i].lock);
603   }
604   spin_lock_init(&pool_lock);
605 }
----------------------------------------------------------------
```

Line 597

The main purpose of this line is to initialize the `page_address_pool` global variable, which is a struct of type `list_head` and point to a list of free pages allocated from `page_address_maps` (line 591). Figure 8.11 illustrates `page_address_pool`.

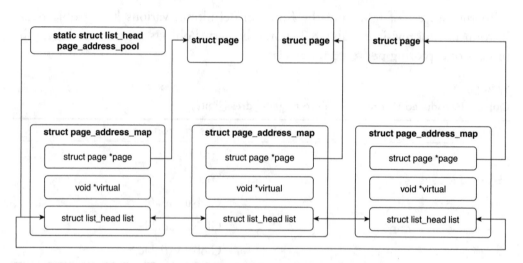

FIGURE 8.11
Data Structures Surrounding the Page Address Map Pool

Lines 598–599

We add each list of pages in `page_address_maps` to the doubly linked list headed by `page_address_pool`. We describe the `page_address_map` structure in detail next.

Lines 600–603

We initialize each page address hash table's `list_head` and spinlock. The `page_address_htable` variable holds the list of entries that hash to the same bucket. Figure 8.12 illustrates the page address hash table.

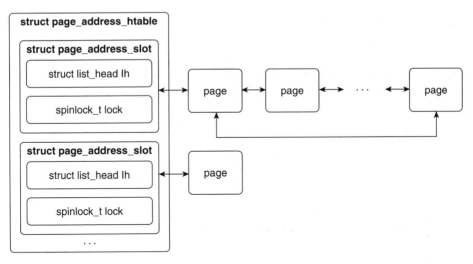

FIGURE 8.12
Page Address Hash Table

Line 604

We initialize the `page_address_pool`'s spinlock.

Let's look at the `page_address_map` structure to better understand the lists we just saw initialized. This structure's main purpose is to maintain the association with a page and its virtual address. This would be wasteful if the page had a linear association with its virtual address. This becomes necessary only if the addressing is hashed:

```
mm/highmem.c
490 struct page_address_map {
491    struct page *page;
492    void *virtual;
493    struct list_head list;
494 };
```

As you can see, the object keeps a pointer to the page structure that's associated with this page, a pointer to the virtual address, and a `list_head` struct to maintain its position in the doubly linked list of the page address list it is in.

8.5.3   The Call to printk(linux_banner)

Line 407

This call is responsible for the first console output made by the Linux kernel. This introduces the global variable `linux_banner`:

```
init/version.c
31  const char *linux_banner =
32   "Linux version " UTS_RELEASE " (" LINUX_COMPILE_BY "@"
LINUX_COMPILE_HOST ") (" LINUX_COMPILER ") " UTS_VERSION "\n";
```

The `version.c` file defines `linux_banner` as just shown. This string provides the user with a reference of the Linux kernel version, the `gcc` version it was compiled with, and the release.

8.5.4   The Call to setup_arch

Line 408

The `setup_arch()` function in `arch/i386/kernel/setup.c` is cast to the `__init` type (refer to Chapter 2 for a description of `__init`) where it runs only once at system initialization time. The `setup_arch()` function takes in a pointer to any Linux command-line data entered at boot time and initializes many of the architecture-specific subsystems, such as memory, I/O, processors, and consoles:

```
arch/i386/kernel/setup.c
1083  void __init setup_arch(char **cmdline_p)
1084  {
1085   unsigned long max_low_pfn;
1086
1087   memcpy(&boot_cpu_data, &new_cpu_data, sizeof(new_cpu_data));
1088   pre_setup_arch_hook();
1089   early_cpu_init();
1090
1091   /*
1092   * FIXME: This isn't an official loader_type right
1093   * now but does currently work with elilo.
1094   * If we were configured as an EFI kernel, check to make
1095   * sure that we were loaded correctly from elilo and that
1096   * the system table is valid. If not, then initialize normally.
1097   */
1098  #ifdef CONFIG_EFI
1099   if ((LOADER_TYPE == 0x50) && EFI_SYSTAB)
1100    efi_enabled = 1;
```

```
1101   #endif
1102
1103   ROOT_DEV = old_decode_dev(ORIG_ROOT_DEV);
1104   drive_info = DRIVE_INFO;
1105   screen_info = SCREEN_INFO;
1106   edid_info = EDID_INFO;
1107   apm_info.bios = APM_BIOS_INFO;
1108   ist_info = IST_INFO;
1109   saved_videomode = VIDEO_MODE;
1110   if( SYS_DESC_TABLE.length != 0 ) {
1111     MCA_bus = SYS_DESC_TABLE.table[3] &0x2;
1112     machine_id = SYS_DESC_TABLE.table[0];
1113     machine_submodel_id = SYS_DESC_TABLE.table[1];
1114     BIOS_revision = SYS_DESC_TABLE.table[2];
1115   }
1116   aux_device_present = AUX_DEVICE_INFO;
1117
1118   #ifdef CONFIG_BLK_DEV_RAM
1119   rd_image_start = RAMDISK_FLAGS & RAMDISK_IMAGE_START_MASK;
1120   rd_prompt = ((RAMDISK_FLAGS & RAMDISK_PROMPT_FLAG) != 0);
1121   rd_doload = ((RAMDISK_FLAGS & RAMDISK_LOAD_FLAG) != 0);
1122   #endif
1123   ARCH_SETUP
1124   if (efi_enabled)
1125     efi_init();
1126   else
1127     setup_memory_region();
1128
1129   copy_edd();
1130
1131   if (!MOUNT_ROOT_RDONLY)
1132     root_mountflags &= ~MS_RDONLY;
1133   init_mm.start_code = (unsigned long) _text;
1134   init_mm.end_code = (unsigned long) _etext;
1135   init_mm.end_data = (unsigned long) _edata;
1136   init_mm.brk = init_pg_tables_end + PAGE_OFFSET;
1137
1138   code_resource.start = virt_to_phys(_text);
1139   code_resource.end = virt_to_phys(_etext)-1;
1140   data_resource.start = virt_to_phys(_etext);
1141   data_resource.end = virt_to_phys(_edata)-1;
1142
1143   parse_cmdline_early(cmdline_p);
1144
1145   max_low_pfn = setup_memory();
1146
1147   /*
1148    * NOTE: before this point _nobody_ is allowed to allocate
1149    * any memory using the bootmem allocator.
1150    */
```

```
1152  #ifdef CONFIG_SMP
1153   smp_alloc_memory(); /* AP processor realmode stacks in low memory*/
1154  #endif
1155   paging_init();
1156
1157  #ifdef CONFIG_EARLY_PRINTK
1158   {
1159    char *s = strstr(*cmdline_p, "earlyprintk=");
1160    if (s) {
1161     extern void setup_early_printk(char *);
1162
1163     setup_early_printk(s);
1164     printk("early console enabled\n");
1165    }
1166   }
1167  #endif
...
1170   dmi_scan_machine();
1171
1172  #ifdef CONFIG_X86_GENERICARCH
1173   generic_apic_probe(*cmdline_p);
1174  #endif
1175   if (efi_enabled)
1176    efi_map_memmap();
1177
1178   /*
1179   * Parse the ACPI tables for possible boot-time SMP configuration.
1180   */
1181   acpi_boot_init();
1182
1183  #ifdef CONFIG_X86_LOCAL_APIC
1184   if (smp_found_config)
1185    get_smp_config();
1186  #endif
1187
1188  register_memory(max_low_pfn);
1188
1190  #ifdef CONFIG_VT
1191  #if defined(CONFIG_VGA_CONSOLE)
1192   if (!efi_enabled || (efi_mem_type(0xa0000) != EFI_CONVENTIONAL_MEMORY))
1193    conswitchp = &vga_con;
1194  #elif defined(CONFIG_DUMMY_CONSOLE)
1195   conswitchp = &dummy_con;
1196  #endif
1197  #endif
1198  }
```

Line 1087

Get `boot_cpu_data`, which is a pointer to the `cpuinfo_x86` struct filled in at boot time. This is similar for PPC.

Line 1088

Activate any machine-specific identification routines. This can be found in `arch/xxx/machine-default/setup.c`.

Line 1089

Identify the specific processor.

Lines 1103–1116

Get the system boot parameters.

Lines 1118–1122

Get RAM disk if set in `arch/<arch>/defconfig`.

Lines 1124–1127

Initialize Extensible Firmware Interface (if set in `/defconfig`) or just print out the BIOS memory map.

Line 1129

Save off Enhanced Disk Drive parms from boot time.

Lines 1133–1141

Initialize memory-management structs from the BIOS-provided memory map.

Line 1143

Begin parsing out the Linux command line. (See `arch/<arch>/kernel/setup.c`.)

Line 1145

Initializes/reserves boot memory. (See `arch/i386/kernel/setup.c`.)

Lines 1153–1155

Get a page for SMP initialization or initialize paging beyond the 8M that's already initialized in `head.S`. (See `arch/i386/mm/init.c`.)

Lines 1157–1167

Get `printk()` running even though the console is not fully initialized.

Line 1170

This line is the Desktop Management Interface (DMI), which gathers information about the specific system-hardware configuration from BIOS. (See `arch/i386/kernel/dmi_scan.c`.)

Lines 1172–1174

If the configuration calls for it, look for the APIC given on the command line. (See `arch/i386/machine-generic/probe.c`.)

Lines 1175–1176

If using Extensible Firmware Interface, remap the EFI memory map. (See `arch/i386/kernel/efi.c`.)

Line 1181

Look for local and I/O APICs. (See `arch/i386/kernel/acpi/boot.c`.) Locate and checksum System Description Tables. (See `drivers/acpi/tables.c`.) For a better understanding of ACPI, go to the **ACPI4LINUX** project on the Web.

Lines 1183–1186

Scan for SMP configuration. (See `arch/i386/kernel/mpparse.c`.) This section can also use ACPI for configuration information.

Line 1188

Request I/O and memory space for standard resources. (See `arch/i386/kernel/std_resources.c` for an idea of how resources are registered.)

Lines 1190–1197

Set up the VGA console switch structure. (See `drivers/video/console/vgacon.c`.)

A similar but shorter version of `setup_arch()` can be found in `arch/ppc/kernel/setup.c` for the PowerPC. This function initializes a large part of the `ppc_md` structure. A call to `pmac_feature_init()` in `arch/ppc/platforms/pmac_feature.c` does an initial probe and initialization of the `pmac` hardware.

8.5.5   The Call to setup_per_cpu_areas()

Line 409

The routine `setup_per_cpu_areas()` exists for the setup of a multiprocessing environment. If the Linux kernel is compiled without SMP support, `setup_per_cpu_areas()` is stubbed out to do nothing, as follows:

```
-------------------------------------------------------------------
init/main.c
317  static inline void setup_per_cpu_areas(void) { }
-------------------------------------------------------------------
```

If the Linux kernel is compiled with SMP support, `setup_per_cpu_areas()` is defined as follows:

```
-------------------------------------------------------------------
init/main.c
327 static void __init setup_per_cpu_areas(void)
328 {
329   unsigned long size, i;
330   char *ptr;
331   /* Created by linker magic */
332   extern char __per_cpu_start[], __per_cpu_end[];
333
334   /* Copy section for each CPU (we discard the original) */
335   size = ALIGN(__per_cpu_end - __per_cpu_start, SMP_CACHE_BYTES);
336 #ifdef CONFIG_MODULES
337   if (size < PERCPU_ENOUGH_ROOM)
338     size = PERCPU_ENOUGH_ROOM;
339 #endif
340
341   ptr = alloc_bootmem(size * NR_CPUS);
342
343   for (i = 0; i < NR_CPUS; i++, ptr += size) {
344     __per_cpu_offset[i] = ptr - __per_cpu_start;
345     memcpy(ptr, __per_cpu_start, __per_cpu_end - __per_cpu_start);
346   }
347 }
-------------------------------------------------------------------
```

Lines 329–332

The variables for managing a consecutive block of memory are initialized. The "linker magic" variables are defined during linking in the appropriate architecture's kernel directory (for example, `arch/i386/kernel/vmlinux.lds.S`).

Lines 334–341

We determine the size of memory a single CPU requires and allocate that memory for each CPU in the system as a single contiguous block of memory.

Lines 343–346

We cycle through the newly allocated memory, initializing each CPU's chunk of memory. Conceptually, we have taken a chunk of data that's valid for a single CPU (`__per_cpu_start` to `__per_cpu_end`) and copied it for each CPU on the system. This way, each CPU has its own data with which to play.

8.5.6 The Call to smp_prepare_boot_cpu()

Line 415

Similar to `smp_per_cpu_areas()`, `smp_prepare_boot_cpu()` is stubbed out when the Linux kernel does not support SMP:

```
------------------------------------------------------------------
include/linux/smp.h
106 #define smp_prepare_boot_cpu()     do {} while (0)
------------------------------------------------------------------
```

However, if the Linux kernel is compiled with SMP support, we need to allow the booting CPU to access its console drivers and the per-CPU storage that we just initialized. Marking CPU bitmasks achieves this.

A CPU bitmask is defined as follows:

```
------------------------------------------------------------------
include/asm-generic/cpumask.h
10 #if NR_CPUS > BITS_PER_LONG && NR_CPUS != 1
11 #define CPU_ARRAY_SIZE    BITS_TO_LONGS(NR_CPUS)
12
13 struct cpumask
14 {
15   unsigned long mask[CPU_ARRAY_SIZE];
16 };
------------------------------------------------------------------
```

This means that we have a platform-independent bitmask that contains the same number of bits as the system has CPUs.

`smp_prepare_boot_cpu()` is implemented in the architecture-dependent section of the Linux kernel but, as we soon see, it is the same for i386 and PPC systems:

```
-------------------------------------------------------------------
arch/i386/kernel/smpboot.c
66 /* bitmap of online cpus */
67 cpumask_t cpu_online_map;
...
70 cpumask_t cpu_callout_map;
...
1341 void __devinit smp_prepare_boot_cpu(void)
1342 {
1343    cpu_set(smp_processor_id(), cpu_online_map);
1344    cpu_set(smp_processor_id(), cpu_callout_map);
1345 }
-------------------------------------------------------------------


-------------------------------------------------------------------
arch/ppc/kernel/smp.c
49 cpumask_t cpu_online_map;
50 cpumask_t cpu_possible_map;
...
331 void __devinit smp_prepare_boot_cpu(void)
332 {
333    cpu_set(smp_processor_id(), cpu_online_map);
334    cpu_set(smp_processor_id(), cpu_possible_map);
335 }
-------------------------------------------------------------------
```

In both these functions, `cpu_set()` simply sets the bit `smp_processor_id()` in the `cpumask_t` bitmap. Setting a bit implies that the value of the set bit is 1.

8.5.7 The Call to sched_init()

Line 422

The call to `sched_init()` marks the initialization of all objects that the scheduler manipulates to manage the assignment of CPU time among the system's processes. Keep in mind that, at this point, only one process exists: the init process that currently executes `sched_init()`:

```
-------------------------------------------------------------------
kernel/sched.c
3896 void __init sched_init(void)
3897 {
3898    runqueue_t *rq;
```

```
3899   int i, j, k;
3900
...
3919   for (i = 0; i < NR_CPUS; i++) {
3920     prio_array_t *array;
3921
3922     rq = cpu_rq(i);
3923     spin_lock_init(&rq->lock);
3924     rq->active = rq->arrays;
3925     rq->expired = rq->arrays + 1;
3926     rq->best_expired_prio = MAX_PRIO;
...
3938     for (j = 0; j < 2; j++) {
3939       array = rq->arrays + j;
3940       for (k = 0; k < MAX_PRIO; k++) {
3941         INIT_LIST_HEAD(array->queue + k);
3942         __clear_bit(k, array->bitmap);
3943       }
3944       // delimiter for bitsearch
3945       __set_bit(MAX_PRIO, array->bitmap);
3946     }
3947   }
3948   /*
3949    * We have to do a little magic to get the first
3950    * thread right in SMP mode.
3951    */
3952   rq = this_rq();
3953   rq->curr = current;
3954   rq->idle = current;
3955   set_task_cpu(current, smp_processor_id());
3956   wake_up_forked_process(current);
3957
3958   /*
3959    * The boot idle thread does lazy MMU switching as well:
3960    */
3961   atomic_inc(&init_mm.mm_count);
3962   enter_lazy_tlb(&init_mm, current);
3963 }
```

Lines 3919–3926

Each CPU's run queue is initialized: The active queue, expired queue, and spinlock are all initialized in this segment. Recall from Chapter 7 that spin_lock|_init() sets the spinlock to 1, which indicates that the data object is unlocked.

Figure 8.13 illustrates the initialized run queue.

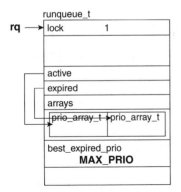

FIGURE 8.13
Initialized Run Queue rq

Lines 3938–3947

For each possible priority, we initialize the list associated with the priority and clear all bits in the bitmap to show that no process is on that queue. (If all this is confusing, refer to Figure 8.14. Also, see Chapter 7 for an overview of how the scheduler manages its run queues.) This code chunk just ensures that everything is ready for the introduction of a process. As of line 3947, the scheduler is in the position to know that no processes exist; it ignores the current and idle processes for now.

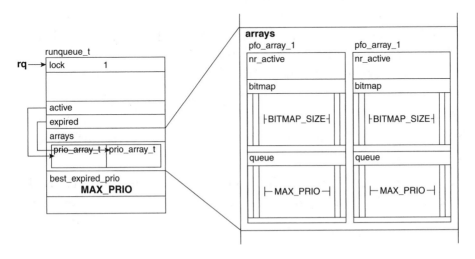

FIGURE 8.14
rq->arrays

Lines 3952–3956

We add the current process to the current CPU's run queue and call `wake_up_forked_process()` on ourselves to initialize current into the scheduler. Now, the scheduler knows that exactly one process exists: the `init` process.

Lines 3961–3962

When lazy MMU switching is enabled, it allows a multiprocessor Linux system to perform context switches at a faster rate. A TLB is a transaction lookaside buffer that contains the recent page translation addresses. It takes a long time to flush the TLB, so we swap it if possible. `enter_lazy_tlb()` ensures that the `mm_struct` `init_mm` isn't being used across multiple CPUs and can be lazily switched. On a uniprocessor system, this becomes a NULL function.

The sections that were omitted in the previous code deal with initialization of SMP machines. As a quick overview, those sections bootstrap each CPU to the default settings necessary to allow for load balancing, group scheduling, and thread migration. They are omitted here for clarity and brevity.

8.5.8 The Call to build_all_zonelists()

Line 424

The `build_all_zonelists()` function splits up the memory according to the zone types `ZONE_DMA`, `ZONE_NORMAL`, and `ZONE_HIGHMEM`. As mentioned in Chapter 6, "Filesystems," zones are linear separations of physical memory that are used mainly to address hardware limitations. Suffice it to say that this is the function where these memory zones are built. After the zones are built, pages are stored in page frames that fall within zones.

The call to `build_all_zonelists()` introduces `numnodes` and `NODE_DATA`. The global variable `numnodes` holds the number of nodes (or partitions) of physical memory.

The partitions are determined according to CPU access time. Note that, at this point, the page tables have already been fully set up:

```
-----------------------------------------------------------------
mm/page_alloc.c
1345  void __init build_all_zonelists(void)
1346  {
1347    int i;
```

```
1348
1349   for(i = 0 ; i < numnodes ; i++)
1350     build_zonelists(NODE_DATA(i));
1351   printk("Built %i zonelists\n", numnodes);
1352   }
```
----

build_all_zonelists() calls build_zonelists() once for each node and
finishes by printing out the number of zonelists created. This book does not go into
more detail regarding nodes. Suffice it to say that, in our one CPU example,
numnodes are equivalent to 1, and each node can have all three types of zones. The
NODE_DATA macro returns the node's descriptor from the node descriptor list.

8.5.9   The Call to page_alloc_init

Line 425

The function page_alloc_init() simply registers a function in a notifier
chain.[6] The function-registered page_alloc_cpu_notify() is a page-draining
function[7] associated with dynamic CPU configuration.

Dynamic CPU configuration refers to bringing up and down CPUs during the
running of the Linux system, an event referred to as "hotplugging the CPU."
Although technically, CPUs are not physically inserted and removed during
machine operation, they can be turned on and off in some systems, such as the IBM
p-Series 690. Let's look at the function:

```
mm/page_alloc.c
1787   #ifdef CONFIG_HOTPLUG_CPU
1788   static int page_alloc_cpu_notify(struct notifier_block *self,
1789       unsigned long action, void *hcpu)
1790   {
1791     int cpu = (unsigned long)hcpu;
1792     long *count;
1793
if (action == CPU_DEAD) {
...
1796     count = &per_cpu(nr_pagecache_local, cpu);
1797     atomic_add(*count, &nr_pagecache);
1798     *count = 0;
```

----

[6]   Chapter 2 discusses notifier chains.

[7]   Page draining refers to removing pages that are in use by a CPU that will no longer be used.

```
1799    local_irq_disable();
1800    __drain_pages(cpu);
1801    local_irq_enable();
1802    }
1803    return NOTIFY_OK;
1804 }
1805 #endif /* CONFIG_HOTPLUG_CPU */
1806
1807 void __init page_alloc_init(void)
1808 {
1809   hotcpu_notifier(page_alloc_cpu_notify, 0);
1810 }
```

Line 1809

This line is the registration of the `page_alloc_cpu_notify()` routine into the `hotcpu_notifier` notifier chain. The `hotcpu_notifier()` routine creates a `notifier_block` that points to the `page_alloc_cpu_notify()` function and, with a priority of 0, then registers the object in the **cpu_chain** notifier chain (`kernel/cpu.c`).

Line 1788

`page_alloc_cpu_notify()` has the parameters that correspond to a notifier call, as Chapter 2 explained. The system-specific pointer points to an integer that specifies the CPU number.

Lines 1794–1802

If the CPU is dead, free up its pages. The variable action is set to CPU_DEAD when a CPU is brought down. (See `drain_pages()` in this same file.)

8.5.10 The Call to parse_args()

Line 427

The `parse_args()` function parses the arguments passed to the Linux kernel.

For example, `nfsroot` is a kernel parameter that sets the NFS root filesystem for systems without disks. You can find a complete list of kernel parameters in `Documentation/kernel-parameters.txt`:

```
kernel/params.c
116 int parse_args(const char *name,
117    char *args,
```

```
118     struct kernel_param *params,
119     unsigned num,
120     int (*unknown)(char *param, char *val))
121 {
122   char *param, *val;
123
124   DEBUGP("Parsing ARGS: %s\n", args);
125
126   while (*args) {
127     int ret;
128
129     args = next_arg(args, &param, &val);
130     ret = parse_one(param, val, params, num, unknown);
131     switch (ret) {
132     case -ENOENT:
133       printk(KERN_ERR "%s: Unknown parameter '%s'\n",
134        name, param);
135       return ret;
136     case -ENOSPC:
137       printk(KERN_ERR
138        "%s: '%s' too large for parameter '%s'\n",
139        name, val ?: "", param);
140       return ret;
141     case 0:
142       break;
143     default:
144       printk(KERN_ERR
145        "%s: '%s' invalid for parameter '%s'\n",
146        name, val ?: "", param);
147       return ret;
148     }
149   }
150
151   /* All parsed OK. */
152   return 0;
153 }
```

Lines 116–125

The parameters passed to parse_args() are the following:

- **name**. A character string to be displayed if any errors occur while the kernel attempts to parse the kernel parameter arguments. In standard operation, this means that an error message, "Booting Kernel: Unknown parameter X," is displayed.

- **args**. The kernel parameter list of form *foo=bar,bar2 baz=fuz wix.*

- **params**. Points to the kernel parameter structure that holds all the valid parameters for the specific kernel. Depending on how a kernel was compiled, some parameters might exist and others might not.

- **num**. The number of kernel parameters in this specific kernel, not the number of arguments in `args`.

- **unknown**. Points to a function to call if a kernel parameter is specified that is not recognized.

Lines 126–153

We loop through the string `args`, set `param` to point to the first parameter, and set `val` to the first value (if any, `val` could be null). This is done via `next_args()` (for example, the first call to `next_args()` with `args` being *foo=bar,bar2 baz=fuz wix*). We set `param` to *foo* and `val` to *bar, bar2*. The space after `bar2` is overwritten with a `\0` and `args` is set to point at the beginning character of *baz*.

We pass our pointers `param` and `val` into `parse_one()`, which does the work of setting the actual kernel parameter data structures:

```
------------------------------------------------------------------
kernel/params.c
46 static int parse_one(char *param,
47      char *val,
48      struct kernel_param *params,
49      unsigned num_params,
50      int (*handle_unknown)(char *param, char *val))
51 {
52   unsigned int i;
53
54   /* Find parameter */
55   for (i = 0; i < num_params; i++) {
56     if (parameq(param, params[i].name)) {
57       DEBUGP("They are equal! Calling %p\n",
58        params[i].set);
59       return params[i].set(val, &params[i]);
60     }
61   }
62
63   if (handle_unknown) {
64     DEBUGP("Unknown argument: calling %p\n", handle_unknown);
65     return handle_unknown(param, val);
66   }
67
68   DEBUGP("Unknown argument '%s'\n", param);
69   return -ENOENT;
70 }
------------------------------------------------------------------
```

Lines 46–54

These parameters are the same as those described under `parse_args()` with `param` and `val` pointing to a subsection of `args`.

Lines 55–61

We loop through the defined kernel parameters to see if any match `param`. If we find a match, we use `val` to call the associated set function. Thus, the set function handles multiple, or null, arguments.

Lines 62–66

If the kernel parameter was not found, we call the `handle_unknown()` function that was passed in via `parse_args()`.

After `parse_one()` is called for each parameter-value combination specified in `args`, we have set the kernel parameters and are ready to continue starting the Linux kernel.

8.5.11   The Call to trap_init()

Line 431

In Chapter 3, we introduced *exceptions* and *interrupts*. The function `trap_init()` is specific to the handling of interrupts in x86 architecture. Briefly, this function initializes a table referenced by the x86 hardware. Each element in the table has a function to handle kernel or user-related issues, such as an invalid instruction or reference to a page not currently in memory. Although the PowerPC can have these same issues, its architecture handles them in a somewhat different manner. (Again, all this is discussed in Chapter 3.)

8.5.12   The Call to rcu_init()

Line 432

The `rcu_init()` function initializes the Read-Copy-Update (RCU) subsystem of the Linux 2.6 kernel. RCU controls access to critical sections of code and enforces mutual exclusion in systems where the cost of acquiring locks becomes significant in comparison to the chip speed. The Linux implementation of RCU is beyond the scope of this book. We occasionally mention calls to the RCU subsystem in our code analysis, but the specifics are left out. For more information on the

Linux RCU subsystem, consult the Linux Scalability Effort pages at
http://lse.sourceforge.net/locking/rcupdate.html:

```
-----------------------------------------------------------------------
kernel/rcupate.c
297 void __init rcu_init(void)
298 {
299   rcu_cpu_notify(&rcu_nb, CPU_UP_PREPARE,
300       (void *)(long)smp_processor_id());
301   /* Register notifier for non-boot CPUs */
302   register_cpu_notifier(&rcu_nb);
303 }
-----------------------------------------------------------------------
```

8.5.13   The Call to init_IRQ()

Line 433

The function init_IRQ() in arch/i386/kernel/i8259.c initializes the
hardware interrupt controller, the interrupt vector table and, if on x86, the system
timer. Chapter 3 includes a thorough discussion of interrupts for both x86 and
PPC, where the Real-Time Clock is used as an interrupt example:

```
-----------------------------------------------------------------------
arch/i386/kernel/i8259.c
410 void __init init_IRQ(void)
411 {
412  int i;
...
422  for (i = 0; i < (NR_VECTORS - FIRST_EXTERNAL_VECTOR); i++) {
423   int vector = FIRST_EXTERNAL_VECTOR + i;
424   if (i >= NR_IRQS)
425    break;
...
430   if (vector != SYSCALL_VECTOR)
431    set_intr_gate(vector, interrupt[i]);
432  }
...
437  intr_init_hook();
...
443  setup_timer();
...
449  if (boot_cpu_data.hard_math && !cpu_has_fpu)
450   setup_irq(FPU_IRQ, &fpu_irq);
451 }
-----------------------------------------------------------------------
```

Lines 422–432

Initialize the interrupt vectors. This associates the x86 (hardware) IRQs with the
appropriate handling code.

Line 437

Set up machine-specific IRQs, such as the Advanced Programmable Interrupt Controller (APIC).

Line 443

Initialize the timer clock.

Lines 449–450

Set up for FPU if needed.

The following code is the PPC implementation of init_IRQ():

```
------------------------------------------------------------------------
arch/ppc/kernel/irq.c
700  void __init init_IRQ(void)
701  {
702    int i;
703
704    for (i = 0; i < NR_IRQS; ++i)
705      irq_affinity[i] = DEFAULT_CPU_AFFINITY;
706
707    ppc_md.init_IRQ();
708  }
------------------------------------------------------------------------
```

Line 704

In multiprocessor systems, an interrupt can have an affinity for a specific processor.

Line 707

For a PowerMac platform, this routine is found in arch/ppc/platforms/pmac_pic.c. It sets up the Programmable Interrupt Controller (PIC) portion of the I/O controller.

8.5.14   The Call to softirq_init()

Line 436

The softirq_init() function prepares the boot CPU to accept notifications from tasklets. Let's look at the internals of softirq_init():

```
------------------------------------------------------------------------
kernel/softirq.c
317 void __init softirq_init(void)
318 {
```

```
319   open_softirq(TASKLET_SOFTIRQ, tasklet_action, NULL);
320   open_softirq(HI_SOFTIRQ, tasklet_hi_action, NULL);
321 }
...
327 void __init softirq_init(void)
328 {
329  open_softirq(TASKLET_SOFTIRQ, tasklet_action, NULL);
330  open_softirq(HI_SOFTIRQ, tasklet_hi_action, NULL);
331 tasklet_cpu_notify(&tasklet_nb, (unsigned long)CPU_UP_PREPARE,
332          (void *)(long)smp_processor_id());
333 register_cpu_notifier(&tasklet_nb);
334 }
```

Lines 319–320

We initialize the actions to take when we get a TASKLET_SOFTIRQ or
HI_SOFTIRQ interrupt. As we pass in NULL, we are telling the Linux kernel to
call tasklet_action(NULL) and tasklet_hi_action(NULL) (in the cases
of Line 319 and Line 320, respectively). The following implementation of
open_softirq() shows how the Linux kernel stores the tasklet initialization
information:

```
kernel/softirq.c
177 void open_softirq(int nr, void (*action)(struct softirq_action*),
void * data)
178 {
179   softirq_vec[nr].data = data;
180   softirq_vec[nr].action = action;
181 }
```

8.5.15 The Call to time_init()

Line 437

The function time_init() selects and initializes the system timer. This function, like trap_init(), is very architecture dependent; Chapter 3 covered this
when we explored timer interrupts. The system timer gives Linux its *temporal* view
of the world, which allows it to schedule when a task should run and for how long.
The **High Performance Event Timer (HPET)** from Intel will be the successor to
the 8254 PIT and RTC hardware. The HPET uses memory-mapped I/O, which

means that the HPET control registers are accessed as if they were memory locations. Memory must be configured properly to access I/O regions. If set in
`arch/i386/defconfig.h`, `time_init()` needs to be delayed until after
`mem_init()` has set up memory regions. See the following code:

```
------------------------------------------------------------------------
arch/i386/kernel/time.c
376 void __init time_init(void)
377 {
...
378 #ifdef CONFIG_HPET_TIMER
379  if (is_hpet_capable()) {
380   late_time_init = hpet_time_init;
381   return;
382  }
...
387 #endif
388  xtime.tv_sec = get_cmos_time();
389  wall_to_monotonic.tv_sec = -xtime.tv_sec;
390  xtime.tv_nsec = (INITIAL_JIFFIES % HZ) * (NSEC_PER_SEC / HZ);
391  wall_to_monotonic.tv_nsec = -xtime.tv_nsec;
392
393  cur_timer = select_timer();
394  printk(KERN_INFO "Using %s for high-res timesource\n",cur_timer->name);
395
396  time_init_hook();
397 }
------------------------------------------------------------------------
```

Lines 379–387

If the HPET is configured, `time_init()` must run after memory has been initialized. The code for `late_time_init()` (on lines 358—373) is the same as
`time_init()`.

Lines 388–391

Initialize the `xtime` time structure used for holding the time of day.

Line 393

Select the first timer that initializes. This can be overridden. (See `arch/i386/`
`kernel/timers/timer.c`.)

8.5.16   The Call to console_init()

Line 444

A computer console is a device where the kernel (and other parts of a system) output messages. It also has login capabilities. Depending on the system, the console can be on the monitor or through a serial port. The function `console_init()` is an early call to initialize the console device, which allows for boot-time reporting of status:

```
-----------------------------------------------------------------------
drivers/char/tty_io.c
2347 void __init console_init(void)
2348 {
2349   initcall_t *call;
...
2352   (void) tty_register_ldisc(N_TTY, &tty_ldisc_N_TTY);
...
2358 #ifdef CONFIG_EARLY_PRINTK
2359   disable_early_printk();
2360 #endif
...
2366   call = &__con_initcall_start;
2367   while (call < &__con_initcall_end) {
2368     (*call)();
2369     call++;
2370   }
2371 }
-----------------------------------------------------------------------
```

Line 2352

Set up the line discipline.

Line 2359

Keep the early `printk` support if desired. Early `printk` support allows the system to report status during the boot process before the system console is fully initialized. It specifically initializes a serial port (`ttyS0`, for example) or the system's VGA to a minimum functionality. Early `printk` support is started in `setup_arch()`. (For more information, see the code discussion on line 408 in this section and the files `/kernel/printk.c` and `/arch/i386/kernel/early_printk.c`.)

Line 2366

Initialize the console.

8.5.17   The Call to profile_init()

Line 447

profile_init() allocates memory for the kernel to store profiling data in. Profiling is the term used in computer science to describe data collection during program execution. Profiling data is used to analyze performance and otherwise study the program being executed (in our case, the Linux kernel itself):

```
-----------------------------------------------------------------
kernel/profile.c
30 void __init profile_init(void)
31 {
32   unsigned int size;
33
34   if (!prof_on)
35     return;
36
37   /* only text is profiled */
38   prof_len = _etext - _stext;
39   prof_len >>= prof_shift;
40
41   size = prof_len * sizeof(unsigned int) + PAGE_SIZE - 1;
42   prof_buffer = (unsigned int *) alloc_bootmem(size);
43 }
-----------------------------------------------------------------
```

Lines 34–35

Don't do anything if kernel profiling is not enabled.

Lines 38–39

_etext and _stext are defined in kernel/head.s. We determine the profile length as delimited by _etext and _stext and then shift the value by prof_shift, which was defined as a kernel parameter.

Lines 41–42

We allocate a contiguous block of memory for storing profiling data of the size requested by the kernel parameters.

8.5.18   The Call to local_irq_enable()

Line 448

The function local_irq_enable() allows interrupts on the current CPU. It is usually paired with local_irq_disable(). In previous kernel versions, the

sti(), cli() pair were used for this purpose. Although these macros still resolve
to sti() and cli(), the keyword to note here is **local**. These affect only the currently running processor:

```
------------------------------------------------------------------
include\asm-i386\system.h

446  #define local_irq_disable()  __asm__ __volatile__("cli": : :"memory")
447  #define local_irq_enable()   __asm__ __volatile__("sti": : :"memory")
------------------------------------------------------------------
```

Lines 446–447

Referring to the "Inline Assembly" section in Chapter 2, the item in the quotes
is the assembly instruction and memory is on the clobber list.

8.5.19   initrd Configuration

Lines 449–456

This #ifdef statement is a sanity check on initrd—the initial RAM disk.

A system using initrd loads the kernel and mounts the initial RAM disk as the
root filesystem. Programs can run from this RAM disk and, when the time comes,
a new root filesystem, such as the one on a hard drive, can be mounted and the initial RAM disk unmounted.

This operation simply checks to ensure that the initial RAM disk specified is
valid. If it isn't, we set initrd_start to 0, which tells the kernel to not use an initial RAM disk.[8]

8.5.20   The Call to mem_init()

Line 457

For both x86 and PPC, the call to mem_init() finds all free pages and sends that
information to the console. Recall from Chapter 4 that the Linux kernel breaks
available memory into *zones*. Currently, Linux has three zones:

- **Zone_DMA**. Memory less than 16MB.

---

[8]   For more information, refer to Documentation/initrd.txt.

- **Zone_Normal**. Memory starting at 16MB but less than 896MB. (The kernel uses the last 128MB.)

- **Zone_HIGHMEM**. Memory greater than 1GB.

The function mem_init() finds the total number of free page frames in all the memory zones. This function prints out informational kernel messages regarding the beginning state of the memory. This function is architecture dependent because it manages early memory allocation data. Each architecture supplies its own function, although they all perform the same tasks. We first look at how x86 does it and follow it up with PPC:

```
--------------------------------------------------------------------
arch/i386/mm/init
445   void __init mem_init(void)
446   {
447     extern int ppro_with_ram_bug(void);
448     int codesize, reservedpages, datasize, initsize;
449     int tmp;
450     int bad_ppro;
...
459   #ifdef CONFIG_HIGHMEM
460     if (PKMAP_BASE+LAST_PKMAP*PAGE_SIZE >= FIXADDR_START) {
461     printk(KERN_ERR "fixmap and kmap areas overlap - this will crash\n");
462     printk(KERN_ERR "pkstart: %lxh pkend:%lxh fixstart %lxh\n",
463     PKMAP_BASE, PKMAP_BASE+LAST_PKMAP*PAGE_SIZE, FIXADDR_START);
464     BUG();
465     }
466   #endif
467
468     set_max_mapnr_init();
...
476     /* this will put all low memory onto the freelists */
477     totalram_pages += __free_all_bootmem();
478
479
480     reservedpages = 0;
481     for (tmp = 0; tmp < max_low_pfn; tmp++)
...
485     if (page_is_ram(tmp) && PageReserved(pfn_to_page(tmp)))
486       reservedpages++;
487
488     set_highmem_pages_init(bad_ppro);
490     codesize = (unsigned long) &_etext - (unsigned long) &_text;
491     datasize = (unsigned long) &_edata - (unsigned long) &_etext;
492     initsize = (unsigned long) &__init_end - (unsigned long) &__init_begin;
493
494     kclist_add(&kcore_mem, __va(0), max_low_pfn << PAGE_SHIFT);
```

```
495    kclist_add(&kcore_vmalloc, (void *)VMALLOC_START,
496      VMALLOC_END-VMALLOC_START);
497
498    printk(KERN_INFO "Memory: %luk/%luk available (%dk kernel code, %dk
reserved, %dk data, %dk init, %ldk highmem)\n",
499      (unsigned long) nr_free_pages() << (PAGE_SHIFT-10),
500      num_physpages << (PAGE_SHIFT-10),
501      codesize >> 10,
502      reservedpages << (PAGE_SHIFT-10),
503      datasize >> 10,
504      initsize >> 10,
505      (unsigned long) (totalhigh_pages << (PAGE_SHIFT-10))
506      );
...
521    #ifndef CONFIG_SMP
522      zap_low_mappings();
523    #endif
524    }
```

Line 459

This line is a straightforward error check so that fixed map and kernel map do not overlap.

Line 469

The function set_max_mapnr_init() (arch/i386/mm/init.c) simply sets the value of num_physpages, which is a global variable (defined in mm/memory.c) that holds the number of available page frames.

Line 477

The call to __free_all_bootmem() marks the freeing up of all low-memory pages. During boot time, all pages are reserved. At this late point in the bootstrapping phase, the available low-memory pages are released. The flow of the function calls are seen in Figure 8.15.

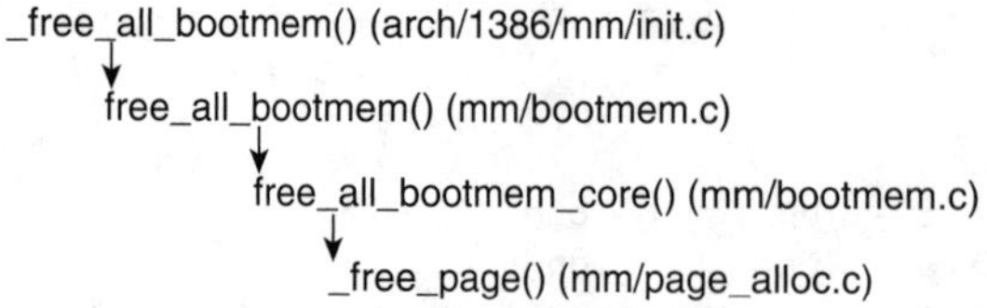

```
_free_all_bootmem() (arch/1386/mm/init.c)
   ↓
   free_all_bootmem() (mm/bootmem.c)
      ↓
      free_all_bootmem_core() (mm/bootmem.c)
         ↓
         _free_page() (mm/page_alloc.c)
```

FIGURE 8.15
__free_all_bootmem() Call Hierarchy

Let's look at the core portion of `free_all_bootmem_core()` to understand what is happening:

```
----------------------------------------------------------------------
mm/bootmem.c
257  static unsigned long __init free_all_bootmem_core(pg_data_t *pgdat)
258  {
259    struct page *page;
260    bootmem_data_t *bdata = pgdat->bdata;
261    unsigned long i, count, total = 0;
...
295    page = virt_to_page(bdata->node_bootmem_map);
296    count = 0;
297    for (i = 0; i < ((bdata->node_low_pfn-(bdata->node_boot_start >>
PAGE_SHIFT))/8 + PAGE_SIZE-1)/PAGE_SIZE; i++,page++) {
298      count++;
299      ClearPageReserved(page);
300      set_page_count(page, 1);
301      __free_page(page);
302    }
303    total += count;
304    bdata->node_bootmem_map = NULL;
305
306    return total;
307  }
----------------------------------------------------------------------
```

For all the available low-memory pages, we clear the `PG_reserved` flag[9] in the `flags` field of the page struct. Next, we set the `count` field of the page struct to 1 to indicate that it is in use and call `__free_page()`, thus passing it to the buddy allocator. If you recall from Chapter 4's explanation of the buddy system, we explain that this function releases a page and adds it to a free list.

The function `__free_all_bootmem()` returns the number of low memory pages available, which is added to the running count of `totalram_pages` (an unsigned long defined in `mm/page_alloc.c`).

Lines 480–486

These lines update the count of reserved pages.

---

[9] Recall from Chapter 6 that this flag is set in pages that are to be pinned in memory and that it is set for low memory during early bootstrapping.

Line 488

The call to set_highmem_pages_init() marks the initialization of high-memory pages. Figure 8.16 illustrates the calling hierarchy of set_highmem_pages_init().

```
set_highmem_pages_init() (arch/1386/mm/init.c)
    ↓
  one_highpage_init() (arch/1386/mm/init.c)
```

FIGURE 8.16
highmem_pages_init Calling Hierarchy

Let's look at the bulk of the code performed in one_highpage_init():

```
-----------------------------------------------------------------------
arch/i386/mm/init.c
253   void __init one_highpage_init(struct page *page, int pfn, int bad_ppro)
254   {
255           if (page_is_ram(pfn) && !(bad_ppro && page_kills_ppro(pfn))) {
256                   ClearPageReserved(page);
257                   set_bit(PG_highmem, &page->flags);
258                   set_page_count(page, 1);
259                   __free_page(page);
260                   totalhigh_pages++;
261           } else
262                   SetPageReserved(page);
263   }
-----------------------------------------------------------------------
```

Much like __free_all_bootmem(), all high-memory pages have their page struct flags field cleared of the PG_reserved flag, have PG_highmem set, and have their count field set to 1. __free_page() is also called to add these pages to the free lists and the totalhigh_pages counter is incremented.

Lines 490–506

This code block gathers and prints out information regarding the size of memory areas and the number of available pages.

Lines 521–523

The function zap_low_mappings flushes the initial TLBs and PGDs in low memory.

The function mem_init() marks the end of the boot phase of memory allocation and the beginning of the memory allocation that will be used throughout the system's life.

The PPC code for `mem_init()` finds and initializes all pages for all zones:

```
----------------------------------------------------------------------
arch/ppc/mm/init.c
393  void __init mem_init(void)
394  {
395   unsigned long addr;
396   int codepages = 0;
397   int datapages = 0;
398   int initpages = 0;
399  #ifdef CONFIG_HIGHMEM
400   unsigned long highmem_mapnr;

402   highmem_mapnr = total_lowmem >> PAGE_SHIFT;
403   highmem_start_page = mem_map + highmem_mapnr;
404  #endif /* CONFIG_HIGHMEM */
405   max_mapnr = total_memory >> PAGE_SHIFT;

407   high_memory = (void *) __va(PPC_MEMSTART + total_lowmem);
408   num_physpages = max_mapnr;  /* RAM is assumed contiguous */

410   totalram_pages += free_all_bootmem();

412  #ifdef CONFIG_BLK_DEV_INITRD
413   /* if we are booted from BootX with an initial ramdisk,
414    make sure the ramdisk pages aren't reserved. */
415   if (initrd_start) {
416  for (addr = initrd_start; addr < initrd_end; addr += PAGE_SIZE)
417   ClearPageReserved(virt_to_page(addr));
418  }
419  #endif /* CONFIG_BLK_DEV_INITRD */

421  #ifdef CONFIG_PPC_OF
422   /* mark the RTAS pages as reserved */
423   if ( rtas_data )
424    for (addr = (ulong)__va(rtas_data);
425     addr < PAGE_ALIGN((ulong)__va(rtas_data)+rtas_size) ;
426     addr += PAGE_SIZE)
427     SetPageReserved(virt_to_page(addr));
428  #endif
429  #ifdef CONFIG_PPC_PMAC
430   if (agp_special_page)
431    SetPageReserved(virt_to_page(agp_special_page));
432  #endif
433   if ( sysmap )
434    for (addr = (unsigned long)sysmap;
435     addr < PAGE_ALIGN((unsigned long)sysmap+sysmap_size) ;
436     addr += PAGE_SIZE)
437     SetPageReserved(virt_to_page(addr));

439   for (addr = PAGE_OFFSET; addr < (unsigned long)high_memory;
440    addr += PAGE_SIZE) {
```

```
441    if (!PageReserved(virt_to_page(addr)))
442      continue;
443    if (addr < (ulong) etext)
444      codepages++;
445    else if (addr >= (unsigned long)&__init_begin
446        && addr < (unsigned long)&__init_end)
447      initpages++;
448    else if (addr < (ulong) klimit)
449      datapages++;
450    }

452  #ifdef CONFIG_HIGHMEM
453    {
454    unsigned long pfn;

456    for (pfn = highmem_mapnr; pfn < max_mapnr; ++pfn) {
457      struct page *page = mem_map + pfn;

459      ClearPageReserved(page);
460      set_bit(PG_highmem, &page->flags);
461      set_page_count(page, 1);
462      __free_page(page);
463      totalhigh_pages++;
464    }
465    totalram_pages += totalhigh_pages;
466    }
467  #endif /* CONFIG_HIGHMEM */

469  printk("Memory: %luk available (%dk kernel code, %dk data, %dk init, %ldk
     highmem)\n",
470      (unsigned long)nr_free_pages()<< (PAGE_SHIFT-10),
471      codepages<< (PAGE_SHIFT-10), datapages<< (PAGE_SHIFT-10),
472      initpages<< (PAGE_SHIFT-10),
473      (unsigned long) (totalhigh_pages << (PAGE_SHIFT-10)));
474    if (sysmap)
475      printk("System.map loaded at 0x%08x for debugger, size: %ld bytes\n",
476        (unsigned int)sysmap, sysmap_size);
477  #ifdef CONFIG_PPC_PMAC
478    if (agp_special_page)
479      printk(KERN_INFO "AGP special page: 0x%08lx\n", agp_special_page);
480  #endif

482    /* Make sure all our pagetable pages have page->mapping
483     and page->index set correctly. */
484    for (addr = KERNELBASE; addr != 0; addr += PGDIR_SIZE) {
485      struct page *pg;
486      pmd_t *pmd = pmd_offset(pgd_offset_k(addr), addr);
487      if (pmd_present(*pmd)) {
488        pg = pmd_page(*pmd);
489        pg->mapping = (void *) &init_mm;
490        pg->index = addr;
```

```
491    }
492    }

493    mem_init_done = 1;
494   }
```

Lines 399–410

These lines find the amount of memory available. If HIGHMEM is used, those pages are also counted. The global variable totalram_pages is modified to reflect this.

Lines 412–419

If used, clear any pages that the boot RAM disk used.

Lines 421–432

Depending on the boot environment, reserve pages for the Real-Time Abstraction Services and AGP (video), if needed.

Lines 433–450

If required, reserve some pages for system map.

Lines 452–467

If using HIGHMEM, clear any reserved pages and modify the global variable totalram_pages.

Lines 469–480

Print memory information to the console.

Lines 482–492

Loop through page directory and initialize each mm_struct and index.

8.5.21   The Call to late_time_init()

Lines 459–460

The function late_time_init() uses HPET (refer to the discussion under "The Call to time_init" section). This function is used only with the Intel architecture and HPET. This function has essentially the same code as time_init(); it is just called *after* memory initialization to allow the HPET to be mapped into physical memory.

8.5.22   The Call to calibrate_delay()

Line 461

The function `calibrate_delay()` in `init/main.c` calculates and prints the value of the much celebrated "BogoMips," which is a measurement that indicates the number of `delay()` iterations your processor can perform in a clock tick. `calibrate_delay()` allows delays to be approximately the same across processors of different speeds. The resulting value—at most an indicator of how fast a processor is running—is stored in `loop_pre_jiffy` and the `udelay()` and `mdelay()` functions use it to set the number of `delay()` iterations to perform:

```
-------------------------------------------------------------------
init/main.c
void __init calibrate_delay(void)
{
   unsigned long ticks, loopbit;
   int lps_precision = LPS_PREC;

186    loops_per_jiffy = (1<<12);

   printk("Calibrating delay loop... ");
189    while (loops_per_jiffy <<= 1) {
     /* wait for "start of" clock tick */
     ticks = jiffies;
     while (ticks == jiffies)
      /* nothing */;
     /* Go .. */
     ticks = jiffies;
     __delay(loops_per_jiffy);
     ticks = jiffies - ticks;
     if (ticks)
      break;
200    }

/* Do a binary approximation to get loops_per_jiffy set to equal one clock
  (up to lps_precision bits) */
204    loops_per_jiffy >>= 1;
   loopbit = loops_per_jiffy;
206    while ( lps_precision-- && (loopbit >>= 1) ) {
     loops_per_jiffy |= loopbit;
     ticks = jiffies;
     while (ticks == jiffies);
     ticks = jiffies;
```

```
    __delay(loops_per_jiffy);
    if (jiffies != ticks)  /* longer than 1 tick */
     loops_per_jiffy &= ~loopbit;
214   }

/* Round the value and print it */
217   printk("%lu.%02lu BogoMIPS\n",
    loops_per_jiffy/(500000/HZ),
219   (loops_per_jiffy/(5000/HZ)) % 100);
}
```

Line 186

Start at 0x800.

Lines 189–200

Keep doubling `loops_per_jiffy` until the amount of time it takes the function `delay(loops_per_jiffy)` to exceed one jiffy.

Line 204

Divide `loops_per_jiffy` by 2.

Lines 206–214

Successively add descending powers of 2 to `loops_per_jiffy` until tick equals jiffy.

Lines 217–219

Print the value out as if it were a float.

8.5.23   The Call to pgtable_cache_init()

Line 463

The key function in this x86 code block is the system function `kmem_cache_create()`. This function creates a named cache. The first parameter is a string used to identify it in `/proc/slabinfo`:

```
arch/i386/mm/init.c
529 kmem_cache_t *pgd_cache;
530 kmem_cache_t *pmd_cache;
531
```

```
532 void __init pgtable_cache_init(void)
533 {
534   if (PTRS_PER_PMD > 1) {
535     pmd_cache = kmem_cache_create("pmd",
536            PTRS_PER_PMD*sizeof(pmd_t),
537            0, 538              SLAB_HWCACHE_ALIGN | SLAB_MUST_H  WCACHE_ALIGN,
539            pmd_ctor,
540            NULL);
541     if (!pmd_cache)
542       panic("pgtable_cache_init(): cannot create pmd c  ache");
543   }
544   pgd_cache = kmem_cache_create("pgd",
545         PTRS_PER_PGD*sizeof(pgd_t),
546         0,
547         SLAB_HWCACHE_ALIGN | SLAB_MUST_HWCACHE_A  LIGN,
548         pgd_ctor,
549         PTRS_PER_PMD == 1 ? pgd_dtor : NULL);
550   if (!pgd_cache)
551     panic("pgtable_cache_init(): Cannot create pgd cache");
552 }
```

```
arch/ppc64/mm/init.c
976 void pgtable_cache_init(void)
977 {
978   zero_cache = kmem_cache_create("zero",
979         PAGE_SIZE,
980         0,
981         SLAB_HWCACHE_ALIGN | SLAB_MUST_HWCACHE_A  LIGN,
982         zero_ctor,
983         NULL);
984   if (!zero_cache)
985     panic("pgtable_cache_init(): could not create zero_cache  !\n");
986 }
```

Lines 532–542

Create the pmd cache.

Lines 544–551

Create the pgd cache.

On the PPC, which has hardware-assisted hashing, pgtable_cache_init() is a no-op:

```
include\asmppc\pgtable.h
685  #define pgtable_cache_init()   do { } while (0)
```

8.5.24   The Call to buffer_init()

Line 472

The `buffer_init()` function in `fs/buffer.c` holds data from filesystem devices:

```
-----------------------------------------------------------------------
fs/buffer.c
3031  void __init buffer_init(void)
{
  int i;
  int nrpages;

3036   bh_cachep = kmem_cache_create("buffer_head",
    sizeof(struct buffer_head), 0,
    0, init_buffer_head, NULL);
3039   for (i = 0; i < ARRAY_SIZE(bh_wait_queue_heads); i++)
    init_waitqueue_head(&bh_wait_queue_heads[i].wqh);

3044   nrpages = (nr_free_buffer_pages() * 10) / 100;
  max_buffer_heads = nrpages * (PAGE_SIZE / sizeof(struct buffer_head));
  hotcpu_notifier(buffer_cpu_notify, 0);
3048   }
-----------------------------------------------------------------------
```

Line 3036

Allocate the buffer cache hash table.

Line 3039

Create a table of buffer hash wait queues.

Line 3044

Limit low-memory occupancy to 10 percent.

8.5.25   The Call to security_scaffolding_startup()

Line 474

The 2.6 Linux kernel contains code for loading kernel modules that implement various security features. `security_scaffolding_startup()` simply verifies that a security operations object exists, and if it does, calls the security module's initialization functions.

How security modules can be created and what kind of issues a writer might face are beyond the scope of this text. For more information, consult Linux Security

Modules (http://lsm.immunix.org/) and the Linux-security-module mailing list
(http://mail.wirex.com/mailman/listinfo/linux-security-module).

8.5.26   The Call to vfs_caches_init()

Line 475

The VFS subsystem depends on memory caches, called SLAB caches, to hold
the structures it manages. Chapter 4 discusses SLAB caches detail. The
vfs_caches_init() function initializes the SLAB caches that the subsystem uses.
Figure 8.17 shows the overview of the main function hierarchy called from
vfs_caches_init(). We explore in detail each function included in this call hierarchy. You can refer to this hierarchy to keep track of the functions as we look at
each of them.

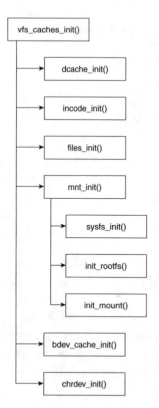

FIGURE 8.17
vfs_caches_init() Call Hierarchy

Table 8.3 summarizes the objects introduced by the `vfs_caches_init()` function or by one of the functions it calls.

TABLE 8.3
Objects Introduced by vfs_caches_init

Object Name	Description
names_cachep	Global variable
filp_cachep	Global variable
inode_cache	Global variable
dentry_cache	Global variable
mnt_cache	Global variable
namespace	Struct
mount_hashtable	Global variable
root_fs_type	Global variable
file_system_type	Struct (discussed in Chapter 6)
bdev_cachep	Global variable

```
-----------------------------------------------------------------------
fs/dcache.c
1623  void __init vfs_caches_init(unsigned long mempages)
1624  {
1625   names_cachep = kmem_cache_create("names_cache",
1626     PATH_MAX, 0,
1627     SLAB_HWCACHE_ALIGN, NULL, NULL);
1628   if (!names_cachep)
1629    panic("Cannot create names SLAB cache");
1630
1631   filp_cachep = kmem_cache_create("filp",
1632     sizeof(struct file), 0,
1633     SLAB_HWCACHE_ALIGN, filp_ctor, filp_dtor);
1634   if(!filp_cachep)
1635    panic("Cannot create filp SLAB cache");
1636
1637   dcache_init(mempages);
1638   inode_init(mempages);
1639   files_init(mempages);
1640   mnt_init(mempages);
1641   bdev_cache_init();
1642   chrdev_init();
1643  }
-----------------------------------------------------------------------
```

Line 1623

The routine takes in the global variable `num_physpages` (whose value is calculated during `mem_init()`) as a parameter that holds the number of physical pages available in the system's memory. This number influences the creation of SLAB caches, as we see later.

Lines 1625–1629

The next step is to create the `names_cachep` memory area. Chapter 4 describes the `kmem_cache_create()` function in detail. This memory area holds objects of size `PATH_MAX`, which is the maximum allowable number of characters a pathname is allowed to have. (This value is set in `linux/limits.h` as 4,096.) At this point, the cache that has been created is empty of objects, or memory areas of size `PATH_MAX`. The actual memory areas are allocated upon the first and potentially subsequent calls to `getname()`.

As discussed in Chapter 6 the `getname()` routine is called at the beginning of some of the file-related system calls (for example, `sys_open()`) to read the file pathname from the process address space. Objects are freed from the cache with the `putname()` routine.

If the `names_cache` cache cannot be created, the kernel jumps to the panic routine, exiting the function's flow of control.

Lines 1631–1635

The `filp_cachep` cache is created next, with objects the size of the file structure. The object holding the file structure is allocated by the `get_empty_filp()` (`fs/file_table.c`) routine, which is called, for example, upon creation of a pipe or the opening of a file. The file descriptor object is deallocated by a call to the `file_free()` (`fs/file_table.c`) routine.

Line 1637

The `dcache_init()` (`fs/dcache.c`) routine creates the SLAB cache that holds dentry descriptors.[10] The cache itself is called the `dentry_cache`. The dentry descriptors themselves are created for each hierarchical component in pathnames referred by processes when accessing a file or directory. The structure associates the

---

[10] Recall that dentry is short for directory entry.

file or directory component with the inode that represents it, which further facilitates requests to that component for a speedier association with its corresponding inode.

Line 1638

The `inode_init()` (`fs/inode.c`) routine initializes the inode hash table and the wait queue head array used for storing hashed inodes that the kernel wants to lock. The wait queue heads (`wait_queue_head_t`) for hashed inodes are stored in an array called `i_wait_queue_heads`. This array gets initialized at this point of the system's startup process.

The `inode_hashtable` gets created at this point. This table speeds up the searches on inode. The last thing that occurs is that the SLAB cache used to hold inode objects gets created. It is called `inode_cache`. The memory areas for this cache are allocated upon calls to `alloc_inode` (`fs/inode.c`) and freed upon calls to `destroy_inode()` (`fs/inode.c`).

Line 1639

The `files_init()` routine is called to determine the maximum amount of memory allowed for files per process. The `max_files` field of the `files_stat` structure is set. This is then referenced upon file creation to determine if there is enough memory to open the file. Let's look at this routine:

```
fs/file_table.c
292  void __init files_init(unsigned long mempages)
293  {
294   int n;
...
299   n = (mempages * (PAGE_SIZE / 1024)) / 10;
300   files_stat.max_files = n;
301   if (files_stat.max_files < NR_FILE)
302     files_stat.max_files = NR_FILE;
303  }
```

Line 299

The page size is divided by the amount of space that a file (along with associated inode and cache) will roughly occupy (in this case, 1K). This value is then multiplied by the number of pages to get the total amount of "blocks" that can be used for files. The division by 10 shows that the default is to limit the memory usage for files to no more than 10 percent of the available memory.

Lines 301–302

The NR_FILE (include/linux/fs.h) is set to 8,192.

Line 1640

The next routine, called mnt_init(), creates the cache that will hold the vfsmount objects the VFS uses for mounting filesystems. The cache is called mnt_cache. The routine also creates the mount_hashtable array, which stores references to objects in mnt_cache for faster access. It then issues calls to initialize the sysfs filesystem and mounts the root filesystem. Let's closely look at the creation of the hash table:

```
-------------------------------------------------------------------------
fs/namespace.c
1137  void __init mnt_init(unsigned long mempages)
{
1139    struct list_head *d;
1140    unsigned long order;
1141    unsigned int nr_hash;
1142    int i;
...
1149    order = 0;
1150    mount_hashtable = (struct list_head *)
1151      __get_free_pages(GFP_ATOMIC, order);
1152
1153    if (!mount_hashtable)
1154      panic("Failed to allocate mount hash table\n");
...
1161   nr_hash = (1UL << order) * PAGE_SIZE / sizeof(struct list_head);
1162    hash_bits = 0;
1163    do {
1164      hash_bits++;
1165      } while ((nr_hash >> hash_bits) != 0);
1166    hash_bits--;
...
1172    nr_hash = 1UL << hash_bits;
1173    hash_mask = nr_hash-1;
1174
1175   printk("Mount-cache hash table entries: %d (order: %ld, %ld bytes)\n",
nr_hash, order, (PAGE_SIZE << order));
...
1179    d = mount_hashtable;
1180    i = nr_hash;
1181   do {
1182     INIT_LIST_HEAD(d);
1183      d++;
1184    i--;
1185    } while (i);
..
1189  }
-------------------------------------------------------------------------
```

Lines 1139–1144

The hash table array consists of a full page of memory. Chapter 4 explains in detail how the routine __get_free_pages() works. In a nutshell, this routine returns a pointer to a memory area of size 2 order pages. In this case, we allocate one page to hold the hash table.

Lines 1161–1173

The next step is to determine the number of entries in the table. nr_hash is set to hold the order (power of two) number of list heads that can fit into the table. hash_bits is calculated as the number of bits needed to represent the highest power of two in nr_hash. Line 1172 then redefines nr_hash as being composed of the single leftmost bit. The bitmask can then be calculated from the new nr_hash value.

Lines 1179–1185

Finally, we initialize the hash table through a call to the INIT_LIST_HEAD macro, which takes in a pointer to the memory area where a new list head is to be initialized. We do this nr_hash times (or the number of entries that the table can hold).

Let's walk through an example: We assume a PAGE_SIZE of 4KB and a struct list_head of 8 bytes. Because order is equal to 0, the value of nr_hash becomes 500; that is, up to 500 list_head structs can fit in one 4KB table. The (1UL << order) becomes the number of pages that have been allocated. For example, if the order had been 1 (meaning we had requested 21 pages allocated to the hash table), 0000 0001 bit-shifted once to the left becomes 0000 0010 (or 2 in decimal notation). Next, we calculate the number of bits the hash key will need. Walking through each iteration of the loop, we get the following:

Beginning values are hash_bits = 0 and nr_hash = 500.

- Iteration 1: hash_bits = 1, and (500 >> 1) ! = 0

  (0001 1111 0100 >> 1) = 0000 1111 1010

- Iteration 2: hash_bits = 2, and (500 >> 2) ! = 0

  (0001 1111 1010 >> 2) = 0000 0111 1110

- Iteration3: hash_bits = 3, and (500 >> 3) ! = 0

  (0001 1111 1010 >> 3) = 0000 0011 1111

- Iteration 4: `hash_bits` = 4, and (500 >> 4) ! = 0

  (0001 1111 1010 >> 4) = 0000 0001 1111

- Iteration 5: `hash_bits` = 5, and (500 >> 5) ! = 0

  (0001 1111 1010 >> 5) = 0000 0000 1111

- Iteration 6: `hash_bits` = 6, and (500 >> 6) ! = 0

  (0001 1111 1010 >> 6) = 0000 0000 0111

- Iteration 7: `hash_bits` = 7, and (500 >> 7) ! = 0

  (0001 1111 1010 >> 7) = 0000 0000 0011

- Iteration 8: `hash_bits` = 8, and (500 >> 8) ! = 0

  (0001 1111 1010 >> 8) = 0000 0000 0001

- Iteration 9: `hash_bits` = 9, and (500 >> 9) ! = 0

  (0001 1111 1010 >> 9) = 0000 0000 0000

After breaking out of the `while` loop, `hash_bits` is decremented to 8, `nr_hash` is set to 0001 0000 0000, and the `hash_mask` is set to 0000 1111 1111.

After the `mnt_init()` routine initializes `mount_hashtable` and creates `mnt_cache`, it issues three calls:

```
fs/namespace.c
...
1189    sysfs_init();
1190    init_rootfs();
1191    init_mount_tree();
1192    }
```

`sysfs_init()` is responsible for the creation of the `sysfs` filesystem. `init_rootfs()` and `init_mount_tree()` are together responsible for mounting the root filesystem. We closely look at each routine in turn.

```
init_rootfs()
fs/ramfs/inode.c
218    static struct file_system_type rootfs_fs_type = {
219      .name    = "rootfs",
220      .get_sb  = rootfs_get_sb,
221      .kill_sb = kill_litter_super,
```

```
222  };
...
237  int __init init_rootfs(void)
238  {
239    return register_filesystem(&rootfs_fs_type);
240  }
```

The `rootfs` filesystem is an initial filesystem the kernel mounts. It is a simple and quite empty directory that becomes *overmounted* by the real filesystem at a later point in the kernel boot-up process.

Lines 218–222

This code block is the declaration of the `rootfs_fs_type file_system_type` struct. Only the two methods for getting and killing the associated superblock are defined.

Lines 237–240

The `init_rootfs()` routine merely register this `rootfs` with the kernel. This makes available all the information regarding the type of filesystem (information stored in the `file_system_type` struct) within the kernel.

```
init_mount_tree()
fs/namespace.c
1107  static void __init init_mount_tree(void)
1108  {
1109    struct vfsmount *mnt;
1110    struct namespace *namespace;
1111    struct task_struct *g, *p;
1112
1113    mnt = do_kern_mount("rootfs", 0, "rootfs", NULL);
1114    if (IS_ERR(mnt))
1115      panic("Can't create rootfs");
1116    namespace = kmalloc(sizeof(*namespace), GFP_KERNEL);
1117    if (!namespace)
1118      panic("Can't allocate initial namespace");
1119    atomic_set(&namespace->count, 1);
1120    INIT_LIST_HEAD(&namespace->list);
1121    init_rwsem(&namespace->sem);
1122    list_add(&mnt->mnt_list, &namespace->list);
1123    namespace->root = mnt;
1124
1125    init_task.namespace = namespace;
1126    read_lock(&tasklist_lock);
1127    do_each_thread(g, p) {
1128      get_namespace(namespace);
```

```
1129    p->namespace = namespace;
1130    } while_each_thread(g, p);
1131    read_unlock(&tasklist_lock);
1132
1133  set_fs_pwd(current->fs, namespace->root,
      namespace->root->mnt_root);
1134  set_fs_root(current->fs, namespace->root,
      namespace->root->mnt_root);
1135  }
```

Lines 1116–1123

Initialize the process namespace. This structure keeps pointers to the mount tree-related structures and the corresponding dentry. The `namespace` object is allocated, the count set to 1, the list field of type `list_head` is initialized, the semaphore that locks the namespace (and the mount tree) is initialized, and the root field corresponding to the `vfsmount` structure is set to point to our newly allocated `vfsmount`.

Line 1125

The current task's (the `init` task's) process descriptor namespace field is set to point at the namespace object we just allocated and initialized. (The current process is Process 0.)

Lines 1134–1135

The following two routines set the values of four fields in the `fs_struct` associated with our process. `fs_struct` holds field for the root and current working directory entries set by these two routines.

We just finished exploring what happens in the `mnt_init` function. Let's continue exploring `vfs_mnt_init`.

```
1641 bdev_cache_init()
fs/block_dev.c
290  void __init bdev_cache_init(void)
291  {
292    int err;
293    bdev_cachep = kmem_cache_create("bdev_cache",
294      sizeof(struct bdev_inode),
295      0,
296    SLAB_HWCACHE_ALIGN|SLAB_RECLAIM_ACCOUNT,
297      init_once,
298      NULL);
```

```
299   if (!bdev_cachep)
300    panic("Cannot create bdev_cache SLAB cache");
301   err = register_filesystem(&bd_type);
302   if (err)
303    panic("Cannot register bdev pseudo-fs");
304   bd_mnt = kern_mount(&bd_type);
305   err = PTR_ERR(bd_mnt);
306   if (IS_ERR(bd_mnt))
307    panic("Cannot create bdev pseudo-fs");
308   blockdev_superblock = bd_mnt->mnt_sb;   /* For writeback */
309   }
```

Lines 293–298

Create the `bdev_cache` SLAB cache, which holds `bdev_inodes`.

Line 301

Register the `bdev` special filesystem. It has been defined as follows:

```
fs/block_dev.c
294   static struct file_system_type bd_type = {
295    .name   = "bdev",
296    .get_sb  = bd_get_sb,
297    .kill_sb  = kill_anon_super,
298   };
```

As you can see, the `file_system_type` struct of the `bdev` special filesystem has only two routines defined: one for fetching the filesystem's superblock and the other for removing/freeing the superblock. At this point, you might wonder why block devices are registered as filesystems. In Chapter 6, we saw that systems that are not technically filesystems can use filesystem kernel structures; that is, they do not have mount points but can make use of the VFS kernel structures that support filesystems. Block devices are one instance of a pseudo filesystem that makes use of the VFS filesystem kernel structures. As with `bdev`, these special filesystems generally define only a limited number of fields because not all of them make sense for the particular application.

Lines 304–308

The call to `kern_mount()` sets up all the mount-related VFS structures and returns the `vfsmount` structure. (See Chapter 6 for more information on setting the global variables `bd_mnt` to point to the `vfsmount` structure and `blockdev_superblock` to point to the `vfsmount` superblock.)

This function initializes the character device objects that surround the driver model:

```
------------------------------------------------------------------------
1642 chrdev_init
fs/char_dev.c
void __init chrdev_init(void)
{
433    subsystem_init(&cdev_subsys);
434    cdev_map = kobj_map_init(base_probe, &cdev_subsys);
435  }
------------------------------------------------------------------------
```

8.5.27   The Call to radix_tree_init()

Line 476

The 2.6 Linux kernel uses a radix tree to manage pages within the page cache. Here, we simply initialize a contiguous section of kernel space for storing the page cache radix tree:

```
------------------------------------------------------------------------
lib/radix-tree.c
798 void __init radix_tree_init(void)
799 {
800   radix_tree_node_cachep = kmem_cache_create("radix_tree_node",
801       sizeof(struct radix_tree_node), 0,
802       SLAB_PANIC, radix_tree_node_ctor, NULL);
803   radix_tree_init_maxindex();
804   hotcpu_notifier(radix_tree_callback, 0);
------------------------------------------------------------------------

------------------------------------------------------------------------
lib/radix-tree.c
768 static __init void radix_tree_init_maxindex(void)
769 {
770   unsigned int i;
771
772   for (i = 0; i < ARRAY_SIZE(height_to_maxindex); i++)
773     height_to_maxindex[i] = __maxindex(i);
774 }
------------------------------------------------------------------------
```

Notice how `radix_tree_init()` allocates the page cache space and `radix_tree_init_maxindex()` configures the radix tree data store, `height_to_maxindex[]`.

`hotcpu_notifier()` (on line 804) refers to Linux 2.6's capability to hotswap CPUs. When a CPU is hotswapped, the kernel calls `radix_tree_callback()`, which attempts to cleanly free the parts of the page cache that were linked to the hotswapped CPU.

8.5.28 The Call to signals_init()

Line 477

The `signals_init()` function in `kernel/signal.c` initializes the kernel signal queue:

```
------------------------------------------------------------------
fs/buffer.c
2565  void __init signals_init(void)
2566  {
2567  sigqueue_cachep =
2568      kmem_cache_create("sigqueue",
2569          sizeof(struct sigqueue),
2570          __alignof__(struct sigqueue),
2571          0, NULL, NULL);
2572   if (!sigqueue_cachep)
2573     panic("signals_init(): cannot create sigqueue SLAB cache");
2574  }
------------------------------------------------------------------
```

Lines 2567–2571

Allocate SLAB memory for `sigqueue`.

8.5.29 The Call to page_writeback_init()

Line 479

The `page_writeback_init()` function initializes the values controlling when a dirty page is written back to disk. Dirty pages are not immediately written back to disk; they are written after a certain amount of time passes or a certain number or percent of the pages in memory are marked as dirty. This init function attempts to determine the optimum number of pages that must be dirty before triggering a background write and a dedicated write. Background dirty-page writes take up much less processing power than dedicated dirty-page writes:

```
------------------------------------------------------------------
mm/page-writeback.c
488 /*
489 * If the machine has a large highmem:lowmem ratio then scale back the
default
490 * dirty memory thresholds: allowing too much dirty highmem pins an excessive
```

```
491 * number of buffer_heads.
492 */
493 void __init page_writeback_init(void)
494 {
495   long buffer_pages = nr_free_buffer_pages();
496   long correction;
497
498   total_pages = nr_free_pagecache_pages();
499
500   correction = (100 * 4 * buffer_pages) / total_pages;
501
502   if (correction < 100) {
503     dirty_background_ratio *= correction;
504     dirty_background_ratio /= 100;
505     vm_dirty_ratio *= correction;
506     vm_dirty_ratio /= 100;
507   }
508   mod_timer(&wb_timer, jiffies + (dirty_writeback_centisecs * HZ) / 100);
509   set_ratelimit();
510   register_cpu_notifier(&ratelimit_nb);
511 }
```

Lines 495–507

If we are operating on a machine with a large page cache compared to the number of buffer pages, we lower the dirty-page writeback thresholds. If we choose not to lower the threshold, which raises the frequency of writebacks, at each writeback, we would use an inordinate amount of `buffer_heads`. (This is the meaning of the comment before `page_writeback()`.)

The default background writeback, `dirty_background_ratio`, starts when 10 percent of the pages are dirty. A dedicated writeback, `vm_dirty_ratio`, starts when 40 percent of the pages are dirty.

Line 508

We modify the writeback timer, `wb_timer`, to be triggered periodically (every 5 seconds by default).

Line 509

`set_ratelimit()` is called, which is documented excellently. I defer to these inline comments:

```
------------------------------------------------------------------------
mm/page-writeback.c
450 /*
451  * If ratelimit_pages is too high then we can get into dirty-data overload
452  * if a large number of processes all perform writes at the same time.
453  * If it is too low then SMP machines will call the (expensive)
454  * get_writeback_state too often.
455  *
456  * Here we set ratelimit_pages to a level which ensures that when all CPUs
are
457  * dirtying in parallel, we cannot go more than 3% (1/32) over the dirty
memory
458  * thresholds before writeback cuts in.
459  *
460  * But the limit should not be set too high. Because it also controls the
461  * amount of memory which the balance_dirty_pages() caller has to write back.
462  * If this is too large then the caller will block on the IO queue all the
463  * time. So limit it to four megabytes - the balance_dirty_pages() caller
464  * will write six megabyte chunks, max.
465  */
466
467 static void set_ratelimit(void)
468 {
469   ratelimit_pages = total_pages / (num_online_cpus() * 32);
470   if (ratelimit_pages < 16)
471     ratelimit_pages = 16;
472   if (ratelimit_pages * PAGE_CACHE_SIZE > 4096 * 1024)
473     ratelimit_pages = (4096 * 1024) / PAGE_CACHE_SIZE;
474 }
------------------------------------------------------------------------
```

Line 510

The final command of `page_writeback_init()` registers the ratelimit notifier block, `ratelimit_nb`, with the CPU notifier. The ratelimit notifier block calls `ratelimit_handler()` when notified, which in turn, calls `set_ratelimit()`. The purpose of this is to recalculate `ratelimit_pages` when the number of online CPUs changes:

```
------------------------------------------------------------------------
mm/page-writeback.c
483 static struct notifier_block ratelimit_nb = {
484   .notifier_call = ratelimit_handler,
485   .next     = NULL,
486 };
------------------------------------------------------------------------
```

Finally, we need to examine what happens when the `wb_timer` (from Line 508) goes off and calls `wb_time_fn()`:

```
mm/page-writeback.c
414 static void wb_timer_fn(unsigned long unused)
415 {
416   if (pdflush_operation(wb_kupdate, 0) < 0)
417     mod_timer(&wb_timer, jiffies + HZ); /* delay 1 second */
418 }
```

Lines 416–417

When the timer goes off, the kernel triggers `pdflush_operation()`, which awakens one of the `pdflush` threads to perform the actual writeback of dirty pages to disk. If `pdflush_operation()` cannot awaken any `pdflush` thread, it tells the writeback timer to trigger again in 1 second to retry awakening a `pdflush` thread. See Chapter 9, "Building the Linux Kernel," for more information on `pdflush`.

8.5.30   The Call to proc_root_init()

Lines 480–482

As Chapter 2 explained, the `CONFIG_*` `#define` refers to a compile-time variable. If, at compile time, the `proc` filesystem is selected, the next step in initialization is the call to `proc_root_init()`:

```
fs/proc/root.c
40  void __init proc_root_init(void)
41  {
42   int err = proc_init_inodecache();
43   if (err)
44     return;
45   err = register_filesystem(&proc_fs_type);
46   if (err)
47     return;
48   proc_mnt = kern_mount(&proc_fs_type);
49   err = PTR_ERR(proc_mnt);
50   if (IS_ERR(proc_mnt)) {
51    unregister_filesystem(&proc_fs_type);
52    return;
53   }
54   proc_misc_init();
55   proc_net = proc_mkdir("net", 0);
56  #ifdef CONFIG_SYSVIPC
57   proc_mkdir("sysvipc", 0);
```

```
58  #endif
59  #ifdef CONFIG_SYSCTL
60    proc_sys_root = proc_mkdir("sys", 0);
61  #endif
62  #if defined(CONFIG_BINFMT_MISC) || defined(CONFIG_BINFMT_MISC_MODULE)
63    proc_mkdir("sys/fs", 0);
64    proc_mkdir("sys/fs/binfmt_misc", 0);
65  #endif
66    proc_root_fs = proc_mkdir("fs", 0);
67    proc_root_driver = proc_mkdir("driver", 0);
68    proc_mkdir("fs/nfsd", 0); /* somewhere for the nfsd filesystem to be
mounted */
69  #if defined(CONFIG_SUN_OPENPROMFS) || defined(CONFIG_SUN_OPENPROMFS_MODULE)
70    /* just give it a mountpoint */
71    proc_mkdir("openprom", 0);
72  #endif
73    proc_tty_init();
74  #ifdef CONFIG_PROC_DEVICETREE
75    proc_device_tree_init();
76  #endif
77    proc_bus = proc_mkdir("bus", 0);
78  }
```

Line 42

This line initializes the inode cache that holds the inodes for this filesystem.

Line 45

The `file_system_type` structure `proc_fs_type` is registered with the kernel.
Let's closely look at the structure:

```
fs/proc/root.c
33  static struct file_system_type proc_fs_type = {
34    .name    = "proc",
35    .get_sb  = proc_get_sb,
36    .kill_sb = kill_anon_super,
37  };
```

The `file_system_type` structure, which defines the filesystem's name simply
as `proc`, has the routines for retrieving and freeing the superblock structures.

Line 48

We mount the `proc` filesystem. See the sidebar on `kern_mount` for more details
as to what happens here.

Lines 54–78

The call to proc_misc_init() is what creates most of the entries you see in the /proc filesystem. It creates entries with calls to create_proc_read_entry(), create_proc_entry(), and create_proc_seq_entry(). The remainder of the code block consists of calls to proc_mkdir for the creation of directories under /proc/, the call to the proc_tty_init() routine to create the tree under /proc/tty, and, if the config time value of CONFIG_PROC_DEVICETREE is set, then the call to the proc_device_tree_init() routine to create the /proc/device-tree subtree.

8.5.31   The Call to init_idle()

Line 490

init_idle() is called near the end of start_kernel() with parameters current and smp_processor_id() to prepare start_kernel() for rescheduling:

```
-------------------------------------------------------------------
kernel/sched.c
2643 void __init init_idle(task_t *idle, int cpu)
2644 {
2645   runqueue_t *idle_rq = cpu_rq(cpu), *rq = cpu_rq(task_cpu(idle));
2646   unsigned long flags;
2647
2648   local_irq_save(flags);
2649   double_rq_lock(idle_rq, rq);
2650
2651   idle_rq->curr = idle_rq->idle = idle;
2652   deactivate_task(idle, rq);
2653   idle->array = NULL;
2654   idle->prio = MAX_PRIO;
2655   idle->state = TASK_RUNNING;
2656   set_task_cpu(idle, cpu);
2657   double_rq_unlock(idle_rq, rq);
2658   set_tsk_need_resched(idle);
2659   local_irq_restore(flags);
2660
2661   /* Set the preempt count _outside_ the spinlocks! */
2662 #ifdef CONFIG_PREEMPT
2663   idle->thread_info->preempt_count = (idle->lock_depth >= 0);
2664 #else
2665   idle->thread_info->preempt_count = 0;
2666 #endif
2667 }
-------------------------------------------------------------------
```

Line 2645

We store the CPU request queue of the CPU that we're on and the CPU request queue of the CPU that the given task `idle` is on. In our case, with `current` and `smp_processor_id()`, these request queues will be equal.

Line 2648–2649

We save the IRQ flags and obtain the lock on both request queues.

Line 2651

We set the current task of the CPU request queue of the CPU that we're on to the task `idle`.

Lines 2652–2656

These statements remove the task `idle` from its request queue and move it to the CPU request queue of `cpu`.

Lines 2657–2659

We release the request queue locks on the run queues that we previously locked. Then, we mark task `idle` for rescheduling and restore the IRQs that we previously saved. We finally set the preemption counter if kernel preemption is configured.

8.5.32 The Call to rest_init()

Line 493

The `rest_init()` routine is fairly straightforward. It essentially creates what we call the init thread, removes the initialization kernel lock, and calls the `idle` thread:

```
init/main.c
388  static void noinline rest_init(void)
389  {
390    kernel_thread(init, NULL, CLONE_FS | CLONE_SIGHAND);
391    unlock_kernel();
392    cpu_idle();
393  }
```

Line 388

You might have noticed that this is the first routine `start_kernel()` calls that is not `__init`. If you recall from Chapter 2, we said that when a function is preceded by `__init`, it is because all the memory used to maintain the function variables and the like will be memory that is cleared/freed once initialization nears completion. This is done through a call to `free_initmem()`, which we see in a moment when we explore what happens in `init()`. The reason why `rest_init()` is not an `__init` function is because it calls the `init` thread before its completion (meaning the call to `cpu_idle`). Because the `init` thread executes the call to `free_initmem()`, there is the possibility of a race condition occurring whereby `free_initmem()` is called before `rest_init()` (or the root thread) is finished.

Line 390

This line is the creation of the `init` thread, which is also referred to as the `init` process or process 1. For brevity, all we say here is that this thread shares all kernel data structures with the calling process. The kernel thread calls the `init()` functions, which we look at in the next section.

Line 391

The `unlock_kernel()` routine does nothing if only a single processor exists. Otherwise, it releases the BKL.

Line 392

The call to `cpu_idle()` is what turns the root thread into the idle thread. This routine yields the processor to the scheduler and is returned to when the scheduler has no other pending process to run.

At this point, we have completed the bulk of the Linux kernel initialization. We now briefly look at what happens in the call to `init()`.

8.6   The init Thread (or Process 1)

We now explore the `init` thread. Note that we skip over all SMP-related routines for brevity:

```
-------------------------------------------------------------------
init/main.c
601  static int init(void * unused)
602  {
603    lock_kernel();
...
612    child_reaper = current;
...
627    populate_rootfs();

629    do_basic_setup();
...
635    if (sys_access((const char __user *) "/init", 0) == 0)
636      execute_command = "/init";
637    else
638      prepare_namespace();
...
645    free_initmem();
646    unlock_kernel();
647    system_state = SYSTEM_RUNNING;

649    if (sys_open((const char __user *) "/dev/console", O_RDWR, 0) < 0)
650      printk("Warning: unable to open an initial console.\n");
651
652    (void) sys_dup(0);
653    (void) sys_dup(0);
...
662    if (execute_command)
663      run_init_process(execute_command);
664
665    run_init_process("/sbin/init");
666    run_init_process("/etc/init");
667    run_init_process("/bin/init");
668    run_init_process("/bin/sh");
669
670    panic("No init found. Try passing init= option to kernel.");
671  }
-------------------------------------------------------------------
```

Line 612

The `init` thread is set to reap any thread whose parent has died. The `child_reaper` variable is a global pointer to a `task_struct` and is defined in `init/main.c`. This variable comes into play in "reparenting functions" and is used as a reference to the thread that should become the new parent. We refer to functions such as `reparent_to_init()` (`kernel/exit.c`), `choose_new_parent()` (`kernel/exit.c`), and `forget_original_parent()` (`kernel/exit.c`) because they use `child_reaper` to reset the calling thread's parent.

Line 629

The `do_basic_setup()` function initializes the driver model, the `sysctl` interface, the network socket interface, and work queue support:

```
------------------------------------------------------------------
init/main.c
551  static void __init do_basic_setup(void)
552  {
553    driver_init();
554
555  #ifdef CONFIG_SYSCTL
556      sysctl_init();
557  #endif
...
560    sock_init();
561
562    init_workqueues();
563    do_initcalls();
564  }
------------------------------------------------------------------
```

Line 553

The `driver_init()` (`drivers/base/init.c`) function initializes all the subsystems involved in driver support. This is the first part of device driver initializations. The second comes on line 563 with the call to `do_initcalls()`.

Lines 555–557

The `sysctl` interface provides support for dynamic alteration of kernel parameters. This means that the kernel parameters that `sysctl` supports can be modified at runtime without the need for recompiling and rebooting the kernel. `sysctl_init()` (`kernel/sysctl.c`) initializes the interface. For more information on `sysctl`, read the man page (`man sysctl`).

Line 560

The `sock_init()` function is a dummy function with a simple `printk` if the kernel is configured without net support. In this case, `sock_init()` is defined in `net/nonet.c`. In the case that network support is configured then `sock_init()` is defined in `net/socket.c`, it initializes the memory caches to be used for network support and registers the filesystem that supports networking.

Line 562

The call to init_workqueues sets up the work queue notifier chain. Chapter 10, "Adding Your Code to the Kernel," discusses work queues.

Line 563

The do_initcalls() (init/main.c) function constitutes the second part of device driver initialization. This function sequentially calls the entries in an array of function pointers that correspond to built-in device initialization functions.[11]

Lines 635–638

If an early user space init exists, the kernel does not prepare the namespace; it allows it to perform this function. Otherwise, the call to prepare_namespace() is made. A namespace refers to the mount point of a filesystem hierarchy:

```
-----------------------------------------------------------------
init/do_mounts.c
383  void __init prepare_namespace(void)
384  {
385    int is_floppy;
386
387    mount_devfs();
...
391    if (saved_root_name[0]) {
392      root_device_name = saved_root_name;
393      ROOT_DEV = name_to_dev_t(root_device_name);
394      if (strncmp(root_device_name, "/dev/", 5) == 0)
395        root_device_name += 5;
396    }
397
398    is_floppy = MAJOR(ROOT_DEV) == FLOPPY_MAJOR;
399
400    if (initrd_load())
401      goto out;
402
403    if (is_floppy && rd_doload && rd_load_disk(0))
404      ROOT_DEV = Root_RAM0;
405
406    mount_root();
407  out:
408    umount_devfs("/dev");
409    sys_mount(".", "/", NULL, MS_MOVE, NULL);
```

---

[11] Refer to http://geek.vtnet.ca/doc/initcall/ for an excellent distillation of the initcall mechanism by Trevor Woerner.

```
410    sys_chroot(".");
411    security_sb_post_mountroot();
412    mount_devfs_fs ();
413    }
```

Line 387

The `mount_devfs()` function creates the `/dev` mount-related structures. We need to mount `/dev` because we use it to refer to the root device name.

Lines 391–396

This code block sets the global variable `ROOT_DEV` to the indicated root device as passed in through kernel boot-time parameters.

Line 398

A simple comparison of major numbers indicates whether the root device is a floppy.

Lines 400–401

The call to `initrd_load()` mounts the RAM disk if a RAM disk has been indicated as the kernel's root filesystem. If this is the case, it returns a 1 and executes the jump to the out label, which undoes all we've done in preparation of a root filesystem from a device.

Line 406

The call to `mount_root` does the majority of the root-filesystem mounting. Let's closely look at this function:

```
init/do_mounts.c
353  void __init mount_root(void)
354  {
355  #ifdef CONFIG_ROOT_NFS
356    if (MAJOR(ROOT_DEV) == UNNAMED_MAJOR) {
357     if (mount_nfs_root())
358      return;
359
360     printk(KERN_ERR "VFS: Unable to mount root fs via NFS, trying
floppy.\n");
361     ROOT_DEV = Root_FD0;
362    }
363  #endif
```

```
364  #ifdef CONFIG_BLK_DEV_FD
365   if (MAJOR(ROOT_DEV) == FLOPPY_MAJOR) {
...
367    if (rd_doload==2) {
368     if (rd_load_disk(1)) {
369       ROOT_DEV = Root_RAM1;
370       root_device_name = NULL;
371     }
372    } else
373     change_floppy("root floppy");
374   }
375  #endif
376   create_dev("/dev/root", ROOT_DEV, root_device_name);
377   mount_block_root("/dev/root", root_mountflags);
378  }
```

Lines 355–358

If the kernel has been configured to mount an NFS filesystem, we execute
`mount_nfs_root()`. If the NFS mount fails, the kernel prints out the appropriate
message and then proceeds to try to mount the floppy as the root filesystem.

Lines 364–375

In this code block, the kernel tries to mount the root floppy.[12]

Line 377

This function performs the bulk of the root device mounting. We now return to
`init()`.

Line 645

The call to `free_initmem()` frees all memory segments that the routines used
up with the __init precursor. This marks our exit from pure kernel space and we
begin to set up user mode data.

Lines 649–650

Open up the initial console.

----

[12] A note on `rd_doload`: This global variable holds a value of 0 if no RAM disk is to be loaded, a value of
1 if a RAM disk is to be loaded, and a value of 2 for a "dual `initrd`/`ramload` setup."

Lines 662–668

The `execute_command` variable is set in `init_setup()` and holds the value of a boot-time parameter that contains the name of the `init` program to call if we do not want the default `/sbin/init` to be called. If an `init` program name is passed, it takes priority over the usual `/sbin/init`. Note that the call to `run_init_process()` (init/main.c) does not return because it ends with a call to `execve()`. Thus, the first `init` function call to run successfully is the only one run. In the case that an `init` program is not found, we can use the bash shell to start up.

Line 670

This panic statement should be reached only if all of our tries to execute various `init` program fails.

This concludes kernel initialization. From here on out, the `init` process involves itself with system initialization and starting all the necessary processes and daemon support required for user login and support.

Summary

This chapter described what happens between power on and kernel bootup. We discussed what BIOS and Open Firmware are and how they interact with the kernel bootloaders. We discussed LILO, GRUB, and Yaboot as some of the more commonly used bootloaders. We overviewed how they work and how they call up the first kernel initialization routines.

We also went through the functions that make up kernel initialization. We traversed the kernel code through its initialization process, touching on concepts that were introduced in previous chapters. More specifically, we traced the Linux kernel initialization through the following high-level operations:

- Starting and locking the kernel
- Initializing the page cache and page addresses for memory management in Linux
- Preparing multiple CPUs
- Displaying the Linux banner

- Initializing the Linux scheduler

- Parsing the arguments passed to the Linux kernel

- Initializing the interrupts, timers, and signal handlers

- Mounting the initial filesystems

- Finishing system initialization and passing control out of `init` and back to the system

As we leave kernel initialization, we must mention that, at this point, the kernel is functional and begins to start many higher level Linux applications, such as X11, sendmail, and so on. All these programs rely on the basic configuration and setup that we have just outlined.

Exercises

1. What's the difference between the Big Kernel Lock (BLK) and a normal spinlock?

2. What `init` script allows you to add extra security features to the Linux kernel?

3. What initializes the data structure for kernel page management?

4. What percentage of pages must be dirty to trigger a background writeback of dirty pages to disk? What percentage triggers a dedicated writeback?

5. Why is `rest_init()` not an `__init` function?

Building the Linux Kernel

In this chapter

Until now, we've seen the subsystems within the Linux kernel and we've explored the system initialization functions. It is also important to understand how the image gets created. This chapter explores the process of compiling and linking the kernel image. We also look at the internals of the Linux build process.

9.1 Toolchain

A **toolchain** is the set of programs necessary to create a Linux kernel image. The concept of the chain is that the output of one tool becomes the input for the next. Our toolchain includes a compiler, an assembler, and a linker. Technically, it needs to also include your text editor, but this section covers the first three tools mentioned. A toolchain is something that is necessary whenever we want to develop software. The necessary tools are also referred to as Software Development Kit (SDK).

A **compiler** is a translation program that takes in a high-level source language and produces a low-level **object language**. The object code is a series of machine-dependent commands running on the target system. An **assembler** is a translation program that takes in an assembly language program and produces the same kind of object code as the compiler. The difference here is that there is a one-to-one correspondence between each line of the assembly language and each machine instruction produced whereas every line of high-level code might get translated into many machine instructions. As you have seen, some of the files in the architecture-dependent sections of the Linux source code are in assembly. These get *compiled down* (into object code) by issuing a call to an assembler.

A **link editor** (or **linker**) groups executable modules for execution as a unit.

Figure 9.1 shows the "chaining" of the toolchain. The linker would be linking the object code of our program with any libraries we are using. Compilers have flags that allow the user the level to which it compiles down. For example, in Figure 9.1, we see that the compiler can directly produce machine code or compile down to assembly source code, which can then be assembled into machine code that the computer can directly execute.

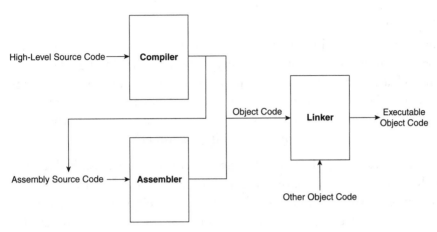

FIGURE 9.1
Toolchain

9.1.1 Compilers

Common compilers also have a "chaining" quality internally whereby they execute a series of phases or steps where the output of one phase is the input of the next. Figure 9.2 diagrams these phases. The first step of compiling is the **scanner** phase, which breaks the high-level program into a series of tokens. Next, the **parser** phase groups the tokens according to *syntactical* rules, and the **contextual analysis phase** further groups them by *semantic* attributes. An **optimizer** then tries to increase the efficiency of the parsed tokens and the **code generation** phase produces the object code. The output of the compiler is a symbol table and **relocatable** object code. That is, the starting address of each compiled module is 0 and must be relocated to its proper place at link time.

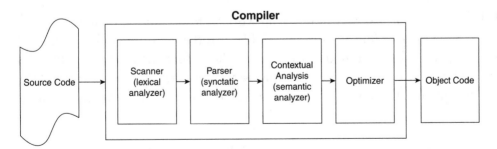

FIGURE 9.2
Compiler Operation

9.1.2   Cross Compilers

Toolkits usually run **natively**, which means that the object code they generate runs on the same system on which it is compiled. If you are developing a kernel on an x86 system to load on another (or the same) x86 system, you can get away with using whatever compiler comes with the system. Power Macs and the myriad of x86 boxes all compile code that runs on their respective architectures. But what if we wanted to write code on one platform and run it on another?

This is not as odd as it sounds. Consider the embedded market. Embedded systems are usually implemented to have just enough memory and I/O to get the job done. Whether it is controlling an automobile, router, or cell phone, there is rarely any room for a full native development environment on an embedded system (let alone monitor or keyboard). The solution is to have developers use their powerful and relatively inexpensive workstations as **host systems** to develop code that they can then download and test on the **target system**. Hence, the term cross compiler!

For example, you might be a developer for a PowerPC-embedded system that has a 405 processor in it. Most of your desktop development systems are x86 based. By using gcc, for example, you would do all of your development (both C and assembler) on the desktop and compile with the -mcpu=405 option.[1] This creates object code using 405-specific instructions and addressing. You would then download the executable to the embedded system to run and debug. Granted, this sounds tedious, but with the limited resources of a target embedded system, it saves a great deal of memory.

For this particular environment, many tools are on the market to assist in the development and debugging of cross-compiled embedded code.

9.1.3   Linker

When we compile a C program ("hello world!," for example), there is far more code than the three or four lines in our .c file. It is the job of the linker to find all these externally referenced modules and "link" them. External modules or libraries originate from the developer, the operating system, or (the home of printf()) the C runtime library. The linker extracts these libraries, fixes up pointers (**relocation**),

---

[1] For more gcc options that are specific to IBM RS/6000 (POWER) and PowerPC, go to http://gcc.gnu. org/onlinedocs/gcc/RS_002f6000-and-PowerPC-Options.html#RS_002f6000-and-PowerPC-Options.

and references (**symbol resolution**) across the modules to create an executable module. Symbols can be global or local. Global symbols can be defined within a module or externally referenced by a module. It is the linker's job to find a definition for each symbol associated with a module. (Note that user space libraries are not available to the kernel programmer.) For common function, the kernel has its own versions available. **Static libraries** are found and copied at link time, while **dynamic libraries** or **shared libraries** can be loaded at runtime and shared across processes. Microsoft and OS/2 call shared libraries dynamic link libraries. Linux provides the system calls `dlopen()`, `dlsym()`, and `dlclose()`, which can be used to load/open a shared library, find a symbol in the library, and then close the shared library.

9.1.4   ELF Object Files

The format of object files varies from manufacturer to manufacturer. Today, most UNIX systems use the Executable and Linking Format (ELF). Many types of ELF files exist, each of which performs a different function. The main types of ELF files are executable files, relocatable object files, and core files or shared libraries. The ELF format allows object files to be compatible across platforms and architectures. Figure 9.3 illustrates an executable and a non-executable ELF object file.

Non-executable ELF Object File   Executable ELF Object File

ELF Header
Program Header Table (optional)
Section 1
Section 2
Section 3
. . .
Section Header Table (sections used for linking)

ELF Header
Program Header Table (sections used for loading)
Section 1
Section 2
Section 3
. . .
Section Header Table (optional)

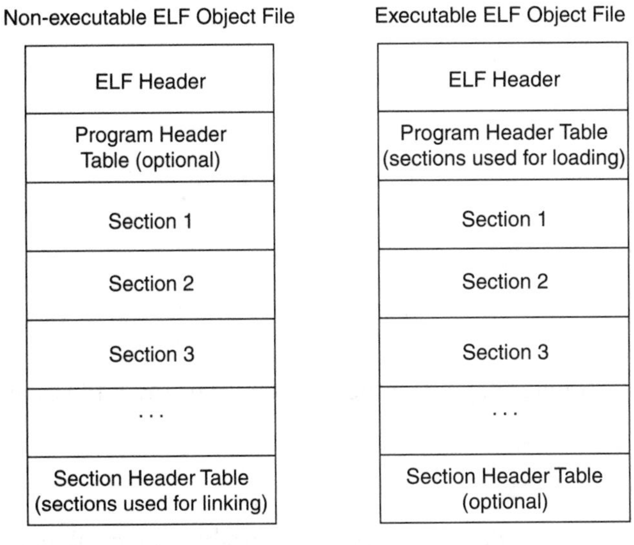

FIGURE 9.3
Executable and Non-Executable ELF Files

The ELF header is always at offset zero within the ELF file. Everything in the file can be found through the ELF header. Because the ELF header is the only fixed structure in the object file, it must point to and specify the size of the substructures within the file. All the ELF files are broken down into blocks of similar data called sections or segments. The non-executable object file contains **sections** and a **section header table**, while the executable object files must contain **segments** and a **program header table**.

9.1.4.1   ELF Header

The ELF header is kept track of in the Linux structure `elf32_hdr` (for a 32-bit system, that is; for 64-bit systems, there is the `elf64_hdr` structure). Let's look at this structure:

```
------------------------------------------------------------------
include/linux/elf.h
234  #define EI_NIDENT  16
235
236  typedef struct elf32_hdr{
237    unsigned char  e_ident[EI_NIDENT];
238    Elf32_Half  e_type;
239    Elf32_Half  e_machine;
240    Elf32_Word  e_version;
241    Elf32_Addr  e_entry; /* Entry point */
242    Elf32_Off   e_phoff;
243    Elf32_Off   e_shoff;
244    Elf32_Word  e_flags;
245    Elf32_Half  e_ehsize;
246    Elf32_Half  e_phentsize;
247    Elf32_Half  e_phnum;
248    Elf32_Half  e_shentsize;
249    Elf32_Half  e_shnum;
250    Elf32_Half  e_shstrndx;
251  } Elf32_Ehdr;
------------------------------------------------------------------
```

Line 237

The `e_ident` field holds the 16-byte magic number, which identifies a file as an ELF file.

Line 238

The `e_type` field specifies the object file type, such as executable, relocatable, or shared object.

Line 239

The `e_machine` field identifies the architecture of the system for which the file is compiled.

Line 240

The `e_version` field specifies object file version.

Line 241

The `e_entry` field holds the starting address of the program.

Line 242

The `e_phoff` field holds the program header table offset in bytes.

Line 243

The `e_shoff` field holds the offset for the section header table offset in bytes.

Line 244

The `e_flags` field holds processor-specific flags.

Line 245

The `e_ehsize` field holds the size of the ELF header.

Line 246

The `e_phentsize` field holds the size of each entry in the program header table.

Line 247

The `e_phnum` field contains the number of entries in the program header.

Line 248

The `e_shentsize` field holds the size of each entry in the section header table.

Line 249

The `e_shnum` field holds the number of entries in the section header, which indicates the number of sections in the file.

Line 250

The `e_shstrndx` field holds the index of the section string within the section header.

9.1.4.2 Section Header Table

The section header table is an array of type `Elf32_Shdr`. Its offset in the ELF file is given by the `e_shoff` field in the ELF header. There is one section header table for each section in the file:

```
------------------------------------------------------------------
include/linux/elf.h
332   typedef struct {
333     Elf32_Word  sh_name;
334     Elf32_Word  sh_type;
335     Elf32_Word  sh_flags;
336     Elf32_Addr  sh_addr;
337     Elf32_Off   sh_offset;
338     Elf32_Word  sh_size;
339     Elf32_Word  sh_link;
340     Elf32_Word  sh_info;
341     Elf32_Word  sh_addralign;
342     Elf32_Word  sh_entsize;
343   } Elf32_Shdr;
------------------------------------------------------------------
```

Line 333

The `sh_name` field contains the section name.

Line 334

The `sh_type` field contains the section's contents.

Line 335

The `sh_flags` field contains information regarding miscellaneous attributes.

Line 336

The `sh_addr` field holds the address of the section in memory image.

Line 337

The `sh_offset` field holds the offset of the first byte of this section within the ELF file.

Line 338

The `sh_size` field contains the section size.

Line 339

The `sh_link` field contains the index of the table link, which depends on `sh_type`.

Line 340

The `sh_info` field contains extra information, depending on the value of `sh_type`.

Line 341

The `sh_addralign` field contains the address alignment constraints.

Line 342

The `sh_entsize` field contains the entry size of the sections when it holds a fixed-size table.

9.1.4.3 Non-Executable ELF File Sections

The ELF file is divided into a number of sections, each of which contains information of a specific type. Table 9.1 outlines the types of sections. Some of these sections are only present if certain compiler flags are set at compile time. Recall that `ELF32_Ehdr->e_shnum` holds the number of sections in the ELF file.

TABLE 9.1
ELF File Sections

Section Name	Description
`.bss`	Uninitialized data
`.comment`	GCC uses this for the compiler version
`.data`	Initialized data
`.debug`	Symbolic debug information in the form of a symbol table
`.dynamic`	Dynamic linking information
`.dynstr`	Dynamic linking strings

continues

TABLE 9.1
Continued

Section Name	Description
.fini	Process termination code, GCC exit code
.got	Global offset table
.hash	Symbol hash table
.init	Initialization code
.interp	Name of where the program interpreter is located
.line	Line numbers for debugging
.note	Compiler uses this for versioning
.plt	Procedure linkage table
.relname	Relocation information
.rodata	Read-only data
.shstrtab	Section names
.symtab	Symbol table
.text	Executable instructions

9.1.4.4   Program Header Table

The header table for an executable or shared object file is an array of structures, each describing a segment or other information for execution:

```
include/linux/elf.h
276  typedef struct elf32_phdr{
277    Elf32_Word  p_type;
278    Elf32_Off   p_offset;
279    Elf32_Addr  p_vaddr;
280    Elf32_Addr  p_paddr;
281    Elf32_Word  p_filesz;
282    Elf32_Word  p_memsz;
283    Elf32_Word  p_flags;
284    Elf32_Word  p_align;
285  } Elf32_Phdr;
```

Line 277

The p_type field describes the type of segment this is.

Line 278

The `p_offset` field holds the offset from the beginning of the file to where the segment begins.

Line 279

The `p_vaddr` field holds the segment's virtual address if used.

Line 280

The `p_paddr` field holds the segment's physical address if used.

Line 281

The `p_filesz` field holds the number of bytes in the file image of the segment.

Line 282

The `p_memsz` field holds the number of bytes in the memory image of the segment.

Line 283

The `p_flags` field holds the flags depending on `p_type`.

Line 284

The `p_align` field describes how aligned the segment is aligned in memory. The value is in integral powers of 2.

Using this information, the system `exec()` function, along with the linker, works to create a process image of the executable program in memory. This includes the following:

- Moving the segments into memory
- Loading any shared libraries that need to be loaded
- Performing relocation as needed
- Transferring control to the program

By understanding the object file formats and the available tools, you can better debug compile-time problems (such as unresolved references) and runtime problems by knowing *where* code is loaded and relocated.

9.2   Kernel Source Build

We now look at how the kernel is compiled into a binary image and gets loaded into memory prior to execution. As a kernel developer, you will be heavily involved with the source code. It is necessary to understand how to navigate the source code and how to edit the build system so you can add your changes.

This chapter is a roadmap to get you from downloading the source code to compiling a kernel image that loads. We cover how the kernel image is created. This is not a detailed, step-by-step instruction manual. There is much comprehensive documentation online about how to build a kernel image, such as the kernel HOWTO (`www.tldp.org/HOWTO/Kernel-HOWTO/`), which is currently under review. This is instead intended to provide the kind of information you need in order to incorporate changes into the build system.

Among developers, build systems or `Makefiles` are never a source of great interest, but as such, we need to understand the kernel build system and how to update it to illustrate changes to the source code. With the 2.6 kernel version, you now have more tools to help you understand all the options that surround the kernel build system. Also, the build system has been significantly cleaned up and redesigned as well as being more effectively documented.

This section covers how the source code is laid out and how the kernel build and `Makefiles` work. The first step is to get the source code. We start by describing the source code structure and where to get it.

9.2.1   Source Explained

The site for Linus's official code release is `www.kernel.org`. The source is available to download in a `.tar.gz` file with gzip compression or a `.tar.bz2` file with `bzip2` compression. These packages contain the source code to all the available architectures.

When a kernel developer makes a change to the kernel source, he submits it to the kernel maintainer. The maintainer then decides whether the changes get incorporated into the next stable tree. Cutting-edge PPC development used to occur in a separate tree maintained at `www.penguinppc.org`. The changes made in the PPC tree would then be submitted to the main tree into which they were (mostly) eventually incorporated. Currently, the Linux PPC community is moving toward working directly on the main tree.

The location of source code is somewhat dependent on your distribution. For example, in a Red Hat system, source code is placed (whether it is by default install or by an RPM) under `/usr/src/linux-<version>/`. If you are cross-compiling— that is, building the kernel for an architecture different to the one you are doing the actual compiling in—the location of the source code might be somewhere under `/opt/<distribution name>` on your host or alternatively in a root filesystem image the user `chroots` into. For example, Montavista, which is a distribution geared toward the embedded Linux market, stores the source code (and the cross compilers) under `/opt/mvista/` by default.

In this section, the root of the source code filesystem is referred to simply as the *root*. In the Red Hat distribution, the root of the source code is located under `/usr/src/linux-<version>`. Figure 9.4 details the hierarchical layout of the source code.

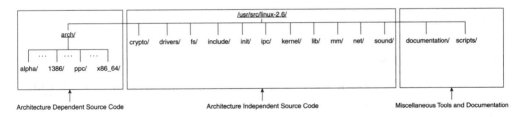

FIGURE 9.4
Source Code Layout

The source code is divided into *architecture-dependent* and *architecture-independent* portions. The `arch/` directory under the root holds all the code that is architecture dependent. Source code downloaded from a mirror of `kernel.org` contains all the supported architectures listed under this subdirectory. Every supported architecture has a directory under `arch/` that contains a further breakdown of the architecture-dependent code. Figure 9.5 shows the supported architectures by means of displaying the listing under the `arch/` directory.

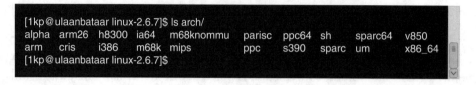

FIGURE 9.5
```
ls /usr/src/linux/arch
```

We begin by looking at the structure of the architecture-independent portion of the source code to understand its breakdown. We then present an overview of the architecture-dependent portion of the source code, followed by a brief summary of miscellaneous files that pertain to neither category.

9.2.1.1   Architecture-Independent Code

The architecture-independent portion of the source code is divided into 11 sub-directories that follow a sensible categorization by functionality. Table 9.2 overviews these subdirectories.

TABLE 9.2
Architecture-Independent Subdirectories

Subdirectory	Description
crypto	Holds code for cryptographic API and various encrypting/decrypting algorithms.
drivers	Code for device drivers.
fs	Code for VFS and all the filesystems supported by Linux.
include	The header files. This directory has a series of subdirectories starting with the prefix asm. These directories hold the architecture-specific header files. The remaining directories hold architecture-independent header files.
init	The architecture-independent portion of the bootstrapping code and initialization code.
ipc	Code for interprocess communication (IPC) support.
kernel	Code for kernel space specific code.

continues

TABLE 9.2
Continued

Subdirectory	Description
lib	Code for helper functions.
mm	Code for the memory manager.
net	Code to support the various networking protocols.
sound	Code for sound system support.

Throughout the various chapters, we have been exploring source code that is located in one or more of these subdirectories. To put them in the proper context, the following sections provide a cursory look at some of the subdirectories. We leave out the ones we have not looked at in more detail.

fs/

The fs/ directory is further subdivided into C source files that support the VFS internals and subdirectories for each supported filesystem. As Chapter 7, "Scheduling and Kernel Synchronization," details, the VFS is the abstraction layer for the various types of filesystems. The code found in each of these subdirectories consists of the code bridging the gap between the storage device and the VFS abstraction layer.

init/

The init/ directory contains all the code necessary for system initialization. During the execution of this code, all the kernel subsystems are initialized and initial processes are created.

kernel/

The bulk of the architecture-independent kernel code is located in the kernel/ directory. Most of the kernel subsystems have their code under here. Some, such as filesystems and memory, have their own directories at the same level as kernel/. The filenames are fairly self-explanatory with respect to the code they contain.

mm/

The mm/ directory holds the memory-management code. We looked at examples of this code in Chapter 4, "Memory Management."

9.2.1.2   Architecture-Dependent Code

The architecture-dependent code is the portion of the kernel source that is directly tied to reference the actual hardware. One thing to remember in your travails through this portion of the code is that Linux was originally developed for the x86. To minimize the complexity of the porting efforts, some of the x86-centric terminology was retained in variable names and global kernel structures. If you look through the PPC code and see names that refer to address translation modes that don't exist in PPC, don't panic.

Doing a listing for both `arch/i386/` and `arch/ppc`, you notice three files that they each have in common: `defconfig`, `Kconfig`, and `Makefile`. These files are tied into the infrastructure of the kernel build system. The purpose of these three files is made clear in Section 9.2.2, "Building the Kernel Image."

Table 9.3 gives an overview of the files and directories shown in a listing of arch/ppc. Once you have gone over the structure of `Makefiles` and `Kconfig` files, it is useful to browse through these files in each of the subdirectories to become familiar with where code is located.

TABLE 9.3
arch/ppc/ Source Code Listing

Subdirectory	Description
`4xx_io`	Source code for MPC4xx-specific I/O parts, in particular, the IBM STB3xxx SICC serial port.
`8260_io`	Source code for MPC8260-communication options.
`8xx_io`	Source code for the MPC8xx-communication options.
`amiga`	Source code for the PowerPC-equipped Amiga computers.
`boot`	Source code related to PPC bootstrapping. This directory also contains a subdirectory called `images`, which is where the compiled bootable image is stored.
`config`	Configuration files for the build of specific PPC platforms and architectures.
`kernel`	Source code for the kernel subsystem hardware dependencies.

continues

TABLE 9.3
Continued

Subdirectory	Description
lib	Source code for PPC specific library files.
math-emu	Source code for PPC math emulation.
mm	Source code for the PPC-specific parts of the memory manager. Chapter 6, "Filesystems," discusses this in detail.
platforms	Source code specific to platforms (boards) on which the PPC chips are mounted.
syslib	Part of the source code core for the general hardware-specific subsystems.
xmon	Source code of PPC-specific debugger.

The directories under arch/x86 hold a structure similar to that seen in the PPC architecture-dependent directory. Table 9.4 summarizes the various subdirectories.

TABLE 9.4
arch/x86 Source Code Listing

Subdirectory	Description
boot	Source code related to the x86 bootstrapping and install process.
kernel	Source code for the kernel subsystem hardware dependencies.
lib	Source code for x86-specific library files.
mach-x	Source code for the x86 subarchitectures.
math-emu	Source code for x86 math-emulation functions.
mm	Source code for the x86-specific parts of memory management. Chapter 6 discusses this in detail.
oprofile	Source code for the oprofile kernel profiling tool.
pci	x86 PCI drivers.
power	Source code for x86 power management.

You may be wondering why the two architecture-specific listings are not more similar. The reason is that functional breakdowns that work well in one architecture may not work well in the other. For example, in PPC, PCI drivers vary by platform and subarchitecture, making a simple PCI subdirectory less ideal than for x86.

9.2.1.3   Miscellaneous Files and Directories

In the source root, a few files are not necessarily pertinent either to the architecture-dependent code or the architecture-independent code. Table 9.5 lists these files.

TABLE 9.5
Miscellaneous Files

File/Directory	Description
COPYING	The GPL license under which Linux is licensed.
CREDITS	List of contributors to the Linux project.
MAINTAINERS	List of maintainers and instructions on submitting kernel changes.
README	Release notes.
REPORTING-BUGS	Describes the procedure for reporting bugs.
documentation/	Directory with partial documentation on various aspects of the Linux kernel and source code. Great source of information, if sometimes slightly out of date.
scripts/	Holds utilities and scripts used during the kernel build process.

9.2.2   Building the Kernel Image

The kernel build system, or kbuild, is the mechanism by which kernel configuration options can be selected when building the kernel. It has been updated for the 2.6 kernel tree. This new kbuild version is much faster than its predecessor and significantly better documented. The kbuild system is highly dependent on the hierarchical structure of the source code.

9.2.2.1   Kernel Configuration Tool

The kernel configuration tool automatically generates the kernel configuration file named .config. This is the first step of the kernel build. The .config file is placed in the source code root; it contains a description of all the kernel options that were selected with the configuration tool. Each kernel build option has a name and value associated with it. The name is in the form CONFIG_<NAME>, where <NAME> is the label with which the option is associated. This variable can hold one of three values: y, m, or n. The y stands for "yes" and indicates that the option should be compiled into the kernel source, or built in. The m stands for "module" and indicates that the option should be compiled as a module separate from the kernel source. If an option is not selected (or its value set to n for "no"), the .config file indicates this by having a comment of the form CONFIG_<NAME> is not set. The .config file options are ordered according to the way they appear in the kernel configuration tool and comments are provided that indicate under what menu the option is found. Let's look at an excerpt of a .config file:

```
-------------------------------------------------------------------
.config
1   #
2   # Automatically generated make config: don't edit
3   #
4   CONFIG_X86=y
5   CONFIG_MMU=y
6   CONFIG_UID16=y
7   CONFIG_GENERIC_ISA_DMA=y
8
9   #
10  # Code maturity level options
11  #
12  CONFIG_EXPERIMENTAL=y
13  CONFIG_CLEAN_COMPILE=
14  CONFIG_STANDALONE=y
15  CONFIG_BROKEN_ON_SMP=y
16
17  #
18  # General setup
19  #
20  CONFIG_SWAP=y
21  CONFIG_SYSVIPC=y
22  #CONFIG_POSIX_MQUEUE is not set
23  CONFIG_BSD_PROCESS_ACCT=y
-------------------------------------------------------------------
```

This `.config` file indicates that the options from lines 4 to 7 are located under the top level, the options from lines 12 to 15 are located under the Code Maturity Level Options menu, and the options from lines 20 to 23 are under the General Setup menu.

Looking at the menus made available through any of the configuration tools, you see that the first few options are at the root level along with the menu items Code Maturity Level Options and General Setup. The latter two get expanded into a submenu that holds those options listed underneath. This is shown in `qconf`, which is the configuration tool that executes when we issue a call to make `xconfig`. The menus the configuration tool shows default to x86. To have it show the PPC-related menus, as shown in Figure 9.6, the parameter `ARCH=ppc` must be appended at the end of the make `xconfig` call.

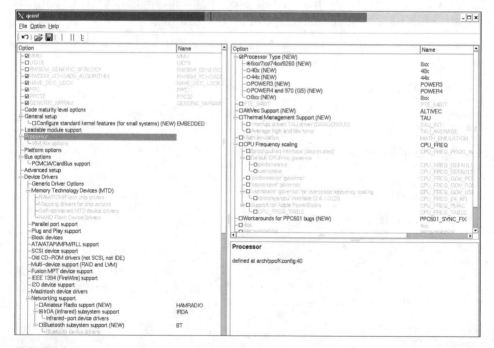

FIGURE 9.6
qconf Snapshot

The `.config` file generated by the configuration tool is read by the root `Makefile` when the image is to be built by the call to make `bzImage`. The root `Makefile` also pulls in information provided by the architecture-specific `Makefile`, which is located under `arch/<arch>/`. This is done by way of the `include` directive:

```
-----------------------------------------------------------------------
Makefile
434   include .config
...
450   include $(srctree)/arch/$(ARCH)/Makefile
-----------------------------------------------------------------------
```

At this point, the `Makefile` has already determined what architecture it is compiling for. The root `Makefile` determines the architecture it is compiling for in three possible ways:

1. By way of the command-line parameter `ARCH`

2. By way of the environment variable `ARCH`

3. Automatically from information received from a call to `uname` on the host the build is executed on

If the architecture being compiled for is different from the native host the compilation is executed on, the `CROSS_COMPILE` parameter has to be passed, which indicates the prefix of the cross compiler to be used. Alternatively, the `Makefile` itself can be edited and this variable is given a value. For example, if I compile for a PPC-based processor on an x86 host machine, I would execute the following commands:

```
lkp:~#make xconfig ARCH=ppc
lkp:~#make ARCH=ppc CROSS_COMPILE=ppc-linux-
```

The `.config` file also generates `include/linux/autoconf.h`, which `#defines` the `CONFIG_<NAME>` values that have been selected and `#undefs` those that were deselected.

9.2.2.2   Sub-Makefiles

The build system relies on sub-`Makefiles` that are located under each subdirectory. Each subdirectory's `Makefile` (called a sub-`Makefile` or `kbuild Makefile`)

defines rules to build object files from source code files located in that subdirectory and only makes appropriate modifications in that directory. The call to each sub-Makefile is done recursively down the tree going into all subdirectories under init/, drivers/, sound/, net/, lib/, and usr/.

Before the beginning of the recursive make call, kbuild needs to make sure a few things are in place, including updating include/linux/version.h if necessary and setting the symbolic link include/asm to point at the architecture-specific files of the architecture for which we are compiling. For example, if we are compiling for PPC, include/asm points to include/asm-ppc. kbuild also builds include/linux/autoconf.h and include/linux/config. After this is done, kbuild begins to recursively descend down the tree.

If you are a kernel developer and you make an addition to a particular subsystem, you place your files or edits in a specific subdirectory and update the Makefile if necessary to incorporate your changes. If your code is embedded in a file that already existed, you can surround your code within an #ifdef(CONFIG_<NAME>) block. If this value is selected in the .config file, it is #defined in include/linux/autoconf.h and your changes are included at compile time.

The sub-Makefile lines have a specific format that must be followed to indicate how the object file is to be built. These Makefiles are straightforward because information such as compiler name and libraries are already defined in the root Makefile and the architecture-specific root Makefile, and rules are defined in the scripts/Makefile.*s. The sub-Makefiles build three possible lists:

- **$(obj-y)** listing the object files that will be linked into built-in.o and later into vmlinux

- **$(obj-m)** listing the object files that will be built as a module

- **$(lib-y)** listing the object files that will be built into lib.a

In other words, when we issue a call to make of type make bzImage, kbuild builds all object files in obj-y and links them. The basic line in a sub-Makefile is of the type.

```
obj-$(CONFIG_FOO) += foo.o
```

If `CONFIG_FOO` is set to `y` in the `.config` file read by the root `Makefile`, this line becomes equivalent to `obj-y += foo.o`. kbuild builds that object file from the corresponding `foo.c` or `foo.S` file in that directory according to rules defined in `scripts/Makefile.build`. (We see more about this file in a moment.) If `foo.c` or `foo.S` do not exist, make complaints with

```
Make[1]: *** No rule to make target '<subdir>/foo.o', needed by
'<subdir>/built-in.o'. Stop.
```

The way that kbuild knows to descend into directories is through explicit additions to `obj-y` or `obj-m`. You can add a directory to set `obj-y`, which indicates that it needs to descend into the specified directory:

```
Obj-$(CONFIG_FOO) += /foo
```

If `/foo` does not exist, make complaints with the following:

```
Make[2]: *** No rule to make target '<dir>/foo/Makefile'. Stop.
```

CML2

Where does the configuration program that you navigate when choosing kernel options get the information? The `kbuild` system depends on CML2, which is a domain-specific language designed for kernel configuration. CML2 creates a rulebase that an interpreter then reads and uses to generate the `config` file. This file covers the syntax and semantics of the language. The CML2 rulebase that is read by configuration programs is stored in files called `defconfig` and `Kconfig`. The `defconfig` files are found at the root of the architecture-specific directories, `arch/*/`. The `Kconfig` files are found in most other subdirectories. The `Kconfig` files hold information regarding the options created, such as the menu it should be listed under, the help information to provide, the `config` name value, and whether it can be built-in only or also compiled as a module. For more information about CML2 and `Kconfig` files, see `Documentation/kbuild/kconfig-language.txt`.

Let's review what we have seen of the kbuild process. The first step is to call the configuration tool with make `xconfig` or `make xconfig ARCH=ppc`, depending on the architecture we want to build for. The selection made in the tool is then stored in the `.config` file. The top `Makefile` reads `.config` when a call such as `make bzImage` is issued to build the kernel image. The top `Makefile` then performs the following before descending recursively down the subdirectories:

1. Updates `include/linux/version.h`.

2. Sets the symbolic link `include/asm` to point at the architecture-specific files of the architecture we are compiling for.

3. Builds `include/linux/autoconf.h`.

4. Builds `include/linux/config.h`.

`kbuild` then descends the subdirectories, calling make on the sub-`Makefiles` and creating the object files in each one.

We have seen the structure of the sub-`Makefiles`. Now, we closely look at the top-level `Makefiles` and see how they are used to drive the kernel build system.

9.2.2.3   Linux Kernel Makefiles

Linux `Makefiles` are fairly complex. This section highlights the interrelationship between all the `Makefiles` in the source tree and explains the make particulars that are implemented in them. However, if you want to expand your knowledge of make, undertaking to understand all the specifics of the `kbuild Makefiles` is a fantastic way to get started. For more information on make, go to `www.gnu.org/software/make/make.html`.

In the source tree, virtually every directory has a `Makefile`. As mentioned in the previous section, the `Makefiles` in subtrees devoted to a particular category of the source code (or kernel subsystem) are fairly straightforward and merely define target source files to be added to the list that is then looked at to build them. Alongside these, five other `Makefiles` define rules and execute them. These include the source root `Makefile`, the `arch/$(ARCH)/Makefile`, `scripts/Makefile.build`, `scripts/Makefile.clean`, and `scripts/Makefile`. Figure 9.7 shows the relationship between the various `Makefiles`. We define the relationships to be of the "include" type or of the "execute" type. When we refer to an "include" type relationship, we mean that the `Makefile` pulls in the information from a file by using the rule `include <filename>`. When we refer to an "execute" type relationship, we mean that the original `Makefile` executes a `make -f` call to the secondary `Makefile`.

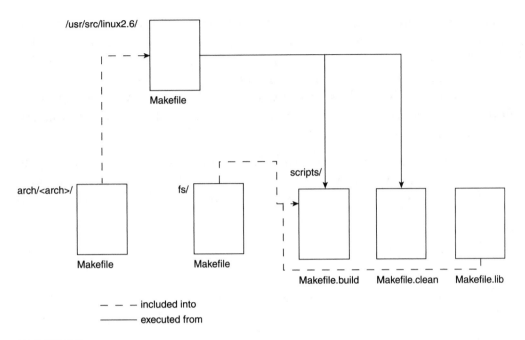

FIGURE 9.7
Makefile Relationships

When we issue a `make` call at the root of the source tree, we call on the root `Makefile`. The root `Makefile` defines variables that are then exported to other `Makefiles` and issues further `make` calls in each of the root-level source subdirectories, passing off execution to them.

Calls to the compiler and linker are defined in `scripts/Makefile.build`. This means that when we descend into subdirectories and build the object by means of a call to `make`, we are somehow executing a rule defined in `Makefile.build`. This is done by way of the shorthand call `$(Q) $(MAKE) $(build)=<dir>`. This rule is the way `make` is invoked in each subdirectory. The `build` variable is shorthand for

```
Makefile
1157  build := -f $(if $(KBUILD_SRC),$(srctree)/)scripts/Makefile.build obj
----------------------------------------------------------------------
```

A call to `$(Q) $(MAKE) $(build)=fs` expands to

```
"@ make -f /path/to/source/scripts/Makefile.build obj=fs".
```

The `scripts/Makefile.build` then reads the `Makefile` of the directory it was passed as parameter (fs, in our example). This sub-`Makefile` has defined one or more of the lists `obj-y`, `obj-m`, `lib-y`, and others. The file `scripts/Makefile.build`, along with any definitions from the included `scripts/Makefile.lib`, compiles the source files in the subdirectory and descends into any further subdirectories defined in the lists mentioned. The call is the same as what was just described.

Let's see how this works in an example. If, under the configuration tool, we go to the File Systems menu and select Ext3 journalling filesystem support, `CONFIG_EXT3_FS` will be set to `y` in the `.config` file. A snippet of the sub-`Makefile` corresponding to `fs` is shown here:

```
Makefile
49  obj-$(CONFIG_EXT3_FS)    += ext3/
------------------------------------------------------------------------
```

When make runs through this rule, it evaluates to `obj-y += ext3/`, making `ext3/` one of the elements of `obj-y`. make, having recognized that this is a subdirectory, calls `$(Q) $(MAKE) $(build)=ext3`.

$(Q)

The `$(Q)` variable prefixes all `$(MAKE)` calls. With the 2.6 kernel tree and the cleanup of the `kbuild` infrastructure, you can suppress the verbose mode of the make output. make prints the command line prior to executing it. When a line is prefixed with the `@`, the output (or echo) of that line is suppressed:

```
------------------------------------------------------------------------
Makefile
254  ifeq ($(KBUILD_VERBOSE),1)
255  quiet =
256  Q =
257  else
258  quiet=quiet_
259  Q = @
260  endif
------------------------------------------------------------------------
```

As we can see in these lines, `Q` is set to `@` if `KBUILD_VERBOSE` is set to 0, which means that we do not want the compile to be verbose.

After the build process completes, we end up with a kernel image. This bootable, compressed kernel image is called `zImage` or `vmlinuz` because the kernel gets compressed with the `zlib` algorithm. Common Linux conventions also specify the location of the bootable image on the filesystem; the image must be placed in `/boot` or `/`. At this point, the kernel image is ready to be loaded into memory by a bootloader.

Summary

This chapter explored the process of compiling and linking and the structure of object files to understand how we end up with code that can be executed. We also looked at the infrastructure surrounding the kernel build system and how the structure of the source code is tied to the build system itself. We gave a cursory glance at how the functional breakdown of the source code is tied to the kernel subsystems we have seen in previous chapters.

Exercises

1. Describe the various kinds of ELF files and what they are used for.

2. What is the point of segments in object files?

3. Look at both `arch/ppc/Kconfig` and `arch/i386/Kconfig` and determine what the supported processors are in each architecture.

4. Look in `arch/ppc` and in `arch/i386`. What files and directories do they have in common? Explore these and list the support they provide. Do they match exactly?

5. If you are cross-compiling the kernel, what parameter do you use to specify the cross-compiler prefix?

6. Under what condition would you specify the architecture through the command-line parameter `ARCH`?

7. What is a sub-makefile? How do they work?

8. Look at the `scripts/Makefile.build`, `scripts/Makefile.clean`, and `scripts/Makefile.lib`. List what they do.

Chapter 10

Adding Your Code to the Kernel

In this chapter

his section is divided into two major parts: "Traversing the Source" and "Writing the Code."

"Traversing the Source" walks through a device driver common to nearly all Linux systems, /dev/random, and shows how the kernel connects with it. During this overview we recap some of the inner workings of the kernel we previously described and show them in a more practical light.

"Writing the Code" walks through building a device driver and delves into common situations that a developer will encounter when writing device drivers.

After those sections, we proceed to describe how you can debug a device driver using the /proc system. Maybe that's the third side to a coin?

10.1 Traversing the Source

This section covers introductory concepts for system calls and drivers (also called modules) under Linux. System calls are what user programs use to communicate with the operating system to request services. Adding a system call is one way to create a new kernel service. Chapter 3, "Processes: The Principal Model of Execution," describes the internals of system call implementation. This chapter describes the practical aspects of incorporating your own system calls into the Linux kernel.

Device drivers encompass the interface that the Linux kernel uses to allow a programmer to control the system's input/output devices. Entire books have been written specifically on Linux device drivers. This chapter distills this topic down to its essentials. In this section, we follow a device driver from how the device is represented in the filesystem and then through the specific kernel code that controls it. In the next section, we show how to use what we've learned in the first part to construct a functional character driver. The final parts of Chapter 10 describe how to write system calls and how to build the kernel. We start by exploring the filesystem and show how these files tie into the kernel.

10.1.1   Getting Familiar with the Filesystem

Devices in Linux can be accessed via /dev. For example, an ls -l /dev/random yields the following:

```
crw-rw-rw- 1 root  root  1, 8 Oct 2 08:08 /dev/random
```

The leading "c" tells us that the device is a character device; a "b" identifies a block device. After the owner and group columns are two numbers that are separated by a comma (in this case, 1, 8). The first number is the driver's major number and the second its minor number. When a device driver registers with the kernel, it registers a major number. When a given device is opened, the kernel uses the device file's major number to find the driver that has registered with that major number.[1] The minor number is passed through the kernel to the device driver itself because a single driver can control multiple devices. For example, /dev/urandom has a major number of 1 and a minor number of 9. This means that the device driver registered with major number 1 handles both /dev/random and /dev/urandom.

To generate a random number, we simply read from /dev/random. The following is one possible way to read 4 bytes of random data:[2]

```
lkp@lkp:~$ head -c4 /dev/urandom | od -x
0000000 823a 3be5
0000004
```

If you repeat this command, you notice the 4 bytes [823a 3be5] continue to change. To demonstrate how the Linux kernel uses device drivers, we follow the steps that the kernel takes when a user accesses /dev/random.

We know that the /dev/random device file has a major number of 1. We can determine what driver controls the node by checking /proc/devices:

```
lkp@lkp:~$ less /proc/devices
Character devices:
 1 mem
```

---

[1]   mknod creates block and character device files.

[2]   head -c4 gathers the first 4 bytes and od -x formats the bytes in hexadecimal.

Let's examine the mem device driver and search for occurrences of "random":

```
drivers/char/mem.c
653 static int memory_open(struct inode * inode, struct file * filp)
654 {
655   switch (iminor(inode)) {
656     case 1:
...
676     case 8:
677       filp->f_op = &random_fops;
678       break;
679     case 9:
680       filp->f_op = &urandom_fops;
681       break;
```

Lines 655–681

This switch statement initializes driver structures based on the minor number of the device being operated on. Specifically, filps and fops are being set.

This leads us to ask, "What is a filp? What is a fop?"

10.1.2   Filps and Fops

A filp is simply a file struct pointer, and a fop is a file_operations struct pointer. The kernel uses the file_operations structure to determine what functions to call when the file is operated on. Here are selected sections of the structures that are used in the random device driver:

```
include/linux/fs.h
556 struct file {
557    struct list_head  f_list;
558    struct dentry    *f_dentry;
559    struct vfsmount  *f_vfsmnt;
560    struct file_operations *f_op;
561    atomic_t     f_count;
562    unsigned int   f_flags;
...
581    struct address_space *f_mapping;
582 };
```

```
include/linux/fs.h
863 struct file_operations {
 864    struct module *owner;
 865    loff_t (*llseek) (struct file *, loff_t, int);
```

```
866    ssize_t (*read) (struct file *, char __user *, size_t, loff_t *);
867    ssize_t (*aio_read) (struct kiocb *, char __user *, size_t, loff_t);
868    ssize_t (*write) (struct file *, const char __user *, size_t, loff_t *);
869    ssize_t (*aio_write) (struct kiocb *, const char __user *, size_t, loff_t);
870    int (*readdir) (struct file *, void *, filldir_t);
871    unsigned int (*poll) (struct file *, struct poll_table_struct *);
872    int (*ioctl) (struct inode *, struct file *, unsigned int, unsigned long);

...
888 };
```

The random device driver declares which file operations it provides in the following way: Functions that the drivers implement must conform to the prototypes listed in the file_operations structure:

```
drivers/char/random.c
1824 struct file_operations random_fops = {
1825    .read   = random_read,
1826    .write  = random_write,
1827    .poll   = random_poll,
1828    .ioctl  = random_ioctl,
1829 };
1830
1831 struct file_operations urandom_fops = {
1832    .read   = urandom_read,
1833    .write  = random_write,
1834    .ioctl  = random_ioctl,
1835 };
```

Lines 1824–1829

The random device provides the operations of read, write, poll, and ioctl.

Lines 1831–1835

The urandom device provides the operations of read, write, and ioctl.

The poll operation allows a programmer to check before performing an operation to see if that operation blocks. This suggests, and is indeed the case, that /dev/random blocks if a request is made for more bytes of entropy than are in its entropy pool.[3] /dev/urandom does not block, but might not return completely random data, if the entropy pool is too small. For more information consult your systems man pages, specifically man 4 random.

---

[3] In the random device driver, *entropy* refers to system data that cannot be predicted. Typically, it is harvested from keystroke timing, mouse movements, and other irregular input.

Digging deeper into the code, notice that when a read operation is performed on /dev/random, the kernel passes control to the function `random_read()` (see line 1825). `random_read()` is defined as follows:

```
--------------------------------------------------------------------
drivers/char/random.c
1588 static ssize_t
 1589 random_read(struct file * file, char __user * buf, size_t
nbytes, loff_t *ppos)
--------------------------------------------------------------------
```

The function parameters are as follows:

- **file**. Points to the file structure of the device.

- **buf**. Points to an area of user memory where the result is to be stored.

- **nbytes**. The size of data requested.

- **ppos**. Points to a position within the file that the user is accessing.

This brings up an interesting issue: If the driver executes in kernel space, but the buffer is memory in user space, how do we safely get access to the data in `buf`? The next section explains the process of moving data between user and kernel memory.

10.1.3   User Memory and Kernel Memory

If we were to simply use `memcpy()` to copy the buffer from kernel space to user space, the copy operation might not work because the user space addresses could be swapped out when `memcpy()` occurs. Linux has the functions `copy_to_user()` and `copy_from_user()`, which allow drivers to move data between kernel space and user space. In `read_random()`, this is done in the function `extract_entropy()`, but there is an additional twist:

```
--------------------------------------------------------------------
drivers/char/random.c
 1: static ssize_t extract_entropy(struct entropy_store *r, void * buf,
 2:          size_t nbytes, int flags)
 3: {
1349 static ssize_t extract_entropy(struct entropy_store *r, void * buf,
 1350          size_t nbytes, int flags)
 1351 {
...
 1452     /* Copy data to destination buffer */
 1453     i = min(nbytes, HASH_BUFFER_SIZE*sizeof(__u32)/2);
 1454     if (flags & EXTRACT_ENTROPY_USER) {
 1455      i -= copy_to_user(buf, (__u8 const *)tmp, i);
 1456       if (!i) {
```

```
1457              ret = -EFAULT;
1458              break;
1459           }
1460        } else
1461           memcpy(buf, (__u8 const *)tmp, i);
```

`extract_entropy()` has the following parameters:

- **r**. A pointer to an internal storage of entropy, it is ignored for the purposes of our discussion.

- **buf**. A pointer to an area of memory that should be filled with data.

- **nbytes**. The amount of data to write to **buf**.

- **flags**. Informs the function whether **buf** is in kernel or user memory.

`extract_entropy()` returns `ssize_t`, which is the size, in bytes, of the random data generated.

Lines 1454–1455

If `flags` tells us that `buf` points to a location in user memory, we use `copy_to_user()` to copy the kernel memory pointed to by `tmp` to the user memory pointed to by `buf`.

Lines 1460–1461

If `buf` points to a location in kernel memory, we simply use `memcpy()` to copy the data.

Obtaining random bytes is something that both kernel space and user space programs are likely to use; a kernel space program can avoid the overhead of `copy_to_user()` by not setting the flag. For example, the kernel can implement an encrypted filesystem and can avoid the overhead of copying to user space.

10.1.4   Wait Queues

We detoured slightly to explain how to move data between user and kernel memory. Let's return to `read_random()` and examine how it uses wait queues.

Occasionally, a driver might need to wait for some condition to be true, perhaps access to a system resource. In this case, we don't want the kernel to wait for the access to complete. It is problematic to cause the kernel to wait because all other system processing halts while the wait occurs.[4] By declaring a wait queue, you can postpone processing until a later time when the condition you are waiting on has occurred.

Two structures are used for this process of waiting: a wait queue and a wait queue head. A module should create a wait queue head and have parts of the module that use sleep_on and wake_up macros to manage things. This is precisely what occurs in random_read():

```
--------------------------------------------------------------------
drivers/char/random.c
1588 static ssize_t
 1589 random_read(struct file * file, char __user * buf, size_t nbytes, loff_t
*ppos)
 1590 {
 1591   DECLARE_WAITQUEUE(wait, current);
...
1597   while (nbytes > 0) {
...
1608     n = extract_entropy(sec_random_state, buf, n,
 1609         EXTRACT_ENTROPY_USER |
 1610         EXTRACT_ENTROPY_LIMIT |
 1611         EXTRACT_ENTROPY_SECONDARY);
...
1618     if (n == 0) {
 1619        if (file->f_flags & O_NONBLOCK) {
 1620          retval = -EAGAIN;
 1621          break;
 1622        }
 1623        if (signal_pending(current)) {
 1624          retval = -ERESTARTSYS;
 1625          break;
 1626        }
...
1632        set_current_state(TASK_INTERRUPTIBLE);
 1633        add_wait_queue(&random_read_wait, &wait);
 1634
 1635        if (sec_random_state->entropy_count / 8 == 0)
 1636          schedule();
 1637
 1638        set_current_state(TASK_RUNNING);
 1639        remove_wait_queue(&random_read_wait, &wait);
...
1645     continue;
 1646   }
--------------------------------------------------------------------
```

Line 1591

The wait queue wait is initialized on the current task. The macro current refers to a pointer to the current task's task_struct.

Lines 1608–1611

We extract a chunk of random data from the device.

Lines 1618–1626

If we could not extract the necessary amount of entropy from the entropy pool and we are non-blocking or there is a signal pending, we return an error to the caller.

Lines 1631–1633

Set up the wait queue. random_read() uses its own wait queue, random_read_wait, instead of the system wait queue.

Lines 1635–1636

At this point, we are on a blocking read and if we don't have 1 byte worth of entropy, we release control of the processor by calling schedule(). (The entropy_count variables hold bits and not bytes; thus, the division by 8 to determine whether we have a full byte of entropy.)

Lines 1638–1639

When we are eventually restarted, we clean up our wait queue.

> NOTE The random device in Linux requires the entropy queue to be full before returning. The urandom device does not have this requirement and returns regardless of the size of data available in the entropy pool.

Let's closely look at what happens when a task calls schedule():

```
-------------------------------------------------------------------
kernel/sched.c
2184 asmlinkage void __sched schedule(void)
2185 {
...
2209   prev = current;
...
2233   switch_count = &prev->nivcsw;
2234   if (prev->state && !(preempt_count() & PREEMPT_ACTIVE)) {
2235     switch_count = &prev->nvcsw;
```

```
2236      if (unlikely((prev->state & TASK_INTERRUPTIBLE) &&
2237          unlikely(signal_pending(prev))))
2238        prev->state = TASK_RUNNING;
2239      else
2240        deactivate_task(prev, rq);
2241    }
2242 ...
```

Line 2209

A pointer to the current task's task structure is stored in the `prev` variable. In cases where the task itself called `schedule()`, `current` points to that task.

Line 2233

We store the task's context switch counter, `nivcsw`, in `switch_count`. This is incremented later if the switch is successful.[5]

Line 2234

We only enter this if statement when the task's state, `prev->state`, is non-zero and there is not a kernel preemption. In other words, we enter this statement when a task's state is not `TASK_RUNNING`, and the kernel has not preempted the task.

Lines 2235–2241

If the task is interruptible, we're fairly certain that it wanted to release control. If a signal is pending for the task that wanted to release control, we set the task's state to `TASK_RUNNING` so that is has the opportunity to be chosen for execution by the scheduler when control is passed to another task. If no signal is pending, which is the common case, we deactivate the task and set `switch_count` to `nvcsw`. The scheduler increments `switch_count` later. Thus, `nvcsw` or `nivcsw` is incremented.

The `schedule()` function then picks the next task in the scheduler's run queue and switches control to that task.[6]

By calling `schedule()`, we allow a task to yield control of the processor to another kernel task when the current task knows it will be waiting for some reason. Other tasks in the kernel can make use of this time and, hopefully, when control

---

[5] See Chapters 4 and 7 for more information on how context switch counters are used.

[6] For detailed information, see the "switch_to()" section in Chapter 7.

returns to the function that called `schedule()`, the reason for waiting will have been removed.

Returning from our digression on the scheduler to the `random_read()` function, eventually, the kernel gives control back to `random_read()` and we clean up our wait queue and continue. This repeats the loop and, if the system has generated enough entropy, we should be able to return with the requested number of random bytes.

`random_read()` sets its state to `TASK_INTERRUPTIBLE` before calling `schedule()` to allow itself to be interrupted by signals while it is on a wait queue. The driver's own code generates these signals when extra entropy is collected by calling `wake_up_interruptible()` in `batch_entropy_process()` and `random_ioctl()`. `TASK_UNINTERRUPTIBLE` is usually used when the task is waiting for hardware to respond as opposed to software (when `TASK_INTERRUPTIBLE` is normally used).

The code that `random_read()` uses to pass control to another task (see lines 1632–1639, `drivers/char/random.c`) is a variant of `interruptible_sleep_on()` from the scheduler code.

```
-----------------------------------------------------------------
kernel/sched.c
2489 #define SLEEP_ON_VAR              \
 2490   unsigned long flags;          \
 2491   wait_queue_t wait;            \
 2492   init_waitqueue_entry(&wait, current);
 2493
 2494 #define SLEEP_ON_HEAD            \
 2495   spin_lock_irqsave(&q->lock,flags);    \
 2496   __add_wait_queue(q, &wait);          \
 2497   spin_unlock(&q->lock);
 2498
 2499 #define SLEEP_ON_TAIL            \
 2500   spin_lock_irq(&q->lock);      \
 2501   __remove_wait_queue(q, &wait);       \
 2502   spin_unlock_irqrestore(&q->lock, flags);
2503
2504 void fastcall __sched interruptible_sleep_on(wait_queue_head_t *q)
 2505 {
 2506   SLEEP_ON_VAR
 2507
 2508   current->state = TASK_INTERRUPTIBLE;
 2509
 2510   SLEEP_ON_HEAD
 2511   schedule();
 2512   SLEEP_ON_TAIL
2513 }
-----------------------------------------------------------------
```

q is a `wait_queue_head` structure that coordinates the module's sleeping and waiting.

Lines 2494–2497

Atomically add our task to a wait queue q.

Lines 2499–2502

Atomically remove the task from the wait queue q.

Lines 2504–2513

Add to the wait queue. Cede control of the processor to another task. When we are given control, remove ourselves from the wait queue.

`random_read()` uses its own wait queue code instead of the standard macros, but essentially does an `interruptible_sleep_on()` with the exception that, if we have more than a full byte's worth of entropy, we don't yield control but loop again to try and get all the requested entropy. If there isn't enough entropy, `random_read()` waits until it's awoken with `wake_up_interruptible()` from entropy-gathering processes of the driver.

10.1.5   Work Queues and Interrupts

Device drivers in Linux routinely have to deal with interrupts generated by the devices with which they are interfacing. Interrupts trigger an interrupt handler in the device driver and cause all currently executing code—both user space and kernel space—to cease execution. Clearly, it is desirable to have the driver's interrupt handler execute as quickly as possible to prevent long waits in kernel processing.

However, this leads us to the standard dilemma of interrupt handling: How do we handle an interrupt that requires a significant amount of work? The standard answer is to use top-half and bottom-half routines. The top-half routine quickly handles accepting the interrupt and schedules a bottom-half routine, which has the code to do the majority of the work and is executed when possible. Normally, the top-half routine runs with interrupts disabled to ensure that an interrupt handler isn't interrupted by the same interrupt. Thus, the device driver does not have to handle recursive interrupts. The bottom-half routine normally runs with interrupts enabled so that other interrupts can be handled while it continues the bulk of the work.

In prior Linux kernels, this division of top-half and bottom-half, also known as fast and slow interrupts, was handled by task queues. New to the 2.6 Linux kernel is the concept of a work queue, which is now the standard way to deal with bottom-half interrupts.

When the kernel receives an interrupt, the processor stops executing the current task and immediately handles the interrupt. When the CPU enters this mode, it is commonly referred to as being in interrupt context. The kernel, in interrupt context, then determines which interrupt handler to pass control to. When a device driver wants to handle an interrupt, it uses request_irq() to request the interrupt number and register the handler function to be called when this interrupt is seen. This registration is normally done at module initialization time. The top-half interrupt function registered with request_irq() does minimal management and then schedules the appropriate work to be done upon a work queue.

Like request_irq() in the top half, work queues are normally registered at module initialization. They can be initialized statically with the DECLARE_WORK() macro or the work structure can be allocated and initialized dynamically by calling INIT_WORK(). Here are the definitions of those macros:

```
----------------------------------------------------------------
include/linux/workqueue.h
30 #define DECLARE_WORK(n, f, d)              \
31    struct work_struct n = __WORK_INITIALIZER(n, f, d)
...
45 #define INIT_WORK(_work, _func, _data)          \
46    do {                \
47       INIT_LIST_HEAD(&(_work)->entry);       \
48       (_work)->pending = 0;          \
49       PREPARE_WORK((_work), (_func), (_data));  \
50       init_timer(&(_work)->timer);        \
51    } while (0)
----------------------------------------------------------------
```

Both macros take the following arguments:

- **n** or **work**. The name of the work structure to create or initialize.

- **f** or **func**. The function to run when the work structure is removed from a work queue.

- **d** or **data**. Holds the data to pass to the function f, or func, when it is run.

The interrupt handler function registered in register_irq() would then accept an interrupt and send the relevant data from the top half of the interrupt handler to the bottom half by setting the `work_struct` data section and calling `schedule_work()` on the work queue.

The code present in the work queue function operates in process context and can thus perform work that is impossible to do in interrupt context, such as copying to and from user space or sleeping.

Tasklets are similar to work queues but operate entirely in interrupt context. This is useful when you have little to do in the bottom half and want to save the overhead of a top-half and bottom-half interrupt handler. Tasklets are initialized with the `DECLARE_TASKLET()` macro:

```
include/linux/interrupt.h
136 #define DECLARE_TASKLET(name, func, data) \
137 struct tasklet_struct name = { NULL, 0, ATOMIC_INIT(0), func, data }
```

- **name**. The name of the tasklet structure to create.

- **func**. The function to call when the tasklet is scheduled.

- **data**. Holds the data to pass to the `func` function when the tasklet executes.

To schedule a tasklet, use `tasklet_schedule()`:

```
include/linux/interrupt.h
171 extern void FASTCALL(__tasklet_schedule(struct tasklet_struct *t));
172
173 static inline void tasklet_schedule(struct tasklet_struct *t)
174 {
175   if (!test_and_set_bit(TASKLET_STATE_SCHED, &t->state))
176     __tasklet_schedule(t);
177 }
```

- **tasklet_struct**. The name of the tasklet created with `DECLARE_TASKLET()`.

In the top-half interrupt handler, you can call `tasklet_schedule()` and be guaranteed that, sometime in the future, the function declared in the tasklet is executed. Tasklets differ from work queues in that different tasklets can run simultaneously on different CPUs. If a tasklet is already scheduled, and scheduled again before the tasklet executes, it is only executed once. As tasklets run in interrupt context, they cannot sleep or copy data to user space. Because of running in interrupt context, if different tasklets need to communicate, the only safe way to synchronize is by using spinlocks.

10.1.6 System Calls

There are other ways to add code to the kernel besides device drivers. Linux kernel system calls (syscalls) are the method by which user space programs can access kernel services and system hardware. Many of the C library routines available to user mode programs bundle code and one or more system calls to accomplish a single function. In fact, syscalls can also be accessed from kernel code.

By its nature, syscall implementation is hardware specific. In the Intel architecture, all syscalls use software interrupt 0x80. Parameters of the syscall are passed in the general registers. The implementation of syscall on the x86 architecture limits the number of parameters to 5. If more than 5 are required, a pointer to a block of parameters can be passed. Upon execution of the assembler instruction **int 0x80**, a specific kernel mode routine is called by way of the exception-handling capabilities of the processor.

10.1.7 Other Types of Drivers

Until now, all the device drivers we dealt with have been character drivers. These are usually the easiest to understand, but you might want to write other drivers that interface with the kernel in different ways.

Block devices are similar to character devices in that they can be accessed via the filesystem. `/dev/hda` is the device file for the primary IDE hard drive on the system. Block devices are registered and unregistered in similar ways to character devices by using the functions `register_blkdev()` and `unregister_blkdev()`.

A major difference between block drivers and character drivers is that block drivers do not provide their own read and write functionality; instead, they use a request method.

The 2.6 kernel has undergone major changes in the block device subsystem. Old functions, such as `block_read()` and `block_write()` and kernel structures like `blk_size` and `blksize_size`, have been removed. This section focuses solely on the 2.6 block device implementation.

If you need the Linux kernel to work with a disk (or a disk-like) device, you need to write a block device driver. The driver must inform the kernel what kind of disk it's interfacing with. It does this by using the `gendisk` structure:

```
------------------------------------------------------------------
include/linux/genhd.h
82 struct gendisk {
83    int major;        /* major number of driver */
84    int first_minor;
85    int minors;
86    char disk_name[32];     /* name of major driver */
87    struct hd_struct **part;  /* [indexed by minor] */
88    struct block_device_operations *fops;
89    struct request_queue *queue;
90    void *private_data;
91    sector_t capacity;
...
------------------------------------------------------------------
```

Line 83

`major` is the major number for the block device. This can be either statically set or dynamically generated by using `register_blkdev()`, as it was in character devices.

Lines 84–85

`first_minor` and `minors` are used to determine the number of partitions within the block device. `minors` contains the maximum number of minor numbers the device can have. `first_minor` contains the first minor device number of the block device.

Line 86

`disk_name` is a 32-character name for the block device. It appears in the `/dev` filesystem, `sysfs` and `/proc/partitions`.

Line 87

`hd_struct` is the set of partitions that is associated with the block device.

Line 88

`fops` is a pointer to a `block_operations` structure that contains the operations `open`, `release`, `ioctl`, `media_changed`, and `revalidate_disk`. (See `include/linux/fs.h`.) In the 2.6 kernel, each device has its own set of operations.

Line 89

`request_queue` is a pointer to a queue that helps manage the device's pending operations.

Line 90

`private_data` points to information that will not be accessed by the kernel's block subsystem. Typically, this is used to store data that is used in low-level, device-specific operations.

Line 91

`capacity` is the size of the block device in 512-byte sectors. If the device is removable, such as a floppy disk or CD, a capacity of 0 signifies that no disk is present. If your device doesn't use 512-byte sectors, you need to set this value as if it did. For example, if your device has 1,000 256-byte sectors, that's equivalent to 500 512-byte sectors.

In addition to having a `gendisk` structure, a block device also needs a spinlock structure for use with its request queue.

Both the spinlock and fields in the `gendisk` structure must be initialized by the device driver. (Go to `http://en.wikipedia.org/wiki/Ram_disk` for a demonstration of initializing a RAM disk block device driver.) After the device is initialized and ready to handle requests, the `add_disk()` function should be called to add the block device to the system.

Finally, if the block device can be used as a source of entropy for the system, the module initialization can also call `add_disk_randomness()`. (For more information, see `drivers/char/random.c`.)

Now that we covered the basics of block device initialization, we can examine its complement, exiting and cleaning up the block device driver. This is easy in the 2.6 version of Linux.

`del_gendisk( struct gendisk )` removes the `gendisk` from the system and cleans up its partition information. This call should be followed by `putdisk (struct gendisk)`, which releases kernel references to the `gendisk`. The block device is unregistered via a call to `unregister_blkdev(int major, char[16] device_name)`, which then allows us to free the `gendisk` structure.

We also need to clean up the request queue associated with the block device driver. This is done by using `blk_cleanup_queue( struct *request_queue)`. Note: If you can only reference the request queue via the `gendisk` structure, be sure to call `blk_cleanup_queue` before freeing `gendisk`.

In the block device initialization and shutdown overview, we could easily avoid talking about the specifics of request queues. But now that the driver is set up, it has to actually do something, and request queues are how a block device accomplishes its major functions of reading and writing.

```
---------------------------------------------------------------
include/linux/blkdev.h
576 extern request_queue_t *blk_init_queue(request_fn_proc *, spinlock_t *);
...
---------------------------------------------------------------
```

Line 576

To create a request queue, we use `blk_init_queue` and pass it a pointer to a spinlock to control queue access and a pointer to a request function that is called whenever the device is accessed. The request function should have the following prototype:

```
static void my_request_function( request_queue_t *q );
```

The guts of the request function usually use a number of helper functions with ease. To determine the next request to be processed, the `elv_next_request()` function is called and it returns a pointer to a request structure, or it returns null if there is no next request.

In the 2.6 kernel, the block device driver iterates through BIO structures in the request structure. BIO stands for Block I/O and is fully defined in `include/linux/bio.h`.

The BIO structure contains a pointer to a list of `biovec` structures, which are defined as follows:

```
---------------------------------------------------------------
include/linux/bio.h
47 struct bio_vec {
48    struct page  *bv_page;
49    unsigned int bv_len;
50    unsigned int bv_offset;
51 };
---------------------------------------------------------------
```

Each `biovec` uses its page structure to hold data buffers that are eventually written to or read from disk. The 2.6 kernel has numerous bio helpers to iterate over the data contained within bio structures.

To determine the size of BIO operation, you can either consult the `bio_size` field within the BIO struct to get a result in bytes or use the `bio_sectors()` macro to get the size in sectors. The block operation type, READ or WRITE, can be determined by using `bio_data_dir()`.

To iterate over the `biovec` list in a BIO structure, use the `bio_for_each_segment()` macro. Within that loop, even more macros can be used to further delve into `biovec` - `bio_page()`, `bio_offset()`, `bio_curr_sectors()`, and `bio_data()`. More information can be found in `include/linux.bio.h` and `Documentation/block/biodoc.txt`.

Some combination of the information contained in the `biovec` and the page structures allow you to determine what data to read or write to the block device. The low-level details of how to read and write the device are tied to the hardware the block device driver is using.

Now that we know how to iterate over a BIO structure, we just have to figure out how to iterate over a request structure's list of BIO structures. This is done using another macro: `rq_for_each_bio`:

```
-------------------------------------------------------------------
include/linux/blkdev.h
495 #define rq_for_each_bio(_bio, rq)   \
496    if ((rq->bio))        \
497       for (_bio = (rq)->bio; _bio; _bio = bio->bi_next)
-------------------------------------------------------------------
```

Line 495

`bio` is the current BIO structure and `rq` is the request to iterate over.

After each BIO is processed, the driver should update the kernel on its progress. This is done by using `end_that_request_first()`.

```
-------------------------------------------------------------------
include/linux/blkdev.h
557 extern int end_that_request_first(struct request *, int, int);
-------------------------------------------------------------------
```

Line 557

The first `int` argument should be non-zero unless an error has occurred, and the second `int` argument represents the number of sectors that the device processed.

When `end_that_request_first()` returns 0, the entire request has been processed and the cleanup needs to begin. This is done by calling `blkdev_dequeue_request()` and `end_that_request_last()` in that order—both of which take the request as the sole argument.

After this, the request function has done its job and the block subsystem uses the block device driver's request queue function to perform disk operations. The device might also need to handle certain `ioctl` functions, as our RAM disk handles partitioning, but those, again, depend on the type of block device.

This section has only touched on the basics of block devices. There are Linux hooks for DMA operations, clustering, request queue command preparation, and many other features of more advanced block devices. For further reading, refer to the `Documentation/block` directory.

10.1.8   Device Model and sysfs

New in the 2.6 kernel is the Linux device model, to which `sysfs` is intimately related. The device model stores a set of internal data related to the devices and drivers on a system. The system tracks what devices exist and breaks them down into classes: block, input, bus, etc. The system also keeps track of what drivers exist and how they relate to the devices they manage. The device model exists within the kernel, and `sysfs` is a window into this model. Because some devices and drivers do not expose themselves through `sysfs`, a good way of thinking of `sysfs` is the public view of the kernel's device model.

Certain devices have multiple entries within `sysfs`.

Only one copy of the data is stored within the device model, but there are various ways of accessing that piece of data, as the symbolic links in the `sysfs` tree shows.

The `sysfs` hierarchy relates to the kernel's `kobject` and `kset` structures. This model is fairly complex, but most driver writers don't have to delve too far into the details to accomplish many useful tasks.[7] By using the `sysfs` concept of attributes, you work with `kobjects`, but in an abstracted way. Attributes are parts of the device or driver model that can be accessed or changed via the `sysfs` filesystem. They could be internal module variables controlling how the module manages tasks

---

[7]   Reference `documentation/filesystems/sysfs.txt` in the kernel source.

or they could be directly linked to various hardware settings. For example, an RF transmitter could have a base frequency it operates upon and individual tuners implemented as offsets from this base frequency. Changing the base frequency can be accomplished by exposing a module attribute of the RF driver to sysfs.

When an attribute is accessed, sysfs calls a function to handle that access, show() for read and store() for write. There is a one-page limit on the size of data that can be passed to show() or store() functions.

With this outline of how sysfs works, we can now get into the specifics of how a driver registers with sysfs, exposes some attributes, and registers specific show() and store() functions to operate when those attributes are accessed.

The first task is to determine what device class your new device and driver should fall under (for example, usb_device, net_device, pci_device, sys_device, and so on). All these structures have a char *name field within them. sysfs uses this name field to display the new device within the sysfs hierarchy.

After a device structure is allocated and named, you must create and initialize a devicer_driver structure:

```
-------------------------------------------------------------------
include/linux/device.h
102 struct device_driver {
 103    char       * name;
 104    struct bus_type    * bus;
 105
 106    struct semaphore   unload_sem;
 107    struct kobject     kobj;
 108    struct list_head   devices;
 109
 110    int  (*probe)   (struct device * dev);
 111    int  (*remove)  (struct device * dev);
 112    void (*shutdown) (struct device * dev);
 113    int  (*suspend)  (struct device * dev, u32 state, u32 level);
 114    int  (*resume)   (struct device * dev, u32 level);
 115};
-------------------------------------------------------------------
```

Line 103

name refers to the name of the driver that is displayed in the sysfs hierarchy.

Line 104

bus is usually filled in automatically; a driver writer need not worry about it.

Lines 105–115

The programmer does not need to set the rest of the fields. They should be automatically initialized at the bus level.

We can register our driver during initialization by calling `driver_register()`, which passes most of the work to `bus_add_driver()`. Similarly upon driver exit, be sure to add a call to `driver_unregister()`.

```
-------------------------------------------------------------------------
drivers/base/driver.c
86 int driver_register(struct device_driver * drv)
 87 {
 88    INIT_LIST_HEAD(&drv->devices);
 89    init_MUTEX_LOCKED(&drv->unload_sem);
 90    return bus_add_driver(drv);
 91 }
-------------------------------------------------------------------------
```

After driver registration, driver attributes can be created via `driver_attribute` structures and a helpful macro, `DRIVER_ATTR`:

```
-------------------------------------------------------------------------
include/linux/device.h
133 #define DRIVER_ATTR(_name,_mode,_show,_store) \
134 struct driver_attribute driver_attr_##_name = {        \
135   .attr = {.name = __stringify(_name), .mode = _mode, .owner = THIS_MODULE
}, \
136   .show = _show,          \
137   .store = _store,         \
138 };
-------------------------------------------------------------------------
```

Line 135

`name` is the name of the attribute for the driver. `mode` is the bitmap describing the level of protection of the attribute. `include/linux/stat.h` contains many of these modes, but `S_IRUGO` (for read-only) and `S_IWUSR` (for root write access) are two examples.

Line 136

`show` is the name of the driver function to use when the attribute is read via `sysfs`. If reads are not allowed, `NULL` should be used.

Line 137

`store` is the name of the driver function to use when the attribute is written via `sysfs`. If writes are not allowed, `NULL` should be used.

The driver functions that implement `show()` and `store()` for a specific driver must adhere to the prototypes shown here:

```
-------------------------------------------------------------------
include/linux/sysfs.h
34 struct sysfs_ops {
35    ssize_t (*show)(struct kobject *, struct attribute *,char *);
36    ssize_t (*store)(struct kobject *,struct attribute *,const char *, size_t);
37 };
-------------------------------------------------------------------
```

Recall that the size of data read and written to `sysfs` attributes is limited to `PAGE_SIZE` bytes. The `show()` and `store()` driver attribute functions should ensure that this limit is enforced.

This information should allow you to add basic `sysfs` functionality to kernel device drivers. For further `sysfs` and `kobject` reading, see the `Documentation/device-model` directory.

Another type of device driver is a network device driver. Network devices send and receive packets of data and might not necessarily be a hardware device—the loopback device is a software-network device.

10.2 Writing the Code

10.2.1 Device Basics

When you create a device driver, it is tied to the operating system through an entry in the filesystem. This entry has a major number that indicates to the kernel which driver to use when the file is referenced as well as a minor number that the driver itself can use for greater granularity. When the device driver is loaded, it registers its major number. This registration can be viewed by examining `/proc/devices`:

```
-------------------------------------------------------------------
lkp# less /proc/devices
Character devices:
  1 mem
  2 pty
  3 ttyp
  4 ttyS
  5 cua
  6 lp
  7 vcs
 10 misc
 29 fb
128 ptm
136 pts
```

```
Block devices:
 1 ramdisk
 2 fd
 3 ide0
 7 loop
 22 ide1
```

This number is entered in `/proc/devices` when the device driver registers itself with the kernel; for character devices, it calls the function `register_chrdev()`.

```
include/linux/fs.h
 1: int register_chrdev(unsigned int major, const char *name,
 2:       struct file_operations *fops)
```

- **major**. The major number of the device being registered. If `major` is 0, the kernel dynamically assigns it a major number that doesn't conflict with any other module currently loaded.

- **name**. The string representation of the device in the `/dev` tree of the filesystem.

- **fops**. A pointer to file-operations structure that defines what operations can be performed on the device being registered.

Using 0 as the major number is the preferred method for creating a device number for those devices that do not have set major numbers (IDE drivers always use 3; SCSI, 8; floppy, 2). By dynamically assigning a device's major number, we avoid the problem of choosing a major number that some other device driver might have chosen.[8] The consequence is that creating the filesystem node is slightly more complicated because after module loading, we must check what major number was assigned to the device. For example, while testing a device, you might need to do the following:

```
lkp@lkp# insmod my_module.o
lkp@lkp# less /proc/devices
1 mem
...
233 my_module
lkp@lkp# mknod c /dev/my_module0 233 0
lkp@lkp# mknod c /dev/my_module1 233 1
```

----

[8] The `register_chrdev()` function returns the major number assigned. It might be useful to capture this information when dynamically assigning major numbers.

This code shows how we can insert our module using the command `insmod`. `insmod` installs a loadable module in the running kernel. Our module code contains these lines:

```
--------------------------------------------------------------------
static int my_module_major=0;
...
module_param(my_module_major, int, 0);
...
result = register_chrdev(my_module_major, "my_module", &my_module_fops);
--------------------------------------------------------------------
```

The first two lines show how we create a default major number of 0 for dynamic assignment but allow the user to override that assignment by using the `my_module_major` variable as a module parameter:

```
--------------------------------------------------------------------
include/linux/moduleparam.h
 1: /* This is the fundamental function for registering boot/module
parameters. perm sets the visibility in driverfs: 000 means it's
not there, read bits mean it's readable, write bits mean it's
writable. */
...
/* Helper functions: type is byte, short, ushort, int, uint, long,
ulong, charp, bool or invbool, or XXX if you define param_get_XXX,
param_set_XXX and param_check_XXX. */
...
 2: #define module_param(name, type, perm)
--------------------------------------------------------------------
```

In previous versions of Linux, the `module_param` macro was `MODULE_PARM`; this is deprecated in version 2.6 and `module_param` must be used.

- **name**. A string that is used to access the value of the parameter.

- **type**. The type of value that is stored in the parameter name.

- **perm**. The visibility of the module parameter name in `sysfs`. If you don't know what `sysfs` is, use a value of 0, which means the parameter is not accessible via `sysfs`.

Recall that we pass into `register_chrdev()` a pointer to a `fops` structure. This tells the kernel what functions the driver handles. We declare only those functions that the module handles. To declare that `read`, `write`, `ioctl`, and `open` are valid operations upon the device that we are registering, we add code like the following:

```
--------------------------------------------------------------------
struct file_operations my_mod_fops = {
  .read = my_mod_read,
```

```
 .write = my_mod_write,
 .ioctl = my_mod_ioctl,
 .open = my_mod_open,
};
```

10.2.2   Symbol Exporting

In the course of writing a complex device driver, there might be reasons to export some of the symbols defined in the driver for use by other kernel modules. This is commonly used in low-level drivers that expect higher-level drivers to build upon their basic functionality.

When a device driver is loaded, any exported symbol is placed into the kernel symbol table. Drivers that are loaded subsequently can use any symbols exported by prior drivers. When modules depend on each other, the order in which they are loaded becomes important; insmod fails if the symbols that a high-level module depend on aren't present.

In the 2.6 Linux kernel, two macros are available to a device programmer to export symbols:

----
include/linux/module.h
```
187 #define EXPORT_SYMBOL(sym)            \
188    __EXPORT_SYMBOL(sym, "")
189
190 #define EXPORT_SYMBOL_GPL(sym)          \
191    __EXPORT_SYMBOL(sym, "_gpl")
```

The EXPORT_SYMBOL macro allows the given symbol to be seen by other pieces of the kernel by placing it into the kernel's symbol table. EXPORT_SYMBOL_GPL allows only modules that have defined a GPL-compatible license in their MODULE_LICENSE attribute. (See include/linux/module.h for a complete list of licenses.)

10.2.3   IOCTL

Until now, we have primarily dealt with device drivers that take actions of their own accord or read and write data to their device. What happens when you have a device that can do more than just read and write? Or you have a device that can do different kinds of reads and writes? Or your device requires some kind of hardware control interface? In Linux, device drivers typically use the ioctl method to solve these problems.

ioctl is a system call that allows the device driver to handle specific commands that can be used to control the I/O channel. A device driver's ioctl call must follow the declaration inside of the file_operations structure:

```
------------------------------------------------------------------
include/linux/fs.h
863 struct file_operations {
...
872 int (*ioctl) (struct inode *, struct file *, unsigned int, unsigned long);
------------------------------------------------------------------
```

From user space, the ioctl function call is defined as follows:

```
int ioctl (int d, int request, ...);
```

The third argument in the user space definition is an untyped pointer to memory. This is how data passes from user space to the device driver's ioctl implementation. It might sound complex, but to actually use ioctl within a driver is fairly simple.

First, we want to declare what IOCTL numbers are valid for our device. We should consult the file Documentation/ioctl-number.txt and choose a code that the machine won't use. By consulting the current 2.6 file, we see that the ioctl code of 'g' is not currently in use. In our driver, we claim it with the following code:

```
#define MYDRIVER_IOC_MAGIC 'g'
```

For each distinct control message the driver receives, we need to declare a unique ioctl number. This is based off of the magic number just defined:

```
------------------------------------------------------------------
#define MYDRIVER_IOC_OP1 _IO(MYDRIVER_IOC_MAGIC, 0)
#define MYDRIVER_IOC_OP2 _IOW(MYDRIVER_IOC_MAGIC, 1)
#define MYDRIVER_IOC_OP3 _IOW(MYDRIVER_IOC_MAGIC, 2)
#define MYDRIVER_IOC_OP4 _IORW(MYDRIVER_IOC_MAGIC, 3)
------------------------------------------------------------------
```

The four operations just listed (op1, op2, op3, and op4) have been given unique ioctl numbers using the macros defined in include/asm/ioctl.h using MYDRIVER_IOC_MAGIC, which is our ioctl magic number. The documentation file is eloquent on what everything means:

```
------------------------------------------------------------------
Documentation/lioctl-number.txt
6 If you are adding new ioctls to the kernel, you should use the _IO
7 macros defined in <linux/ioctl.h>:
8
9  _IO an ioctl with no parameters
10  _IOW an ioctl with write parameters (copy_from_user)
```

```
11  _IOR an ioctl with read parameters (copy_to_user)
12  _IOWR an ioctl with both write and read parameters.
13
14  'Write' and 'read' are from the user's point of view, just like the
15  system calls 'write' and 'read'. For example, a SET_FOO ioctl would
16  be _IOW, although the kernel would actually read data from user space;
17  a GET_FOO ioctl would be _IOR, although the kernel would actually write
18  data to user space.
```

From user space, we could call the `ioctl` commands like this:

```
ioctl(fd, MYDRIVER_IOC_OP1, NULL);
ioctl(fd, MYDRIVER_IOC_OP2, &mydata);
ioctl(fd, MYDRIVER_IOC_OP3, mydata);
ioctl(fd, MYDRIVER_IOC_OP4, &mystruct);
```

The user space program needs to know what the `ioctl` commands are (in this case, `MYDRIVER_IOC_OP1 ... MY_DRIVER_IOC_OP4`) and the type of arguments the commands expect. We could return a value by using the return code of the `ioctl` system call or we could interpret the parameter as a pointer to be set or read. In the latter case, remember that the pointer references a section of user space memory that must be copied into, or out of, the kernel.

The cleanest way to move memory between user space and kernel space in an `ioctl` function is by using the routines `put_user()` and `get_user()`, which are defined here:

```
Include/asm-i386/uaccess.h
* get_user: - Get a simple variable from user space.
* @x: Variable to store result.
* @ptr: Source address, in user space.
  ...
* put_user: - Write a simple value into user space.
* @x: Value to copy to user space.
* @ptr: Destination address, in user space.
```

`put_user()` and `get_user()` ensure that the user space memory being read or written to is in memory at the time of the call.

There is an additional constraint that you might want to add to the `ioctl` functions of your device driver: authentication.

One way to test whether the process calling your `ioctl` function is authorized to call `ioctl` is by using capabilities. A common capability used in driver authentication is `CAP_SYS_ADMIN`:

```
------------------------------------------------------------------------
include/linux/capability.h
202 /* Allow configuration of the secure attention key */
 203 /* Allow administration of the random device */
 204 /* Allow examination and configuration of disk quotas */
 205 /* Allow configuring the kernel's syslog (printk behavior) */
 206 /* Allow setting the domainname */
 207 /* Allow setting the hostname */
 208 /* Allow calling bdflush() */
 209 /* Allow mount() and umount(), setting up new smb connection */
 210 /* Allow some autofs root ioctls */
 211 /* Allow nfsservctl */
 212 /* Allow VM86_REQUEST_IRQ */
 213 /* Allow to read/write pci config on alpha */
 214 /* Allow irix_prctl on mips (setstacksize) */
 215 /* Allow flushing all cache on m68k (sys_cacheflush) */
 216 /* Allow removing semaphores */
 217 /* Used instead of CAP_CHOWN to "chown" IPC message queues, semaphores
 218 and shared memory */
 219 /* Allow locking/unlocking of shared memory segment */
 220 /* Allow turning swap on/off */
 221 /* Allow forged pids on socket credentials passing */
 222 /* Allow setting readahead and flushing buffers on block devices */
 223 /* Allow setting geometry in floppy driver */
 224 /* Allow turning DMA on/off in xd driver */
 225 /* Allow administration of md devices (mostly the above, but some
 226 extra ioctls) */
 227 /* Allow tuning the ide driver */
 228 /* Allow access to the nvram device */
 229 /* Allow administration of apm_bios, serial and bttv (TV) device */
 230 /* Allow manufacturer commands in isdn CAPI support driver */
 231 /* Allow reading non-standardized portions of pci configuration space */
 232 /* Allow DDI debug ioctl on sbpcd driver */
 233 /* Allow setting up serial ports */
 234 /* Allow sending raw qic-117 commands */
 235 /* Allow enabling/disabling tagged queuing on SCSI controllers and sending
 236 arbitrary SCSI commands */
 237 /* Allow setting encryption key on loopback filesystem */
 238
 239 #define CAP_SYS_ADMIN 21
------------------------------------------------------------------------
```

Many other more specific capabilities in `include/linux/capability.h` might be more appropriate for a more restricted device driver, but `CAP_SYS_ADMIN` is a good catch-all.

To check the capability of the calling process within your driver, add something similar to the following code:

```
if (! capable(CAP_SYS_ADMIN)) {
 return -EPERM;
}
```

10.2.4   Polling and Interrupts

When a device driver sends a command to the device it is controlling, there are two ways it can determine whether the command was successful: It can poll the device or it can use device interrupts.

When a device is polled, the device driver periodically checks the device to ensure that the command it delivered succeeded. Because device drivers are part of the kernel, if they were to poll directly, they risk causing the kernel to wait until the device completes the poll operation. The way device drivers that poll get around this is by using system timers. When the device driver wants to poll a device, it schedules the kernel to call a routine within the device driver at a later time. This routine performs the device check without pausing the kernel.

Before we get further into the details of how kernel interrupts work, we must explain the main method of locking access to critical sections of code in the kernel: spinlocks. Spinlocks work by setting a special flag to a certain value before it enters the critical section of code and resetting the value after it leaves the critical section. Spinlocks should be used when the task context cannot block, which is precisely the case in kernel code. Let's look at the spinlock code for x86 and PPC architectures:

```
-----------------------------------------------------------------
include/asm-i386/spinlock.h
32 #define SPIN_LOCK_UNLOCKED (spinlock_t) { 1 SPINLOCK_MAGIC_INIT }
33
34 #define spin_lock_init(x)  do { *(x) = SPIN_LOCK_UNLOCKED; } while(0)
...
43 #define spin_is_locked(x)  (*(volatile signed char *)(&(x)->lock) <= 0)
44 #define spin_unlock_wait(x)  do { barrier(); } while(spin_is_locked(x))

include/asm-ppc/spinlock.h
25 #define SPIN_LOCK_UNLOCKED  (spinlock_t) { 0 SPINLOCK_DEBUG_INIT }
26
27 #define spin_lock_init(x)  do { *(x) = SPIN_LOCK_UNLOCKED; } while(0)
28 #define spin_is_locked(x)  ((x)->lock != 0)
while(spin_is_locked(x))
29 #define spin_unlock_wait(x)  do { barrier(); } while(spin_is_locked(x))
-----------------------------------------------------------------
```

In the x86 architecture, the actual spinlock's `flag` value is 1 if unlocked whereas on the PPC, it's 0. This illustrates that in writing a driver, you need to use the supplied macros instead of raw values to ensure cross-platform compatibility.

Tasks that want to gain the lock will, in a tight loop, continuously check the value of the special flag until it is less than 0; hence, waiting tasks spin. (See `spin_unlock_wait()` in the two code blocks.)

10.2   Writing the Code

2.5-28 ⟶ Cli, sti are phased out
       & Spinlocks are
                  introduced.

583

Spinlocks for drivers are normally used during interrupt handling when the kernel code needs to execute a critical section without being interrupted by other interrupts. In prior versions of the Linux kernel, the functions cli() and sti() were used to disable and enable interrupts. As of 2.5.28, cli() and sti() are being phased out and replaced with spinlocks. The new way to execute a section of kernel code that cannot be interrupted is by the following:

```
-----------------------------------------------------------------
Documentation/cli-sti-removal.txt
 1: spinlock_t driver_lock = SPIN_LOCK_UNLOCKED;
 2: struct driver_data;
 3:
 4: irq_handler (...)
 5: {
 6: unsigned long flags;
 7: ....
 8: spin_lock_irqsave(&driver_lock, flags);
 9: ....
10: driver_data.finish = 1;
11: driver_data.new_work = 0;
12: ....
13: spin_unlock_irqrestore(&driver_lock, flags);
14: ....
15: }
16:
17: ...
18:                    ⟶ bottom-half
19: ioctl_func (...)
20: {
21: ...
22: spin_lock_irq(&driver_lock);
23: ...
24: driver_data.finish = 0;
25: driver_data.new_work = 2;
26: ...
27: spin_unlock_irq(&driver_lock);
28: ...
29: }
-----------------------------------------------------------------
```

Line 8

Before starting the critical section of code, save the interrupts in flags and lock driver_lock.

Lines 9–12

This critical section of code can only be executed one task at a time.

Line 27

This line finishes the critical section of code. Restore the state of the interrupts and unlock `driver_lock`.

By using `spin_lock_irq_save()` (and `spin_lock_irq_restore()`), we ensure that interrupts that were disabled before the interrupt handler ran remain disabled after it finishes.

When `ioctl_func()` has locked `driver_lock`, other calls of `irq_handler()` will spin. Thus, we need to ensure the critical section in `ioctl_func()` finishes as fast as possible to guarantee the `irq_handler()`, which is our top-half interrupt handler, waits for an extremely short time.

Let's examine the sequence of creating an interrupt handler and its top-half handler (see Section 10.2.5 for the bottom half, which uses a work queue):

```
#define mod_num_tries 3
static int irq = 0;
...
int count = 0;
unsigned int irqs = 0;
while ((count < mod_num_tries) && (irq <= 0)) {
 irqs = probe_irq_on();
 /* Cause device to trigger an interrupt.
  Some delay may be required to ensure receipt
  of the interrupt */
 irq = probe_irq_off(irqs);
 /* If irq < 0 multiple interrupts were received.
  If irq == 0 no interrupts were received. */
 count++;
}
if ((count == mod_num_tries) && (irq <=0)) {
 printk("Couldn't determine interrupt for %s\n",
   MODULE_NAME);
}
```

This code would be part of the initialization section of the device driver and would likely fail if no interrupts could be found. Now that we have an interrupt, we can register that interrupt and our top-half interrupt handler with the kernel:

```
retval = request_irq(irq, irq_handler, SA_INTERRUPT,
     DEVICE_NAME, NULL);
if (retval < 0) {
 printk("Request of IRQ %n failed for %s\n",
   irq, MODULE_NAME);
 return retval;
}
```

`request_irq()` has the following prototype:

```
arch/ i386/kernel/irq.c
590 /**
 591 *  request_irq - allocate an interrupt line
 592 *  @irq: Interrupt line to allocate
 593 *  @handler: Function to be called when the IRQ occurs
 594 *  @irqflags: Interrupt type flags
 595 *  @devname: An ascii name for the claiming device
 596 *  @dev_id: A cookie passed back to the handler function
...
622 int request_irq(unsigned int irq,
 623     irqreturn_t (*handler)(int, void *, struct pt_regs *),
 624     unsigned long irqflags,
 625     const char * devname,
 626     void *dev_id)
```

The `irqflags` parameter can be the ord value of the following macros:

- `SA_SHIRQ` for a shared interrupt

- `SA_INTERRUPT` to disable local interrupts while running `handler`

- `SA_SAMPLE_RANDOM` if the interrupt is a source of entropy

`dev_id` must be `NULL` if the interrupt is not shared and, if shared, is usually the address of the device data structure because `handler` receives this value.

At this point, it is useful to remember that every requested interrupt needs to be freed when the module exits by using `free_irq()`:

```
arch/ i386/kernel/irq.c
669 /**
670 *  free_irq - free an interrupt
671 *  @irq: Interrupt line to free
672 *  @dev_id: Device identity to free
...
682 */
683
684 void free_irq(unsigned int irq, void *dev_id)
```

If `dev_id` is a shared `irq`, the module should ensure that interrupts are disabled before calling this function. In addition, `free_irq()` should never be called from interrupt context. Calling `free_irq()` in the module cleanup routine is standard. (See `spin_lock_irq()` and `spin_unlock_irq`.)

At this point, we have registered our interrupt handler and the `irq` it is linked to. Now, we have to write the actual top-half handler, what we defined as `irq_handler()`:

```
void irq_handler(int irq, void *dev_id, struct pt_regs *regs)
{
 /* See above for spin lock code */
 /* Copy interrupt data to work queue data for handling in
  bottom-half */
 schedule_work( WORK_QUEUE );
 /* Release spin_lock */
}
```

If you just need a fast interrupt handler, you can use a tasklet instead of a work queue:

```
void irq_handler(int irq, void *dev_id, struct pt_regs *regs)
{
 /* See above for spin lock code */
 /* Copy interrupt data to tasklet data */
 tasklet_schedule( TASKLET_QUEUE );
 /* Release spin_lock */
}
```

10.2.5   Work Queues and Tasklets

The bulk of the work in an interrupt handler is usually done in a work queue. In the last section, we've seen that the top half of the interrupt handler copies pertinent data from the interrupt to a data structure and then calls `schedule_work()`.

To have tasks run from a work queue, they must be packaged in a `work_struct`. To declare a work structure at compile time, use the `DECLARE_WORK()` macro. For example, the following code could be placed in our module to initialize a work structure with an associated function and data:

```
...
struct bh_data_struct {
 int data_one;
 int *data_array;
 char *data_text;
}
...
static bh_data_struct bh_data;
...
static DECLARE_WORK(my_mod_work, my_mod_bh, &bh_data);
...
```

```
static void my_mod_bh(void *data)
{
 struct bh_data_struct *bh_data = data;

 /* all the wonderful bottom half code */
}
```

The top-half handler would set all the data required by `my_mod_bh` in `bh_data` and then call `schedule_work(my_mod_work)`.

`schedule_work()` is a function that is available to any module; however, this means that the work schedule is put on the generic work queue "events." Some modules might want to make their own work queues, but the functions required to do so are only exported to GPL-compatible modules. Thus, if you want to keep your module proprietary, you must use the generic work queue.

A work queue is created by using the `create_workqueue()` macro, which calls `__create_workqueue()` with a second parameter of 0:

```
kernel/workqueue.c
304 struct workqueue_struct *__create_workqueue(const char *name,
 305            int singlethread)
```

`name` can be up to 10 characters long.

If `singlethread` is 0, the kernel creates a `workqueue` thread per CPU; if `singlethread` is 1, the kernel creates a single `workqueue` thread for the entire system.

Work structures are created in the same way as what's been previously described, but they are placed on your custom work queue using `queue_work()` instead of `schedule_work()`.

```
kernel/workqueue.c
97 int fastcall queue_work(struct workqueue_struct *wq, struct work_struct
*work)
98 {
```

`wq` is the custom work queue created with `create_workqueue()`.

`work` is the work structure to be placed on `wq`.

Other work queue functions, found in `kernel/workqueue.c`, include the following:

- **queue_work_delayed()**. Ensures the work structure function is not called until a specified number of jiffies has passed.

- **flush_workqueue()**. Causes the caller to wait until all scheduled work on the queue has finished. This is commonly used when a device driver exits.

- **destroy_workqueue()**. Flushes and then frees the work queue.

Similar functions, `schedule_work_delayed()` and `flush_scheduled_work()`, exist for the generic work queue.

10.2.6 Adding Code for a System Call

We could edit the `Makefile` in `/kernel` to include a file with our function, but an easier method is to include our function code in an already existing file in the source tree. The file `/kernel/sys.c` contains the kernel functions for the system calls and the file `arch/i386/kernel/sys_i386.c` contains x86 system calls with a nonstandard calling sequence. The former is where we add the source code for our syscall function written in C. This code runs in kernel mode and does all the work. Everything else in this procedure is in support of getting us to this function. It is dispatched through the x86 exception handler:

```
--------------------------------------------------------------------
kernel/sys.c
 1: ...
 2: /* somewhere after last function */
 3:
 4: /* simple function to demonstrate a syscall. */
 5: /* take in a number, print it out, return the number+1 */
 6:
 7: asmlinkage long sys_ourcall(long num)
 8: {
 9: printk("Inside our syscall num =%d \n", num);
10: return(num+1);
11: }
--------------------------------------------------------------------
```

When the exception handler processes the `int 0x80`, it indexes into the system call table. The file `/arch/i386/kernel/entry.S` contains low-level interrupt handling routines and the system call table `sys_call_tabl`. The table is an assembly code implementation of an array in C with each element being 4 bytes. Each element or entry in this table is initialized to the address of a function. By convention, we must prepend the name of our function with sys_. Because the position in the table determines the syscall number, we must add the name of our function to the end of the list. See the following code for the table changes:

```
------------------------------------------------------------------------
arch/i386/kernel/entry.S
 : .data
608: ENTRY(sys_call_table)
  .long sys_restart_syscall /* 0 - old "setup()" system call, used for
restarting*/
...
  .long sys_tgkill  /* 270 */
  .long sys_utimes
  .long sys_fadvise64_64
  .long sys_ni_syscall /* sys_vserver */
  .long sys_ourcall  /* our syscall will be 274 */
884: nr_syscalls=(.-sys_call_table)/4
------------------------------------------------------------------------
```

The file include/asm/unistd.h associates the system calls with their positional numbers in the sys_call_table. Also in this file are macro routines to assist the user program (written in C) in loading the registers with parameters. Here are the changes to unistd.h to insert our system call:

```
------------------------------------------------------------------------
include/asm/unistd.h
 1: /*
 2: * This file contains the system call numbers.
 3: */
 4:
 5: #define __NR_restart_syscall 0
 6: #define __NR_exit    1
 7: #define __NR_fork    2
 8: ...
 9: #define __NR_utimes    271
10: #define __NR_fadvise64_64  272
11: #define __NR_vserver    273
12: #define __NR_ourcall    274
13:
14: /* #define NR_syscalls 274 this is the old value before our syscall */
15: #define NR_syscalls   275
------------------------------------------------------------------------
```

Finally, we want to create a user program to test the new syscall. As previously mentioned in this section, a set of macros exists to assist the kernel programmer in loading the parameters from C code into the x86 registers. In

/usr/include/asm/unistd.h, there are seven macros: _syscall**x**(type, name,..), where **x** is the number of parameters. Each macro is dedicated to loading the proper number of parameters from 0 to 5 and syscall6(...) allows for passing a pointer to more parameters. The following example program takes in one parameter. For this example (on line 5), we use the _syscall1(type, name,type1,name1) macro from /unistd.h, which resolves to a call to int 0x80 with the proper parameters:

```
-------------------------------------------------------------------
mytest.c
 1: #include <stdio.h>
 2: #include <stdlib.h>
 3: #include "/usr/include/asm/unistd.h"
 4:
 5: _syscall(long,ourcall,long, num);
 6:
 7: main()
 8: {
 9: printf("our syscall --> num in=5, num out = %d\n", ourcall(5));
10: }
-------------------------------------------------------------------
```

10.3 Building and Debugging

Adding your code to the kernel typically involves cycles of programming and bug fixing. In this section, we describe how to debug the kernel code you've written and how to build debugging-related tools.

10.3.1 Debugging Device Drivers

In previous sections, we used the /proc filesystem to gather information about the kernel. We can also make information about our device driver accessible to users via /proc, and it is an excellent way to debug parts of your device driver. Every node in the /proc filesystem connects to a kernel function when it is read or written to. In the 2.6 kernel, most writes to part of the kernel, devices included, are done through sysfs instead of /proc. The operations modify specific kernel object attributes while the kernel is running. /proc remains a useful tool for read-only operations that require a larger amount of data than an attribute-value pair, and this section deals only with reading from /proc entries.

The first step in allowing read access to your device is to create an entry in the /proc filesystem, which is done by create_proc_read_entry():

```
-----------------------------------------------------------------------
include/linux/proc_fs.h
146 static inline struct proc_dir_entry *create_proc_read_entry(const char
*name,
147   mode_t mode, struct proc_dir_entry *base,
148   read_proc_t *read_proc, void * data)
-----------------------------------------------------------------------
```

*name is the entry of the node that appears under /proc, a mode of 0 allows the file to be world-readable. If you are creating many different proc files for a single device driver, it could be advantageous to first create a proc directory by using proc_mkdir(), and then base each file under that. *base is the directory path under /proc to place the file; a value of NULL places the file directly under /proc. The *read_proc function is called when the file is read, and *data is a pointer that is passed back into *read_proc:

```
-----------------------------------------------------------------------
include/linux/proc_fs.h
44 typedef int (read_proc_t)(char *page, char **start, off_t off,
45        int count, int *eof, void *data);
-----------------------------------------------------------------------
```

This is the prototype for functions that want to be read via the /proc filesystem. *page is a pointer to the buffer where the function writes its data for the process reading the /proc file. The function should start writing at off bytes into *page and write no more than count bytes. As most reads return only a small amount of information, many implementations ignore both off and count. In addition, **start is normally ignored and is rarely used anywhere in the kernel. If you implement a read function that returns a vast amount of data, **start, off, and count can be used to manage reading small chunks at a time. When the read is finished, the function should write 1 to *eof. Finally, *data is the parameter passed to the read function defined in create_proc_read_entry().

Summary

This chapter covered device drivers, modules, and system calls. We described the variety of ways that Linux uses device drivers.

More specifically, we covered the following topics:

• We described the /dev tree in the Linux filesystem and explained how to determine what device is controlled by what device driver.

- We explained how device drivers use file structures and file operations structures to handle filesystem I/O.

- We discussed the difference between user-level memory and kernel space memory and how device drivers need to copy data structures between the two.

- We examined the wait queue construct of the Linux kernel and demonstrated how it is used when a device driver needs to wait for a particular resource to become available.

- We explored the theory behind wait queues and interrupts, which are the methods that the Linux kernel uses to cleanly interrupt the processing of device drivers when the CPU needs to be yielded to another process.

- We introduced Linux system calls and outlined their basic functions.

- We covered the differences between block and character device drivers and the new device model that was introduced in Linux 2.6. This involved a quick tour of `sysfs`.

In the first part of Chapter 10, these topics were talked about from an abstract level, and we traced a specific device driver, `/dev/random`, through the topics described. The second part of Chapter 10 provided more concrete examples and sample code for how to actually construct a device driver.

More specifically, we detailed the following concepts:

- We showed how to construct nodes in `/dev` that could be attached to a device driver and how to construct dynamic modules.

- We described the new methods in Linux 2.6 to export symbols from device driver modules.

- We demonstrated how a device driver provides IOCTL functions that allows the device to interact with Linux via the filesystem.

- We explained how interrupts and polling occur and the difference between spinlocks in the x86 and PPC architecture.

- We explained how to add a simple system call to the Linux kernel.

Chapter 10 provides a solid basis for developing device drivers in Linux 2.6 and combines, in a practical fashion, the ideas and concepts we introduced previously in this book.

Exercises

1. See Chapter 3, "Processes: The Principal Model of Execution," on building the kernel and user code. Recompile the kernel and compile `mytest.c`. Run `mytest.c` and observe the output.

2. Add another parameter to `ourcall`.

3. Make a system call from within `ourcall`.

4. Explain the similarities and differences between system calls and device drivers.

5. Why can't we use `memcpy` to copy data between user space and kernel space?

6. What is the difference between a top-half and bottom-half routine?

7. What's the difference between a tasklet and a `work_queue`?

8. When a device can handle more than simply read and write requests, how does Linux interact with it?

9. What is the numerical value of an unlocked spinlock on x86 architecture? On PPC?

10. In one sentence, describe the difference between block drivers and character drivers.

Bibliography

Aas, Josh. "Understanding the Linux 2.6.8.1 CPU Scheduler." *Linux 2.6.8.1 CPU Scheduler Paper*. 17th February 2005. http://josh.trancesoftware.com/linux/.

Corbet, J., and A. Rubini. *Linux Device Drivers*. 2nd edition. Sebastopol, CA: O'Reilly and Associates, 2001.

Cormen, T., C. Leiserson, and R. Rivest. *Introduction to Algorithms*. Cambridge, MA: MIT Press, 1996.

Detmer, R. *Introduction to 80x86 Assembly Language and Computer Architecture*. Sudbury, MA: Jones and Bartlett Publishers, Inc., 2001.

Goodheart, B., and J. Cox. *The Magic Garden Explained: The Internals of UNIX System V Release 4*. Englewood Cliffs, NJ: Prentice Hall, 1994.

Gorman, M. *Understanding the Linux Virtual Memory Manager*. Englewood Cliffs, NJ: Prentice Hall, 2004.

IBM Corp. *Book I: PowerPC User Instruction Set Architecture*. Version 2.02. IBM Corp., 2003. http://www-128.ibm.com/developerworks/eserver/library/es-archguide-v2.html.

IBM Corp. *Book II: PowerPC Virtual Environment Architecture*. IBM Corp., 2003. http://www-128.ibm.com/developerworks/eserver/library/es-archguide-v2.html.

IBM Corp. *Book III: Operating Environment Architecture.* IBM Corp., 2003. http://www-128.ibm.com/developerworks/eserver/library/es-archguide-v2.html.

IBM Corp. *PowerPC Microprocessor Family: The Programming Environments for 32-bit Microprocessors.* IBM Corp., 2000. http://www-3.ibm.com/chips/techlib/techlib.nsf/techdocs/852569B20050FF778525699600719DF2.

IBM Corp. *The PowerPC Architecture: A Specification for a New Family of RISC Processors.* 2nd Edition. San Francisco: Morgan Kaufmann Publishers, Inc. May 1996.

Intel Corp. *IA-32 Intel Architecture Software Developer's Manual, Volume 1: Basic Architecture.* Intel Corp., 2005. http://www.intel.com/design/pentium4/manuals/index_new#sdm_vol1.

Intel Corp. *IA-32 Intel Architecture Software Developer's Manual, Volume 2: Instruction Set Referenece Manual.* Intel Corp., 2005. http://www.intel.com/design/pentium4/manuals/index_new#sdm_vol2.

Intel Corp. *IA-32 Intel Architecture Software Developer's Manual, Volume 3: System Programming Guide.* Intel Corp., 2005. http://www.intel.com/design/pentium4/manuals/index_new#sdm_vol23.

Kerninghan, B., and D. Ritchie. *C Programming Language.* Englewood Cliffs, NJ: Prentice Hall PTR, 1998.

Lions, J. *Lion's Commentary on UNIX 6th Edition with Source Code.* Charlottesville, VA: Peer-to-Peer Communications, 1977.

Love, R. *Linux Kernel Development.* Indianapolis, Indiana: Sams Publishing, 2001.

Maxwell, S. *Linux Core Kernel Commentary.* Scottsdale, AZ: Coriolis Press, 1999.

McKusick, Marshal Kirk. *The Design and Implementation of the 4.4 BSD Operating System.* Boston, MA: Addison-Wesley Professional, 1996.

Patterson, D., and J. Hennessy. *Computer Organization and Design: The Hardware/Software Interface*. San Francisco, CA: Morgan Kaufmann Publishers, Inc., 1994.

Plauger, P.J. *The Standard C Library*. Englewood Cliffs, NJ: Prentice Hall PTR, 1991.

Silberschatz, A., P. Gavin, and G. Gagne. *Operating Systems Concepts*. 7th Edition. John Wiley and Sons, 2001.

Tanenbaum, Andrew. *Modern Operating Systems*. 2nd edition. Englewood Cliffs, NJ: Prentice Hall, 2001.

Index

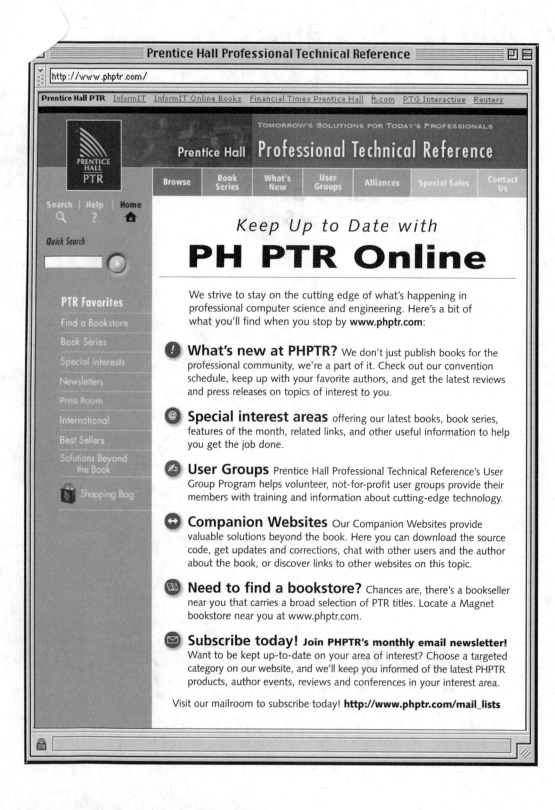

Prentice Hall Professional Technical Reference

http://www.phptr.com/

Prentice Hall PTR   InformIT   InformIT Online Books   Financial Times Prentice Hall   ft.com   PTG Interactive   Reuters

TOMORROW'S SOLUTIONS FOR TODAY'S PROFESSIONALS

Prentice Hall **Professional Technical Reference**

Browse | Book Series | What's New | User Groups | Alliances | Special Sales | Contact Us

Search | Help | Home

Quick Search

PTR Favorites

Find a Bookstore

Book Series

Special Interests

Newsletters

Press Room

International

Best Sellers

Solutions Beyond the Book

Shopping Bag

Keep Up to Date with
PH PTR Online

We strive to stay on the cutting edge of what's happening in professional computer science and engineering. Here's a bit of what you'll find when you stop by **www.phptr.com**:

What's new at PHPTR? We don't just publish books for the professional community, we're a part of it. Check out our convention schedule, keep up with your favorite authors, and get the latest reviews and press releases on topics of interest to you.

Special interest areas offering our latest books, book series, features of the month, related links, and other useful information to help you get the job done.

User Groups Prentice Hall Professional Technical Reference's User Group Program helps volunteer, not-for-profit user groups provide their members with training and information about cutting-edge technology.

Companion Websites Our Companion Websites provide valuable solutions beyond the book. Here you can download the source code, get updates and corrections, chat with other users and the author about the book, or discover links to other websites on this topic.

Need to find a bookstore? Chances are, there's a bookseller near you that carries a broad selection of PTR titles. Locate a Magnet bookstore near you at www.phptr.com.

Subscribe today! Join PHPTR's monthly email newsletter! Want to be kept up-to-date on your area of interest? Choose a targeted category on our website, and we'll keep you informed of the latest PHPTR products, author events, reviews and conferences in your interest area.

Visit our mailroom to subscribe today! **http://www.phptr.com/mail_lists**

inform**IT**

YOUR GUIDE TO IT REFERENCE

Articles

Keep your edge with thousands of free articles, in-depth features, interviews, and IT reference recommendations – all written by experts you know and trust.

Online Books

Answers in an instant from **InformIT Online Book's** 600+ fully searchable on line books. For a limited time, you can get your first 14 days **free**.

Safari
POWERED BY
TECH BOOKS ONLINE

Catalog

Review online sample chapters, author biographies and customer rankings and choose exactly the right book from a selection of over 5,000 titles.